Parents Are Our Other Client

Parents Are Our Other Client: Ideas for Therapists, Social Workers, Support Workers, and Teachers stands out among the vast literature on counseling children and families by finally giving therapists, social workers, support workers, and teachers the tools necessary to work with the single most significant influence on children: the parents.

This book:

- Explains in an accessible and readable format how parenting patterns are learned unconsciously during early childhood and emerge later, when people become parents.
- Delivers a comprehensive and practical guide for professionals working to help parents see their children differently and change the way they interact with their children.
- Clarifies why directing attention to the non-verbal areas of a parent's brain with techniques such as imaging is essential for achieving a shift away from early learned patterns.
- Examines how a professional's own childhood experience influences the way he or she works with parents and how professionals can shift to more positive responding even with the most resistant parent.
- Provides informative clinical illustrations based on current research and the authors' extensive clinical and supervisory experience.

Sandra Wieland, PhD, was a psychologist, play therapist, trainer, and consultant in Victoria, Canada. She was previously a classroom teacher, special education teacher, and school counselor. Dr. Wieland taught internationally on trauma and working with parents, had written books and chapters on therapy with children and adolescents, and recently had edited *Dissociation in Traumatized Children and Adolescents, Second Edition* (Routledge, 2015). She received the Woman of Distinction Award and the Cornelia B. Wilbur Award for clinical excellence. In 2016 she was 'blanketed' by the Hulitan First Nations Family for her work with their therapists, children, and parents.

Sandra Baita is a clinical psychologist and EMDR therapist living and working in private practice in Buenos Aires, Argentina. She has written several book chapters and articles, co-authored a book on child sexual abuse for Judges and Prosecutors, and authored a book on complex trauma and dissociation in children. She gives regular training on child abuse, developmental trauma, and dissociation in both her country and Latin America.

Parents Are Our Other Client

Ideas for Therapists, Social Workers, Support Workers, and Teachers

Sandra Wieland
(in collaboration with Sandra Baita)

NEW YORK AND LONDON

First published 2017
by Routledge
711 Third Avenue, New York, NY 10017

and by Routledge
2 Park Square, Milton Park, Abingdon, Oxon OX14 4RN

Routledge is an imprint of the Taylor & Francis Group, an informa business

© 2017 Taylor & Francis

The right of Sandra Wieland to be identified as the author of this work has been asserted by her in accordance with sections 77 and 78 of the Copyright, Designs and Patents Act 1988.

All rights reserved. No part of this book may be reprinted or reproduced or utilised in any form or by any electronic, mechanical, or other means, now known or hereafter invented, including photocopying and recording, or in any information storage or retrieval system, without permission in writing from the publishers.

Trademark notice: Product or corporate names may be trademarks or registered trademarks, and are used only for identification and explanation without intent to infringe.

Library of Congress Cataloging-in-Publication Data
Names: Wieland, Sandra, author. | Baita, Sandra, author.
Title: Parents are our other client : ideas for therapists, social workers, support workers, and teachers / Sandra Wieland ; in collaboration with Sandra Baita.
Description: New York, NY : Routledge, 2017. Includes bibliographical references.
Identifiers: LCCN 2016040751 | ISBN 9781138832572 (hardback) | ISBN 9781138832565 (pbk.)
Subjects: LCSH: Family social work. | Parents—Services for. | Social work with children. | Child welfare.
Classification: LCC HV697 .W534 2017 DDC 362.82/53—dc23
LC record available at https://lccn.loc.gov/2016040751

ISBN: 978-1-138-83257-2 (hbk)
ISBN: 978-1-138-83256-5 (pbk)
ISBN: 978-1-315-73595-5 (ebk)

Typeset in Minion
by Apex CoVantage, LLC

Cover art by Dominique Whelan.

To my parents: Marjorie & John
&
To the three I parented: Bruce, Marjorie, Ken

Contents

	Introduction	xi
1	**The Parents and Us**	1
	Who Are the Parents?	1
	What Do Parents Bring to Our Work with Them?	2
	What Parents Want	2
	Where Parents May Get Caught	2
	Patterns of Interaction	6
	Who Are We?	8
	What Do We Bring to Our Work with Parents?	9
	What We Want	9
	Where We May Get Caught	9
	How Child Professionals Can Work with Parents	12
	Summary	14
	Chapter 1—Points to Remember	14
2	**Learning About the Parent and About Us**	17
	Referral Phone Call	17
	Developmental Interview	18
	Present Concern	19
	Child's Development	19
	Child in the Present	25
	Parent's Own Experiences	29
	Parent's Early Emotional Experiences	30

Drawing Genograms	34
Observing Parent-Child Dynamics	35
In an Office	36
In a Home	37
Recognizing Parent-Us Dynamics	39
Becoming Aware of the Dynamics Occurring between Ourselves and the Parent	39
Becoming Aware of the Experiences We Had Growing Up	39
How Our Early Experiences Influence Our Interactive Experiences with Parents	41
One More Question	43
Summary	43
Chapter 2—Points to Remember	44
3 How Parenting Patterns Are Held in the Brain	**47**
Attachment	48
Brain Patterns	52
How One Is Parented Becomes Part of the Neuronal Patterns within the Brain	53
Where in the Brain/Body Many of These Patterns Are Held	55
Limbic System	55
Prefrontal Cortex	59
Right Hemisphere	61
Autonomic Nervous System	63
How Understanding the Brain Can Help Guide Our Therapeutic Interactions	65
Engaging Deep Right Cortices—Our Relationship with the Parent	65
Engaging Right Hemisphere—Dyadic Art and Sand-Tray Activity	66
Engaging Motor Activity and Right Hemisphere Processing—Imaging	67
Engaging Orbital Medial Prefrontal Cortex—Emotional Regulation; Mindfulness; Mentalization	71
Engaging Dorsal Lateral Prefrontal Cortex—Focus; Working Memory; Problem-Solving	73
Regulating the Autonomic Nervous System—Window of Receptivity	74
Summary	76
Chapter 3—Points to Remember	76
4 Attending to Attachment Relationships	**79**
Intergenerational Transmission of Attachment	79
Our Relationship with the Parent	81
Attunement	85
Mindfulness	86
Mentalization	91
Nonverbal Interaction—Play	96

	Nonverbal Interaction—Imaging	97
	Nonverbal Interaction—Attachment Activities	102
	Summary	103
	Chapter 4—Points to Remember	103
5	**Using the Skills We Already Have**	**105**
	Getting Starting	105
	Attunement	107
	Emotional Regulation	113
	Validation	118
	Providing and Strengthening New Experiences for the Parent	125
	Present Safety	125
	Strengthening an Internal Resource	129
	Building External Supports	133
	Summary	134
	Chapter 5—Points to Remember	135
6	**Helping Parents Move Out of Negative Interactive Patterns**	**137**
	Habits Underlying Negative Parenting Patterns	138
	Beliefs Underlying Negative Parenting Patterns	144
	Values Underlying Negative Parenting Patterns	150
	Emotions Underlying Negative Interactive Parent-Child Patterns	151
	Blockages to Positive Parenting Patterns	161
	Triggers	161
	Mismatched Temperaments	163
	Rejection of Ideas Presented	165
	'Preaching' Parenting	171
	Overactive Therapist	173
	Parent Exhaustion	174
	Summary	177
	Chapter 6—Points to Remember	177
7	**When the Home is an Adoptive Home**	**179**
	The Meeting between the Child's Previous Experience and Parents' Expectations	179
	Gathering Information: What Do We Need to Know and How Can We Use This Information?	187
	Helping Adoptive Parents	191
	Attach to Their Children	191
	Understand Their Child's Emotions and Behaviors	193
	Helping the Child Mourn the Past and Attach to the Present	202
	Understanding the Role of Disorganized Attachment	209
	Child's Disorganized Attachment May Activate Parents' Old Disorganized Attachment Patterns	210
	Child's Controlling Behavior May Disorganize Parents	215

x   Contents

	Working with Foster Parents	220
	Foster Care is a Temporary Situation	220
	Foster Parents are Often Overwhelmed by Multiple Demands	222
	Visits with Birth Parents	223
	Providing Ideas for Foster Parents	227
	Finding Out about the Foster Parents	229
	Summary	232
	Chapter 7—Points to Remember	233
8	**Our Experience**	**235**
	Where Countertransference Comes From; Why We Need to Pay Attention to It	236
	What is Going On in Our Own Lives at That Particular Moment	236
	Our Past Experiences	238
	Our Triggers	238
	Our Values	241
	Our Vulnerabilities	242
	Replay of Parents' Past Relationship Dynamics	243
	Ambivalent Attachment Pattern	244
	Avoidant Attachment Pattern	247
	Disorganized Attachment Pattern	249
	Our Attachment Pattern	251
	Other Early Parental Patterns	252
	Shifting Countertransference Reactions	254
	Managing Countertransference	255
	Relationship Responses	256
	Intellectual Responses	263
	Verbalizing What Is Happening	264
	Linking the Present with the Past	266
	Recognizing the Emotion Underlying Behaviors	268
	How We Decide Which Countertransference Response to Use	271
	Summary	272
	Chapter 8—Points to Remember	272
9	**Concluding Thought—Super-Vision, Peer-Vision, Self-Vision**	**275**
	Bibliography	277
	Index	287

Introduction

Through my many years of working with children—first as a classroom teacher, then a special education teacher and a school counselor, and for the last 30 years as a child clinical psychologist—I have often been asked the question, "What is the hardest part of your work?" And I have consistently answered, "Working with the parent." That is the reason for this book. If we are to help a child, the parent, as well as the child, needs to be our client.

Why was the work so hard? Because I knew I was not being as effective as I might be, no matter how hard I tried to be available to parents and to give them ideas for parenting their child. I realized that it was not parenting ideas or family therapy they needed—there are multitudinous books and websites available on those. Rather, they needed more positive attachment experiences and experiences of being aware of themselves, their past, their children, and the future they wanted for themselves and their children. They needed recognition of the negative parenting they had learned from their parents. And, as I learned more about the brain, I began to understand why my past efforts had not worked and to develop new ways to work with the parent.

"But," said a colleague to me recently, "teachers, day care workers, child/youth support workers, doctors and nurses don't work with parents, they work with the child or youth." My answer: "They interact with parents every day as the parent drops off or picks up the child, they interact via phone conversations or parent interviews—no matter how short. And in every interaction there is a potential for helping that parent develop a more positive way of interacting with his or her child." We need to use that potential.

As professionals concerned with children, the focus of our training has been on how to work with children and family systems. Unfortunately this training all too often skips over a crucial part of the child's world—the parent, the parent's own experience of being parented and, most importantly, how we can work with the parent. We, as child professionals, shall come and go in the child's life—the parent is there for a long time. Working with children can be greatly enhanced or obstructed by how professionals engage the parent or other primary caregiver. How we interact with our 'other client'—that is, how we interact with a child's parents—can ultimately determine the outcome of our work with a child.

This is a book for child therapists and counselors, but it is not about child therapy or counseling. It is a book for teachers and principals but not a book about teaching. It is a book for child support workers and social workers but not about their work with children. It is a book for pediatricians and nurses but not about medical services. This book is about creating healthy interactions between ourselves—professionals working with children—and parents. It is about giving parents the type of interactive experiences we want them to be able to give to their children—interactions that give an experience of being 'seen' and 'heard,' of being valued. We want to create interactions that strengthen the parents' ability to be present for their children and to change negative parenting patterns taught to them years earlier by their parents.

Parents Are Our Other Client: Ideas for Therapists, Social Workers, Support Workers, and Teachers will be a valuable and practical tool for professionals interacting with parents. Both experienced clinicians and those new to the field need a straightforward and practical guide that can help them understand the parent's experience, help them build a relationship with the parent and help them work with the parent to build a healthier relationship with his or her children—a relationship crucial to the child's success. While this book talks about parenting, it is *not* a book on parenting. Rather it is a book for the professional striving to be more effective in his or her work with the parent.

While research related to attachment, brain functioning, imaging, and countertransference will be described, the emphasis of the book will be a practical one—what a child professional can do in her or his work with parents. Case studies and practical examples make this book both readable and easily transferable into practice.

We shall start our journey, in Chapter 1, by taking a look at who the parents are and what they bring with them as they become parents and, indeed, as they become 'our other client.' We will notice that, however much they want to be 'good' parents and may want to be different from their own parents, they get caught in old patterns. At the same time, we will need to look at who we are, what we want, and where we, as professionals and humans, get caught. Every relationship has two sides. It is important that we do not overlook how our own past experiences shape our work with parents.

Then, being efficient and trained child professionals, we will, in Chapter 2, consider the developmental assessment. This assessment is somewhat different from the standard assessment taught in counseling or social work courses. The assessment not only asks about the child but also asks the parents to remember back to their own growing up. We introduce the fact that each of us has parenting behaviors—those we did not like as well as those we did like—patterned into us long before we became parents. And we, the professionals, also have patterns that need to be examined. We shall talk briefly about genograms and about using our observations of the dynamics between the parent and the child, and the parent and ourselves, as part of the assessment process. Teachers and child care workers may not, unfortunately, have the time to do this type of work. There are, however, a number of ideas that will be of interest to them.

Chapter 3—please do *not* skip this chapter even if you are allergic to brain terminology. This is not a lengthy neuroscience lecture but rather an explanation of why those early experiences we did not like and did not want are caught in our brains and come out when we least want or expect them to. Then we talk about how this information can help guide our work with parents just as it has done, over the last decade, in our work with children. We shall be talking about both brain and body responses. We will introduce the idea of using imaging in our work with parents. Imaging has been shown to be a very powerful training tool for athletes, musicians, and doctors. And it is easily available to us for our work with parents.

Then we shall move beyond the brain information to what we can do together with parents (Chapter 4). We shall look at our relationship with the parent and talk about attunement, mindfulness, and mentalization. We shall emphasize nonverbal interaction—more discussion about imaging as well as play and attachment activities. Many of the skills we need we already have, and Chapter 5 talks about how to use those skills as we interact with parents. Then comes Chapter 6—another chapter not to skip—"Helping Parents Move Out of Negative Interactive Patterns." We have already talked about why those negative patterns are there. Here we will talk about what holds parents in these patterns, why they are so difficult to shift, and—most importantly—many, many ideas for shifting the negative patterns.

Extra challenges arise for adoptive parents, and these will be discussed together with ideas for working with these parents in Chapter 7. There is also a short discussion of some of the challenges facing us as we work with foster parents and ideas for how we can help them.

Finally we circle back to the beginning and look again at our relationship with the parent—how we 'play out' what we have learned (our past experiences, our vulnerabilities and triggers) as parents 'play out' what they have learned. This is our countertransference to the parent. We describe ideas as to how we can identify and then use this countertransference to help the parent. And our journey ends with acknowledging that throughout our career we need assistance in the work we do, whether with children or parents—it is hard work and important work.

There are many different people who fill the parental role for children—relatives, foster parents, group home workers, Big Sisters and Big Brothers, support workers, teachers, other school and community workers, neighbors, or the parents of friends. For simplicity's sake, the single term "parent" will be used in this book to encompass all of these important individuals. And while there are many different people working with the child and parents, again, for simplicity's sake, a single term, "child professional," will often be used. The goal of this book is to help *all those who work with parents* to become more skilled in helping those parents become the parents they wish to be.

As you flip through the pages, you will quickly realize this book is full of dialog examples. These examples come from a wide range of socioeconomic groups and include families of Caucasian, Black, First Nation, and Asian backgrounds. Gray shading is used to designate the professional's experience, thinking, and intended intervention. At the end of each chapter, there are "Points to Remember." These are *not* the main points of the chapter—those are already listed in bold print and in the table of contents. Rather, these "Points to Remember" are additional ideas important for us, as child professionals working with parents. They are ideas we need to keep in mind even as we focus on the main content of the chapter.

As always, there are many people to thank when writing a book. Without Dr. Mike Dadson, this book never would have been started; without Dr. Sandra Baita, cases and ideas would not have been debated and written out; and without Nancy Miller-Stone, the book would not have been finished. A special thanks to Dominique Whelan and Chris Orchard, who listened to my ideas and figured out visual ways to portray them. My thanks to Joan Tuttle, Susan Breiddal, Pauline Barrett, and Bea Elwood for their reading and comments. My thanks to Chris Whelan for his patience and constant support. And my thanks to all the counselors, therapists, teachers, social workers, and support workers who have brought and worked through cases with me. And thank you most of all to the many, many parents who have taught me so much.

CHAPTER 1

The Parents and Us

As we start this conversation, we need to define who we are and whom we are working with. As explained in the introduction, this book is written for all professionals working with children—teachers, support workers, day care providers, social workers, pediatricians, spiritual leaders, counselors, and therapists. If you are working with children in any capacity, you will be working with parents. And that is very fortunate! If we can help parents create a more secure and positive relationship with their children, the emotional lives of these children will be changed far more than by any direct work we do with the child. Parents are the most important people in a child's life. A positive change in their relationship with their child has the potential of creating more positive relationships for the child throughout his or her life.

This is not a book about parenting although undoubtedly ideas about parenting will come in. It is a book about child and youth professionals and how we can work with the parents. The type of work we do with parents—support or therapy—will depend on our field of expertise and the training we have. But in all interactions—support or therapy—there is the potential for a positive effect.

Who Are the Parents?

The Oxford dictionary defines 'parent' as "a person's father or mother" (Parent [Def. 1], 2016). Webster's defines 'parent' as "one that begets or brings forth offspring" (Parent [Def. 1a], 2016); "the material or source from which something is derived" (Parent [Def. 2b], 2016). While not challenging these definitions, we would like to expand these definitions. A parent is someone who used to be someone else's child and now has a child.

You may ask, why ask for this extension of the dictionary definition? Without this extension we miss a very important component of each parent's ability to parent. In our conversations with parents we need to look beyond what they have learned (or not learned) from books, from talking with friends, from courses about parenting, about what children need, and about how best to interact with their children. We need to be aware of what these parents have brought from their time as a child to their present-day parenting. Most importantly, what did they experience from their parents—how were they parented? This is a teaching about how to be a parent that parents are often least aware of—it is 'taught' long before the individual is aware of being taught. And yet, in many cases the ways the parent was parented is the most influential part of how they parent their own child.

You will notice in the last paragraph that the active verb changed from 'learned' to 'taught.' 'Learned' implies a choice—we can read or not read a book, we can decide to listen to a friend or not. 'Taught' implies something done to us—we do not have a choice as to the parenting pattern surrounding us as we grow up. And being an infant, a child, or even a youth observing and experiencing a parenting pattern, we do not have a choice as to whether this parenting influences us—it does because that is how humans work.

If we do not recognize the parents' early experiences of being parented and we do not address it in our work with them, their parenting is unlikely to change in significant ways. They may, indeed, learn new ways of responding, new ways of disciplining, new ways of supporting. But without some shift in processing[1] that early experience of being parented, parents are all too likely to continue with old, and possibly destructive, interactive patterns.

As we talk about parents, what we say applies to all parents whether biological parent, adoptive parent, foster parent, members of the extended family, or group home parents. We shall be talking more directly about adoptive families in Chapter 7 and at that point will talk about some of the extra complications that come into their relationships with their children. For our beginning discussions, let's stay as simple as we can—and, as you will find, that is not very simple. We need to look at parents and we need to look at ourselves. We need to look at attachment and interactive patterns, we need to look at neurobiology and how we can best shift patterns already engrained in the brain. We need to look at our own reactions and what they mean and how they can help us in our work.

What Do Parents Bring to Our Work with Them?

What Parents Want

First and foremost, most parents want to be good parents. They may define[2] being good parents as providing a healthy and safe world for their child. They may define being good parents as having children who follow rules and succeed in school. They may define being good parents as having children who are happy all the time. Or their definition may include having their own needs met by their child.

The other thing they want is for us to 'fix their child.' Fix their child in such a way that they will, indeed, be the 'good parent' they have envisaged. There will be some parents who are in our office or have invited us into their homes because they want to change, but they are the minority and they are not the parents we shall be talking about in this book.

Where Parents May Get Caught

At the same time as they want to be good parents, parents are caught in their own story. If their story is primarily a healthy one, they may be coming to see us about some stumbling spot—their child experiences a temperament very different from their own and, as a result, they are finding themselves in a struggle with their child (Thomas et al., 1968). Their child may have a learning disability or a mental health challenge and they want to learn skills for helping their child. Their child may have experienced a frightening or traumatic event and they want help for their child or for their child and themselves.

If, however, the parents' stories are not healthy ones, they may be coming to see us to help them relate in a different way to their child. They may be coming to see us because someone else (perhaps, protective services) has told them they have to. In the former case—wanting help to relate in a different way—they are likely to be at least moderately receptive. In the latter case—being told they have to—they are unlikely to be receptive. Receptive or not, they are there and we are there with them.

We will meet all of these parents—those with healthy stories and those with unhealthy stories, those who want to be there and those who don't want to be there—in the pages ahead. Each will bring challenges but each will also bring opportunities to make a difference for them and their children. That's a confounding statement—"difference for them and their children." Parents are not usually in our office because they want to be 'different'; they are there because they want their child to be 'different'—more compliant, less difficult, less anxious, less frightened or traumatized.

These parents who come to our offices with their children or allow us to come into their homes are in a state of distress. Whether they describe it as 'worry' or 'concern' or use stronger terms such as 'anger' or 'desperation,' underneath this terminology there will be powerful emotions.

Perhaps disappointment—not being the 'perfect parent' they had determined they would be, not having the 'perfect child' they wanted to have, not continuing with the exciting life they wished for. Perhaps fear—fear they have failed; fear something cannot be repaired. Guilt or even shame may be experienced—guilt they did something wrong; shame that they need to ask for help. There may also be the very strong emotion of disgust (Tomkins, 1963)—disgust with themselves, disgust that they are not the parents they wanted to be. In order not to experience these emotions of disappointment, fear, shame, and disgust with themselves, parents all too often, and not consciously, project these feelings onto their child. There is something wrong with their child—fix it.

Trained as professionals to help children, we may, all too easily, follow the parent's diversion and focus on the child, not the parent. We have been trained to tune to the child and even when the child is not in the room (for example, during an intake interview or a developmental interview), our underbrain (not the unconscious but that part of the brain which holds the agenda for a particular session, the hypotheses we are developing, and the questions that need to be asked) is focused on the child. For those of us who work in agencies or institutions, we are going to need to complete a report about the child or the child's situation. Yes, there will be references to the parent but the report is not about the parent, it is about the child and so, being efficient professionals, we focus there. For those of us who work in private practice, we are going to need to provide feedback to the parents and they do not want to know about themselves—there is a reason they project their disappointment, fear, shame, disgust onto the child—they want to know what is 'wrong' with their child.

There is another reason some of us follow the parent's diversion. We chose to work with children because that is where our interest lies—not with adults/parents. Indeed, we may even dislike the idea of focusing on the parent. It is not so much that we do not know how, we do not even want to work with them. If only the parent had been more attentive, more sensitive, more aware, the child would not have been caught in a negative situation. If only the parent were more flexible, more open, the child would not be experiencing this level of frustration. We may feel antagonism, even anger, at the parent and not want to be in the same room as the parent.

But if we follow diversion away from the parent, we miss what could be our best resource for helping the child—the child's attachment experience with his parent. Attachment (the child-parent interactive connection) has been described as a psychological immune system (Schore, 2012; Siegel & Hartzell, 2003; see also Chapter 4, this volume)—the more secure (steady and supportive) the attachment, the more resilient the child can be when faced with disappointments, threats, traumas. The more unbalanced (shifting, denying, disorganized or what is known in the psychological community as 'insecure' attachment), the less resilient the child is when faced with negative encounters.

In our training to work with children, we learn to establish a trust relationship with the child. Then the child will be able to tell us—either in words or in behaviors—about his experiences, his struggles, his pain or fright. As we work with the child and with his environment, the child starts to calm, experiences more regulated arousal, and becomes more aware of safety in his world. As we interact with the child and provide him with space to show us his story, the child experiences relief and a stronger sense of self.

But our interaction, whatever our role, with the child is not an ongoing relationship. It can provide a new experience of a relationship, and one that we hope the child will be able to internalize and hold and, as a result, come to believe more in himself and in others who are trustworthy. Through the relationship, the child hopefully gains an expanded window of tolerance[3] so he does not move as quickly into hyperarousal or hypoarousal. The relationship, hopefully, gives him a safe space to experience and integrate enough bits of prior distress or trauma so he can move ahead without the distress or trauma shaping each new experience. The relationship gives him a positive experience of himself in which he can believe. Then the child leaves. But if the parent has not changed, the family does not change. And the child's negative experiences are all too likely to continue.

The child may, because of the positive therapeutic, supportive, or educational experience, be more open to the parent, more responsive to the parent, less anxious, less scared. But what about the parent? Is the parent able to be open to the child? As the child settles, parents often settle, and they are able to engage in more attuned, supportive interaction with their child. As the parent is more consistently attuned to the child, the child will be better able to trust and thus go to the parent for support—a support that will be more consistently available. There will be a movement toward a more positive and secure attachment between child and parent. That is the fantasy—and sometimes reality—story of professional interventions with children.

It is the other stories that we are concerned with in this book. It is the stories where the distress of the parents blocks their ability to be adequately available to their children. And while the child and we may be able to interrelate, it is the relationship between the child and the parent that is the important one, the one the child is craving and the one the child needs for continued growth.

MARIE (21 YEARS OLD)—mother of a 6-year-old boy sits rigid on the couch as the 6-year-old puts his head on her shoulder. The professional meeting with Marie finds herself going tight inside—what's wrong, doesn't Marie see that Jimmy is frightened and unsure as to what he should do, doesn't she see that he needs reassurance, needs some physical response from her? No wonder he is creating stories about a fantasy world in which there are two parents and several siblings.

But Marie is not here for therapy. She is completing school, working part time, and raising her son—far more than her mother ever did.

JOHN (45 YEARS OLD)—father of a 10-year-old boy—engages the school counselor in animated conversation about the contents of the office while his son flips through the pages of a magazine. The school counselor finds herself floundering as to how to redirect the conversation back to why they are here without cutting John off. No wonder the 10-year-old has rages.

John definitely is not here for therapy. He tells the school counselor he has his world 'all together.' Although it is a struggle to be a single father with two children, he is doing his best to raise his children, and they have wonderful times together. If his son would just do what he is told, there would be no problem.

JOCELYN (34 YEARS OLD)—mother of a 13-year-old girl—responds with minimal information or the statement, *"That's not relevant,"* to all the social worker's questions. Although the social worker knows it is relevant, he finds himself tongue-tied and really wanting to just end this session and get back to the activity room where the 13-year-old is willing to engage with the art supplies. No wonder Delia is withdrawn and verbally uncommunicative while being behaviorally intrusive with other children.

Jocelyn is only meeting with the social worker because protective services said this was necessary for her family to stay out of their files. We will be discussing the cases of Marie, John, and Jocelyn further in the pages to come.

JOAN (40 YEARS OLD)—foster parent of a 14-year-old girl who is now in her ninth placement in as many years—tells about how 'attached' she is to her new foster daughter. Joan realizes that this is the 'honeymoon stage,' but she and Annie have connected so well that she knows they will be able to survive the more difficult times. She feels a real connection with Annie and is so thrilled with this chance to make a difference for Annie. The professional suppresses the urge to list the problems ahead. Realism is going to be more helpful than fantasy, but the professional needs to work with Joan, not in opposition to her.

Joan is happy to meet with the professional, but the therapy is for Annie and not related to her. As she sees it, the professional will work to help Annie—and her foster placement will be the one to make the difference for Annie.

Although Marie and Jocelyn's disengagement from their children and the therapist is most obvious, all four parents are clearly disengaged. All the children are experiencing some form of insecure attachment as a result of less than optimal growing-up environments. All the children may, indeed, profit from some form of intervention, either directly with the child or indirectly with the family, and their emotional distress may be able to settle. But if the relationship in which they are living (child-parent relationship) does not improve, their emotional distress is unlikely to go away. They will not have a chance to experience a positive and consistent sense of self in relation to their parent. Without this positive sense of self and parent, it is difficult for a child to achieve a positive and consistent sense of self in relation to the world. It will be difficult for this child, in the future, to have a positive, consistent relationship with a partner and eventually with his or her own children. The insecure attachment and the 'less than optimal growing-up environment' experienced with his or her parent will pass intergenerationally to his or her children.

Patterns of Interaction

Patterns of parent-child interaction may come from parents' recall of their own interaction with their parents if what they remember is a 'happy childhood' or it may come from 'how they are going to do it differently' if their active memory[4] holds negative experiences from childhood. While this image of the good parent-child relationship is important, unfortunately—or in some cases fortunately—it is not necessarily the determinant of how they are going to parent. Far more influential will be what they actually were taught—experiential memory—as they grew up.

As soon as we start talking about teaching and learning, we are talking about the brain, about the neuronal firing within the brain as an individual has a variety of experiences. With these neuronal firings, neurochemicals are released that cause dendritic changes and the formation of synapses—the connections between neurons—which determine the future pattern of firing when these neurons are stimulated. This pattern of neuronal firing may relate to information about safety or lack of safety in the world, about safety with one person and not another, about how different people respond, and about what behavior follows another behavior. The neuronal firing may provide information related to the somatic sensations or emotional reactivity connected with these activities, and the child is taught (again, neuronal firing) to attend to or to ignore these signals. The neuronal patterns holding the experiences of safety and attachment experienced from when one is an infant or young toddler occur within the child's brain at a very deep level, and primarily within the right hemisphere (Schore, 2001, 2003, 2012). They are held at what can be referred to as an 'unconscious' level—a level that does not include ongoing awareness (Mancia, 2006). These neuronal patterns are the initial learning within the child's brain related to parenting—patterns that are there *not because the child chose them but because the child experienced them*.[5]

They may be positive—patterns that hold safety and secure attachment—or they may be negative—patterns that hold fright and insecure attachment. The child cannot choose. These patterns not only shape the infant/toddler concept of self in relation to self and others but also hold their 'knowledge' of how parenting is to be done. Years later, when the child becomes a parent, these patterns emerge. For the parents who experienced brain neuronal patterns related to positive parenting, they become, for the most part, positive parents like their parents. For the parents who experienced brain neuronal patterns related to negative parenting, they are likely to become negative parents like their parents. For most parents, they will have received both positive and negative responses from their parents. We want to help parents notice both—one set to recognize and hold on to and the other to recognize and shift.

Some parents with early learned negative parenting patterns recognize that they want to do parenting differently from how their parents did. They read about parenting, they talk about parenting, and they make decisions about how they will do it differently. Then they become parents, and when things are going well, their new chosen way of parenting works well. But when things do not go well—as is inevitable with parenting—and the parent becomes agitated, becomes upset, new thought-out patterns are harder to hold. Without calm thinking and reflection, old neuronal patterns take over without the parent ever wanting this to happen. This old pattern 'takeover' is also likely to happen when something similar to their experience as a child happens in the present. Perhaps their child behaves in a way similar to the way they behaved as a child; perhaps their child shows a characteristic that is similar in some way to a characteristic of their own parent.[6]

The pattern most relevant to parenting is the attachment pattern. Attachment, defined as the seeking of safety and comfort together with the giving of safety and comfort (Schore, 2003), has been found to be an instinctual pattern in both animals and humans (Bowlby, 1969).[7] Some of the parents we will meet in the pages ahead will have been able to establish secure attachment patterns with their children, but the majority of the parents we work with will have experienced insecure (insecure avoidant, insecure ambivalent, insecure disorganized) attachment and will carry many of these patterns on to their attachment interactions with their own children. As we will discuss in more detail in Chapter 4, insecure avoidant patterns occur when the parents distance themselves in some way from the infant/child, and as a result the infant/child learns to hold more of her needs and feelings inside in order not to want what she cannot get. Insecure ambivalent patterns occur when the parent is inconsistent in his or her reactions to the child—sometimes trying to meet all the infant/child's needs but, because this is very exhausting and actually beyond what any parent is capable of, sometimes not meeting the infant/child's needs. The infant/child, having experienced all his needs being met, becomes more and more demanding, and the parent in exhaustion becomes more and more ambivalent in responding. Insecure disorganized is the most difficult attachment pattern for the infant/child. Within this pattern the parent swings from caretaking to angry and/or neglectful, and—within the extreme situations—from abusive, to frightened, to frozen. These changes (often a result of an internal trigger or flashback) in the parent occur without the child being aware of any cause. As a result, the child is left in a state of confusion. Am I loved and cared for? Am I hated and hurt? Am I the one who caused hurt to my parent? The child is left with contradictory beliefs about himself—I am loved, I am hated; I

8 The Parents and Us

am good, I hurt others. The contradictions are so extreme that the beliefs cannot connect together and may lead to the child experiencing dissociation. These attachment patterns will be looked at in more detail in the chapters ahead.

We will also be talking about patterns of emotional expression. As with the attachment pattern, there is a biological element underlying how each of us expresses emotion,[8] together with a pattern learned from the world around us—our first teachers being our parents. We shall be talking about parents who are able to be open but contained with their emotions, the parent who is dismissive of emotions, the parent who has dissociated emotions, and parents who are overwhelmed by their emotions and unable to contain themselves when with their child.

We have been talking about parents—who they are, what they bring, and their patterns of interaction. Now let's look at the other side of the equation—ourselves, the child professionals.

Who Are We?

As noted in the introduction, there are many different professionals working with children—from day care providers to protective service workers, from child and youth support workers to child psychiatrists, from foster and adoptive workers to child therapists—and all these individuals come in contact with parents.

As we view the Child's Helping System (see Chart 1.1), we find the child in the middle of three concentric ovals. The child, as our primary client, is in the center oval. The second oval includes parents. This may be a fairly narrow space with just one or two parents, or it may be expanded with extended family members (siblings, grandparents, aunts) or alternative sets of parents (foster, group home parents, adoptive parents). For some children a narrow second oval (two parents) may imply a healthy setting, while for other children a narrow second oval may imply a rigid, unhealthy setting where outside assistance is all too often blocked.

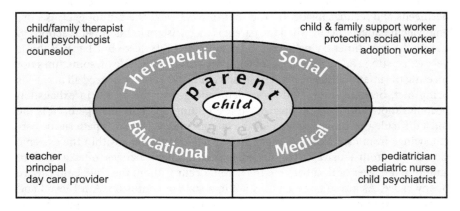

Chart 1.1 The Child's Helping System.

The outer oval includes ourselves, the many different professionals who come in contact with the child and, thus, with the parent. Some of us (family support workers, foster and adoptive workers) already have the parent as our primary client, but most of us consider the child as our primary concern. 'We' are anyone who is working with or on behalf of children.

Being in the outside oval we have the opportunity to work directly or indirectly with the child, and we have the opportunity, if we take it, to work directly with the parent. If we ignore the oval between us and the child, we lose not only a primary resource for helping the child, but we also lose the *ongoing* resource for helping each child.

We will come and go in a child's life; the parent is there day after day, month after month, and—we hope—year after year.

What Do We Bring to Our Work with Parents?

What We Want

Just as parents want to be good parents, so we want to be good therapists, good pediatricians, good child or family support workers, good protection workers, good teachers. We may have chosen this area of work because we enjoy being with children, because we are fascinated by family dynamics, or because we want to make a positive difference for another person. Some of us may be here because our experience of being parented was a negative one and we want to make it better for children in the future. Some of us may be here because our experience of being parented was a positive one and we want to offer something to the generations ahead. Whatever the reason, we want to do our job well—otherwise, why read this book?

We also want to be able to go home at the end of the day to our own life—a life that will involve taking care of ourselves and may involve taking care of partners, children, and perhaps even parents. To do this we need, at the end of our work day, to know that we have engaged in as healthy a manner as possible (given the constraints of our job and perhaps limited capabilities of the individuals with whom we are working, we need always to focus on the possible not the ideal) with the people with whom we work. We have listened[9] to the children and to their parents, we have noticed the hurt and struggle inside them, and we have honored[10] this hurt and struggle while at the same time nudging the children and parents forward to examine their own experiences and to experiment with change.

Where We May Get Caught

Just as with parents, we may be caught in the experiences we had growing up—both good experiences and bad experiences. Again, similar to parents, some of these experiences are well known to us (within our active memories) and some we are unaware of (within our experiential memories). We shall be talking more about that in the next chapter, "Learning about the Parent and about Us," and then again in Chapter 8.

One area we do know about but tend, far too often, to overlook is our cultural background. Cultural background can refer to the history of the racial group in which we grew up. For some of us it is quite privileged—economically or educationally—and for others of us it has not been privileged. Whichever is the case, many of the parents with whom we are working will not have had the same experiences as our own. As a result, they are likely to view many situations from a different perspective than our own. While we may not agree with their perspective, we do need to respect their perspective (see Chapter 6 for further discussion). Cultural background also refers to the belief structure (religious, political, ethical, gender) within which we grew up. Again, we may not agree but do need to respect.

And we have an advantage most parents don't have—our professional training. For those of us whose training has included therapeutic skills, there has been quite a shift over the last hundred years. Therapeutic professional training during the 1900s focused, for the most part, on a disease model—what was wrong with the child. Early conversations were influenced by Freud and psychoanalysis and focused on 'projection,' 'transference,' and 'projective identification.' There was some limited conversation about 'countertransference': the analyst's experience. Then the focus switched to learning and 'classical conditioning,' 'operant conditioning,' and 'reinforcement.'

Only toward the end of the twentieth century did attention start to shift more directly to ourselves, to the other side of the interaction. Interaction (even if mostly one-sided) always has two sides. We may be considered professionals, but we are also human—thank heavens, because it is our humanness that gives us the greatest possibility for successful work with whomever we are working (Brandell, 1992; Gelso & Hayes, 2007; Wieland, 1997). University courses and continuing education workshops have started talking about 'countertransference': about the reactions we have when we are interacting with another person. These reactions can give us a great deal of information about the other person, but they also hold information related to ourselves. We need to learn how to separate these two pieces of information in order that our personal reaction (our attachment pattern, our style of emotional expression, and many other elements outside the purview of this book) does not interfere with what we are reacting to in the other person. It is only when we do this separation accurately that we are able to empathize and resonate with the child or parent with whom we are working (see Chapter 8).

The explosion of research in neuroscience over the last two decades has affected all areas of psychology and education. Understanding how the brain develops and how it is affected by experiences is particularly important for those of us working with children and parents. It is during the childhood years—the years when parents are the major influence—that tremendous growth occurs within the central and peripheral nervous system. Thus, understanding brain development, how parent-child interaction affects brain development, and—for our discussion here—how understanding the brain can help us be more effective in our interactions with parents is important for our work with parents.

The content of our professional training differs depending on the role we are going to be playing with children or families. We may be going into the field of teaching. We may be focusing on the protection of children or on work with the entire family unit. Our training may come through academic courses, internships, continuing education, reading, or supervision. This training helps us build our understanding and our skills in relation to the many issues related to child and family development and to working with children and families. Training also helps us build our communication and interactive skills.

But along the way, even with excellent training, there will be many places where we may get caught—political mandates, agency requirements, job descriptions, parental demands, and both parent and child resistance. In this book we shall be focusing on parental demands and parental resistance.

Within our training we learn about observation and assessment of children. We watch children's physical response to different places, different situations, and different people, including their parents and ourselves. We notice how they interpret our questions, how they respond to requests, and how they use toys and other materials. We notice what increases their anxiety and what reassures them. We notice how they do or do not turn to their parents, how they respond to their parents' responses, and how they react to their parents' reactions.

We learn about connecting to children—about attuning with the child's wariness or anger or perhaps the child's relief or excitement at meeting with us. We learn how to use the child's language in order that the child feels understood but not talked down to. If we are teachers, we learn to develop lessons that will engage the child's interest and challenge her to try something new. If we are support workers or counselors, we learn to keep our office or play area as consistent as possible so the child can learn to trust us. We learn when to keep our comments within the metaphor of the child's activity and when to expand our comments to include the child's real world in order neither to overwhelm the child nor ignore the pain in the child's real world.

What we need along with learning to connect with the child is how to connect with the child's parent. We learn about parenting styles and ideas for more positive and supportive parenting interaction. We learn about attachment and the errors that can lead to insecure attachment patterns. But seldom are there opportunities for learning how to interact with parents in a way that can change the parent's ability to interact with her or his children—and so we get caught trying to teach parents 'how to parent.'

Unfortunately, parenting is not a skill like drawing or throwing a ball. There are not certain steps to be learned and then to practice. Parenting is an interactive process that all of us experienced as children—for some of us, mostly a good experience, and for others, mostly a negative experience. It is that experience parents bring forward to their interaction with their children. In order for parents with a negative experience to move forward to a new way of parenting, they need more than being told what to do. They need to experience something different. And this is where we, as professionals committed to helping children, can play an important role. We can offer the parents a new and more positive experience of being heard, being seen, and being valued.

To offer parents 'a new and more positive experience of being heard, being seen, and being valued' we are going to need all the knowledge and skills we have already developed through our training (see Chapter 5) together with new knowledge (see in particular Chapters 3 and 8) and new skills (see Chapter 6). We will need to notice the parents' reactions to us (transference)[11] and our own reactions to them (countertransference, see Chapter 8). We will need to notice which of our reactions are a result of what is going on in our own lives at that particular moment, which are a result of some earlier experience of our own we have not adequately processed, and which is a result of reverberation with the parent's own state. In our work with parents we want to be able to notice the differences between these two internal reactions—and then, to move away from those that belong to us and to address those that come from the parent.

Because we are the child's advocate and support, we are likely to become acutely aware of a parent's inability to see what the child needs in a particular moment. We become acutely aware of the parent's effort to change the child to her or his image of what the child should be. This awareness brings up in us an impatience and criticism—criticism of the parent. And criticism, even when unvoiced, is sensed by the parent and, in most situations, creates a defensive response. The parent, the person whom we need as part of the team for helping the child, draws away from us. We are left with fewer resources for helping the child or, in some situations, the child may even be pulled out of his work with us. In either case, the child has lost an opportunity for positive repair and we, as the child's advocate, have lost an opportunity to help make a child's world better.

In the pages ahead, we will be asking you—as you become aware of a parent's inability to see what his or her child needs—also to be aware that that parent did not have a parent who saw what he or she needed. Keeping that piece of information clear in our minds helps us be less judgmental, less blaming. Asking parents questions about what they notice in their child, rather than giving them statements about what we have noticed in their child or what we think they should do, lets parents know we want them as part of a team working with us to help the child, not the enemy to be resisted. Feelings of impatience and criticism make sense but are unproductive. An effort to see parents differently—this is not what they wanted for their child or for themselves—is more productive.

How Child Professionals Can Work with Parents

As child professionals, we are well aware of the importance of helping children experience more secure attachment. We are also aware from the research on attachment (Schore, 2003, 2012) that helping a child develop secure attachment cannot be based on the child or even on the events around the child. Secure attachment is based on the interaction between the 'individual and the important other' (the seeking of safety and comfort together with the giving of safety and comfort; Schore, 2003).

For a child, this means child-parent interaction. As we look at this interaction, we also look at how it has been determined by the way the parent as a child was parented. For the child-parent experience of an insecure attachment to shift to secure, the parent-figure's own experience of interpersonal interaction needs to shift from insecure to secure. Where is this new experience to come from? Maria, John, Jocelyn, and Joan have all moved away from their own parents. They have moved into their own homes and they have become parents. They have contacted a variety of professionals, but not for themselves. They came to have the child professional fix their child.

As discussed in Chapter 3, neuronal activity related to attachment patterns occurs in the deep cortices of the right hemisphere (Schore, 2003, 2012). When we can talk about the deep right cortices, when we analyze and explain about attachment, we are activating the outer cortex of the brain, not the deep right cortices. These analyses and explanation will not change attachment patterns or behavior. The deep cortices of the right hemisphere are areas of the brain affected by experience and in particular relationship experiences (Schore, 2012; Schore & Schore, 2014). If these children are to have a chance at a more secure attachment experience, then their parents need to have a new and more positive attachment experience—an experience they are not seeking or asking for but which they very much need.

In the ideal world, individual therapy would be available free of charge for all the parents who bring their children for help. The parent's individual therapist could be given the job of creating/providing a new positive relationship experience for the parent. Thanks to the parent's therapist, the parent—as she or he engaged in a positive therapeutic relationship with recognition, attunement, and responding and as she or he recognized and processed her or his own difficult experiences—would bit by bit develop new neuronal connections within the deep right cortices related to secure attachment and sensitive interrelating. These new neuronal patterns would then be available as the parent interacted with his or her child. The parent would be able to notice when the child needed more comforting or increased security and when the child needed space to move off on his own. The parent would be able to attune and respond to his or her child. And the child, in turn, would develop neuronal connections related to secure attachment and positive interrelating.

But this is not the ideal world; there is not an individual therapist for every parent, and even where there is the possibility of individual therapy, many parents choose not to engage in the therapy. Creating a new positive relationship experience for the parent is left to us, the child professionals.

This is probably the most difficult part of being a child professional. We chose to work with children because we felt a particular affinity with or interest in children, because we recognized the importance of the childhood years. We spent years studying child development and learning to be observant of child behavior and child learning. We did not become child professionals in order to work with adults, and particularly not with resistant adults. It is all too easy for us to see the mistakes the parents have made and still are making. Often we become angry with parents for their mistakes and impatient that they have not changed their parenting. We cringe as we hear them criticize their child or order their child around. Indeed, the most difficult countertransference reactions we encounter are not, in most situations, with the children with whom we work but with their parents (see Chapter 8).

This book is for child professionals who see working with parents as an important part of their job. It is also for child professionals who want nothing to do with working with parents but yet recognize that it is important if they are to be able to help the child. In the chapters ahead we will look at how we can learn about the parent and what they may have missed in their own experience of being parented. This helps us know what we are going to need to bring to them in our work. We will find out that not only do we need to learn about the parent, we also need to learn about ourselves if we are to be able to help the parent (Chapter 2). We shall then take a step away from our story of working with the parent to take a look at the brain (Chapter 3), since that is where the early learning about parenting is held. We shall look at the roles of attachment and emotional management in parenting. Holding this new information about the brain and parenting, we shall look at the skills we already have and can use in our work with parents (Chapter 5) and ideas for helping parents out of negative parenting patterns (Chapter 6).

We shall briefly talk about some of the special challenges in homes where the child has been adopted (Chapter 7). Our own experience of the work with parents will be referred to several times during the coming chapter but will be discussed in detail in Chapter 8.

Summary

As parents come into our classrooms or offices, as they open their doors to let us come into their homes, they are seldom seeking help for themselves. But in most cases, they need help, and because they are meeting with us we have the opportunity to provide that help. And as we provide that help we are helping their children.

As our relationship with the parent becomes stronger and more positive, neuronal networks supporting stronger, more positive interrelating are created and strengthened. A new, more secure attachment experience between parent and child becomes possible.

Chapter 1—Points to Remember

- Our choice of words is important—"learned" implies that we chose to hold a way of doing something; "taught" implies that we experienced something and, as a result, that way of doing something is held in our neuronal networks.
- Most parents want to be good parents.
- Remembering to focus on parents takes effort.
- If we are not careful, our cultural background shapes the way we see the world.
- Our work is easier and more successful if we see the parent as someone who does not know how to make his or her child's world better than it is, not as someone who is doing it all wrong.

Notes

1 "Processing" is a word that is used quite loosely in psychological literature. It implies far more than just thinking about something. There needs to be a change in the experiencing (on both the conscious and the unconscious level) of something for there to be true processing. Many examples of this will be given in later chapters.

2 "Defining" implies an explicit verbal statement. Here we are referring to an internal nonverbal statement (one the parent may or may not be aware of) and, thus, one that we need to decipher not only from what the parent says but also from their voice tone and from the behaviors we notice (Siegel & Hartzell, 2003). The internal statement may be congruent with the external one or it may be very different.

3 The 'window of tolerance' refers to the range of arousal within the autonomic nervous system, within which individuals are able to interact successfully with themselves and with others (see pages 63 and 74 for further discussion).
4 The term "active memory" is being used here in place of "explicit memory"—that which the individual can remember with words and thus is actively accessible. The term "experiential memory" will be used for "implicit memory"—that which the individual remembers through emotion and experience but not declarative learning. Implicit memory affects how we react and behave but without our conscious awareness (Tulving & Craik, 2000).
5 As discussed further in Chapter 3, mammalian brains have neurons referred to as 'mirror neurons.' These neurons fire when an individual (infant, child, adolescent, adult) observes someone else doing something. The firing of a neuron means that the neuron is learning/practicing that behavior. Thus, the parent's reactions experienced by the infant are learned without any conscious awareness.
6 In the psychological literature this is referred to as a "trigger."
7 John Bowlby's close observations in the mid-1900s of mother-infant interaction in both animal and human species (Bowlby, 1969, 1973, 1980) highlighted the biological and instinctual nature of attachment bonding (the seeking of safety and comfort together with the giving of safety and comfort; Schore, 2003, 2012) between an infant and a caregiver. Bowlby described these attachment dynamics and highlighted the effect of these dynamics on the child's internal working models of self and other. Over the half-century since Bowlby wrote there has been extensive research in this field—first observational research, then more rigorous research within an experimental setting (the Strange Situation) which led to identification of attachment classifications (secure, insecure ambivalent, insecure avoidant, insecure disorganized; George & Solomon, 1999), then larger, longer-term studies, some of which have included intergenerational groupings (Shah et al., 2010). More recently researchers have moved back to the micro-level and started to look at the neurological mechanism behind attachment (Schore, 2003, 2012). While our neurological knowledge is still very limited, it can help us in our own understanding and, most importantly, it can help us develop more successful ways to work with parents.
8 Early work by Cannon in the 1920s and Selye in the 1930s (see brief review in Porges, 2009) highlighted how both the autonomic nervous system (ANS) and the central nervous system (CNS) play primary roles in the 'experience' of an emotion and, in particular, in fight-flight reactivity. Porges (2004, 2011) expanded our understanding of the ANS with his identification of the reactive freeze response and the development of the polyvagal theory of affect expression (reviewed in Chapter 3). As with attachment patterns, this understanding makes us aware that we experience 'emotions' at a physiological level as well as a cognitive level.

Research in the 1960s by Thomas et al. (1968) identified nine temperament traits that have a physiological basis but are tempered by interaction with parents and others as the child grows up. Temperament (that which is biological and that which is learned) affects our way of expressing emotion.
9 Remembering that 'listening' includes observation of play, of body shifts, and of voice tone in the individual with whom we are interacting and within ourselves.
10 As we will talk about in Chapters 4, 5, 6, and 7, naming, while at the same time attuning with and validating the parent's struggles around the many hurts connected with parenting, provides for the parent an honoring of their experiences.
11 'Transference' here refers to individuals in the parents' lives—very likely their own parents—whom they are reminded of, usually on an unconscious level, when they interact with us. The emotions and reactions from this earlier relationship (positive or negative) are then transferred onto us and acted out in their interactions with us as if we were that earlier person. If it is a positive transference, it can assist us in our work with the parent. If, however, it is a negative transference, it will likely create numerous blocks in our work with them.

CHAPTER 2

Learning About the Parent and About Us

Sandra Wieland & Sandra Baita

The importance of learning about the life of an individual child, not just a child with a problem or a diagnosis, is emphasized more and more in our training as professionals working with children and families. In this chapter we will look at both formal (assessment questions and genograms) and informal (observing parent-child interaction; experiencing parent-us interaction) ways of gathering information about the parent. While teachers and other individuals within the educational and the medical sectors of the Child's Helping System (p. 8) may find items of interest in this chapter, the chapter is not written for them. It is written for those of us who have specialized training in understanding and supporting parents who need new and more positive ways to connect with their children. Some of us have additional therapeutic skills, while others have focused more on how to provide support and assistance for parents negotiating the bureaucratic systems involved with adoption or protection issues. Both of these groups—those of us who focus on counseling and those of us who focus on navigating the bureaucratic systems—need to know more about the parent.

We shall first be talking about the process of getting to know about the child and parent, and most particularly the parent's parents. And then we shall talk about the importance of getting to know about ourselves and about how we react with parents. Only when we are aware of what we were taught as children and of how we normally react with parents will we be able to be alert to what a particular reaction to a particular parent means.

Referral Phone Call

Our first chance to get to know the parent is the referral phone call. Whether this call is taken by ourselves or a receptionist, it is helpful to note who is making the call (mother, father, grandparent, social services) and the individual's tone of voice (distressed, anxious, flat, angry, impatient, matter-of-fact) as well as the referral reason and other general information. Which parent calls highlights who is (and more importantly who is not) taking responsibility for the child's present experience. The tone of voice and the way the concern is described starts to give us an indication of the parent's experience of the present situation.

When scheduling the initial appointment with the parents, it is important, if the child is living with both parents, that both parents be present. So often mothers take on the responsibility of seeking and arranging therapy for a child and indicate that the father is too busy to attend appointments. If we go along with this, we are missing not only an important piece of information on the child's early years but also an important partner in helping the child. Even if it means delaying the beginning of therapy for several weeks, inclusion of both parents is an important message to convey to parents right at the start.

The father, however, may be adamant that, even though he gives his consent for support or therapy for his child, he thinks this is a waste of time. He does not want others 'messing with his family,' he thinks the problem is not serious enough to seek help, or he just does not want to be involved. In such a situation, we may be able to encourage him to come in on his own in order to obtain his formal consent. This would offer an occasion to highlight not only the importance of support or therapy but also that we are able to be respectful of him and able to listen closely to his objections *without* contradicting them. We can invite him to get in touch with us at any point in the future when he might wish to do so. If the referral has a legal component to it, this approach obviously would need to be adapted to the legal requirements.

If the child is living in two homes, we will want to meet separately with each parent. Other significant parent-figures (live-in partners, grandparents) could be included in sessions along with a parent. If there were not questions regarding 'significant others' during the referral call interview, these questions would need to be included in the Developmental Interview.

Developmental Interview

Our second chance to get to know the parents and to begin a relationship with them is at the initial appointment[1], which is scheduled for gathering information on the pregnancy/birth of the child; on the child's infant/toddler years; on the child's experiences at home, at school, in the neighborhood; on the teen years; and behaviors in the present. This is a parent's usual understanding of what will be included during the Developmental Interview. We are, however, going to need a great deal more information than this if we are to be able to help the child. As mentioned in Chapter 1, part of helping the child is enabling the parent to be more positively and consistently present to the child. And to do this we need to know about the parent.

Yet, we must remember that the parents did not come asking for help for themselves—they are not here to talk about themselves. We must always be respectful of this. Our first questions should focus on the child and the parent's concern related to the child. As we start to gather developmental information related to the pregnancy and to the child's infant years, we can ask how those times were for the parent. In this way, we start to highlight that the parent's experiences were relevant for the child's development. Also, from the parent's responses we start to get a glimpse of the parent's learned attachment pattern, pattern of emotional expression, and ways of handling stress.

The following discussion includes only a few of the questions that need to be asked about the child. We are focusing in this book on work with parents and, thus, in this chapter on "Learning about the Parent," we shall be concentrating on the questions related to the parents—their experiences of parenting and their experiences of being parented.

Present Concern

As we start our conversation with the parents, we will want to refer to the information given in the referral phone call. This assures the parents that we are already focusing on them and their concerns and they are not just another name on a list given to us.

In the referral phone call you mentioned—, tell me more about that. . . . When did you become concerned about this? . . . Who was first concerned about this? . . . Who is most concerned now? . . . Do you agree that this is a problem? . . . How do each of you talk with your child about this? . . . Why is it that each of you think this is happening? . . . What is it that each of you is hoping that [protective services, support services, therapy] will be able to achieve?

We are focusing here on how each of the parents experiences their child, their level of concern with regard to the present problem, and how they do or do not work together with regard to the problem. This also provides us with a chance to join with each parent in relation to her or his concern. If only the mother is there, asking about the father highlights the value we are placing on the father's contribution to parenting and also enables us to better grasp the mother's attitude toward the father.

Child's Development

It is helpful to ask whether the pregnancy was planned, whether it was mom's first pregnancy, whether it was dad's first pregnancy, how they felt about the pregnancy, and what that period of time was like for each of them and for their relationship. Considerable information related to the parents' relationship at that time will come from these questions. Of particular importance will be questions related to any losses or frightening events experienced during the two years before and after the child's birth.[2] Further questions related to where and how the parent managed during that time and whether the parent received, or did not receive, support (both physical help and emotional support) during that time provide information on what resources the parent does or does not have and the parent's ability to seek and use help.

Questions related to the baby's temperament, how the parent soothed the baby, and, most particularly, where the parent was taught this way of being with the baby are important. The latter question highlights that caring for babies is not an innate ability but rather one that is taught to them—either from the parenting the parents received or from a conscious effort by the parent to do things differently.

We can ask who was living in the home where the child grew up and about tensions in the home between the various adults and older children, recognizing that tension can be caused by economic strain, by differing attitudes toward babies/toddlers/children, by differing degrees of willingness to be involved in care for the child, by instances of physical or emotional violence between the couple or toward the child, by interference from outsiders (perhaps family or protection services), or by health challenges such as feared miscarriages or postpartum depression.

Florence & Ted, 6 Years Old

> **REFERRAL:** Ted was referred by his school for play therapy because of disruptive behavior on the playground and in the classroom. Ted's father had left the home when he was 2 years old.

THERAPIST: *Was Ted a quiet and calm baby or did he cry and have a difficult time settling?*[3]

FLORENCE: *Oh, goodness, no! Quiet? Calm? He would cry all day all night, I was exhausted!*

THERAPIST: *[Speaks with a heaviness in his voice.]*[4] *What was that like for you?*

FLORENCE: *I felt like a failure because I was unable to calm him down. It reminded me what my mother told me when I got pregnant, "You won't know how to hold your child."' I felt like "Oh my God, she was right!" I used to think she was looking at me from her grave [her mother had unexpectedly died two months prior to the birth of Ted] and laughing at me, like, you know, 'I told you!,' and that made me feel even worse. She used to say I was a whiny baby, I don't know what she did to manage me. I thought it was fate, if I used to be a whiny baby I deserved to have a whiny baby. That's why I didn't want any help. I had this neighbor, she was so nice, she would come to talk to me. But then I refused to have her around. I didn't feel comfortable—she would hold Ted and he would smile at her but not at me—so I started making excuses not to see her, and one day she stopped coming over. I'm a mess, aren't I [Laughs]?*

THERAPIST: *What a hard time! No, you're not a mess. Sounds as if your mother was very negative—as if you may never have had a chance to learn ways of calming from her as you grew up. Knowing how to calm either ourselves or our babies is not something anyone is born knowing how to do. Each of us is taught it from the way our parent did or did not soothe us. And how hard it is when someone else, like your neighbor, was taught a skill you wish you had been taught. I can understand your feeling uncomfortable with* *your neighbor calming Ted. [Validates.] [Florence nods.] Tell me, how is Ted now? Did anything change?*

FLORENCE: *No, not at all. He is still a whiny child, only now he's 6, he's no longer a baby, he should be able to control himself. Sometimes it's so unbearable that I lock myself in my room and leave him whining until he gets tired. I don't know what to do. I don't think he's going to change, I'm not going to change. Well, here we are—do you think you can change him?*

THERAPIST: *No, I can't change him, but I do think the two of us working together can bring more calmness into your and Ted's lives. Your describing so clearly what it was like when Ted was a baby and what it is like now lets me know how much you want to be a different mother from your mother—not a mother who criticizes but a mother who calms her child.*

How careful we have to be. Florence's comments offer several opportunities for us to offer suggestions or to talk about her learning different ways of doing things. But doing that will most likely be experienced by Florence as criticism—we would be repeating her experience from her mother (see Chapter 8 on countertransference responses). Rather, we want to give parents a positive experience about themselves (how much Florence wants to be different from her mother)—only then will the parent be able to give the child a positive experience about him or herself. And Florence's positive experience with us will also help us build a working relationship with her.

Notice our therapist's use of the word "taught" rather than "learned." "Taught" places the negative behavior with the parent's parent rather than with the parent. Infants and toddlers cannot choose what they learn—they learn what they experience. The experience is the teaching given by the parent's parent. Words imply responsibility. "Learning" places the action with the parent and implies that she or he is responsible. But early learning is not a choice, it is the way the brain works.[5] "Taught" places the action, and thereby the responsibility, with the parent's parent.

The one question related to Ted's infancy and then a second one about his current situation provided considerable information—Ted's high state of tension as a child, Mom's difficulties in soothing him, her own mother as a ghost[6] predicting she would fail, Florence's sense of inadequacy, and a probable disorganized attachment between Florence and her mother as well as between Florence and Ted. A hypothesis with regard to the parent-child attachment pattern is an important step in starting to work with a parent. When interacting with a parent who has experienced avoidant attachment, it is particularly important to be attentive and available; for a parent with ambivalent attachment, it is important to state clear boundaries and be absolutely consistent; and for a parent with disorganized attachment it is particularly important to be structured and organized in one's work. The parent's way of interacting with us will make these guidelines quite a challenge (see Chapter 8 for further discussion).

Florence's reluctance to accept help probably reflects her fear of inadequacy and her present sense of hopelessness (the feeling that she is unable to change).

Florence's description of her mother and herself as well as herself and Ted supports our hypothesis that she experienced (i.e., was taught) a pattern of disorganized attachment; from her choice of words (e.g., "looking at me from her grave," "I deserved," "I'm a mess") and voice tone we can recognize an emotional style of being overwhelmed; and from Florence's account of her interactions with her neighbor we can notice her inability to either build or use a support system.

As we pursue questions about the child's first year of life, we ask how the parents soothed the child and where they had been taught that skill. If they had difficulty soothing the child as a baby or as a toddler, it would be important to ask what that experience was like for them. What emotions did they experience, and was there anyone who helped them through that time? What upsetting things happened for the child and/or the parent, how were they handled, what changes did they notice in their child around that time?

Tom, Sara, & Maya, 12 Years Old

> **REFERRAL:** Tom and Sara referred themselves and their daughter Maya to the local child and family agency for support services because of high tension in the home.

FAMILY SUPPORT WORKER: *You said that Maya had a hard time sleeping when she was a baby. I imagine that her constantly interrupted sleep cycles would have been very distressing for the both of you. How did you manage this situation?*

SARA: *Tom was so angry—I could understand—he had to go to work the next day—it was so—I don't remember the word.*

TOM: *"Irritating," you can say the word I used. I used to say I felt irritated by this baby. But that was so upsetting for Sara; she felt like I didn't love our daughter. And it wasn't like that; of course I loved Maya. I was just sleep deprived! And then we would end up fighting.*

FAMILY SUPPORT WORKER: *I can understand.* [Speaks slowly.] *Being sleep deprived is distressing for everyone; it was distressing for Maya as a baby, and it was distressing for you and Sara as her parents. Not knowing what else to do, not being able to sleep well. How did you, Sara, manage Maya at those moments?*

SARA: [Upset] *Well, in so many different ways. Sometimes I brought her to our bed; sometimes, I went to her bedroom, staying by her crib, singing songs; sometimes I talked to her . . . "Sweetie, you have to sleep, Daddy needs to go to work tomorrow, and he is so tired." Some things did work, some others did not. I had nobody to ask for advice* [Sara was the only child of immigrants, and both parents had died when she was in her 20s]*, another woman, you know? I read all the books, and they gave me ideas, but I think I needed somebody showing me how to do this, not just telling me.*

TOM: *I tried to take Sara's place on weekends, so she could rest a little bit, but she didn't let me, it was like she felt she had to be a perfect mom! My family was willing to help, but again, Sara would not let anyone else take Maya. And now all we do is fight, and mostly about Maya.*

FAMILY SUPPORT WORKER: [Speaks to Tom.] *Yes, Tom, you tried when you could. Seems like you were both trying so hard, and that in itself is exhausting. And it's important what Sara said about needing someone there to model for her how to manage.* [Turns to Sara.] *And still, Sara, you kept trying.*

SARA: *She was my baby. I had to keep trying.*

Tom and Sara had different backgrounds. While Tom was the youngest of four siblings and was raised surrounded by several women (his mother, an aunt, his grandmother), Sara was the only child of an immigrant couple who had placed value on being able to manage by themselves. In Sara's family culture, 'kids belonged to their mothers,' which meant that women were supposed to know what to do with their children, and they were to do it right. Having lost her mother long before becoming a mom herself meant for her that she—as a mom—was somehow incomplete or imperfect. Nobody was there to model the role of mom, and books were not enough. She had not learned within her family growing up how to rely on others—outsiders—for support. She was convinced she had to do it by herself and that she also had to take care of her husband, another learning from her culture. Tom's background allowed him to discuss his mistakes and his angry feelings openly, but this just raised Sara's anxiety and feelings of failure. Knowing this background helps the support worker understand both Sara and Tom.

This is a tricky position—wanting to support both parents—with Tom replying before the support worker had a chance to respond to Sara. Notice how the family support worker would go back to something Sara had said and give some support before asking another question. This is an opportunity for learning more about the couple and their tensions—certainly not a time for teaching or for taking sides.

And what has our family support worker learned? Both Sara and Tom seemed to have been able to be available to baby Maya some of the time, but not consistently, which may mean, but not necessarily, an insecure ambivalent attachment pattern. They are able to be open about their experience, although there is a sense that each of them feels alone in what is going on. While Tom seems to be able to call on outside support (his extended family), Sara appears in need of more support.

We also want to know about *positive moments* from when the child was an infant. When asking or being referred for therapy or other help, it is easy for the parents to get connected only with bad memories, with negative information, with negative beliefs. Sometimes parents do not expect to talk about positive things, maybe because they do not think positive things matter for those who are offering support or maybe because they are so consumed by the present problems that they are unable to focus on positive times.

But positive memories do matter. They remind us that there were good times, good moments, and that these good times can come back. These positive memories remind both us and the parent that the parents have, along with all the problems, done positive parenting. Emphasizing these moments not only strengthens the parent but also strengthens the relationship between us and the parents. Remembering positive moments gives hope to the parent and the child. These memories provide us with information that we can use to encourage both the parent and the child when the relationship seems stuck in a negative pattern.

FAMILY SUPPORT WORKER: *During the first years of Maya's[7] life, what did you enjoy most about being with Maya?*

The next question provides us with more information regarding the parent's internal experience of attachment with her or his child. How the parent reacted to, felt about, and handled the early difficult times tells us a great deal about the parents and the parents' capacity to reflect on or mentalize[8] their child.

FAMILY SUPPORT WORKER: *And which were the worst moments, the ones you feared the most? Tell me more about those moments.*

The next few questions relate to *times of separation*, perhaps the first time the parent and child were separated—a time when someone else, perhaps a stranger (for example, a nanny) or a relative took care of the infant.[9] These questions can help us understand the feelings and responses of both parent and child at the earliest moments of separation and reunion. They assist us in our initial hypothesis related to the early attachment relationship between parent and child.

FAMILY SUPPORT WORKER: *Was Maya cared for by anyone else? . . . When? . . . What was the reason Maya was cared for by—? . . . For how long were you separated from Maya? . . . What was it like for you when you left Maya with—? . . . What was it like for Maya when you came back? Was Maya whiny, was Maya angry, was Maya delighted to see you, did Maya ignore you? . . . [If the response was negative] How was that for you? . . . How did you feel at that point—upset, angry, indifferent, distressed, numb? . . . What did you do then?*

In order to better understand the parents' early relationship with their child, it is helpful to ask for specific examples.[10] Asking about the parent's internal reactions during different parts of an experience helps us understand the connection between parent and child. Did the parent experience delight, trepidation, discouragement, and how might those emotions have influenced the parent's interaction with the child? The more detailed the description—as if we were right there—the more information we will gain.

FAMILY SUPPORT WORKER: *I would like to know a little bit more about the two of you and Maya when she was a toddler. Sara, how would you* describe your relationship with her when she was 2–3 years old? Tell me about a specific time you did something together.

SARA: *Oh, she was my little princess! Around the end of the first year, Maya's sleep improved, and I finally got the baby I had always dreamed about. I loved to dress Maya and comb her hair. She was very polite, you know? I felt so happy! And she was also very clever, everybody told me that.*

FAMILY SUPPORT WORKER: *And you, Tom, what was your relationship with Maya like? What would you do with her?*

TOM: *I wish I could have spent more time with her, but my job was too demanding. I think I tried to manage, especially on weekends. I loved to take her to the park and do things kids do, you know? She enjoyed so much going to the park. I wanted to let her feel free and run and climb, and get her clothes dirty! You can't do these things when you grow up, well, unless you become a parent, of course.*

Tom and Sara again provide us with an example of how parents can see their child in very different ways and how these views can shape their relationships with their child. For Sara, it was that Maya had finally become the child she had always dreamed about. Her appreciation of Maya's politeness and cleverness is undoubtedly related to the values she learned within her own family. Her enjoyment of Maya seems to be related with the things she, as a mom, loved to do—dressing Maya and combing her hair. Tom, instead, seemed more attuned to Maya as an energetic toddler. Growing up with three siblings had given Tom the chance to play with other kids. He was now enjoying those types of experiences again, but as a parent. Sara's early experiences of interpersonal connections seemed to have been limited to her parents.

Child in the Present

Depending on the age of the child, there will then be questions related to preschool, to learning and social experiences both in and out of school, reactions with the birth of siblings, changes in parental relationships, and other major experiences. Again we will want to know about the parent's relationship with the child. By asking for an example, as we did before, we gain a better understanding of the parent's attitude and feelings toward the child.

Jenny & Agnes, 9 Years Old

> **REFERRAL:** Agnes was referred by her teacher to the school counselor because of the problems she was having getting along with the other children in her class. Agnes has lived with her single mom, Jenny, since she was born.

SCHOOL COUNSELOR: *How would you describe your relationship with Agnes?*

JENNY: *Well, good I guess.*

SCHOOL COUNSELOR: *Tell me about a specific time you and Agnes did something together.*

JENNY: *Well, we play cards together. She helps me with the household chores. She's a nice, obedient child.*

SCHOOL COUNSELOR: *And as you are doing those things together, what do you notice about the way you are feeling?*

JENNY: *Well, I feel proud, of course!*

SCHOOL COUNSELOR: *And with that feeling of pride, what are the thoughts you notice coming up inside you?*

JENNY: *My thoughts? I guess I think I'm a good mom. If you have a good child you might be a good parent, am I right?*

Notice how tentative Jenny is, unsure about her relationship with Agnes but, most of all, she seems unsure about herself. She is seeing her daughter from her own perspective and not from her daughter's perspective—an indicator of limited ability to mentalize.[11] Jenny's relationship with Agnes is tied closely to Agnes meeting her mother's needs and expectations. Jenny seems to be able to speak positively of Agnes because Agnes is "nice and obedient." In this situation, we would ask Jenny what happens when Agnes misbehaves and how she, Jenny, reacts. The answers to these questions will help us understand the attachment relationship between parent and child at the time of referral—does Jenny stay available to Agnes (secure attachment), does she pull away (insecure avoidant), or does she waffle between the two (insecure ambivalent). Jenny appears to have meshed herself and Agnes together and to be using Agnes as an outside support for her own self-image.

The next set of questions asks the parent to focus exclusively on the child. We want to know the parent's *ability to see the child as a person separate from the parent's* desires, needs, and expectations and if the parent can 'see' more of the child than the present difficulty.

SCHOOL COUNSELOR: *Describe Agnes. . . . Tell me about a time she was* [names one of the adjectives the parent had used in her description].

If the parent gives a description of both positive and negative qualities, it is best to ask first for an example of the positive qualities. In case the parent only gives a negative description of the child, we could ask:

SCHOOL COUNSELOR: *Tell me something you [others] like about Agnes. Describe a time she did that.*

If the parents are so negatively involved in their perception of the child that asking them about a positive quality seems impossible or even potentially conflictual, we can change the 'you' to 'others.' A negative attitude from a parent is certainly informative, but we also need to know if the parent is able to connect to something positive in her child that can open the door to hope for change. Another way to frame the question would be:

SCHOOL COUNSELOR: *Do you think other people see things they like about your child, even if you disagree or even if you don't like that particular characteristic?*

John & Mark, 10 Years Old

> **REFERRAL:** Mark was referred to the counselor because of disruptive behavior during class. Mark lives with his father and younger sister. His mother left the family when he was 5 years old.

SCHOOL COUNSELOR: *How would you describe Mark?*

JOHN: *Mark is a devil. Not in a real sense of course. But he acts like one, and he does it because he wants to.*

SCHOOL COUNSELOR: *Tell me about a time when Mark acted like a devil.*

JOHN: *I have thousands. He's always trying to break rules—at home, at school, in the neighborhood. He doesn't care about others, he is disrespectful. He lies a lot, he calls his sister names; sometimes he can be really nasty to her.*

SCHOOL COUNSELOR: *And are there any good times? Times you enjoy being with him.*

JOHN: *Well, he is smart—but only for doing negative things. He never uses his intelligence to do well. You know, the kind of intelligence offenders have! Like those who keep committing crimes without being caught.*

SCHOOL COUNSELOR: *Do other people mention things they like about Mark even though you may disagree?*

JOHN: *Well, everybody says he is funny. Like, he is a good joker; one teacher said he could become a good comedian. I don't know . . . I think he's always trying to fool others.*

SCHOOL COUNSELOR: *That's tricky, isn't it—what is good humor and what is fooling others.*

While exploring the other perspective (positive if the parent is primarily negative or negative if the parent is primarily positive) is important, it is equally important to let parents know that their opinion is heard and is respected.

The next set of questions is related to *limit setting*—the way in which parents help their children learn right from wrong, set consequences following negative actions, and how they encourage their children to explore the world in a safe way.

Limit setting is influenced by cultural and community standards, by what parents hear in the media, and by the disciplining they experienced from their parents (wishing to repeat what their parents did, wishing to avoid what their parents did, repeating unintentionally what their parents did).

> SCHOOL COUNSELOR: *When do you have to set limits for Mark? . . . How do you do this? . . . Has it always been this way or did it change at some point? . . . When was that and why do you think it changed then? . . . Where were you taught this pattern of limit setting? . . . How did your parents set limits with you when you were a child?*

One more suggested question:

> SCHOOL COUNSELOR: *Who is it in your past or present that Mark reminds you of?*

We will be listening here not just to the answer to this question but also to the speed with which the parent responds and the tone of voice. If it is an immediate response, we know that this is a clear, and perhaps already acknowledged, connection in their mind. If the response is slow, it may be a connection they may not have made before. Tone of voice lets us know something about the parent's relationship with that person—positive or negative. The parent's relationship with that person is all too likely to have pervaded his experience with his child. This helps us understand *how the parent experiences his child.*

> SCHOOL COUNSELOR: *Whom does Mark remind you of?*
>
> JOHN: *[Voice becomes louder and harsher.] My older brother! He was awful, constantly getting me into trouble.*
>
> SCHOOL COUNSELOR: *What was that like for you: your brother getting you into trouble?*
>
> JOHN: *And my parents always took his side. I mean I was younger, why didn't they stop him?*

John's resentment of his parents' inability to support him when he was little likely plays a role in his present anger with Mark. It will have a negative effect on his ability to feel close to Mark and to help Mark navigate difficult situations. If we do not identify this dynamic, we won't have the possibility, in future conversations, to help John separate Mark from his uncle (John's brother).

In a Future Conversation between John and the School Counselor

> SCHOOL COUNSELOR: *As you talk about Mark's problems here at school and being upset with the meeting with the principal, I am reminded of how,*

when you were a kid, your brother used to get you into trouble. How are Mark and your brother different?

Parent's Own Experiences

As we discussed in Chapter 1, a parent's own experience of being parented forms the base on which their parenting is built. The following questions are designed not only to help us, as professionals working with the child or family, to know more about the parent but also to help the parents start making a connection between their way of parenting and the way they were parented by their parents. Being aware that one has unknowingly been taught something—that a behavior is not 'just the way I am' but is 'something that influenced me without my wanting it to'—is the first step to being able to change something.

> *I am going to ask a few questions about your experience growing up and what you remember about the way your parents parented you. Our brains have neurons called 'mirror neurons' that fire—that means they are learning to do a behavior—when we watch or hear someone else doing the behavior. How our own parents cared for us or didn't care for us, talked to us or didn't talk to us, taught us to do that same behavior. What our parents did with us or didn't do with us plays a major role in how we care for our children—*[speaks slowly and carefully] *even when we may not want it to.*
>
> *Our talking about how your parents parented you will help you and me sort out which parts of that early learning from your parents help your parenting now and which parts might be getting in the way of how you want to parent.*
>
> *Who was the person who had the greatest impact on you as you were growing up? . . . Why?*

These questions may bring considerable resistance[12] from some parents—we are switching away from their agenda—'Fix my child—if I want therapy I will go see my own therapist.' If we sense that the parent may be resistant, it would be wise to introduce the idea that we will be changing the topic before we actually change it.

> *These next questions may seem strange to you and you may wonder how it is even relevant. I am going to ask a few questions about your parents and how they parented you.* [Then continue as suggested earlier.]

If their resistance catches us by surprise, then we will want to take a step back.

> *You are absolutely right, I switched my questioning without checking with you first. You came here to get some help for Mark. When thinking about Mark and all of the problems he is running into, I am certainly aware that you, not I, are the person who can help him most. Figuring out the help your parents were able or not able to give you as you grew up will help you and me to know what you were taught—without any choice on your part—about how to help children. Knowing that, will help us figure out how you, yourself, may want to help Mark.*

30   *Learning About the Parent and About Us*

First we agree with them, then we explain why we have done something. If the resistance is too great, we move on to another topic. What we have accomplished is the introduction of a new idea—they were taught patterns of parenting that they may not wish to have, that they had no choice but to learn because that is the way brains work. And if they become aware of these patterns, they can then choose to stay with the pattern or change the pattern. It is best to leave the topic and not ask their permission to talk about it, since if they say "no," this topic, which we will want to pursue again in the future, will be closed.

Most parents will answer the question about who had the greatest impact on their growing up by referring to an adult—perhaps a parent, a grandparent, a nanny, or even a neighbor or teacher. Some may, however, refer to a sibling or other child. At this point, we want to know about the relationship with an adult, so we would then ask for an adult figure. We can later ask more about the siblings or peers. We are purposefully asking about "a person," not a parent, since for some people the important figure may not have been a parent.

> *What word or phrase best describes your relationship with this person. . . . Tell me about a memory that led you to choose that particular person.*[13] *. . . Is there an image or maybe a body reaction that comes up when you focus on your relationship with this particular parent/person?*

When we ask the parent for a word or a sentence, we are inviting their conscious (explicit memory, see Chapter 3) brain to answer. By asking the parent for an image or body reaction, we are seeking to activate a more implicit or unconscious recall of that relationship. Remember our discussion in Chapter 1 related to early attachment memories being held primarily in the right hemisphere (see Chapter 1, pages 6 and 13 and further discussion in Chapter 3) which functions primarily in images and sensations.

> *What about your parent* [if the adult named was not a parent: *other parent/stepparent/guardian*]? *Tell me about him/her.* [Repeat earlier questions.]

Parent's Early Emotional Experiences

The next questions are phrased to help us and the parent become more aware of the parent's emotional experiences as a child—most importantly, how did the parent learn to recognize, or not recognize, to express, to tolerate, and to modulate his or her own emotions? Who was the model who helped the parent balance his or her emotional world, and how did this other person act?

> *All children are sad or lonely sometimes. When might this have happened for you as a child? . . . Were you allowed to show those feelings? . . . How might you have shown feelings of sadness or loneliness? . . . What do you remember your parents doing when that happened? . . . What would that have been like for you? . . .*

What about feelings of anger; what would have made you angry when you were a child? . . . How would you have shown anger? . . . What do you remember your parents doing when that happened? . . . What would that have been like for you? . . .

And scared feelings, what are some of the things that scared you as a child? How would you have shown fear? What do you remember your parents doing when that happened? . . . What would that have been like for you? . . .

And for some of us there were very scary or hurtful things that happened when we were children—fighting between parents, severe drinking or drug use by parents, sexual or physical abuse of someone—maybe you—in the family, emotional abuse, or abuse from outside the family. Was this part of your experience? . . . Were your parents aware of this experience? . . . How did your parents respond to your experience? . . .

If it was a negative response:

Thinking back to that incident now, what was it like for you with your mom/dad responding that way? . . . How do you wish they had responded? . . . How might that have helped you? . . . If your child were in a similar situation, how would you like to respond? . . . How could that make your child's world different from the one you experienced? (See Chapter 6 for ideas on how to follow up from this conversation.)

These questions help parents—without actually going back to process the incident (which is what a parent's individual therapist would do)—focus on how their parent did or did not support them, how that affected them, and how, if they were in a similar situation with their child, they might like to do it differently. This highlights not only that they are different from their parents but also that they can act differently from their parents.

How have you, over the years, managed this experience? . . . Are these events coming back in your thoughts or dreams now? . . .

Did you experience frightening medical procedures, separations from your parents, an accident or other frightening events? Have people important to you died? . . . How did you manage that experience? . . . Were your parents able to be helpful to you at those times? . . . Are these events coming back in your thoughts or dreams now?

We ask these questions, not to start a therapeutic process, but in order that negative parental experiences can be an open topic between the parent and ourselves. Unresolved past trauma and loss has been found to correlate with disorganized attachment between a mother and child (Lyons-Ruth & Jacobvitz, 1999) and, thus, we want to be aware of situations where this may have happened. When appropriate, we would suggest to the parent that she seek some individual therapy for herself.

We can also introduce further questions related to how their parents expressed emotions and how they dealt with stress. Encouraging the parents to reflect on what they observed—that is, what they learned, 'thanks or no thanks' to mirror neurons—from their parents provides a first step toward their possibly changing those patterns.

What are the experiences from your childhood that you most want your child to have? . . . Which are the ones you do not want your child to have? . . . How do you wish your parent had responded to you when those things happened?

At this point in the Developmental Interview, we may want to ask how the parent thinks his experience of being parented has affected the way he parents. If, however, the parent has been defensive during the preceding conversation, it would be best not to ask this question but rather to 'store' the information the parent has shared with us and then, when relevant, be able to refer back to the parent's own personal experience as a child.

Do you think your own experiences of being parented have impacted your way of parenting your child? . . . How? . . . Would you like to change anything? . . . How would you like to change that? . . . And all those changes are possible.

Ann & Jonah, 4 Years Old

> **REFERRAL:** Ann and Jonah were referred to a play therapist by the pediatrician because of Jonah's out-of-control and demanding behaviors with his mother, Ann. Jonah, since his parents' separation when he was 3, has lived during the week with his mother and every other weekend with his father. These behaviors are not present with Dad or at day care. Ann and the play therapist meet together for the Developmental Interview.

PLAY THERAPIST: *We have been talking about how your parents reacted when you were little and you were feeling upset or angry or scared. Do you think their reactions to you have affected in any way how you react with Jonah?*

ANN: *I never thought about that—I guess everyone's experience affects them in some way. I don't know how to answer that—can you give me a clue?*

PLAY THERAPIST: *How did your dad or your mom react when you felt sad or upset or angry? Is any of that similar to your reaction with Jonah?*

ANN: *Well, I told you that my dad didn't want me to cry; he would threaten me if I cried. And now I'm thinking about it, I hate it when Jonah cries. It makes me anxious. No, not anxious, it scares me. If he cries it may mean he is in pain, he might be suffering—so I do whatever it takes to stop him from crying. I give him whatever he wants.*

PLAY THERAPIST: [Nods thoughtfully to indicate understanding of Ann's position—attunement—and then speaks with a note of curiosity in his voice.] *And is that the way you want things to be, giving him whatever he wants?*

ANN: *I guess the right answer is "no," but I'm not sure. What if he cries because he is suffering and I do nothing to stop the suffering and crying?*

PLAY THERAPIST: [Validates and then continues with curiosity.] *You're a careful mother. My guess is that you can check whether there is anything that is hurting him. If there is nothing hurting him, what might you do then?*

ANN: *But I get scared. And then I can't think and I might not notice something.*

PLAY THERAPIST: [Again validates and again continues with curiosity.] *That scared feeling is really hard. Did your dad scare you when he threatened you not to cry? . . . I wonder if the scared feeling comes more from the past than from the 'now' incident with Jonah? . . .* (see Chapter 6 for more ideas).

As we come to the end of the Developmental Interview, we want to finish on a positive note and with a sense that we, together with the parents, will be able to help their child. If the parent has disclosed painful experiences from her own past, we need to acknowledge this and the courage and effort she is making.

PLAY THERAPIST: *As we come to the end of our time today, is there anything else you would like to tell me about Jonah or about your experience of parenting? . . . Thank you so much for coming today and for sharing your experiences of your child and also experiences that you had when you were little and your parents were parenting you. We have talked about some really difficult times. What are you noticing inside you right now? . . . [If the feelings are difficult. . . .] Stay with that feeling for just a bit and let that feeling know that you and I are going to be able to work together to help Jonah and to help you and Jonah together. . . . I hope you will have some time after you leave today to walk around a little bit or have a cup of tea—just something to give your system a bit of a rest before you pick up Jonah.*

I admire your decision to call us and to come in today. As I said, we have talked about some very difficult times, and that lets me know that you want things to be different for your child. I look forward to working together with you to help your child.

While it may feel early in our relationship with the parent to include these personal questions, including them right at the beginning highlights the major role the experiences of 'being parented' play in how each of us parent. This will continue to be a theme as we follow our story of working with our other client—the parent.

The Developmental Interview we have been talking about can be quite long. Given the time limitations that each of us has for doing an assessment, we are going to have to make choices as to which questions we include and which we skip over. Information from the referral phone call and from the answers given during the interview will help guide us with these choices. What we must *not* skip over is asking some questions about how the parent was parented. It is easier to introduce the importance of this experience as part of a standard assessment than it may be to bring it up later when the parent may feel that the questions imply something wrong about her particular family.

Drawing Genograms

Another way to identify familial patterns of reacting is to create a genogram[14] with the parent or with the parent and child. Many of us will have been trained in the use of genograms and include them in the notes we take as we talk with parents. Seldom, however, are we encouraged to draw the genogram together with the parent. Creating genograms together with the individual with whom we are working—parent, adolescent, or child—provides an opportunity for individuals themselves to identify patterns that have occurred within the nuclear family and between the generations (Wieland, 1998).

Genograms are particularly valuable for tracing behavioral patterns including varied forms of abuse. When the occurrence of abuse is viewed across multiple generations, it becomes something that happened within a system and not just something that happened to that child or that parent. "It becomes something that happened because of events and decisions outside the child, not because of the child" (Wieland, 1998, p. 80).

McGoldrick et al. (2008) describe in detail[15] how to draw genograms and use a variety of symbols to highlight the varied relationships between people in the family. They use short descriptions next to the relevant family members that focus on whatever issue is being examined. In our work with parents, we would highlight the emotional and behavioral patterns relevant for attachment and emotional expression that were taught by a parent's parent. We would not be asking for or noting on the genogram the amount of details related to each member of the family, as one would when doing a genogram during individual therapy.

This genogram (Chart 2.1), which would have taken between 10 and 15 minutes to complete, gives us quite a bit of information. John would have been taught

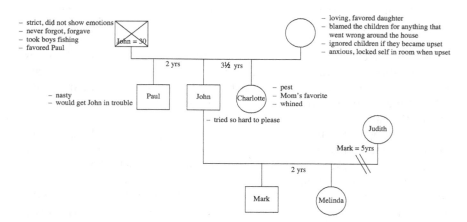

Chart 2.1 Genogram for John and Mark—squares are for males and circles are for females.

by his parents that adults do not need to accept responsibility for things that go wrong. Other people can be blamed. He would also have been taught that having favorites is normal in families. John would not have been taught positive ways of dealing with emotions or even that having emotions is healthy and can be talked about with other people. Most likely we are looking at either an avoidant or an ambivalent-insecure attachment pattern. All of this John would have brought with him into the family he created together with Mark's mother. On top of that would be the many stresses that are experienced when a relationship fails and are experienced when raising children on one's own.

These hypotheses are going to help the support worker and social worker to be alert for these characteristics and, therefore, less negatively reactive if John starts to blame them for Mark's problems or even for his own problems. They could, *without challenging*, be curious as to where the tendency to blame came from. They might pull out the genogram and ask John what he notices. A support worker or a social worker without therapeutic training would go no further than that. But their understanding from the genogram would have given them the ability not to get into a dispute over blame and also not to want to get rid of the case. And this might be a new and important experience for Mark—someone who could listen to him.

The hypotheses are certainly going to help the therapeutically trained social worker, counselor, or therapist. When blame comes up with words or maybe just in John's tone of voice, they are going to be able to ask John to notice it. They can remember what was noted on the genogram and ask John how it felt when things were blamed on him, what he wished his parents had done. How he, himself, and not 'he shaped by his parents,' wants to do it. And then, after reading the next several chapters, our social worker, counselor, or therapist can ask John to image himself doing it differently.

Up to this point, we have been talking about formal parts of an assessment—the Developmental Interview and drawing of genograms. Many agencies and individual professionals also have questionnaires for parents to complete that ask about family medical, educational, and emotional histories. Equally important for giving us information on parents and their experiences of attachment and emotional expression are informal observations—what are the dynamics between the parent and child? What are the dynamics between the parent and us?

Observing Parent-Child Dynamics

The type of interaction that occurs between the parent and child helps us understand their attachment relationship. Does the parent notice and respond to the child's experience of being in a strange place and with a strange person? Are there reassuring words or gestures? Does the child look to the parent for expected reassurance (secure attachment) or avoid the parent and present as a separate individual rather than part of a child-parent pair (avoidant attachment) or cling to the parent as if unsure as to how the parent is going to react (ambivalent attachment) or try with either manipulative or aggressive behaviors to control the situation (disorganized attachment—see, for example, Grimminck, 2011).

36   *Learning About the Parent and About Us*

Unfortunately, determining an attachment pattern is not this simple. But noticing these initial interactions is definitely a start and does give us information about both the child's experience and the parent's experience. Are emotions openly discussed between them? Does the parent notice the child's emotions, or is he too preoccupied with himself and his own experience to notice the child? How does each of them respond to the other? How do they manage the stress of meeting with a child professional? This may be part of our normal day, but it is a stressful experience for both the parent and the child.

In an Office

Our first meeting with the child may be in the home, at the school or day care setting, or in an office. If it is at an office, in most situations the parent-figure[16] comes in with the child (up to adolescence[17]) at the beginning of the session. First, we will want to observe what is occurring in the waiting area when we go to greet the child and parent. Is there any interaction between them and, if so, what is the quality of it? How do they interact on the way to our office? Is the parent more attentive to us and socially engaging with us or more attentive to the child and responding to any anxiety the child may be experiencing?

As they enter the room, who determines where they sit? Who is it that may change this initial placement and how is it done? Is there any physical contact between them and, if so, what is the quality of the contact—is it a corrective touch or a reassuring touch? As the session goes on, what is the interaction between parent and child? Do they have any eye contact? If so, who initiated it and how was it established? If not, who seemed to be avoiding it?

We may start with an open-ended question such as, "*What was it like coming here today?*" "*What type of conversation did the two of you have before coming today?*" Is it the parent who responds or the child? What is the tone of voice?

Sienna & Gavin, 11 Years Old

> **BACKGROUND INFORMATION:** *Mom (Sienna) has registered Gavin for an after-school activity facility. They have just finished walking around the facility for their initial visit.*

AFTER-SCHOOL CARE PROVIDER: *Mom, you have come by before and seen what our activities are like, but I am wondering what it was like for you, Gavin, coming to a new place.*

MOTHER: [Speaks quickly before Gavin has a chance to reply.] *Remember I told you about the gym and all the games they play here.*

GAVIN: *Yeah. And I told you I could do that at home—the games. I don't have to come here.*

MOTHER: *And what happens when you are home by yourself?*

GAVIN: *I'm old enough.*

MOTHER: *Sure* [sarcastic tone], *but what happens?*

AFTER-SCHOOL CARE PROVIDER: *Gavin, it sounds as if you would really like to just go home after school, but, Mom, you seem worried about that, so you are trying to work something else out. I'm wondering, Gavin, what would be the hardest thing about having to come here?*

The child professional starts by trying to connect with Gavin; she has already spent time with Mom. Immediately she is learning about the relationship between Mom and Gavin. Mom is disrespectful of Gavin (answering a question directed to Gavin), and Gavin is confrontational with Mom. Both of them become easily triggered into heightened emotions. The care provider acknowledges both of them and again tries to connect with Gavin. She asks a question that acknowledges and highlights that Gavin is finding this situation difficult.

As the session progresses, the care provider, doctor, or therapist—whoever is meeting with the parent and child—will probably ask to have some time alone with the child. Who finds this idea most difficult—the parent or the child? The child may move closer to Mom or may start looking around the room. Mom may say, "*Why, yes, of course,*" at the same time as tightening her hand on the child's shoulder. How does the child respond to this contradictory statement? Who is most anxious with the idea of separation, how is the anxiety expressed, does the other person recognize this anxiety, and how does the other person respond?

Indeed, information related to the parent-child dynamics may feel like it is coming so quickly and so strongly that the child professional may feel a bit overwhelmed—how to notice all of this and at the same time respond in a helpful manner? It will be important to remember that there are going to be many occasions over the weeks ahead to interact with both parent and child—together or individually. Forming some connection with *each* of them is the most important task at that moment.

In a Home

If the first meeting is in the child's home, we are confronted with many challenges. The home may be very different from the homes we have known—we may find ourselves in the middle of a level of poverty that we have never experienced. The cleanliness of the home and, indeed, safety may be well below what we consider 'acceptable.' There may be no place to sit down, and the volume from the television, which the family tunes out, may, for us, block the parents' and children's voices. There may be smoking or evidence of use of drugs or alcohol, which we will, inevitably, find distracting. Indeed, our whole system may go into hyperarousal.

Before we can accurately observe any of the parent-child dynamics, we are going to need to calm ourselves and remind ourselves that we are not there to judge but to get to know the parents, the children, and their reality. We need to remind ourselves that we are intruding on their world; we are 'guests' in their home. Luckily, if we remember, we do have many calming and grounding ideas—the ideas we teach to others and also need ourselves.

While home visits are challenging, they are also very helpful. We are better able to identify poverty or drug issues with which the family needs assistance before they will have the energy even to consider their relationship with their children. Although we do not work in those areas, we can be advocates for the family and help them locate other resources.

Once our system has settled, we can start to observe the same dynamics that we focused on in the office session: What is the physical proximity between the parent and child—who establishes it and who changes it; is there eye contact; what is the tone of voice as they speak to each other—do they even speak to each other, and, more importantly, do they hear each other? Who seems to tune to whom—the parent to the child or the child to the parent? These dynamics very likely reflect dynamics that the parents themselves experienced when they were children. Some of the dynamics will be positive, and we can notice and support those. Some of the dynamics will be negative. As we become aware of what the parent was taught 20 or 30 years earlier, we can help the parent become aware of these behaviors. And remember, awareness is the first step toward change. Recognition that parents did not have a choice as to what we were taught helps to relieve parental guilt and, thus, leaves more energy for change. Then comes recognition that parents now do have a choice as to which behaviors they continue. This can enable parents to move toward change.

Whether in the office or the home, there will also be an opportunity to observe how the child relates to us—in a relaxed manner, wary and suspicious, or frightened by the encounter. Are these dynamics similar to what the child displayed with the parent or different from her interaction with the parent? We will want to build the child's trust in us. But more important than that will be helping the parent become a more trustworthy figure and helping the child build trust in her parent.

At the same time we are noticing the parent-child interaction, we can become aware of our experience of our interaction with the parent. Just as the parent's interaction with the child tells us about the parent and the parent's experience with her or his own parent, so our experience of our interaction with the parent is going to tell us a great deal about the parent. But we need to be careful! Information about the parent is accurate only if we separate out the interactive information that relates to ourselves. We will talk more about this in Chapter 8.

Recognizing Parent-Us Dynamics

What was the time in the room with the parent like for us? Did we find ourselves leaning slightly back or slightly forward? Was the backward movement because we felt bombarded, overwhelmed, or rejected? These are very different pieces of information. Was the movement forward because we felt comfortable and were responding to a sense of connection or because we felt ineffective and were trying to draw more information from the parent—again, very different information. Was this the type of experience the child has with the parent? Was this the type of experience the parent had with his own parent? And there is another question to be asked—what, in our own experiences of having been parented (or responded to by other important people in our lives), did the experience remind us of?

When we talk about our experience of an interaction with a child or parent, we are talking about countertransference—"The entirety of the [child professional's] emotional reactions to the individual within the [interactive] situation" (Bouchard et al., 1995, p. 719). We shall be talking more about countertransference—what it is, where it comes from, and how we can work with it—in Chapter 8. Our focus here is on (1) becoming aware of the dynamics occurring between ourselves and the parent and (2) becoming aware of the experiences we had growing up and how they influence our present interactive experiences.

Becoming Aware of the Dynamics Occurring between Ourselves and the Parent

Was our movement (slightly back or slightly forward) a response to the parent's way of being or a result of our past experiences or, indeed, a mixture of the two? Do we easily become overwhelmed; was rejection a theme as we grew up? Do we tend to easily feel comfortable with others; do we overtry in tasks we have set for ourselves?

We need to be aware of our body movement, our voice tone, and our eye contact as we work with parents. Even more important than these outward responses are our internal responses—tightening of muscles, distracted thoughts, sense of fatigue or even boredom. Do we become disorganized in our thinking or in the interviewing process? Do we become irritated with the parent, are we feeling critical or criticized? Do we feel comfortable because we sense a similarity in values or uncomfortable because the parent espouses a worldview that differs from our own? Do we unknowingly shift into a teaching or lecturing mode rather than listening and reflecting? Do we like the parent; do we dislike the parent? Why are these particular reactions occurring?

Becoming Aware of the Experiences We Had Growing Up

Just as we are asking parents to be aware of their early experiences, so we need to be aware of our early experiences and what our parents taught us without our realizing it and without our having any choice as to what we took in. The very questions that we asked parents about the person in their life who had the greatest impact on them and the questions about how their parents handled situations, we need to ask of ourselves.

As we answer these questions and explore our own early experiences, we become more attuned to ourselves and how we react with other people—in both our personal lives and our professional lives. Did we learn to be open to others or to be critical of others? We may find that even though we wish to be open—this is, after all, part of being an individual working in a 'helping profession'—we are often critical of how the parent has parented. *"If only they were not . . ., had not . . ., did not . . ., their child would be fine."* These thoughts, even though not verbalized, can be sensed by parents. The possibility of a positive working relationship with the parent decreases if those feelings persist.

Just as drawing a genogram with a parent can help the parent become aware of patterns of behavior that were passed from generation to generation, so too drawing our genogram can help us become aware of patterns we have 'inherited' from the influential people in our lives (Aponte & Carlsen, 2009; Kaslow & Schulman, 1987).

Family therapists have been encouraged to pursue family of origin questions and genograms regarding themselves during supervision time (Aponte & Carlsen, 2009; Bowen, 1972; McGoldrick, 1982; Timm & Blow, 1999) in order to avoid therapist 'blind spots'[18] and negative countertransference reactions. Timm and Blow (1999) suggest that understanding one's own issues also enables a therapist to be more compassionate and understanding of the individuals with whom we are working. Similar training has not generally been highlighted for child professionals. And yet as child professionals we are always dealing with family issues—either through the child's experience, the parent's struggles, or the family interactions. Indeed, the interaction with parents is likely to activate—on a deep unconscious level—issues related to our experiences of being parented.

How do we become more aware of those early experiences? Just like the parents with whom we are working, we do not have explicit memories from infancy and early toddler years. But we do have stories from that time, we do know what our interactions with each parent were like as we grew up, and we do know the way our parents were with other people. Asking our parents to talk about their own growing up, their experiences of their parents (our grandparents), and their experiences of being young parents as they raised us can give us considerable information about the judgments, tensions, and unspoken messages passed down to us.

Drawing our own genogram and asking ourselves the same questions we would ask parents can also be helpful. Exploration of one's genogram can be done on one's own but is far more productive if done with a group of supportive colleagues. Others are able to ask the questions that are most difficult and, therefore, unlikely to occur to us. *"What would that have been like for the 'toddler you' who wanted so much to be accepted by your father?"*

When our genogram is completed, we can reflect on the unspoken messages conveyed by the patterns of behavior noticed through the generations in our family. Until those messages are verbalized, we have little control over them. Once they are identified and spoken, we are better able to see where they intrude into our thinking, our reacting to others, and into our work with parents. We also want to be aware of our personal attachment pattern. Is it secure, avoidant, ambivalent, disorganized, or, more likely, some combination of several of these? And it may be different with different people in our world—those who are close and those who are distant, those who are female and those who are male. How our own personal attachment pattern affects our work with parents will be discussed in more detail in Chapter 8.

How Our Early Experiences Influence Our Interactive Experiences with Parents

Personal therapy was required as part of training within the early tradition of psychoanalytic psychotherapy and continues to be recommended, although not required, for both counselors and therapists.[19] It is not, however, considered as necessary for other child professionals and, thus, is seldom pursued. Personal therapy is a process in which the majority of people are unable (e.g., financially, lack of availability) or unwilling (e.g., do not need because I have not experienced trauma; do not have time for) to participate. And even for those who pursue personal therapy, not all therapies look at the early teaching each of us received within our family of origin. This process that enables individuals to become more self-aware and, thus, better able to focus on the issues of the individuals with whom we are working (Timm & Blow, 1999) is missing for the majority of us. We are left on our own to seek out what we were unknowingly taught. Those of us who seek it out are less likely to repeat it, either with our own children or with the individuals with whom we work.

Becoming introspective about one's responses to the other person is not generally part of the training within an education or medical program or, indeed, many sections of social work or child and youth care programs. It is, however, always available to us as part of our own internal work. And it enables us to be open to and communicate in a more positive way with the individuals with whom we would otherwise find it very difficult to work. A parent's harshness toward his or her child and toward us will always create a negative response in us. Recognizing that this harshness is a result of the parent's own experiences and internal struggles, not an 'open choice'[20] of how the parent wishes to be, enables us to be less judgmental and more sympathetic to the parent. Knowledge of our own stuck spots with parenting creates empathy. This stance enables us to work in a more positive way with the parent. As we continue through the chapters ahead, there will be many examples of this.

Fran, Alex, & Joshua (4 Years Old)

> **REFERRAL:** Fran had called the agency requesting play therapy for Joshua, who was refusing to leave his mother to go to day care. The therapist meets with Fran and Alex for the Developmental Interview.

42   Learning About the Parent and About Us

THERAPIST: Describe for me what it was like in the home when Joshua was first born.

ALEX: Well, it was really busy. We had two little children and now a baby.

FRAN: Alex, you are forgetting how well organized we were. My parents helped with the older two, and I could focus on Joshua.

THERAPIST: [Feels a high level of irritation at Fran—why does she keep dominating the conversation? It is not unusual for one parent to dominate the conversation, but usually this does not cause so much irritation. Also notices a negative reaction to Fran's size. Although Fran and Alex are the same height, it feels as if Fran is the larger of the two, and for some reason this is bothersome.]

As the Developmental Interview continues, our therapist learns that Fran had encouraged Joshua as an infant to attach to her and took him everywhere she went. She presently helps Joshua calm and go to sleep at night by lying with him and letting him curl his fingers in her hair. Fran clearly likes this role and does not see any need to change it. She does not connect this behavior with what happens every morning, when Joshua refuses to leave her side.

FRAN: It is so frustrating! He just clings to me and tries to climb up on me, even grabbing for my hair. Somehow Alex is going to have to figure out how to get Joshua to go get in the car with him.

THERAPIST: [Thinks Fran is being absolutely self-centered and unreasonable. Notices that thought but moves it away in order to be attentive to both Fran and Alex. Then notices that he is consistently redirecting his questions back to Alex when Fran answers first. His negative reaction to Fran is not obediently staying away.]

After Fran and Alex leave, the therapist completes his notes from the session. He easily identifies the emergence of his critical side (he had grown up with a very critical father). He then tries to figure out who it is Fran is reminding him of—certainly not his father, nor his mother. He goes through this exercise several more times during the week but does not come up with any answer. The next time Fran came in, even though the therapist had not figured out where the block he had experienced between himself and Fran had come from, his reaction to Fran had changed. Just the puzzling and the acknowledgement that the difficulty came from him and not Fran had shifted his reaction to Fran. Fran felt more like a friend who needed some help because of being caught in a negative pattern and not someone who had centered on her own needs and not her child's needs, someone in need of correction. What had shifted? What allowed it to shift?

The therapist's experience with Fran illustrates how recognition of one's own role within an interactive relationship allows an opening of ourselves to the other person. Hopefully we are able to identify what has been triggered within ourselves and, in this way, be able to attend to our own distress and earlier negative experiences. Even when we are unable to identify the source of the negative reaction, being aware of the reaction and willing to 'own it' as a personal reaction, not something wrong with the parent, enables us to be more open to the parent. This openness will translate into a more positive relationship and, therefore, better working relationship with the parent. We will talk about this further in Chapter 8.

One More Question

And this question is for ourselves, NOT to be asked of the parent—

"How did the parent experience the last hour?"

We are aware of our experience, but if we are truly to work with this parent—as a teacher, a therapist, a social worker, a doctor—not just meet with her, we need to be constantly aware of what her experience of us is. This is mentalization[21] (see Chapter 4), what we want parents to be able to do with their children. Why not ask them? They are likely to respond in a 'socially correct' manner or in a defensive irritated manner, and neither of those will help our relationship. Our mentalization will help the relationship.

If *their* experience has been negative—and often it is, particularly if they did not choose to meet with us—how can we shift our interactions with the parent so that her experience is a positive one? That is what the rest of the book is about!

Summary

Providing assistance to a child always includes interaction with a parent-figure. The better we know the parent and the parent's own experiences, the better we are able to work with that particular parent and, thus, with that particular child. In this chapter, we have reviewed the various ways we can learn about the parent—conducting assessment interviews, drawing genograms, observing the dynamics between the parent and child, and also observing the dynamics between the parent and ourselves. In order to understand the dynamics between the parents and ourselves, we need to be aware of our own early interactive experiences, particularly our experiences with our parents. Being aware of our own experiences enables us to be more open to the responses we experience when interacting with parents and able to recognize that these responses belong not only to the parent's presentation but also to us. As we recognize and process what belongs to us, we are better able to set this part of the response aside and become more receptive to the parent. The discussion of our responses and how to process them will continue in Chapter 8.

As we continue with our conversation about working with parents, we will look at the skills we already have and how we can use them with parents (Chapter 4). Then we will move on to new ideas for building the child's relationship with the parents (Chapter 5). To strengthen both the skills we already have and the new ones we want to build, we need the most recent research on learning and the brain. For this reason Chapter 3 will be a detour into the functioning of the brain. Chapter 7 will look briefly at working with parents if the child is adopted. In Chapter 8 we shall focus again on ourselves and what we can learn from our experience of the parent. We shall consider in more detail how to provide support and learning for ourselves in this very important work.

Chapter 2—Points to Remember

- It is important to introduce the concept of 'parents parent as they were parented' at the very beginning of working with a parent.
- Caring for babies is not an innate ability but rather one taught to parents—either from the parenting they received or from a conscious effort by the parent to do things differently.
- Asking for specific examples gives more helpful information with regard to the parent-child interactions.
- When there is 'resistance':
  – 'resistance' indicates the individual is feeling threatened;
  – first we accept their position and, if possible, agree with it;
  – then we explain why we are asking something;
  – if continued, we switch topics.
- Giving parents a positive experience about themselves will help them be able to give their child a positive experience about herself or himself.
- Remembering positive moments gives hope to the parent and the child.
- Drawing genograms together with the parent saves time and provides information.

Notes

1. In most situations, the Developmental Interview occurs prior to the initial assessment interview with the child. If there is a question as to whether abuse toward the child has occurred and we might be asked for our opinion with regard to this, then it is best to meet first with the child in order that our observations not be affected by any outside information. If it is a teen who has been referred, then the teen would be invited to the Developmental Interview.
2. Having lost a significant individual or experienced a trauma during the two years prior to the birth of the child and/or during the two years following the child's birth has been found to be highly correlated with the presence of disorganized attachment between the parent and child (Lyons-Ruth & Jacobvitz, 2008). The parent's preoccupation with grief and distress would lead to the secretion of stress neurochemicals within the pregnant mother (and thus possible deleterious effects on the fetus) and, following the birth of the baby, could interrupt the parent's ability to be available to the baby and, in particular, hinder the parent's ability to soothe and emotionally regulate the infant (Schore, 2012).
3. For parents who were taught as children that they were not to complain or be dramatic, it can be helpful to name the negative behaviors the parents may have experienced. This gives them permission to complain.
4. Grey shading indicates that these are the child professional's thoughts or intended interventions, not spoken words.

5 Recall note 5 in Chapter 1 (p. 15) regarding mirror neurons.
6 See Fraiberg et al. "Ghosts in the Nursery" for an excellent description of how past important figures influence one's ability to parent.
7 The name of the child in the most recent example will be used for our sample questions. The name obviously changes with each family you see.
8 Mentalizing refers to an individual's ability to hold their own mind and the mind of another within their awareness (Fonagy et al., 2012). See further discussion on mentalizing in Chapter 4, pages 91–96.
9 This would be a real world example of Ainsworth's Strange Situation (Ainsworth et al., 1978). The Strange Situation was developed as a parent-child measure for determining attachment category. The parent and child play together, the parent leaves, a stranger enters and engages with the child, then leaves, and the parent returns. The child's response on the parent's return is used as a measure of the attachment relationship.
10 This is a pattern of questioning proposed by the Adult Attachment Interview (George et al., 1985) and has been found to provide a more accurate view of experiences than do general questions.
11 Holding Jenny's mind in her mind. Ability to mentalize has been found to correlate with secure attachment patterns (see further description of mentalization in Chapter 4).
12 Messer (2002) highlights that resistance is not "the enemy of therapy . . . [but] the inevitable expression of the person's manner of relating to their inner problems and to others. The resistance is what we have to work *with*, not against, in therapy" (page 158). Viewing it in this light helps us be more accepting in our reaction to 'resistant' parents.
13 This question is framed similarly to several of the questions in the Adult Attachment Interview (George et al., 1985). The degree of concordance between the memory and word helps us understand the early attachment between the parent and the parent's parent (Hesse, 1999).
14 A genogram is a multigenerational chart of a family in which a particular trait, behavior pattern, or disease is traced over several generations (Genogram, 2016). Murray Bowen (1978), basing his work on both family and systems theories, urged therapists to use genograms to help them understand intergenerational patterns. McGoldrick and Gerson (1985) developed a format that has been generally accepted and is now further developed (McGoldrick et al., 2008) to show multiple interactional patterns between generations.
15 While McGoldrick et al. (2008) have a very detailed explanation on how to complete a genogram, a simpler and quicker explanation and one that suffices for our present usage is offered by Wieland (1998).
16 When the child is living in a group home, the parent-figure might be the group home parents. If there are not group home parents, then it should be the primary worker for the child. Having the child brought by a different worker each time is counter-productive to the work we are trying to do. Attachment is an important part of the work any of us do with a child. Having contact with a variety of workers encourages indiscriminate attachment—a type of disorganized attachment—not a positive, more secure attachment.
17 Adolescents would be asked whether they want the parent to come in with them or whether they prefer to come in on their own.
18 A therapist 'blind spot' refers to issues that activate the therapists' own triggers and thereby limit the ability to hear and understand the individual with whom they are working.
19 Although personal therapy is not required for counselors and therapists, it is the position of the present authors that it is absolutely essential for someone to be careful and effective in this work.
20 'Open choice' implies that the parent had both positive experiences and negative experiences growing up and was able to choose between the two as to what to continue with

his child. A 'closed choice' occurs when the parent had only one experience (in this situation a negative one) on which to model his relationship with his child.
21 Mentalization is the ability to be aware of the other person's experience of something as well as one's own experience—something we want a parent to be able to do with her child and therefore something the parent needs to experience from someone else.

CHAPTER 3

How Parenting Patterns Are Held in the Brain

As parents interact with their children, they are responding from many different areas of their brain. Many of these areas of activity are outside awareness—automatic responding from neuronal networks shaped years earlier as the 'parent as child' observed and interacted with his or her own parents. As mentioned in the previous chapter, for some parents the early learning was positive, and they are able to respond to their infant or child in a healthy and positive manner. For others, and most likely the majority of parents who come to our offices, some of the early learning was not positive. While many of the parents who experienced negative learning from their parents' style of parenting have thought through how they themselves want to parent,[1] others just assumed that wanting to be good parents was enough to create good parenting responses. For those who rely on their wish to be good parents, old negative patterns sculpted into their brains are, all too often, stronger than positive wishes.

And, indeed, what does a 'good parent' mean? For some, it means recognizing one's child as he or she is developing into a unique self, providing the soothing and alerting needed at each developmental stage, being a steady secure attachment figure, and maintaining a healthy life of one's own. But for others—and especially for those who have had negative interactions with their parents—it may mean being a provider who pays for the shelter and food and toys, it may mean being a clear disciplinarian who has an obedient child, it may mean being a parent who meets the child's every wish, or it may mean being the parent who has a child who meets the parent's needs.

Even for those parents who thought through how they want to be different from their own parents, once difficult parent-infant/child interactions occur—as always happens during parenting—and a parent's system goes into overarousal, it is 'early brain learning,' not 'recent brain thought,' that takes over.

If we are to help parents shift in their responding, it is important to understand—within the limits placed on us by present neuroscience knowledge—where within the brain the early parent-child learning took place, how it was formed, and, therefore, based on this information, how the parenting pattern may be able to be changed. With that as a basis, we can then start to explore the type of interactions we, as child professionals, need to have with parents in order to help them build new neuronal patterns related to parenting.

In this chapter we will look at early caregiver-infant/child attachment and early learning. We will be considering the areas of the brain that appear to be most involved in attachment dynamics and in early learning of parenting. We will look at the autonomic nervous system (ANS) and how caregiving affects this system. Then we will consider ideas for shifting parental patterns. While acknowledging that some children are not raised by a parent, we will be using the term "parent" rather than "care-giver" in the following discussion to mean all individuals who raise children.

Attachment

As the fetus develops in the womb, growth develops upward from the spinal cord up through the brain stem. At the time of birth, the brain stem, mid-brain, right-lateralized limbic areas and deep cortices of the right hemisphere are actively functioning—processing and encoding information, as seen in Diagram 3.1 (see also Chiron et al., 1997; Schore, 2012).

With amazing speed, the other areas of the brain are also developing and strengthening as the baby's system is stimulated from within (hunger, fatigue) and from the outside (interpersonal stimulation and soothing). For the developing infant, interpersonal interactions consist primarily of touch (body sensation), voice tone, and eye contact. These interactions are processed and encoded in neuronal networks deep within the right hemisphere (Schore, 2001, 2003, 2012). These early developed areas of the brain have been identified as also holding the neuronal networks related to early attachment patterns.

Attachment was described by Bowlby (1969) as an infant's biological drive to seek safety and comfort together with the parent's movement to provide safety and comfort

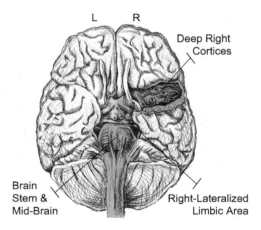

Diagram 3.1 View of brain from the bottom. Dark shading on the brain stem, mid-brain, right-lateralized limbic area and deep right cortices (see area within the imagined cut into the right hemisphere) indicates the areas actively functioning (processing and encoding information) at birth. Development is starting to occur throughout the brain.

for the infant. While clearly interactive and often initiated by infant need, the initial pattern of the attachment is shaped more by the parent's behavior than the infant/child's. For some parents the caregiving response may be thought out and, therefore, a conscious action. For the most part, however, caregiving responses are unconscious behaviors that come from a parent's already formed neuronal networks, networks formed during her or his early attachment experiences with her or his parents. This neuronal network developed when the 'parent as infant'[2] sought safety and comfort and was or was not responded to, cared for, and protected by her or his parent.

If there was sufficient attending/caring/protecting for the 'parent as infant' or sufficient repair when the attending was ruptured (Siegel, 2003; Tronick, 1989), then the 'parent as infant' would have experienced (had stimulated within his or her own brain) neuronal activity that regulated the 'parent as infant's' affect (Schore, 2012). With each positive interactive experience—soothing when the infant is agitated; stimulating when the infant is lethargic—the neuronal pattern for a healthy range of affect in the 'parent as infant' would strengthen. This neuronal pattern fits within the category known as secure attachment.

Schore (2012), in his extensive review of the literature on infant development, tells us that numerous areas of the infant's nervous systems are activated in early affect regulation—right limbic area, right cortical association areas, the hypothalamus-pituitary axis (HPA), and the autonomic nervous system (ANS). As noted earlier, this activation—arousal or soothing—may be initiated internally or externally (see Diagram 3.2).

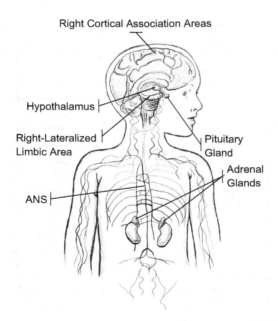

Diagram 3.2 Activation within the infant/child during affect stimulation or soothing—right limbic area, right cortical association areas, HPA and ANS.

50 How the Brain Holds Parenting Patterns

These multiple early learned neuronal patterns of responding reflect the world the 'parent as infant/child' experiences. Since this is his knowledge of the world and indeed his knowledge of himself, these neuronal patterns provide, over time, not only an expectation of what the world is going to be like but also his internal concept of self (Bowlby's internal working model, 1973). With the expectation of positive responding (i.e., secure relationships) the 'parent as child' will respond positively when interacting with others. When the child confronts, as he surely will at some point, negative relationships, this individual will typically seek help. Over time, the child, having repeatedly experienced from the parent this pattern of positive arousal together with repair from negative (either over- or under-) arousal, develops an internal ability to provide this regulation on his own (see Chart 3.1, Secure Attachment). The child's system can on its own—without the intervention of an outside caregiver—provide positive arousal and repair from negative (too much or too little) arousal, a characteristic of secure attachment. That which was stimulated from the outside is now part of the child's own neuronal network patterns within the child's right limbic area, the right cortical association areas, the HPA, and the ANS system.

If the early experiences of the 'parent as infant' included a parent who was only sometimes available to attend/care/protect, then the 'parent as infant' would have experienced limited external regulation of affect. If the infant did not encounter experiences causing extreme ranges of arousal (overarousal or underarousal), the infant's own system may have been able to maintain healthy arousal regulation. This pattern of regulation that was experienced and therefore held within multiple neuronal

	Secure attachment	Avoidant attachment	Ambivalent attachment	Disorganized attachment
Infant behavior	Crying, thrashing, unresponsive	Crying, thrashing, unresponsive	Crying, thrashing, unresponsive	Crying, thrashing, unresponsive
Parent response	Rocking, soothing playing with	Limited soothing limited playing	Inconsistent soothing inconsistent stimulation	Unregulated and shifting parental affect
Infant response	Quieting with parent's quieting laughing with parent's activity	Quieting on own activating on own	Inconsistent quieting inconsistent alerting	Unregulated responding
Infant/child neuronal patterns	Supports interactive regulation of arousal	Supports self-regulation shut-down	Supports inconsistent interactive arousal	Supports aberrant arousal shifts
Child's internal working model	I am OK the world is safe & dependable	I am OK on my own the world is not dependable	I am only sometimes OK the world is only sometimes safe	I am not OK the world is not safe
Child behavior	Positive responding seeks help	Avoids others does not seek help	Over-demanding over-seeking of help	Tries to control others

Chart 3.1 Attachment patterns: Infant/child-parent responding.

networks would not, however, include interactive or seeking of another person for closeness and safety (see Chart 3.1, Avoidant Attachment). When, in the future, this infant, now child, confronts a negative situation or relationship, the child would be unlikely to seek help but would, based on the already developed neuronal patterns of self-regulation, rely on himself for calming or alerting. If this child, because of temperament or because of chaos within the home, abuse, or extreme neglect, experienced extreme ranges of over arousal or underarousal and insufficient external caring and comforting, the child's system would have to close down. Patterns of neuronal activity leading to emotional/physiological shutdown would develop within the right limbic, right cortical, HPA, and ANS neuronal areas. This form of responding—overreliance on self-regulation or shut-down—is known as insecure avoidant attachment (Main et al., 1985) (see Chart 3.1, Avoidant Attachment).

In other situations, the parent of the 'parent as infant' may not have had the resources to respond consistently with attending, comforting, protecting to her or his infant/child's over- or underarousal experiences. With an inconsistent response (sometimes responding and sometimes not responding), as opposed to lack of response (see preceding discussion), the 'parent as infant' does experience some positive responding. Because this is a positive experience, it is one the 'parent as child' will continue to seek. While heightened seeking can be handled by a caregiver with adequate resources, for the parent without adequate resources inconsistency increases—the caregiver sometimes providing soothing or alerting but at other times withdrawing and leaving the infant/child in an unregulated state. This 'parent as infant/child' develops behaviors that overseek attention and comfort. This attachment pattern is labeled as insecure ambivalent (Main et al., 1985) (see Chart 3.1, Ambivalent Attachment).

The most difficult experience for an infant/child is disorganized responding by the caregiver. This occurs when the parent of the 'parent as child' not only cannot provide adequate soothing and stimulation for the infant/child but he or she experiences extreme and unregulated affect—extreme anger, extreme fright, extreme withdrawal, and perhaps extreme engagement. In that an infant/child's neuronal system synchronizes with the parent's system (Schore, 2012; Siegel, 2012), the infant/child's system reverberates with responses—anger, fright, withdrawal, engagement—similar to those of the parent. Owing to this dysregulation, it is only natural that these children develop behaviors (both aggressive and caregiving) that try to control situations. This is referred to as a disorganized attachment pattern (Solomon & George, 1999) (see Chart 3.1, Disorganized Attachment). Given the danger inherent in anger, fright, and withdrawal, the infant/child tries to avoid the very individual whom she needs to approach for care and engagement (Hesse et al., 2003; Main & Hesse, 1990; Schuengel et al., 1999). The caregiver within this disorganized attachment pattern has an ANS that goes into overarousal or underarousal, an HPA system and cortisol response that reverberates with over- or underarousal, and has within her or his deep right hemisphere neuronal patterns of dysregulation. Beebe and her colleagues in their research (2010) found that caregivers exhibiting disorganized attachment patterns were not without empathy for their infant but that they, because of their own experiences, were triggered by their infant's needs and, therefore, unable to tolerate the infant/child's distress.

The caregiver, for his or her own survival, disengages from the infant/child. These caregivers have been observed to smile when the infant was in distress and not to respond when the infant smiled (Hughes & Baylin, 2012). The infant/child is left in a world that feels out of control and responds by trying to control others.

Chart 3.1 presents the scenarios and eventual child behaviors following similar infant behavior (crying, thrashing, unresponsive). But, of course, all infants are different. Some are more sensitive to stimulation than others; some are easier to calm than others. Thus, parents are presented with a wide variety of challenges. The chart is designed to provide an overview of how infant/child-parent interactions affect a child's neuronal and conceptual world and, therefore, the child's behavior with the parents and others. Most parents and children will experience a combination of attachment patterns (e.g., secure avoidant). We will want to identify the most prominent pattern and the one that most needs shifting for the parent and child to experience a stronger and more secure relationship.

As described by Schore (2012), "internal working models[3] of the attachment relationship with the primary caregiver, stored in the right brain, encode strategies of affect regulation that non-consciously guide the individual through interpersonal contexts" (p. 77). The infant/child who experienced primarily secure attachment holds an internal working model (neuronal networks formed from experiences) that informs the child/adult that people are available to care for and help, that being with people provides safety, and that the child is worthwhile. The infant/child who experienced primarily insecure avoidant attachment holds a model that people are not available, that avoiding people means safety, and that the child has to prove his worth. For the infant/child who experienced primarily insecure ambivalent attachment, the internal working model would include information that people are not dependable, it is necessary to grab onto people in order to be safe, and the self is unworthy. For the infant/child who has experienced a parent who is sometimes frightening (and therefore the parent is dangerous), sometimes frightened (and therefore the child himself must be dangerous), sometimes unavailable (and therefore the child is worthless), and sometimes a caring parent (and therefore the child is worthwhile), the internal working model holds the information that people (even seemingly caring people) may be dangerous and/or unavailable, that he must control others to be safe (others do not keep one safe), and that there is confusion as to whether he has worth. A child who experiences a disorganized attachment pattern, in order to feel safe, will try to control interactions—not only interactions with the parent but also interactions with other adults and children. The pattern of controlling may vary from constant refusal and/or aggressive behaviors to caretaking and overly solicitous behaviors (Cicchetti et al., 1990; Main & Cassidy, 1988).

Brain Patterns

To understand what is meant by the terminology we have been using, 'held in neuronal networks in the brain,' we need to look at learning and brain functioning. For those of us who are fascinated by the brain and by the recent findings in the area of neuroscience, this next section will be fun to read. For those who become overwhelmed by brain terminology, be reassured you do not need to learn any of this terminology. But understanding the role of the brain in relation to parenting can help guide us in our work with parents. We need to understand how the parents' own experience of having been parented becomes part of the neuronal networks within the parents' brains/bodies and how these neuronal patterns then affect the way they themselves parent. In the last section of the chapter, we will discuss how this information can help us in our work with parents.

How One Is Parented Becomes Part of the Neuronal Patterns within the Brain

As we experience something, we are taking information in through seeing, hearing, body movement, and affect. With each of these dimensions there will be firing in several areas of the brain. If the information is new, the neurons involved fire in such a way that new dendritic growth occurs, thus enabling new synaptic connections with the axon of other neurons and, in some situations, the formation of new neurons (see more detailed description: Cozolino, 2010). These synapses (one neuron may form up to 10,000 synapses with other neurons) may be excitatory or inhibitory, and as they interact with other neurons, specific patterns of firing occur. If the information is old, a neuronal firing pattern that was previously formed reoccurs, thereby strengthening the synaptic connections and possibly the stability of the neurons within the firing pattern. These neuronal patterns can stretch between many areas of the brain/body, some having axons as long as six feet (Doidge, 2007). Given that we are talking here about early experiences and experiences based on touch, voice tone, and eye contact, we are looking at neuronal patterns primarily within the right hemisphere—the part of the brain most reactive in the first months of life.

When we talk about parents co-regulating their infant/child, we are talking—within the secure attachment scenario—about neuronal reactions within the parent initially speeding up (the parent of a crying baby experiences anxiety) or slowing down (the parent of the lethargic baby experiences heaviness) in a manner that matches the infant/child's state. The parent in the secure attachment scenario then readjusts her own system—calms the anxiety or activates the heavy feeling. This shift in the parent's presentation stimulates a similar shift within the infant's brain—a calming or an energizing. With this process, the parental neuronal patterns for regulation have stimulated infant neuronal patterns for regulation.

Our understanding of the transmission of behavior from person to person increased considerably with the identification of mirror neurons (Ramachandran, 2011). In the mid-1990s, researchers started identifying specific activity neurons within the brain that fired when an individual observed another person doing that particular activity. This meant that neuronal patterns having to do with a particular activity were being created or strengthened when a person was observing an activity, even though the person was not actually doing that particular activity. These neurons—mirror neurons—not only hold information with regard to a specific physical activity (e.g., the raising of a hand) but also information related to the intent of the movement (e.g., to wave to the other person or to hit the other person).

As mentioned earlier, a parent responding to an infant/child with a secure attachment pattern response stimulates neuronal networks underlying positive soothing or positive alerting within the infant/child brain. As these networks are stimulated, the parent within the secure attachment pattern matches the infant/child's facial expression, voice tone, gestures, and body stance, thereby re-enforcing the child's neuronal pattern of positive response. This child's internal experience (the basis of the child's internal working model; Bowlby, 1971; Schore, 2012) is one of affect regulation and of a world that responds positively to himself/herself.

The parent who provides little responding (an avoidant attachment pattern) stimulates fewer positive interactive neuronal networks within the infant/child. The infant/child needing soothing/alerting becomes dependent on his own system (builds neuronal networks that are self-directed for soothing/alerting). Since this pattern is successful—the child either solves the problem or, if overwhelmed, shuts down and does not need a solution—it is reinforced. This child's internal working model holds information related to needing to rely only on oneself.

When a parent is sometimes available and sometimes not available (ambivalent attachment pattern), the neuronal networks related to soothing/alerting stimulated within the infant/child will include information that interaction with the parent occurs if one just persists long enough. This way of behaving—persisting or clinging—does in the end bring success for the child, and thus the neuronal network related to persistence and clinging is reinforced. The child's internal working model holds information related to help being inconsistently available and being dependent, not on the child's need, but on the child's persistent demand.

If the parent's responses alternate between anger-fright-neglect-support, the infant/child's neuronal networks encode all these states and, thus, are left with internal chaos (disorganization). As the parent responds to the infant's distress with a smile or shows no response when the infant smiles (see discussion earlier), the child's neuronal networks have no reinforcement of their own experience but rather a reinforcement of a contradictory world. This creates for many infants a vulnerability to dissociation which, if further activated by continued attachment trauma or other trauma, can develop into a dissociative disorder (Liotti, 2009; Wieland, 2015a).

Trauma that is beyond what the infant/child's system is able to deal with and where there is no relief, comforting, or reestablishment of safety leads to a division within the self. This division (dissociation), which keeps the knowledge, emotions, and physical experience of the trauma separate from the child, enables the child to function day by day (Braun, 1988; Silberg, 2013; van der Hart et al., 2006; Waters, 2016; Wieland, 2015a). The division may lead to experiences of depersonalization, derealization, and/or amnesia (American Psychiatric Association, 2013; Wieland, 2015a). When the dissociation is such that the emotions, somatic sensations, or memories related to the trauma take over the child/adult's functioning with the individual being aware that it is happening, it is referred to as a dissociative disorder not elsewhere classified (American Psychiatric Association, 2013; Wieland, 2015a). When these changes occur without the child/adult having any awareness of what is happening, it is referred to as dissociative identity disorder (American Psychiatric Association, 2013; Wieland, 2015a).

Where in the Brain/Body Many of These Patterns Are Held

The following discussion is an simplification of brain processing. Every human function and emotional reaction engages multiple areas of the brain. To understand this in detail, we (both authors and readers) would need to return to university for several years. And that would leave waiting, unnecessarily, both the children and the parents we are trying to help. What we need to understand are the areas that have been found to have a primary role in different mental (both cognitive and emotional) experiences related to parenting.

Limbic System

The limbic 'system,'[4] that area in the very middle of the brain that we share with both mammals and reptiles, creates responding without thinking, as well as responding modified by thinking (see Diagram 3.3).

The amygdala, a primary structure within the limbic system, evaluates the environment for danger or safety. This structure, which is often referred to as the anger/fear center of the brain (Damasio, 1994), is fully developed by the eighth month of gestation (Cozolino, 2010) and thus plays a major role in the infant's early experiences of the world. If danger is detected, the amygdala alerts both the hypothalamus-pituitary-adrenal axis (HPA), which leads to secretion of cortisol[5] (stress hormone) by the adrenal gland, and the ANS, which activates the sympathetic nervous system and prepares the body for danger (see Diagram 3.2, p. 49). The infant cries and thrashes around, thereby alerting the parent. The parent's response—soothing behavior, anxious or worried behavior, angry behavior—determines the infant's subsequent experience and early emotional learning about the world. The amygdala, together with the basal ganglia and perceptual cortices, holds early learning and, later, highly stressful, traumatic learning in implicit (without words) format (see discussion further on). The hippocampus, (also part of the limbic system), which is associated with explicit memory, does not

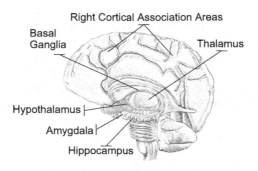

Diagram 3.3 Areas related to early emotional learning and control—amygdala, hypothalamus, basal ganglia—and areas through which stimuli from both the body and the outside world enter the brain—thalamus—are labeled.

complete development until somewhere between 1½ years and 3 years and it does not function under high levels of traumatic stress (for further information, see Cozolino, 2010).

The parent serves as an external cortex for the infant/child (Swain, 2008; Swain et al., 2014) until the child's cortex develops neuronal connections capable of calming the amygdala. If the parent offers a soothing response, the infant/child's HPA, ANS, and amygdala settle, and the infant/child learns the world is safe. If the parent becomes overly anxious with the infant's distress, the reactivity within the infant/child's HPA, ANS, and amygdala is likely to continue, and the infant/child's system becomes sensitized to activation. If there is yelling and chaos surrounding the infant, the infant's amygdala, HPA, and ANS will likely go into an overaroused state. This may lead to oversensitivity of the amygdala and, if high arousal continues, the dorsal vagal parasympathetic nervous system (see p. 64) is likely to be triggered and, when extreme, dissociation may occur (Perry et al., 1995; Schore, 2003, 2012).

As the child's cortex and, in particular, the orbital-medial prefrontal cortex (OMPFC)—an area that has the capability of developing extensive neuronal connections with the amygdala—develops, the child can acquire an ability to calm the amygdala. Research has shown that as activity in the OMPFC increases, the activation within the amygdala—and therefore the experiencing of anger/fear—decreases (Damasio, 1994; Grecucci et al., 2015; Hariri et al., 2003). Diagram 3.4 provides a schematic portrayal of hypothesized neuronal activity between the OMPFC and the amygdala. With age and with the development of emotional regulation, activity in the OMPFC increases,[6] 'messages' are passed to the amygdala, and high activation of the amygdala settles. When the child or adult perceives danger and the amygdala is activated, 'messages' are passed to the OMPFC that interrupt OMPFC functioning—the individual is less able to calm.

Strengthening the functioning of the OMPFC is clearly going to be important in our work (see discussion further on) whether we are with the child or with the child's parent.

Before we leave the discussion of the amygdala, it will be helpful for us to understand and, therefore, be able to explain to parents the role the amygdala plays in sudden and intense, but unwarranted—there is no danger at that moment—reactions (i.e., trigger reactions). The thalamus, another structure within the limbic system, serves as the gateway for sensory stimuli coming from the outside world or from inside the body to the brain (see Diagram 3.3). This information travels from the thalamus on two different pathways through the brain: the first is direct from the thalamus to the amygdala and the second is from the thalamus through the hippocampus (memory function) and frontal cortex (analysis function) to the amygdala (LeDoux, 2002).

If the stimulus is indeed dangerous then that first, direct pathway to the amygdala, which results in an immediate response that activates arousal within the HPA and ANS, is important. If, however, the stimulus has a similarity to something that has in the past been frightening but is not now dangerous, then the fast activation via the amygdala to the ANS can cause difficulty. By the time the stimulus information has passed via the second pathway through the hippocampus (memory: this is not the same as the stimulus in the past) and the cortex (reflection: this is not

How the Brain Holds Parenting Patterns   57

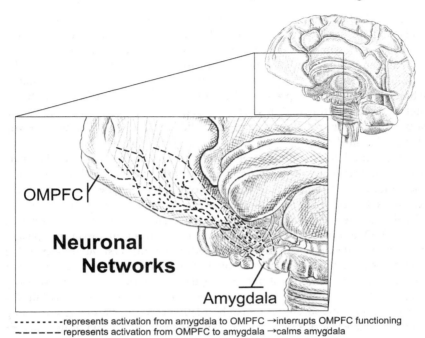

- - - - - - - - represents activation from amygdala to OMPFC →interrupts OMPFC functioning
— — — — — represents activation from OMPFC to amygdala →calms amygdala

Diagram 3.4 Schematic portrayal of hypothesized brain activity between the orbital-medial prefrontal cortex (OMPFC) and amygdala.

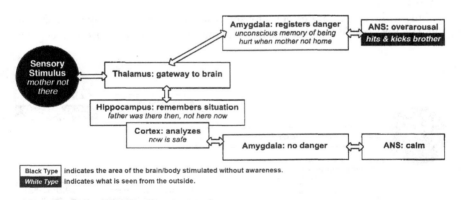

Chart 3.2 Trigger reaction—child becoming aware that his mother is not there (thalamus), amygdala announcing danger and alerting ANS. By the time the information is able to travel to the hippocampus (memory—Dad is gone) and the frontal lobe (analysis—world is safe now), then to the amygdala, the ANS is already in full alert.

dangerous), the body is in full arousal and possibly unable to think and take in this new information (see Chart 3.2).

A 6-year-old child now living in safety is playing with his brother. He looks around, does not see mother, and goes into high fright. He starts kicking and hitting his brother. Outside stimuli: mother not there → thalamus → amygdala: emotional reaction from early years when mother was not there and child was abused by father = amygdala registers danger. When mother comes back in room, the child runs and hides. He is unable to explain (no verbal understanding) why he hit his brother. Later (hippocampus: remembers father is no longer living in the home; cortex: analyzes present safety → amygdala: no danger) child is able to regret he did the hitting and to say he is sorry. Because, however, the amygdala works at an implicit, reactionary level, the child has no understanding as to why he behaved as he did.

Even as an adult, regardless of new and safe experiences, the amygdala networks continue to focus on "what they perceive as interpersonally threatening and anxiety inducing" (Ginot, 2007, p. 323). A mother is helping her 5-year-old learn to tie shoes. He tries and tries, but it just does not work, and in his frustration he yanks off his shoe and throws it, picks up his other shoe, and throws it as well (see Chart 3.3). One of the shoes passes close to mom's head, mom startles, pushes her son away, and runs screaming into her bedroom (outside stimulus: something being thrown at her; amygdala: emotional memory from early childhood when alcoholic father threw things at her → amygdala registers danger). Five-year-old is frightened by mother and starts to cry, goes to his room and crawls into his bed. Later (mom's hippocampus remembers father (not son) throwing something means she will get hurt; mom's cortex analyzes son is not trying to hurt her → mom's amygdala: no danger) mom cuddles son to calm her system and to calm his system. Mom is confused—why did she get so frightened? Child is confused—first Mom shoves him (angry), then Mom runs away (frightened), then Mom soothes him (caretaking).

Only if the mom puzzles out why she reacted like she did (Siegel & Hartzell, 2003) will she understand her reaction and may be able, in the future, to recognize

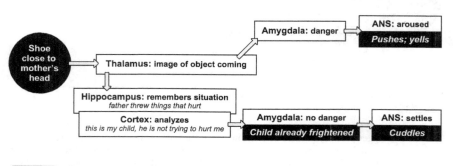

Chart 3.3 Mother's trigger response.

her emotional and somatic reactivity and interrupt her responding in such a way that she can react differently to the boy's throwing response.

Prefrontal Cortex

Cozolino, in his discussion of brain functions, compares the amygdala and the ANS to soldiers in the field who are ready to fight and survive, while the prefrontal cortex plays the role of the general who reviews what is happening, updates strategy, and communicates (sometimes well and sometimes poorly) with the soldiers in the field (Cozolino, 2010, p. 156). The prefrontal cortex is divided into four general regions: starting just behind the eyes—orbital prefrontal, ventral or medial prefrontal, lateral prefrontal, dorsal prefrontal (see Diagram 3.5).

Starting at the area just behind the eyes is the orbital prefrontal cortex, which has been found to play a primary role in emotional regulation, self-soothing, and social regulation (Damasio, 1994; Rempel-Clower, 2007). Moving up from there is the ventral or medial prefrontal cortex (mPFC), which is related to reflection and self/other awareness. (Hughes & Baylin, 2012) and is activated as we engage in social situations. Above the mPFC is the lateral prefrontal cortex, which is active in directing attention and activating working memory. The top area, labeled the dorsal prefrontal cortex, is particularly active when an individual is engaging in problem-solving.

As can be noticed from this description, the orbital-medial prefrontal cortex (OMPFC) is engaged primarily with emotional and social tasks and is part of the processing needed for understanding not only how we ourselves feel but also how

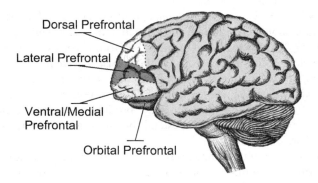

Diagram 3.5 Prefrontal lobes—orbital: important role in emotional and social regulation; medial: important role in self-reflection and awareness; lateral: important role in attention and activating working memory; dorsal: important role in problem-solving.

others feel. The right hemisphere OMPFC is active in observing and taking in information, including the facial expressions and somatic responses of other people and of the self. The left OMPFC is more engaged with explicit information—what the other person said or the events that happened. Working together with the right OMPFC, the left OMPFC has the capacity to develop an ability to use internal and external information to understand one's own feelings as well as the feelings of others. This area of the brain has the capability to develop extensive neuronal connectivity with the amygdala (see Diagram 3.4) and, therefore, the capacity—if developed and if the implicit and explicit information received is congruent—to calm and regulate the amygdala.

The dorsal-lateral prefrontal cortex (DLPFC) engages more in cognitive tasks (focusing attention, engaging working memory,[7] reappraising situations, and problem-solving) with the right DLPFC processing observation-based information and the left DLPFC centering more on verbally learned information (for a more detailed description see Cozolino, 2010; Hughes and Baylin, 2012). Similar to the OMPFC, the DLPFC can calm the amygdala, but this calming is achieved through cognitive processing—distraction, reasoning, avoidance—as opposed to the emotional regulation process (calming) of the OMPFC. Based on his review of the research, Cozolino (2010) concludes that a task primarily emotional in content will tend to activate the OMPFC, while a task with high cognitive demands will increase activation in the DLPFC and decrease activation in the OMPFC.

An overly activated infant/child creates distress for a parent. Depending on the parent's own personal experiences and, therefore, the parent's reactivity to the infant/child's crying, her orbital prefrontal cortex (see Diagrams 3.6a, 3.6b) provides some evaluation along the continuum from "*calm*" ← → "*can't stand this.*" Based on the level of reflection and mindfulness the parent has developed, her medial prefrontal cortex responds along a continuum from "*I can stay calm, I can hold and rock him*" ← → "*Everything is out of control.*" The lateral prefrontal cortex directs attention along a continuum from "*I can notice his responses, I can understand this*" ← → "*I can't focus.*" And the dorsal prefrontal cortex provides problem-solving, also along a continuum from "*I think the ear infection has come back, I'll look at the drops from his last infection and see if the expiry date is still all right*" ← → "*If he cries long enough, he will fall asleep.*" These responses reflect activity from many areas of the brain—no thought is the product of an exact location. This description is to help the reader understand the importance of processing within the prefrontal areas.

While the specifics of the parent's response are based on the infant/child behavior of the moment, the manner of responding is dictated by the parent's earlier experiences as a child.[8] As professionals working with the child and parent, we need to determine if the parent has the ability to emotionally regulate, to be mindful of what is happening, to direct attention to what is pertinent, and to integrate present information with what the parent already knows in such a way that a problem situation can be resolved. Which is the weak capability—emotional regulation,

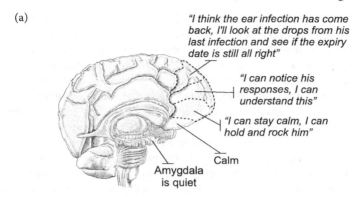

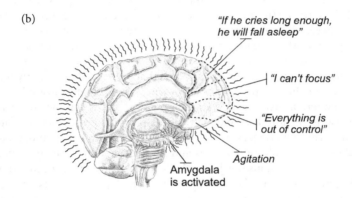

Diagram 3.6a and Diagram 3.6b Simplified conceptualization of parent's left prefrontal cortex[9] responding to an infant/child crying—brain on the top (3.6a) is in a calm state; brain on the bottom (3.6b) is in a highly agitated state.

mindfulness, attention, integration of information? Then we can direct our attention to that area/s needing assistance (see Chapters 4, 5, 6).

Right Hemisphere

Because neuronal networks related to attachment start building early in development, they exist primarily within the right hemisphere (Schore, 2003, 2012)—that part of the brain that is developing most rapidly at birth (see Diagram 3.1, p. 48). Recent research has extended our understanding of the right hemisphere. The right hemisphere is identified as the primary location of implicit memory (reviewed in Mancia, 2006), nonconscious awareness (Schore, 1994, 2012), self-awareness (Ginot, 2007; Keenan et al., 2005; Keenan & Gorman, 2007), and attachment (Schore, 2001, 2012).

Implicit memory—that which is encoded without conscious awareness and held without words—as opposed to explicit memory (encoded with awareness and able to be verbally expressed), is active from birth and perhaps before birth (Ginot, 2007). While vital for survival and constantly in use, implicit memory cannot be actively recalled. Implicit memory holds the sights, sounds, smells, movements, body responses (e.g., heart rate, pain) that are recorded within us (neuronal connections) without active attention and impinge on us without active awareness. Implicit memory is often emotion based. What implicit memory does not, for the most part, have is contextual detail (Brewin, 2005). It does not place an event according to when it happened—in the past, the present, or possibly the future. It exists in the moment. Early attachment patterns as part of implicit memory are experienced as if they are part of our present relationships (with our partners, with our colleagues, with our children). Thus, the dynamics we were taught when we were young are likely to replay (unless we are conscious of them and consciously make distinctions between then and now) within our present relationships—including our parenting relationship. This is one reason why we highlighted in the last chapter the importance of child professionals doing their own therapeutic work.

Another characteristic of implicit memory is that it does not necessarily match explicit memory. Explicit memory consists of what one is taught through outside (as opposed to internal) experiences. Explicit memory holds consciously learned information that is anchored as being part of the past, the present, or the future. The individual who experiences a dissonance between explicit memory (good grades in school; being told one is safe) and implicit memory (being treated as not capable; experiencing abuse) is left with a confused and unclear sense of self. Because the implicit memory (lack of capability, lack of safety) is outside of conscious awareness, it impinges on one's actual experience or explicit memory (good grades in school; being told one is safe) without the possibility of the individual being able to refute or modify the sense of incapability or the sense of unsafety. Because the implicit memory is based earlier in life and is there without understanding, it—in most situations—has a greater impact on the individual. People often experience this as I 'know' I can do well (explicit knowing) but it is *only because* I am lucky, have worked hard (implicit sensing); I 'know' I am safe (explicit knowing) but I don't 'feel' safe (implicit sensing).

Schore's research (summarized in Schore, 2012) has highlighted the interconnections between body response, in particular the ANS, and right hemisphere neuronal networks via the brain stem and limbic system (see Diagram 3.2). These dense interconnectivities link early interpersonal experiences (e.g., caretaking or physical/sexual abuse) that impact both the physical body and the peripheral nervous system—thus, one's state of arousal—to the right hemisphere, where information is held in a sensed but not verbal form. These primarily right-lateralized networks hold sensory, arousal, and emotional information encoded without awareness and held outside consciousness. Later in life, these same sensory, arousal, and emotional reactions may be activated (i.e., triggered, see p. 56) without awareness and outside consciousness. Mancia (2006) refers to this as the "unrepressed unconscious"—because an individual is not consciously aware of the information, the individual is unable to repress the information and, therefore, it continues to intrude even when present world information contradicts it. It is these "presymbolic and preverbal experiences of the primary mother-infant relations . . . that form the nucleus of self" (Mancia, 2006, p. 83).

Keenan et al., in a review of right hemisphere functioning (2005), noted that it is the right, not left, hemisphere that holds an individual's self-awareness and ability to reflect on one's own thinking and on the thinking of other people—a process important for mentalization.[10] The unconscious awareness of self-image has been found to occur primarily within the right hemisphere (Theoret et al., 2004), and Schore (2012) has speculated that an infant/child/adult's internal working model of self is held "at levels beneath conscious awareness" (p. 236) within the right hemisphere. One's internal working model of self and the world affects how each of us interacts with the world without conscious awareness.

A parent comes home from a long and difficult day at work and is looking forward to an excited and warm hug from his or her 9-year-old (see Chart 3.4). The child, however, was involved in what he was doing and did not even come to the door to greet his parent. A parent with a right hemisphere-held internal working model of being a capable and lovable person would call out a greeting and ask the child what he is up to. At dinner that evening, parent and child would share anecdotes from their days. A parent with a right hemisphere-held internal working model of being inadequate and an unlovable person would feel hurt and rejected and might not even call a greeting to the child. At dinner that evening, the parent would not ask the child about his day but instead would find fault with the child's table manners.

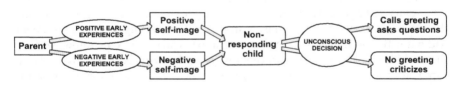

Chart 3.4 Parent's response as shaped by early formed self-image.

Autonomic Nervous System

The brain and the body are intimately interconnected, with both areas holding genetic and environmental information. Ogden et al. (2006) describe early sensorimotor experiences and traumatic sensorimotor experiences as being held in the brain/body in the form of sounds, smells, and physical sensations including pain, energizing, constriction, relaxation, and numbing even though the individual has no words to describe the experience. These reactions may be activated when the body, because of stress related to present-day personal or interpersonal interactions, moves out of 'the window of tolerance' (Ogden et al., 2006). This window of tolerance refers to an individual's optimal arousal zone—not too high, not too low—in which the individual is able to tolerate, think about, and make reasoned decisions related to what is going on (similar to the infant/child's optimal level of arousal that we discussed earlier). When an individual's arousal level is too high, he or she becomes hypervigilant, emotionally reactive, physically tense, and disorganized in his or her thinking. When the arousal level is too low, the individual experiences little sensation, a numbing of emotions, slowed movement, and, often, disabled thinking. Arousal level refers to the functioning of the ANS (control of heartbeat, breathing rate, digestive processes, and other involuntary musculature of the body).

Porges (2011) has delineated three subsystems within the ANS: one sympathetic or energizing subsystem and two parasympathetic or slowing-down subsystems: one which is mediated by the dorsal vagal nerve and the other which is mediated by the ventral vagal nerve—thus the name 'polyvagal theory.' At birth, the sympathetic nervous system and the dorsal vagal parasympathetic system are functioning. The infant can be aroused and the infant can close down. As the infant's physiological system matures, the ventral vagal nerve myelinates, and the infant/child develops what Porges refers to as the 'social engagement system.' This system helps to maintain a level of arousal within a range that permits engagement with other people and the environment without (1) overactivating the sympathetic system (hyperarousal leading to fight or flight) or disengaging from people and from the reflecting/thinking parts of the brain or (2) activating the dorsal vagal parasympathetic system (hypoarousal leading to numbing) and disengagement. For an individual to be able to stay within the ventral vagal social engagement system when something anxiety-provoking occurs, the individual needs to experience an internal sense of safety (Porges, 2011).

Porges (2004) has proposed the term "neuroception" to describe "how neural circuits distinguish whether situations or people are safe, dangerous, or life threatening" (p. 19). Neuroception is an internal processing of the environment without active awareness that lets us, and in particular our ANS, know whether the world is safe or not. The neuroception system is particularly sensitive to facial expressions, voice tone, and gesture. If our neuroception senses that the world is dangerous, our body goes into either sympathetic arousal (negative 'gut response') or dorsal vagal parasympathetic closing down (numbing)—both of these being defensive responses. Early positive experiences build an internal sense of safety, which means that future experiences will be judged as safe (defensive reactions will not occur) unless there is reason (actual threat) related to safety. With early negative experiences, which create an oversensitized system, there is no internal sense of safety. This individual's neuroception system is likely to misread cues, such that situations which are safe are 'misread' as unsafe. There are also situations in which a young child experiences chaos and danger to such an extent that his or her neuroception system becomes immune—what is unsafe becomes familiar, expected, and therefore not judged as unsafe. This child/then adult's neuroception is likely to misread cues such that unsafe places or people are 'misread' as safe and safe places or people may be misread as unsafe.

When positive early attachment occurs, parents provide their child with arousal regulation experiences that contribute to the strengthening of the infant/child's social engagement system. If there is abuse or chaos—witnessing violence, in particular domestic violence—within the early experiences, the ANS of the infant/child is overly activated and the sympathetic (fight/flight) system becomes more reactive. This child, later adult, tends to react to undesirable situations quickly with angry and aggressive—as opposed to thought-out and reasonable—responses. If there is abuse/chaos beyond what can be tolerated or severe neglect within the early experiences, the ANS, by means of the dorsal vagal parasympathetic system, slows down the body systems. This child, later adult, when stressed, is more likely to respond by shutting down or dissociating. The individual has difficulty evaluating situations accurately and often presents as depressed, nonresponsive, or dissociated.

How Understanding the Brain Can Help Guide Our Therapeutic Interactions

Given what we know about the brain and the body, how can we, as individuals committed to helping children and parents, create experiences which will help parents build within their brains neuronal networks that underlie more secure, positive parenting? What makes this work exciting is that recent research has demonstrated the brain's ability to change (Doidge, 2007, 2015). Our interactions with parents have the potential to contribute toward a change in parenting neuronal networks.

As an activity happens, the brain neurons underlying that activity—for example, an attachment experience—are stimulated. If there is a new quality to the experience—this is positive, this is safe—new neuronal connections (synapses) are stimulated. Because of simultaneous firing, these neuronal networks—attachment and safety—build linkages (Doidge, 2007).[11] If *repeated and repeated*, these synaptic connections become stronger and more dense. The older connections—for this situation, synaptic connections to negative attachment outcome—if not retriggered, become weaker.

To encourage positive attachment changes, stimulation is needed within those areas of the brain/body that have been found to be the primary holders of neuronal patterns related to attachment (deep right cortices), to self-awareness and the internal working model of self (right associative cortical areas), to the ability to be mindful, reflect, and mentalize (OMPFC), to the ability to focus attention, engage working memory, and problem solve (DLPFC), to recognition of danger and safety (*amygdala*), and to the ability to regulate emotional arousal (OMPFC, mid-brain areas, ANS).

Engaging Deep Right Cortices—Our Relationship with the Parent

Because the parent's early attachment interactions taught by their parents—teaching that forms the basis of the parent's knowledge about parenting—is held deep in the right hemisphere, a part of the brain that is more reactive to what people do than to what people say, we need to be as attentive to what we do and how we do it as we are to what we say. We need to pay attention to our body position—alert, interested as opposed to slack, disinterested. We also need to pay attention to our voice tone—engaged, supportive as opposed to monotone, disapproving—and to our eye gaze—direct, ready to engage as opposed to shifting and disinterested. While we—as individuals[12]—may experience disapproval or even repulsion in relation to the parent's manner of interacting with his or her child, we—as someone who wants to help children—need to have an open, 'ready-to-hear-their-story' stance with parents if we are to provide a positive interpersonal experience for them.

While reading and talking about attachment may modify one's understanding of attachment, it is only through positive reciprocal interactions within an ongoing relationship that neuronal networks related to attachment patterns can be modified (Alexander, 1992; Blizard, 2003; Cozolino, 2010; Schore, 2012). Our relationship with the parent is, therefore, of paramount importance if we are to help parents build neuronal networks that underlie secure and supportive interactive behaviors. These secure and supportive neuronal networks are then available within the parents as they interact with their child.

The parent who experienced negative parenting when young is going to be keenly aware of our reactions—in our position as a child professional, we become similar to her or his parent. We need, therefore, to be aware of our reactions to the parent. We will be discussing our reactions (countertransference) in more detail in Chapter 8. Here we want to focus on how, if we are to provide new experiences—and, therefore, new synaptic firing—in an effort to counter early insecure attachment neuronal networks the parent may have embedded in his or her right hemisphere, we need to attend carefully to how we respond to the parent. More important than the explicit information (words) we say will be the implicit information from our body response (movement forward, not backward), our facial expressions (acceptance-approval, not dismissal-disapproval), our voice tone and speed (acceptance and interest, not dismissal and withdrawal), our eye contact (direct acknowledging, not indirect avoiding). It is this implicit information that engages the right hemisphere and the neuronal connections relevant to interpersonal relationships. Attunement to and support of the parent (see Chapter 5) is going to be as important as attunement to and support for the child.

Engaging Right Hemisphere—Dyadic Art and Sand-Tray Activity

Because parenting style is based on a parent's internal working model of self (I can trust others ←→ I have to be in control) and the world (the world is safe ←→ the world is dangerous), we need to involve right hemisphere—the location of one's internal working model—processing in our work with parents. As we work with children in their homes, in school, and in therapy settings, we encourage play, art, movement, and sand tray exploration as ways to engage the child's right hemisphere (Chapman, 2014).[13] With adults who have come for individual help, art, movement, and sand tray work can similarly be encouraged. But with adults who have brought their children for help, this is seldom an option unless it is included within the work with the child. Parents can be encouraged to follow the child's direction within a play scenario or while painting pictures. As the play progresses, both child and parent gain a sense of togetherness (the activity) and safety (the setting established by the professional). As is described in Chapter 5, parents working together with children in therapy can be encouraged to draw or do a sand tray representing a safe place or a particular internal resource they want to strengthen. When recognizing that parents are struggling with anxiety or particular fears—as often is true of parents of children with anxiety and fears—therapists can encourage the parent, along with the child, to use drawings as a way of exploring old fears or new situations.

Images or pictures referring to positive shared moments can be used to remind both parent and child about good memories, strengths, and inner resources. The parent and child can be encouraged to create a 'Book of Life' in which the parent narrates the story of the child through images and stories starting from the experience of expecting the child, through his birth, special moments shared by the family, and important milestones (learning to walk, to ride a bike, first day at school, graduation from school). The child and parents can search for photos or other pictures that represent those times and then bring them to their appointments with a support worker or therapist for inclusion within the 'Book of Life.'

For children who have a history of trauma, this work should be done by a trained therapist. The therapist can create, with the parent's help, a story of the child's early frightening experiences together with the body sensations, emotions, and possible thoughts experienced at that time, followed by the new and positive experiences since that time. This story, which may be verbally presented to older children or visually presented in a cartoon strip for younger children, can be presented with bilateral stimulation as part of an Eye Movement Desensitization and Reprocessing (EMDR) session (Lovett, 2005; Wieland & Silberg, 2013).

Engaging Motor Activity and Right Hemisphere Processing—Imaging

Another way to initiate right hemisphere engagement is to encourage visualization and imaging. Visualization of oneself doing an activity stimulates neuronal activity within the brain similar to the neuronal activity that occurs when one is actually doing the activity (Doidge, 2007, 2015; Holmes & Collins, 2001; Jeannerod & Decety, 1995; Lang, 1979). Visualization provides effective practice for doing that particular activity in real life (see Louridas et al., 2015). Thus, a parent imaging himself or herself within a positive interaction with a child can stimulate neuronal synapses that support that particular interaction and thus enable it to happen more easily in the future.

Over the past century, mental imaging or visualization has been increasingly recognized as a way to stimulate change within the brain. Freud speculated that mental activity leads to changes in neuronal connections (referenced in Doidge, 2007), and Pierre Janet talked about using positive images related to the self as a means to relieve traumatically caused conditions (referenced in van der Kolk & van der Hart, 1989). In the 1960s and 1970s, Lang (1979), having observed increased muscle tension when someone imaged themselves lifting weights and increased heart rate when someone imaged a frightening scene, proposed that an "image is a prototype in the brain for overt responding" (p. 500). In this way imaging leads to an alteration in both cognitive and motor structures, thereby creating the basis for a significant behavioral change (Lang, 1979).

Introduction of visualization as a way to enhance more positive and productive thinking (Gawain, 2002) as well as increased athletic performance (Holmes & Collins, 2001) became popular in the 1970s and 1980s. Mental imaging became an increasingly important therapeutic component within cognitive therapy (Beck et al., 1985) and was used in psychodynamic therapy for trauma survivors (Grove & Panzer, 1991; Hyde, 1990; Wieland, 1998). The shift observed in EMDR processing (Shapiro, 1995) from dark, depressive, and clear negative scenes to lighter, more positive, or hazy/distant negative scenes as negative cognitions are resolved highlights the connection between images and internal cognitions or beliefs.

At the beginning of the twenty-first century, imagery re-scripting was increasingly being used therapeutically with individuals struggling with numerous serious psychopathologies including posttraumatic stress disorder (Holmes et al., 2007). Focusing based on imagery has been found to have more impact on emotions and emotional states than verbal focusing (Holmes & Mathews, 2010). As described by Kindt et al. (2007), it is not the perceptual processing but the conceptual processing related to imaging that effects a positive therapeutic change. Imagery training with doctors has indicated not only improved surgical performance following mental imaging practice but also better retention of this skill in an emergency situation when stress levels (heart rate and cortisol secretion) were elevated (Louridas et al., 2015).

Can imaging help us in our work with parents? Clearly, from this review, imaging has the potential to teach and strengthen new activities as well as increasing the individual's ability to maintain self-regulation when under stress (see sports and medical training research). Maintaining self-regulation during stressful times is certainly relevant for our work in that, for the parents we see, parenting is a highly stressful activity. Although the actual process of imaging engages both right and left hemispheres and in some cases more left than right (Behrmann, 2000), it is the right hemisphere that is active for the conceptual (meaning-making), as opposed to the perceptual, processing of content from mental images (Kindt et al., 2007). The research of Holmes and Mathews (2010) supports the close connection between imagery and autobiographical memory, a primarily right hemisphere function (Cozolino, 2010; Schore, 2012). Parents imaging themselves within a positive interaction (perceptual processing) with their child while noticing what this would mean (conceptual processing) for both them and their child has the potential of stimulating neuronal growth that can underlie new and more positive activity within the motor areas—shifting from a stiff arm to an arm around the child's shoulders; stopping a slapping movement—and the right cortices—sensing support and love of self and child—of the brain. This neuronal growth within the right cortices supports more positive attachment, implicit memory of positive times, and a more positive internal working model of themselves in relation to their child.

Because imaging is not an activity adults often engage in and may, indeed, be reluctant to do, we need to be able to explain to them why we are asking for this. We can explain that doing something related to parenting in a new way (a different way of talking with the child, a different way of responding to the child's 'fits,' a different way of sitting with the child during a difficult incident) takes practice, just as learning to swing a tennis racket in a new way takes practice. When we practice (image) new behaviors in our mind's eye, the neurons related to the muscles involved in those actions and the neurons related to the interpersonal interaction involved in those actions actually fire. As those neurons fire, they strengthen. They start to build the new responding pattern the parent wants. We can talk about the research with sports, musical instruments, and surgery that show that imaging increases one's ability to respond in a particular way. No matter how much we may want to change, without some practice, our brain cells related to how we are already doing something—the parenting response we want to get rid of—that has had lots of practice from the past are most likely to take over.

Our parent undoubtedly wishes that his or her left hemisphere words, *"I want to be a calm, loving parent. I want to . . .,"* would overwrite the negative early parenting pattern. And we agree with them; after all, our job would be much easier if this were true. But the brain does not work that way. The early unconsciously taught parenting neuronal patterns are far stronger than recently learned words and wishes. Words and wishes can work well when the parent is calm but once the parent is agitated, the early taught neuronal patterns take over.

Heather & Bill, 8 Years Old

> **BACKGROUND INFORMATION:** *Mom (Heather) has been telling the woman who is providing day care for Bill after school about the awful times she has with Bill at bedtime. Evenings seem to be going well, but as soon as Mom says it is time to get ready for bed, Bill starts yelling at and hitting her. The day care provider, remembering some of the bedtime problems she had with her children, sympathizes with Mom and wonders if there is anything about bedtime or the bedroom that is scaring Bill. Nothing unusual seems to be evident, but Bill has learned that if he screams then he can stay up longer and longer.*

DAY CARE PROVIDER: *What would you like to do when he doesn't get into bed, when he starts yelling and hitting?*

HEATHER: *The getting ready for bed goes all right—it is the getting into bed. I'd like to be able to just walk out of the room and not go back in until he is in bed and quiet. But when he starts yelling, I yell—it's like it is automatic, I hate it. My parents always yelled at me, and I said I wouldn't do it and here I am!*

DAY CARE PROVIDER: *What a good idea—going out of the room and not back in until he is quiet. What could you give him to reassure him that you will come back when he is quiet?*

HEATHER: *I suppose I could write it on a card. I used to put cards in his lunch box when he was in grade one. You know, something like "Mom will be back when you stop yelling and then I'll kiss you good night." I could give that to him. Guess I better go into the bathroom and gag my mouth so I don't yell through the door.*

DAY CARE PROVIDER: *Sounds like a plan—but not the gag, how about some good magazines? But I know how hard it is to do something new and different when everyone is upset—and those times are certainly upsetting. Having some practice would help.*

One way to practice is to visualize the situation in your head and watch yourself doing the plan—taking a breath, telling Bill you are leaving and will be back when he is quiet, giving him the card that you have already written out, and then going into the bathroom where you have some magazines to read.

HEATHER: *I'm really not interested in visualizing anything. It just needs to work tonight when Bill, like always, goes out of control.*

DAY CARE PROVIDER: *Absolutely, you want it to work. Here is my concern—without some practice for the new way of responding, tonight when Bill starts yelling or hitting, your brain is likely to go to the old pattern of yelling back that you were taught by your parents. Research with athletes shows us that when we visualize ourselves and feel ourselves doing an activity, the muscles related to those activities actually contract—that is, the muscles practice the activity. And an activity that has been practiced is more likely to happen. Would you be willing to give it a try?* (See more examples in Chapter 6.)

As we work with parents, we want not only to have the parent learn a new way of reacting but to have this new pattern of reacting occur to them when difficult situations happen—when the child, the parent, or both are in overarousal. This means that the practice imaging needs to include the child and/or the parent in a state of overarousal.

Within the imaging, we can ask parents to bring up an image of the negative interaction with the child, notice the tension that comes in to their body, have them describe that tension to be sure they are actually experiencing it, have them take a deep breath—breathing slows down the ANS and allows movement to the ventral vagal 'social engagement' system—have them image themselves doing the new planned reaction, have them notice what happens for their child, and have them notice the shift in their own tension level. We need to be sure to carry the activity all the way through to its end—for the example here, the mother would watch herself explaining to Bill what would happen, giving him the card, going into the bathroom and sitting there listening to Bill's yelling, waiting while the yelling continues, listening for the end of the yelling, and then watch herself coming back out and the child's response after she is back with him. If the child, within the parent's image, continues in a highly activated mode, we most likely have not come up with a sufficiently reassuring plan. We would want to do some more problem-solving together with the parent as to what might help reassure the child, and then try the imaging once again. This process could be repeated until the child in the parent's image has been able to settle. We can then ask the mother to image herself and the child doing something positive together.

If we are trained in therapeutic skills, we would ask the mom how the experience was for her. What were the emotions and sensations that she experienced during the imaging? What were the emotions and sensations she thought the child might experience? What was it about her behavior that led to a change in the child's behavior? As the child's behavior changed, what happened for her, what happened for him?

The mom has gained practice in maintaining her own emotional regulation (see further discussion later), practice of a new active response to the child's agitation, practice of believing in her child's ability to calm, and practice of a positive connection with the child. Our questions following the imaging encourage mentalization, a pattern of thinking that has been found to correlate with secure attachment interactions.

If we are working with parents in a group setting, roleplay can be used to provide the practice that imaging provides when working with an individual parent. Roleplay has had a long history as a successful therapeutic technique in group work.

Engaging Orbital Medial Prefrontal Cortex—Emotional Regulation; Mindfulness; Mentalization

As we engage parents and their children in calming activities (see p. 127) and as we remain calm when we are with them—remembering that attuning with emotions means recognizing and naming emotions, not engaging in the emotion (Hughes, 2009)—we are engaging and stimulating neuronal activity in the parent's OMPFC. While our emphasis will be on right hemisphere functioning—emotional and somatic responses—left hemisphere engagement—talking about emotional regulation, calming and safety, about being mindful and considering the effect of oneself on other people—is also relevant. As long as the information to the two hemispheres is not discordant, left hemisphere reasoning can help strengthen right hemisphere experiencing.

For parents to become more positive in relation to their child, they need to have the experience of someone being more positive with them. Although we are inevitably going to have a negative response to the parents' anger and frustration with their child, we need to identify and focus on some positive characteristic. The parent has come to seek help for her child and her family. We can focus on and respect this seeking of help. As we do this, we are not only being mindful—internal awareness—of our own responses but also mentalizing. As we recognize our own state of mind and the effect it is having on our behavior, we want also to recognize the parents' state of mind and the effect it is having on their behavior and on our behavior (Fonagy et al., 1991). Being mindful and mentalizing activates our mPFC (Frith & Frith, 2006).[14] Then, with the action of mirror neurons, as we become more mindful and mentalize, the parent with whom we are interacting is likely to experience more moments of mindfulness and mentalization.

We can encourage parents to engage either together with us, together with their child, or on their own in thinking that fosters mindfulness and mentalization. As they do, there is the potential for new synaptic connections within their mPFC—that area of the brain that has the capability for dense neuronal connections to the amygdala (Cozolino, 2010) and therefore better control of anger/fear reactivity.

Mindfulness, defined as "paying attention in a particular way: on purpose, in the present moment and nonjudgmentally" (Kabat-Zinn, 1994, p. 4) has been recognized as an effective means of increasing self-awareness and emotional regulation. As such, it can be very helpful for us as professionals working with children and parents and for the parents with whom we are working. Mindfulness is utilized in a variety of different therapies including dialectical behavioral therapy, cognitive therapy, dynamic psychotherapy, and attachment-focused psychoanalysis (Grecucci et al., 2015). It is used within these therapies as a means to help individuals control their emotional reactivity and to focus their attention on what is going on in the present moment as opposed to the past, thereby helping individuals stay away from destructive thoughts related to the past. As past negative thoughts and events arise, the individual is invited to observe them from the outside and not become involved.

Relevant to our discussion here are the results of neuroimaging studies of mindfulness practice that show a negative correlation between increased activation of the mPFC and the cingulate cortex (particularly important for maintaining attention) and decreased activation in the amygdala (reviewed in Grecucci et al., 2015). Also evident is activation of the insula—an area related to somatic processing and emotions. Interestingly, the neuroimaging studies of experienced meditators—as opposed to those using a less structured mindfulness practice—showed decreased activation in both prefrontal and limbic areas. This is hypothesized (Grecucci et al., 2015) as indicating that emotional regulation—decreased activation of the amygdala—through practiced meditation is facilitated by detachment—taking both the mPFC and the amygdala offline—as opposed to cognitive regulation—increased medial prefrontal activity with concomitant decreased amygdala activity. Further discussion and case examples of the use of mindfulness are included in the next chapter (Chapter 4, pages 86–90). It always helps to take a stance of curiosity and exploration as we work with parents (Karterud & Bateman, 2012).

For those of us trained in therapeutic skills, we can encourage mental reflection or mentalization in parents—how is it that they came to have that feeling, that idea, or engage in that behavior; how is it that their child came to have that feeling, that idea, or engage in that behavior? To encourage this, we can explain our own mental processes as we try to understand the parent's experience:

> "I've been thinking about what it might have been like for you when I had to end our phone call so suddenly the other day; I knew why I had to stop talking, but

you did not have that information, so I have been trying to understand how it might have felt for you."

We want the parent to be able to focus both inward—how something affected them; what was going on for them when . . . ?—and outward—how did that affect Johnny; what was happening for Johnny that he responded in that way? Questions are more helpful than statements.

The way we phrase our questions to parents can help them become more reflective (see Karterud & Bateman, 2012).

- *Why do you think you reacted in that way at that point?*
- *That was a really big feeling you experienced; why do you think your reaction was so big?*
- *What do you think made Jane say/do that?*
- *Yes, it is possible she said/did that to hurt you, but I am wondering, could there be other reasons as well?*
- *I hear that you felt very hurt by what she did; it was really hard to have that happen. I am wondering what was happening for her that she would behave in that way.*

If the parent is having difficulty exploring something from the child's perspective,[15] we can, after first recognizing her or his experience of the situation, make some suggestions as to what the child's experience might have been. We need, however, to be careful not to make statements. We will want to be curious about the parent's or the child's motives or mental states and not get caught up in details about what happened in the particular situation.

As the neuronal connections from the OMPFC to the amygdala are strengthened and, as a result, the amygdala experiences less time within overly alert arousal, we can hypothesize that the sensitivity of the amygdala shifts. As triggers—both the parent's and the child's—are better understood (left hemisphere processing) and experienced within a safe setting (right hemisphere processing), the immediate danger reaction (thalamus → amygdala) can lessen, and the second route (thalamus → hippocampus & cortex → amygdala) strengthen (see Chart 3.2).

Engaging Dorsal Lateral Prefrontal Cortex—Focus; Working Memory; Problem-Solving

As we encourage parents to mentalize about their children, we are building their capacity to focus—maintain attention, a lateral prefrontal activity—on their children. We want their responses to their children not to be 'knee-jerk' reactions but rather reactions that take the child's past experiences and present situation into consideration. In other words, we want the parent to hold in his or her mind what his or her child needs—to activate working memory and consider the perspective of another person, a dorsal-lateral prefrontal activity (Tachibana et al., 2012). And we want parents to consciously consider different ways of reacting—how they were parented, how they wish they had been parented, what they read now in parenting books, how they want to parent. This recognition and comparison of alternatives involves problem-solving—an activity of the dorsal lateral prefrontal cortex (DLPFC) (Pochon et al., 2002).

Similar to our earlier discussion about the importance of us being mindful and mentalizing as a way to help build the parent's ability to be mindful or to mentalize, we need to focus on parents and their responses even when we are talking about the child. We need to hold the parents—their experiences and their needs—in our mind as we react to them. When we refer to the parents' past experiences and present situation as we work with them, we are modeling the process we want them to use when they are making decisions for their child.

Hughes and Baylin (2012), in their discussion of how to engage a parent's 'meaning-making system' (DLPFC) as opposed to reactivity system (limbic/amygdala), highlight the important role of curiosity. Curiosity enables us to wonder about alternatives without judgment of what the parent is already doing.

Some of the parents we work with will become overly emotional when talking about or relating to their child (increased OMPFC activity), while others will disconnect emotionally and relate to their children like an academic problem to be solved (increased DLPFC activity). Neither approach on its own facilitates a healthy interaction between parent and child or between the parent and us. When a parent appears stuck in OMPFC activity, we can ask him what he remembers about his childhood or about how he himself was raised and how thinking about that helps him decide what to do next, thereby activating more DLPFC activity (see Diagram 3.5, p. 59). When parents appear stuck in DLPFC activity, we can ask about the emotions they are feeling toward their child and the emotions they experienced in their relationship with their parents, and then ask them to take a breath as they notice these emotions, thereby activating more OMPFC activity. The detached parent—responding with primarily DLPFC activity—will have difficulty noticing any emotions. We can be curious, while acknowledging their DLPFC activity as to what they think their emotion might be 'if' they were to experience an emotion (see Chapter 6, pages 151–160, for example).

Regulating the Autonomic Nervous System—Window of Receptivity

When we talked earlier about the ANS (see pages 15, 48–49, 63–65), we referred to the window of tolerance, that range of arousal in which an individual is able to tolerate interactive situations (day-by-day incidents or therapeutic interactions) without becoming so hyper- or hypoaroused that the individual is not able to think (Ogden et al., 2006; Schore, 2012; Siegel, 2012). When considering our work with parents, we might be better to talk about this window as the 'the window of receptivity.' It is only when the parent is within this window and engaging with us from their ventral vagal system (social engagement; Porges, 2011) that they are able to receive what we are saying. One must be able to receive information before one can make use of it.

As we interact with parents, we need to be attentive to their muscular tension (facial muscles, body positioning, hand movement), breathing rate, eye gaze, facial expression, and voice tone and speed. An increase in any of these areas lets us know that the parent is experiencing some hyperarousal and is unlikely to be able to receive and process anything we say. It is at that point that we need to pause, take a breath, and find a way to provide some comfort or calming for the parent. We may want to recognize how the conversation is really difficult, how hard they are trying to create a better world for their child, and that we appreciate their willingness to work with us. If we know them well enough and are trained in therapeutic skills, we might ask them to notice what they are experiencing inside and then validate that experience. If these efforts are unable to calm the parent, we can shift the focus of the conversation away from emotional topics and toward information gathering. Based on present understanding of prefrontal lobe activity, this will increase DLPFC (cognitive) processing and decrease OMPFC (emotional) processing, thereby decreasing the experienced hyperarousal (Cozolino, 2010). Only when the parent is back in the window of receptivity will we be able to work productively with her or him (see Chapter 6, p. 147 for an example).

Other parents may find the conversation with us so difficult that they move into hypoarousal (cutting off all feeling or responding; Porges, 2011) or dissociation[16] (switching to another aspect of themselves; Dell, 2009; Silberg, 2013; Turkus & Kahler, 2006; van der Hart, 2006; Wieland, 2015a).

At this point, we need to find a way to reengage them (if in hypoarousal) or to engage with the presenting self-state (if they have dissociated). With the former (hypoarousal) we will not want to continue with the parenting discussion until the individual is feeling safer with us (see discussion on attunement and validation, Chapter 5) and able to be within his or her window of receptivity. With the latter (dissociation), we need to remember that, although many parents with dissociation will have a positive parental self-state, they are also likely to have negative self-states that take over when they are with their child. It is, therefore, important as someone who works with children to be aware of and (if trained in therapeutic skills) able to connect with all parts of a parent with dissociation. If we notice an abrupt dissociative switch in a parent, we can enquire as to what the parent has noticed—the trigger for the dissociative switch—and how this relates to his or her child. A particularly important piece of work with parents with dissociation is recognizing how the child may trigger the parent. Helping the parent become aware of these triggers enables the parent to have better control over switching. Helping these parents find effective personal therapy will also be important.

Equally important to noticing the state of the parent's ANS will be noticing the state of our own ANS. Are we becoming anxious or overly irritated; are we closing down? Just as the parent has a 'window of receptivity,' so do we. And if we are not within our own 'window of receptivity,' we will not be able to 'hear' the parent. And if we cannot 'hear' them as people, we will not be able to provide them with what they need to become more supportive for their child. If we have become anxious or overly irritated, we can take a breath and remember that what the parent needs more than anything else is to be heard and appreciated. This we can do. And then later, after the time with the parent, we can examine why we experienced that anxiety or irritation (see discussion of countertransference, Chapter 8).

How the Brain Holds Parenting Patterns

If we have become tired and experience hypoarousal, we can remind ourselves as to why we have chosen to work with children and their parents. We can also be patient with ourselves—we cannot be at our best all the time. And again, after the time with the parent, we can examine why we experienced hypoarousal at that particular time.

Summary

We started our discussion related to the brain/body and parenting by talking about how attachment patterns are held in the brain/body of the parent. We talked about how these attachment patterns are duplicated in the brain/body of the parent's child just as the parent had been 'taught' an attachment style by her or his parents.[17] Similarly, the patterns of parenting experienced by the children we work with—and held at a level below awareness—will determine the way these children will someday parent.

Our discussion of how parenting patterns are held in the brain was certainly a simplification of what goes on within the brain. This simplification helped us focus on areas particularly relevant to interpersonal interactions—the limbic system, prefrontal cortices, right hemisphere, and ANS. The most important part of the chapter was the last section, in which we posed the question: Given the importance of these brain/body areas, what activities can best activate positive change?

We discussed the importance of our interactions with the parent and the need for us to attend not only to our words but also to the nonverbal information relayed by our bodies, our voice tone, and our eye contact. The importance of the right hemisphere in the holding of parenting patterns led us to a discussion of nonverbal activities with the parent or with the parent and child. We discussed the importance of using imaging as a way to provide the parents with the practice needed for creating new ways to interact with their child. We talked about the role of the prefrontal cortices in helping parents to become more aware of their own emotions and more aware of their child's experience. The importance of emotional regulation, mindfulness, and strengthening the ability to mentalize was discussed. Helping the parent to balance emotional responding with more cognitive reacting was considered.

We suggested the term 'window of receptivity' be used in regard to the ANS. Only when both our system and the parent's system are within the social engagement parasympathetic range and able to receive words, actions, or ideas can we be of assistance to the parent.

Chapter 3—Points to Remember

- Patterns of attachment are stored in the deep right cortices of the brain without our choosing and without our knowledge until we look.
- Early experiences prime the body (ANS, HPA) for calm, agitated, or dissociated responses to later experiences.
- Wanting one's behavior to be different does not change the neuronal networks holding the behavior pattern.

- To encourage more secure attachment, stimulation is needed within those areas of the brain/body that are the primary holders of neuronal patterns related to attachment (deep right cortices, right associative cortical areas), the ability to self-regulate (OMPFC, mid-brain areas, ANS, amygdala) and to mentalize (OMPFC).
- Trigger reactions are a result of fast thalamus to amygdala responses (result of earlier experience), not thought-through (thalamus to hippocampus/cortex to amygdala) responses.
- Once the amygdala (and therefore the autonomic nervous system) is in high arousal, it is difficult to calm; activity in prefrontal cortex *decreases*.
- It is *increased* OMPFC activity that can calm the amygdala.
- We need an open, 'ready-to-hear-their-story' stance with parents *even* if we dislike the parent. Questions (stance of curiosity) are more helpful than statements.
- For a parent to be able to initiate a positive interaction with a child, the parent needs to have had an experience of the positive interaction.
- What the parent needs more than anything else is to be heard and appreciated.
- Imaging can stimulate neuronal connections supporting new positive patterns of parenting.

Notes

1. One parent described this as "conscious parenting"—where one decides what to do rather than just doing. Conscious parenting takes not only a great deal of thought but also a great deal of energy. It is also likely to run into difficulty when the parent is under high stress and, as a result, has difficulty accessing reasoned-out thinking.
2. 'Parent as infant' or 'parent as child' is used to refer to parents when they were babies and when they were young children.
3. Bowlby (1971, 1973), in his seminal work on child development and attachment, described the child as creating inside him or herself "working models" of the self, of mother, of mother in relation to self, of the world, and of self within the world. These internal concepts are generally referred to as "internal working models" (Schore, 2012).
4. Technically, the part of the brain that has historically been known as the limbic system is not a system but rather a grouping of structures between the cerebral hemispheres and the brain stem. While some of the structures such as the amygdala play a major role in emotions, others are more closely connected with autonomic functioning and memory consolidation.
5. When the amygdala is alerted, a 'message of danger' is sent to the hypothalamus, which in turn activates the pituitary gland and from there the adrenal gland within the body. In response to this activation, the adrenal gland produces cortisol (a glucocorticoid). There are glucocorticoid receptors throughout the body, including the brain. As cortisol arrives in any particular area, it energizes the body/brain to deal with (fight/flight) whatever was the emergency. If, however, the 'message of danger' extends over a prolonged period of time or comes when not needed, the level of cortisol production is unnecessarily high. High levels of cortisol disrupt protein synthesis, and thus, when prolonged, have a detrimental effect on those areas affected. Both the hippocampus (memory formation/retrieval) and the frontal lobes (executive functioning) are greatly affected by cortisol and, therefore, negatively affected when prolonged stress occurs.
6. This can also occur as the individual learns mindfulness (see pp. 71–72, 86–90).

7. Working memory refers to the ability to actively recall, update, and hold information while using it to guide behavior (Baddeley, 1992).
8. A primary exception to this occurs when the parent has done his or her own therapy and thus become aware of and able to shift trigger responses.
9. The prefrontal cortex in both hemispheres would be stimulated. This diagram shows the left hemisphere prefrontal since it works more in words, which are easier to indicate on a diagram, while the right works more in images and conceptualizations.
10. Mentalization, the ability to recognize another person's thinking separate from one's own, is a characteristic that differentiates mothers who provide secure attachment relationships with their children from mothers who provide insecure attachment relationships (see page 91–96).
11. Freud talked about the "law of association by simultaneity," hypothesizing that if neurons fire at the same time, they become linked. Hebb's (1949) most quoted phrase, "cells that fire together, wire together," similarly refers to the neuronal action that links new information with old information. Doidge (2007, 2015) has summarized recent work illustrating how the brain, based on this concept, is able to change and to heal.
12. Our reaction as an individual with our own experiences and our own values is part of a countertransference experience. This will be discussed in Chapter 8.
13. Chapman (2014), in her book *Neurobiologically Informed Trauma Therapy with Children and Adolescents: Understanding Mechanisms of Change*, discusses therapeutic approaches for children and adolescents that engage right hemisphere processing.
14. The mPFC is not the only area of the brain activated during mentalization—no mental process is so specific—but it is a primary area and therefore will be our focus in this discussion.
15. It will be helpful for us to recall Beebe et al.'s research (2010) that showed that parents who have experienced disorganized attachment do experience empathy but, because they are triggered by their child, are unable to respond appropriately (see discussion p. 51).
16. Although a dorsal vagal response and a dissociative switch may look similar, they are quite different. The dorsal vagal freeze is an ANS response, while a dissociative switch, as part of dissociation, is a defensive response which appears to be based in right hemisphere functioning (Schore, 2012). Some, but not all, individuals who experience dissociation will have a dissociative state which presents as being frozen.
17. This is referred to as the intergenerational transmission of attachment parenting patterns (Bretherton, 1990; Shah et al., 2010).

CHAPTER 4

Attending to Attachment Relationships

The subject of attachment has already come up multiple times in the last couple of chapters, and be assured it will come up many more times. Attachment is based on a biological instinct (Bowlby, 1973)—nature—and it is shaped by environmental influences—nurture. It describes how each of us learned from those who cared for us how to connect with others and, thus, formed the prototype for connections we make with others. It is central not only to parenting—the connection from the parent (our other client) to his or her child (our client)—but also to our work with the parent—the connection from us to the parent. This may be labeled as a 'professional relationship,' but it is also, and very importantly, an 'attachment relationship.'

In this chapter we will look just briefly at some of the research related to attachment that can assist us in our work with parents. Then we will focus on our primary means of affecting the parent's attachment pattern—that is, our interactive/attachment pattern with the parent. Most important within this relationship is our attunement to the parent. As we talk about attunement, we will consider how mindfulness (both ours and the parents') and mentalization (both ours and the parents') can have a positive effect on parents. The importance of the right hemisphere within attachment dynamics will lead our discussion to a more detailed description of the use of nonverbal interventions, with particular attention to imaging with parents and children and with parents alone. Also discussed, but briefly since there are numerous resources already available, will be dyadic attachment activities for the parent and child.

Intergenerational Transmission of Attachment

Research and clinical work over the last 50 years has highlighted the pivotal role attachment patterns play in the emotional, social, and physical health of both children and adults. In the 1990s, researchers began to look at the transmission of attachment patterns between generations. Peter Fonagy, together with Miriam and Howard Steele (1991), found that the attachment style of pregnant mothers (measured with the Adult Attachment Interview; George et al., 1985) correlated closely with the attachment pattern measured 15 months later (Strange Situation procedure; Ainsworth et al., 1978) in their children. Further longitudinal research has supported this finding but has emphasized that it is not necessarily the parents' early experience that determines the parents' attachment pattern at the time they are parents and, therefore, the pattern they engage in with their child. Rather, it is the parents' internal working model of attachment at the time of parenting that is passed to their child (van IJzendoorn & Bakermans-Kranenburg, 1997). While this model is initially formed from the parents' early experiences with their parents, it can be affected either negatively or positively by subsequent important relationships (Bowlby, 1988; Steele & Steele, 2008; van IJzendoorn & Bakermans-Kranenburg, 1997).

This is important for us to keep in mind, for we have the potential, in our work with the child's parent, to form a positive relationship with the parent (Cozolino, 2010; Siegel, 2007). This relationship will probably not have the intensity or importance of the relationship formed within individual therapy, but it does have the potential of being positive, of creating for the parent a new interpersonal experience, and, therefore, of stimulating new neuronal patterns within those areas of the brain and body relevant to attachment. And our relationship with the parent—whether we are social workers, family support workers, teachers, or therapists—may, indeed, be the only helping relationship available to the parent.

As we consider intergenerational transmission of attachment, we need to address the perennial question as to whether the transmission of attachment is a nature or nurture effect. Holmes (2014), in his review of research in this area, concludes that the intergenerational transmission of attachment is a result of gene X environment. Some infants/children have what is referred to as a robust genome and, thus, as a result of a more relaxed temperament and lower biological reactivity to stress, are able to achieve some degree of attachment security and psychological health even with adverse parenting and/or trauma. Other infants/children having a 'plasticity gene'—greater biological reactivity to environmental influences and a genetic tendency toward anxiety—are highly affected by interaction with their parent (Steele & Siever, 2010). For these children, the parental pattern—internal working model of attachment—is highly influential on the child's attachment pattern. It is going to be, for the most part, these children with the 'plasticity gene' whose parents hold an insecure attachment internal working model—negative gene X + negative environment—who end up in our offices. And it will be their parents with whom we are working.

Considerable research has looked at the differences between the experiences of mothers who show secure attachment patterns with their children and mothers who show insecure and, in particular, disorganized attachment patterns. Instances of high levels of early chaos/trauma and/or significant loss during the year before and after birth of the baby have been found to differentiate significantly between these two groups (Lyons-Ruth & Jacobvitz, 1999). Although therapeutic work related to a parent's childhood chaos/trauma or loss is not part of our work as professionals working with the child, knowing this information helps us be alert for the negative parenting patterns likely to intrude into the parent's behavior without the parent even being aware.

Attachment research of particular interest to those of us working with parents is the research looking at differences between mothers who had troubled childhoods and yet were able to raise children with secure attachment and mothers with troubled childhoods who were not able to do so (Fonagy et al., 1991). Ability to mentalize—to see one's child as separate from oneself, to recognize that each affects the other's behavior and beliefs, and to recognize that one's beliefs may be prone to error (Fonagy et al., 2002; Holmes, 2014)—has been found to differentiate between these two groups. Mothers from troubled childhoods who were able to raise their children within a secure attachment pattern scored significantly higher on mentalization.

Our Relationship with the Parent

As discussed in Chapter 3, to be most effective in our work with parents we need to focus on strategies that activate those areas of the brain most relevant for parenting. It is only when we activate neuronal networks relevant to interpersonal functioning—and parenting is the most basic of our interpersonal functions—that we have the potential of changing patterns held within those networks (Doidge, 2007; Siegel, 2012). As we interact with the parents from the first phone call to the last good-bye, we are activating—for better or for worse—these networks. There is a possibility for neuronal firing that stimulates positive, supportive synapses related to interpersonal functioning, and there is a possibility for neuronal firing that strengthens negative, dismissing synapses related to interpersonal functioning. We want to be sure we are stimulating positive, supportive synapses. And this is a challenge when the parent is someone who demeans and criticizes her or his child or someone who demeans and criticizes us—someone with whom we would not normally choose to have a relationship. But it is these parents who need our help the most.

The interaction within a helping relationship is a unique one. Whether one is the individual seeking help or the one who is bringing the child for help—as is a parent—one is exposing oneself. As discussed in Chapter 1, our initial reaction to the parent as a professional trained to work with children may be negative. But if we respond from that reaction—and there are many innate reasons to do so—we lose an important opportunity to help the child. If we are, on the other hand, able to provide the parent with a safe relationship in which he or she feels (1) attunement,[1] (2) experiences some emotional regulation (Chapter 5), and then (3) is engaged in some positive interpersonal interaction (Chapters 5 and 6), new firing occurs in neuronal networks related to interpersonal connectivity (Siegel, 2012). This new neuronal firing creates the possibility of new synaptic connections. These connections are then present—in very embryonic form but with the potential of becoming stronger—when the parent interacts with his or her child.

Siegel (2003) lists five elements that are essential for developing a secure attachment: a contingent communication, a reflective dialog, repair, emotional communication, and a coherent narrative. We want these five elements as part of our communication with parents.

By contingent communication, Siegel (2003) refers to perceiving signals from the other person, making sense of those signals, and responding to the signals. As we interact with parents, this means we need to be alert both to what the parent says and to what the parent's body expresses. Some parents will verbally agree with us, but their bodies pull back or stiffen. Siegel highlights the need to make sense of these signals. In this situation, they are mixed signals. The words of agreement are likely the polite, learned response, while the body reaction tells us that the parent does not feel comfortable with what we said. For our communication with the parent to be contingent, we need to respond to the discrepancy we notice. It would be so much easier to base our response on the parent's agreement but that will not build a positive relationship with the parent. If we respond by noticing both the agreement and the reluctance and then wondering about and encouraging discussion of both responses, we are starting to build a strong relationship.

TEACHER/SOCIAL WORKER/THERAPIST: *As you agreed with me just now that it would be good if Susan spent more time working on her project, I noticed that your body stiffened a bit. I'm wondering if, even though it sounds like a good idea, getting her to do that is not something you want to do. Or maybe you are agreeing with me because that's the easiest way* [smiles] *to get me 'off your back.'*

To build a positive relationship, we need to be sure that we, ourselves, do not send mixed messages. We have learned accepting phraseology—"*Yes, that makes sense*"; "*How difficult for you*"; "*I understand.*" For contingent communication, accepting phraseology—recognized by the parent's left hemisphere—is not enough. Our body posture, our voice tone, and our facial expression—recognized by the parent's right hemisphere—must also be accepting. And that can genuinely happen[2] only when we recognize and accept that the way the parent is feeling—however inconceivable to us—has a real and valid basis to it. We need to remember that the parents' reaction to their child comes from the way their parent reacted to them.[3] Knowing something about the parents' experiences growing up (see Chapter 2) can help us recognize and accept the limitations they may have in their ability to relate to their child. Not only knowing that information but being sensitive to how either the child or we, ourselves, may trigger the parent enables us to be mindful of a parent's limited ability to support her or his child. We also need to be mindful of our initial reaction to the parent, which may be a response to someone of whom the parent reminds us or may be a response to the parent's negative manner toward her or his child and not a response to the parent's needs. Only when we are mindful of our reaction are we able to step away from that reaction and back to the parent's needs. This step away (mindfulness) enables us to settle our system sufficiently to be truly contingent in our communication.

Siegel (2003, 2012) writes about the importance of a 'reflective dialog.' Our interaction with parents must always be two-way, a dialog—our hearing of their concerns as well as our expression of our concerns related to their child or family.

And it needs to be reflective—focusing on both thoughts and emotions; wondering where a particular reaction (either the child's or the parent's) came from:

> *"As we talk about your reaction with your son, I can see some tension in your body. I know it can be hard to talk about these things. What do you notice? Do you remember having felt like this before?"*

As we wonder, we encourage the parent also to wonder and thus become more reflective (see discussion later on mentalization). Hughes and Baylin (2012) have highlighted the importance of curiosity both for the teacher, social worker, or therapist with the parent and for the parent with the child. For many of us, making statements is a more familiar way of talking than asking questions. As we think about an upcoming appointment or a casual exchange with a parent, we can write down questions we might ask. We can take the idea we would like to convey to the parent and rephrase it as a question—this is the practice we, ourselves, need as we learn to interact in a more positive way with parents.

And then, because we, just like parents, make mistakes in our attunement and in our interactions with parents, there will always be the need for some repair of the relationship. The first step in the repair is some acknowledgement of the error—"My comment clearly did not recognize accurately what has been happening, I am sorry"; "Annie's therapy has not been as helpful as you or I had hoped."
We then make a renewed effort to connect and work more cooperatively. To be able to do this, we need first to calm ourselves. Whether we recognized the error because of the parent's anger response or our own discomfort with what we said or did, it is likely we will be agitated—our ANS will be activated. After all, we do not like making errors. Or maybe we do not think we have made an error—it is the parent who is in error, who is refusing to understand what needs to happen. What we must remember is that if a parent is 'refusing to understand,' we have not attuned accurately to the parent. However accurate an observation may be, not attuning is an error.

Jacob & Shawn, 12 Years Old

> **BACKGROUND INFORMATION:** *Shawn's teacher had invited Jacob to come in and talk about Shawn not turning in any assignments.*

JACOB: *Shawn just won't get off his butt. I told him the other day that he is just lazy and will amount to nothing unless he changes.*

TEACHER: *Calling Shawn 'lazy' is not helping him. It just gives him a label that he may use as an excuse.*

JACOB: *[angry tone of voice] Well, you certainly are not helping him.*

TEACHER: *[Body tightens, last thing he needed was a fight with Shawn's father. But he is right—labeling a child does not help, why doesn't the* father understand that? Takes a breath—what else could be going on? Maybe he is worried about Shawn and doesn't know how to help him. Takes another slow breath—] *I am noticing how much you want things to be different for Shawn; you want him to succeed at something.*

JACOB: *Yes, cuz he is a kid with potential—just too lazy. He spends all his time daydreaming and never gets anything done.*

TEACHER: *I wonder how we could use that daydreaming in a positive way—what does he daydream about?*

JACOB: *I don't know, never asked him. Guess I could ask him.*

TEACHER: *That could be a connection between the two of you. Then if you let me know—ask Shawn if it is okay for me to know—I could create an assignment around some topic that he dreams about.*

The teacher taking a breath helped him slow down his agitated ANS response. And, as he took a breath, Jacob may also have taken a breath—mirror neurons can be wonderful helpers. This creates a pause in what is happening. Our acknowledgement of our error—to the parent or maybe just to ourselves—and our recognition that we need to better understand the parent's perspective can help open the door to better connection with the parent.

TEACHER: *"Help me understand better what it is like for you when Billy explodes"; "What are your thoughts as to what Annie needs?"*

Within the repair, we need to be careful to respect parents and always recognize that their role as parent is far more important than is our role as teacher, support worker, therapist, or protection worker.

Siegel (2003) highlights that communication facilitating a secure attachment pattern between parent and child—or, in our situation, between ourselves and the parent—needs to have emotional content. Within our interaction with the parent, this emotional content needs to include not only a discussion of the child's emotions but also the parent's emotions and, when appropriate, our emotions. Both negative (right hemisphere held) and positive (left hemisphere held) emotions need to be acknowledged. The discussion needs to identify both the affect and the somatic experience of emotion (Ogden et al., 2006). Many of the parents with whom we work would have, as children, needed either to take care of their parents or to avoid their parents. In both cases, they would have needed, for self-protection, to move away from—deny—their own emotions. Thus, the parents we work with may have little sense of their own emotions or may become overwhelmed whenever emotions do arise. They have little understanding of where emotions come from and even what emotions are.

Helping parents recognize and appreciate both positive emotions—*"When you talk about your daughter, your face lights up. Being with her certainly brings you a feeling of joy"*—and negative emotions—*"How sad it is for you to remember those moments of not knowing what to do." "Anger does come up toward our children. You have made so much effort to help him and then he does this."* Learning about emotions is an important part of our work with them. Parents who block their own feelings will not be able to help their child with his or her feelings.

Siegel's last element needed for a secure attachment relationship is a coherent narrative (2003). A coherent narrative[4] refers to the story of a person's life that acknowledges both the positive and negative experiences and how these experiences played a role in who he or she is now as an adult. To help a parent who does not already experience a secure attachment pattern move toward a coherent narrative, we need to have some awareness of the parent's story growing up (see Chapter 2). Then, as we work with parents around their interactions with their child, we can help them recognize how those early negative experiences are affecting their present interaction with their child. We can be curious as to whether this is what they want for themselves or their child. As a reflective dialog develops, the possibility for a more coherent narrative and earned secure attachment (Siegel, 2012) increases. This increased reflection with regard to both themselves and their child provides a basis for a more secure attachment.

Attunement

Attunement has been defined as being in harmony with another being (Attunement, 2016). Schore (2012) talks about the attuned mother as "synchronizing the spatiotemporal patterning of her exogenous sensory stimulation with the infant's spontaneous expressions of her endogenous organismic rhythms" (p. 75).[5] So we—as the attuned therapist, social worker, or support worker—need to synchronize our body and voice reactivity with the parent's spontaneous expressions of her or his internal distress or internal delight. We need to feel, not just intellectually know, some of the distress the parent is feeling. As we do, the parent will sense validation, not judgment. Judgment from us increases a parent's fear and defensiveness. Validation from us decreases a parent's fear and defensiveness—the parent (similar to the infant in Schore's example) can have the experience of being 'seen.'

Daniel Hughes warns us that our attunement needs to match the other person's emotional state but without the "intensity of affect" (Hughes & Baylin, 2012, p. 149). Our words—the tone, intensity, rhythm—are to match the parent's experience but without the intensity of anger, fear, disappointment, or hopelessness that the parent is experiencing. This can provide, for the parent, a sense of being experienced and, at the same time, create a possibility for calming. Attunement is quite distinct from empathy in that empathy is an understanding of the other person's experience and emotions. Attunement includes not just an understanding—a cognitive response—but also a somatic responding that matches the physical experience of the other individual.

In the next chapter, we will expand on the concept of attunement and provide several examples. Before doing that, however, it will be helpful to understand the role mindfulness and mentalization can play in our ability to be attuned to the children and the parents with whom we are working.

86 *Attending to Attachment Relationships*

Mindfulness

As we encourage self-awareness in parents or in ourselves, we are talking about mindfulness (see page 72). As we pay attention in the present moment and without judgment, we become more aware of our body responses, our emotional reactions, and our cognitive appraisal. When we are able to hold this awareness nonjudgmentally, we experience increased emotional regulation (Brown & Ryan, 2003; Grecucci et al., 2015). Duncan et al. (2009), in their model of mindful parenting, proposed five dimensions to mindful parenting: (1) listening with full attention; (2) nonjudgmental acceptance of self and child; (3) emotional awareness of self and child; (4) self-regulation in the parenting relationship; and (5) compassion for self and child.

These ideas do not apply only to parents. Our listening with full attention, nonjudgmental acceptance, emotional awareness, self-regulation, and compassion enables us to 'hear' the parents with whom we work even while we may disagree with their way of parenting. By practicing mindfulness, we are better able to attune with both the cooperative parent and the uncooperative parent.

Holly & Jacob, 6 Years Old

> **REFERRAL:** Holly had referred herself and her son to the neighborhood family service agency for support related to their relationship. The family support worker has already met with Holly for the Developmental Interview and for two family sessions. Today Holly has come in on her own.

HOLLY: *Things are not any better. Jacob did not use any of the ideas like breathing or looking me in the eye like you taught him last week. Those ideas just don't work.*

FAMILY SUPPORT WORKER: [Heart starts to pound—what does she expect—she has to encourage him, she has to attune with him first—I'm so irritated. But my heart pounding—that's an old reaction—being told I'm not doing well—take a breath, another one—this is my experience, I can look at it later—breathe—what's her experience—she's really anxious—she's anxious; I'm anxious; Jacob's anxious—breathe, that's okay—that's why we are here—something's going on for her right now; something is going on for me right now—I can listen to her—I can listen to me later.] *Sounds like you are really disappointed. I realize how much you are wanting Jacob to do better.*

As we calm our systems, we will be better able to hear and appreciate the parent's experience. A mindfulness exercise with the parent should always be done in a session separate from a young child. It is possible to do mindfulness exercises together with a parent and youth.

FAMILY SUPPORT WORKER: *Let's try something. I invite you to stay just as you are; there is no need to do anything. This is going to be a moment of*

> silence and observation for yourself. Your only job will be to just notice, you don't even have to talk to me, just notice. . . . I want you to look in your mind's eye at Jacob, just look at him. What is he doing right now in that image in your mind's eye? And notice your body, from the top of your head to the tip of your toes; is there any tension? Is there any urge to do something, or say something? Notice if it is possible for you to not do anything or say anything. . . . Your mind may be distracting you with thoughts, with opinions, your mind may be telling you to do things. Just notice that this is what is happening right now. . . . Just notice whatever emotions or thoughts arise. You may not want to feel this way, but see if it is possible to stay with that feeling, even though you don't like it, for a while.
>
> [Pauses.] What was that like?
>
> **HOLLY:** *I really didn't want to do it. I kept saying inside my head, "I'm wasting my time," but somehow—I can't explain—I feel calmer now. It was hard for me to stay with the emotions; I wanted to get rid of them, not to let them be! But it is strange, I actually calmed down.*

Parents who have practiced mindfulness have experienced increased emotional regulation, decreased stress, improved anger management and decreased negative states (Coatsworth et al., 2015). Several small studies in which mothers of children with behavioral difficulties were taught mindfulness found that not only did the mothers experience improved interactions with their children and increased satisfaction with their parenting but that the children—for whom no direct intervention had occurred—showed a decrease in aggressive and noncompliant behavior (see Singh et al., 2010). Patterns of attachment were not studied, but we can hypothesize that with increased emotional regulation and increased satisfaction with parenting, there would be a strong possibility of more positive attachment experiences.

Coatsworth et al. (2015) reported on a study of 432 families with youth divided into three groups. One group was offered the Strengthening Families Program (SFP) for youth and parents, the second group was offered SFP with the inclusion of mindfulness training for parents, and a third group served as a control with assigned readings. Significant improvement on varied dimensions of parenting was reported by both mothers and youth for the two SFP groups (with mindfulness and without mindfulness), with little variance between the two SFP groups. Interestingly, fathers in the STP + mindfulness group reported greater emotional awareness and more compassion for their youth than the fathers in both the control group and the STP group without mindfulness. It may be that the mothers were already more mindful than the fathers and, therefore, did not profit in the same way as the fathers when mindfulness was directly taught. The fathers needed formal mindfulness training in order to learn how to listen attentively and be emotionally aware of their youth. Undoubtedly, more research will be done in this area over the next decade.

As professionals working with children, we can introduce mindfulness exercises to parents as we work jointly with the child and the parent. Often we only include the parent in these exercises if the child with whom we are using mindfulness is unable to separate from the parent. We are suggesting that the parent be included as often as possible, not just for the child's benefit but also for the parent's benefit. Children experiencing anxiety for which mindfulness can be of assistance often have parents who also experience anxiety. We might choose to do a breathing exercise or a body awareness exercise.

Cinder & Alicia, 11 Years Old

> **REFERRAL:** Alicia was referred for therapy by her pediatrician because of increasingly intrusive negative thoughts. Her mother, Cinder, was very skeptical but was willing to give it a try. They have been meeting for the last month. Cinder comes in with Alicia at the beginning of each session.

THERAPIST: *Alicia, we have been talking about some of the worries you have. What do you notice in your body as we have this conversation? . . .; Does anything change as we talk about it? Where did it change? . . .; And that feeling in the stomach, what is it like? . . . Is it getting tight, is it getting jagged, is it getting full of butterflies? . . .; And as you notice that feeling in the stomach, does it get stronger or weaker, does it speed up, or does it slow down? . . .; What do you notice now, Alicia? . . .*

And, Mom, as you have been here with Alicia, what have you noticed in your body? Did anything change? . . .

I noticed a slight shift in your face; I wonder if it was worry for Alicia and all the difficult sensations she is having inside, or maybe it was admiration that she was working really hard on noticing what is happening inside. What did you notice in your stomach, your chest, your arms, your head? . . .; Notice that sensation; what is happening with it right now? . . . Is it expanding or is it staying the same? . . .; Now take a breath into that feeling in your chest. . . . What did you notice when you did that? . . .

Both of you have done some really good noticing inside. Before we stop today, let's just do some breathing together. With your eyes open or with your eyes closed, take a breath in through your nose and out through your mouth. Take another breath in and up to the top of your head and out again.

Alicia, where do you want to breathe in to now? . . . Let's do it together. Feel it go all the way down to ___ and out.

Mom where do you want to breathe in to? . . . Let's do it together. Feel it go all the way down to ___ and out.

Once introduced together with the child, mindfulness can be reintroduced and encouraged when meeting with parents alone as something they can do with their child and on their own. At those times it will be important to ask parents how they experience the mindfulness exercise and to be attuned to possible discomfort while complimenting them on their willingness to try something new for their child.

Those of us trained in therapeutic skills can, when working with the parent alone, ask questions as to whether the sensation the parent is experiencing is a new sensation or an old sensation, when he or she felt it before, how old he or she feels when having that sensation. We can ask how he or she can help his or her younger self who first had that sensation.

Mindfulness with messages of loving-kindness and compassion (see example Chapter 7, p. 198) as well as openness to both positive and negative feelings can be emotional and can be soothing (Neff & Dahm, 2015).

Anna & Mila, 8 Years Old

> **REFERRAL AND PRESENT SITUATION:** Anna has referred herself and her daughter, who is constantly defiant and aggressive towards Anna. Anna struggles with wanting to stay away from her daughter.

ANNA: *Good mothers don't run away from their children. But Mila is so awful to me.*

THERAPIST: *I can see you are so tired and sad. Sometimes when we feel this way, it's hard to have our minds clear and try to do something different. I would like to try a brief exercise; it's about giving ourselves and others—you and Mila, for example—some peace, some loving-kindness; we all deserve that. What do you think?*

ANNA: *Well, I'm not sure if I can do this right now. I feel too upset. What if I can't get involved in your exercise?*

THERAPIST: *[Feels tension coming into his body and recognizes this as also the tension Anna is feeling—attunement. Takes a slow breath to moderate that tension.] Well, the good news is that there is no way to do this wrong. It's just about observing and allowing whatever happens to happen without trying to shape it or change it. You may feel something or nothing, you may engage or feel disconnected. We cannot know that in advance, we cannot predict how this experience is going to be for you or even for myself. It's all about letting ourselves stay with whatever might arise. Would you give it a try?*

ANNA: *OK. I trust you. Do I have to close my eyes? I don't like these things where you have to close your eyes.*

THERAPIST: *Of course you can keep your eyes open. But in order to avoid any distraction, why don't you focus your eye gaze in one spot, like the wall or the carpet?*

ANNA: *OK. Are you going to close your eyes?*

THERAPIST: *What do you prefer? I could stay with my eyes open or close them.*

ANNA: *No. I'm fine. That's okay, do whatever you want.*

THERAPIST: *Okay. I would like to invite you to take a couple of breaths, letting yourself feel the sensations of the air coming in and out, . . . the movement of your chest, . . . the temperature of the air. . . . What about the position of your body? . . . Is it comfortable? . . . Is it holding any unnecessary tension?. . . .* [Focuses on relaxing his own body—using his own settling from the initial attunement to Anna's tension to help Anna settle.] *Let's focus on the breath just one more time. . . . Now, I would like to invite you to remember a moment in which you felt good and positive about yourself. It doesn't need to be a current moment or a special moment, just the first one that comes to your mind, a moment in which you felt joy or tranquility or happiness. You may be alone or you may be with someone. . . . Try to stay with this memory and see if you can send to yourself kind words like "May I be joyful. May I be peaceful." See if it is possible to stay with this image of yourself and with these words for a little more time. . . . Now I would like you to bring a picture into your mind of Mila feeling happy or calm and notice whatever feelings and sensations arise when you have this picture in your mind. . . . Now try to see if it is possible for you to send to her a wish for more happiness, saying words like "May you be joyful. May you be peaceful."*

Are you OK? Can we go on?

ANNA: *Yes, it's so nice to feel this way. I've almost forgotten Mila's moments of being happy.*

THERAPIST: *Let yourself stay with this feeling a little longer, sending Mila your wish for her to be happy. . . . Now try to bring to your mind a moment in which you felt distressed or sad, it can be either a current moment or a past one.*

ANNA: [Starts to cry] *When I was a child I used to feel angry most of the time. But I guess deep inside I felt very sad.*

THERAPIST: [Also holds an image of a sad little Anna.] *Try to stay with that picture of yourself, the sad little you, and see if it is possible for you to send the little you a wish for happiness. You could say words like, "May this little me be free of this suffering." "May this little me be peaceful and joyful."*

ANNA: *It's so strange. Suddenly the image changed and I can only see Mila, she's sad.*

THERAPIST: *See if it is possible for you to stay for a moment with that picture of Mila feeling sad. Then send her your loving-kindness using words like "May you be free of this suffering." "May you be peaceful and joyful."*

ANNA: *I wish I could hug her.*

Attending to Attachment Relationships   91

THERAPIST: *You can try picturing yourself hugging Mila. What does the picture look like? ... How does it feel? ... Stay with whatever feeling or sensation arises.*

ANNA: *I don't think I'm such a bad mom.*

If parents are unable to bring up a happy or even calm image of themselves or their child, then the therapist would ask them *not* to artificially create such an image but just to let that sense of not being able to connect with a positive image be there and to know that it is all right because that is their experience at the moment. Then the therapist would invite them to offer compassion to themselves for being caught in this feeling (Neff & Dahm, 2015).

ANNA: *I can't bring in a picture of Mila. I'm so mad at her right now. I'm sorry.*

THERAPIST: *That makes sense, not being able to connect with Mila because you are feeling so angry. Try to stay with that feeling for a moment.* [Feels tension coming into his body and, knowing that he is feeling—attuning—to Anna's anger, allows it to be there.] *Where in your body do you feel this emotion—this 'madness'—right now?*

ANNA: *I'm just feeling my body so tense. I shouldn't feel this way. I'm her mom. I should be able to do this!*

THERAPIST: *None of us is perfect, Anna. Everyone feels inadequate sometimes, angry when we think we shouldn't be, overwhelmed when we think we should be handling things. This is a human experience, this is something we all share, it's okay.*

[Takes a breath to settle himself.] *Let's try giving to you, as Mila's mom, some loving-kindness words in the same way you would give those words to a friend or someone you care about. Try to say these words to yourself. "May I be peaceful." "May I be kind to myself." "May I accept myself as I am." Just try to stay with whatever feeling or sensation comes when you say these kind words to yourself once again, "May I be peaceful." "May I be kind to myself." "May I accept myself as I am."*[6]

ANNA: *I feel a little better. Thanks.*

For parents interested in and willing to participate in mindfulness activities, we can encourage them to use mindfulness to understand more clearly the negative interactions that occur between themselves and their children (Duncan et al., 2009; Kabat-Zinn & Kabat-Zinn, 1997). Mindfulness exercises written for children can be practiced by both parent and child in our offices and at home.

Mentalization

Fonagy et al. (2012) have introduced us to another important concept—'mentalization'—that can be of considerable help as we try to attune with parents. Mentalization is defined as the ability to understand (1) how a person's mental state affects that person's behavior, (2) how the mental state of another person affects our behavior, and (3) how our mental state affects the other person's behavior (see Chapter 3, p. 63 for discussion of brain functioning related to mentalization). A parent who mentalizes recognizes her infant/child as a separate individual with needs, feelings, and desires separate from the parent.

Parents may have gained the ability to mentalize their child because the parent's parent mentalized them. Possibly one parent or possibly both saw them as individuals with their own needs, feelings, and desires; as a result, they are able to see both themselves and others as individuals with their own needs, feelings, and desires, and they are able recognize that each person affects the other. Other parents may not have received this experience from their parents but had sufficient experience of being mentalized by other individuals—perhaps teachers, coaches, grandparents or other relatives, partners, friends—in their lives. For others, having been held in someone else's mind as a separate individual with needs and feelings of their own is an unknown experience. And without having had this experience themselves, it is difficult for parents to see their infant/child as a separate being and not just an extension of themselves. It is difficult for these parents to recognize how their mental state and their behavior affects their infant/child and to recognize that their child's mental state affects how they themselves are behaving.

If these parents are to gain the ability to mentalize their child, they need the experience of being mentalized and they need to be encouraged to see situations from their child's perspective. This is an experience we can give them.

Marie & Jimmy

> **REFERRAL:** Initial session with Marie & Jimmy is described in Chapter 5, pages 105–109 This session is with Mom alone.

MARIE: *Jimmy was at his grandpa's for the weekend. I really needed relief. It was much better when he came back. Then this morning when he woke up, he came in and lay down on my bed next to me. I felt suffocated.*

THERAPIST/SOCIAL WORKER/SUPPORT WORKER: [Struggles with a feeling of how much Jimmy needed closeness at that moment, but not saying anything about it for fear Marie would pick up on his disapproval—his mentalization. Rather focuses on attunement to Marie.] *Feeling better and then right back again to that suffocated feeling. How hard for you—you and Jimmy were in such totally different spaces. Let's look at what was going on for you and what was going on for him.*

MARIE: *Closeness feels scary for me. Then I pull away just like my grandpa used to do with me.*

Attending to Attachment Relationships 93

THERAPIST/SOCIAL WORKER/SUPPORT WORKER: *There's that early learning, isn't it? You are getting really good at recognizing it. What about Jimmy?* [Highlights that Jimmy is separate from Marie.] *What was happening for him?*

MARIE: *I guess he had missed me. He hadn't wanted to go away for the weekend. I think he gets scared. And then I told him to get up off the bed.*

THERAPIST/SOCIAL WORKER/SUPPORT WORKER: *Do you think that scared him? His experience was so different from yours.*

MARIE: *Yes, probably, and he should get over it.*

THERAPIST/SOCIAL WORKER/SUPPORT WORKER: [Learned very early in the work with Marie that if there was not first a response to Marie's reaction, Marie would reject any comment made about Jimmy—mentalizing of Marie.] *Wouldn't that be great if he could get over being scared?* [Wants to highlight that Marie's reaction affects Jimmy—again mentalizing.] *What might help him feel less scared?*

MARIE: *Well, I guess I could have told him I was going to get up and we would have breakfast together.*

THERAPIST/SOCIAL WORKER/SUPPORT WORKER: *Good idea. You are right—your letting him know when the two of you would be together would decrease his fear of not being wanted. It's tricky, isn't it—what we say and what we do affects how our kids feel.*

Our way of talking—whether with the parent alone or with the parent and child together—about the parent and child can highlight (1) parent-child separateness and (2) how the mental state and behavior of one affects the mental state and behavior of the other.

Marie & Jimmy together (Next Appointment)

THERAPIST/SOCIAL WORKER/SUPPORT WORKER: *Jimmy, your mom was telling me that you went to your grandpa's for the weekend so she could have some time on her own. How was that for you?*

JIMMY: *Okay.*

THERAPIST/SOCIAL WORKER/SUPPORT WORKER: *I was asking because it can feel really different for each person. You had wanted to have a friend over and to do something with your mom and your mom had wanted to have time on her own. For you, it might even have felt like you were being pushed out by your mom, while for her it felt like catch-up time. How was it for you?*

JIMMY: *Okay.*

THERAPIST/SOCIAL WORKER/SUPPORT WORKER: *What I am noticing now is that the more I push you to tell me how something feels for you, the more you don't tell me. What I do certainly affects what you do, don't you think so?*

JIMMY: *If you say so.*

THERAPIST/SOCIAL WORKER/SUPPORT WORKER: *There I did it again. Mom, you would think I would learn, wouldn't you? Does this happen at home—the more you push one way, the more Jimmy pushes the other way?* [Highlights how Mom's behavior affects Jimmy's behavior—mentalizing.]

MARIE: *All the time.*

THERAPIST/SOCIAL WORKER/SUPPORT WORKER: *So what you and I do affects what Jimmy does. And my guess is that whether we are feeling approving or critical of Jimmy also affects how he behaves.*

MARIE: *Well, when I am fed up with Jimmy, his behavior just gets worse—that's why I need a break.*

THERAPIST/SOCIAL WORKER/SUPPORT WORKER: *Jimmy, you probably feel Mom's irritation and fatigue, and that's upsetting and, as happens with all of us when we are upset, our behavior gets worse. Sounds like a vicious circle, doesn't it. How could we change it?*

While our conversation with the parent and child can encourage mentalization, the most important factor in parents learning to mentalize in relation to their child is their experience of being mentalized. "The [professional's] sensitivity to the presenting parent will be a mutative ingredient in helping the parent to be more sensitive to her child. Professionals need to tune into and identify parents' feelings, to contain and hold them, to acknowledge and soothe where appropriate" (Holmes, 2014, p. 60).

Alexandra (20 Years Old) & Mary (4 Years Old)

> **REFERRAL AND BACKGROUND INFORMATION:** Alexandra had contacted a family service agency wanting play therapy for Mary and wanting to learn better parenting skills. Alexandra had gone into a rehabilitation program related to drugs and alcohol shortly after Mary's birth. Mary lived with Alexandra's mother. When Mary was 1 year old, Alexandra started having visits. Each time Alexandra left after a visit, Mary became quite anxious and withdrawn. By the time Mary was 2 years old, Alexandra was living full time with Mary and grandmother.
>
> **PRESENT SITUATION:** Alexandra's new boyfriend has asked her to a weekend outing, and Alexandra is undecided as to whether she should go or not. She is meeting individually with the play therapist.

PLAY THERAPIST: *What a hard decision! How wise of you to want to look at how your decision will affect how you feel and how your decision will affect how Mary feels* [Defines mentalization]. *What if you decide to go: How will this affect you and how will it affect Mary?* [Alexandra talks about how she will feel guilty and how Mary may get scared.] *What if you decide not to go: How are you going to feel and how might that feeling in you affect Mary* [Encourages mentalization]?

ALEXANDRA: *I simply have no fun anymore. I spend all my time taking care of Mary or working. Jack is patient, but I want to spend more time with him.*

PLAY THERAPIST: *You have given up so much for Mary. Of course you want to have fun and you want to be with Jack. A normal reaction, if you stayed home, would be resentment* [Attunes]. *Let's say you decided to stay home so as not to scare Mary and not to feel guilty. That feeling of resentment, even if you tell yourself not to feel that way, is going to come in* [Mentalizes]. *How do you think the feeling of resentment could affect your behavior with Mary* [Encourages mother to mentalize]?

ALEXANDRA: [Voice raised a bit and talking faster.] *Well, I wouldn't let it affect my behavior!*

PLAY THERAPIST: *You're right, you wouldn't want it to affect your behavior, but the way we feel does alter the way we say something—our tone of voice—the way we hold ourselves, even how much time we spend with the other person* [Educating related to mentalizing]. *You did not like my comment about possibly feeling resentful. Even though you and I work well together, my comment irritated you* [Mentalizes]—*did you notice, your voice got a bit louder and you talked a bit faster? Your reaction—not liking what I said—changed the way you spoke. That's not a problem here, but if I were Mary, if I were 4 years old, I might have felt I had done something wrong* [Establishes Mary as a separate person].

The family support worker and Alexandra then talk about how Alexandra being away for a weekend could scare her child. As they work out a way Alexandra can tell Mary about the weekend away and can reassure Mary that Mom is coming back, the family support worker encourages Alexandra to mentalize. The family support worker uses questions to help Alexandra reflect on how Mary may react.

PLAY THERAPIST: *What do you think may happen inside Mary when you tell her you are going away?*

ALEXANDRA: *I feel so guilty with all the times I left her in the past.*

PLAY THERAPIST: *Yes, that is the feeling that comes up inside you, a guilty feeling. But inside Mary, I wonder what will come up inside her* [Effort to help Alexandra separate her daughter's experience from her experience]?

ALEXANDRA: *Oh, she will get scared.*

PLAY THERAPIST: *Scared of what?*

ALEXANDRA: *That I'm not coming back.*

PLAY THERAPIST: *How do you let Mary know you are coming back?*

ALEXANDRA: *Well, I tell her!*

PLAY THERAPIST: *How can we let Mary know that the 'now going away' is different from the going away when you were still caught in the use of drugs? My guess is you told Mary back then that you were coming back—which you did, but it was after a long time. Mary probably needs something to separate 'now going away' from the 'then going away.'*

ALEXANDRA: *I was sick then, and I'm okay now. I have a job now and I do things with Mary now!!!*

PLAY THERAPIST: *How might you include these ideas you have recognized in a statement about coming back?*

ALEXANDRA: *I will tell Mary I am well now, I play with you now, I take care of you now, I come back to be with you.*

The more we are able to mentalize in our work with parents, the more likely it is that the parents will be able to mentalize with their child. And as we mentalize—recognizing parents as individuals separate from us and having experiences different from our experiences, recognizing that there are reasons behind their negative reactions to their child, and that as we struggle (and often it is a struggle) to understand those reasons we are able to provide them with a positive experience—we are modeling that which we want them to be able to do with their child.

Nonverbal Interaction—Play

As we talk with a parent about how they want to do something, neuronal activity is occurring primarily in the parent's left hemisphere. Yet, most of our early learned parenting patterns are held in the right hemisphere (see discussion on p. 14), the hemisphere that is primarily dependent on nonverbal processing. Trained as child professionals, we are at an advantage. Working with children for whom talking is not the primary mode of learning and processing, we have learned to engage in nonverbal (primarily right hemisphere) functioning with emphasis on movement, play, and art. We can bring this learning to our work with parents, helping them shift from old and often unconscious negative patterns of responding held primarily within their right hemispheres.

We may encourage parents to do sand trays or paintings with their child not only as an attachment activity but also as an activity that helps parents understand the fears or other issues with which their child is struggling.[7] In that parents have come for help for their child, not themselves, suggesting that they draw or create a sand tray on their own is unlikely to be successful. Having them image how they would like to interact with their child is far more likely to be accepted, and this process of visualization does, indeed, activate right hemisphere functioning.

Nonverbal Interaction—Imaging

As discussed in Chapters 2 and 3, we can explain to parents how the negative parenting patterns they were taught, without ever wanting to learn them, are held at an unconscious level primarily within the deep right cortices of the brain (see Diagram 4.1.a). While the parent may have decided they wish to do parenting, or some part of parenting, differently from how his or her parents did, this is a thought-out (conscious) logical decision involving primarily the left hemisphere. When everything is going smoothly, this decision usually works quite well (see Diagram 4.1.b). Because there is no stress at that moment, the new thought-out words come easily and the old experience within the deep right cortices stays 'quiet.' But once tension occurs, as inevitably happens with parenting, parents are seldom able to stay with the logical pattern. The early negative patterns taught to them by their parent's behavior when they were young and held deep within the right cortices erupt (see Diagram 4.1.c). Nonverbal activity is needed to stimulate the growth of new neuronal patterns in the right cortices.

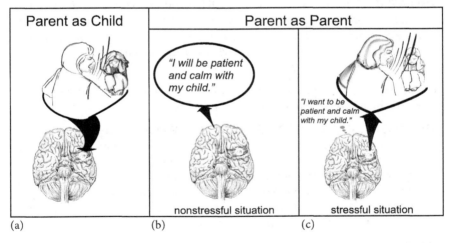

Diagram 4.1 Views into the brain from the bottom, with logical thought-out parenting developed primarily in the left prefrontal lobe, but early taught parenting patterns held in the deep right cortices: 4.1.a—parent as child, negative parenting is experienced and encoded in the deep right cortices; 4.1.b and 4.1.c—parent as parent. 4.1.b is a nonstressful situation, when thought-out parenting developed primarily in the left prefrontal area can occur, and 4.1.c is a stressful situation, when the early deep right hemisphere learning, the negative parenting patterns, is demonstrated instead.

As we talk with parents about how they would like to respond to their child, we can ask them to visualize the scene in their mind's eye. It is important that this not be an abstract picture but one that is very specific—seeing themselves and their child in a specific place and engaged in a specific activity. The child's refusal or emotional upset would be an important part of the imaged scenario.

Marie & Jimmy

> MARIE: *I have been trying to do things with Jimmy—even sitting together to watch a video—but he refuses to sit with me and then, well, I just don't care, so I go and watch the video in my room. And then he gets angry at me, so I stay away from him, and that's not what I want. I want us to do things together, really I do.*
>
> THERAPIST / SOCIAL WORKER / SUPPORT WORKER: *You are really trying hard to do things together with Jimmy. But it sounds like his saying "no"— and he is really good at saying "no"—discourages you. It makes sense to me that it discourages you* [Attunes]. *You keep trying and nothing seems to change* [Validates].
>
> MARIE: *So I just go away and do my thing, but then he becomes more and more uncooperative. I would rather not go away. I'd rather stay in the living room and watch the video with him.*
>
> THERAPIST / SOCIAL WORKER / SUPPORT WORKER: *Saying "no" is Jimmy's habit, and doing things separately is the habit Grandpa taught you. But you have told me that it is not the way you want to parent; you would rather the two of you do things together. What would you rather do when Jimmy says he won't watch the video with you?*
>
> MARIE: *I'd rather just stay in the living room and turn on the video there. Then he might come sit by me. But as soon as he says "no," I'm out of there.*
>
> THERAPIST / SOCIAL WORKER / SUPPORT WORKER: *So something is happening—probably way down inside you—when Jimmy says "no" that takes you away from what you want to do. Unfortunately, you don't have any experience of people staying with other people when things go bad. It takes practice to do something new and, as you already know, you can't get that practice with Jimmy in real life. Visualizing yourself staying with Jimmy when he says "no" could give you some practice.*
>
> MARIE: *What's the point of that—I know I want to stay. I just don't.*
>
> THERAPIST / SOCIAL WORKER / SUPPORT WORKER: *Knowing something, knowing you want to stay is a very conscious—and important—decision you have made. Things we decide—like wanting to stay with Jimmy even when he says "no"—happen primarily in the left side of our brain. But parenting patterns like 'don't stay with a child' that were taught by Grandpa when you*

Attending to Attachment Relationships 99

were really little are held primarily in the right side of our brain. They happen without our thinking, without our wanting them to. As soon as we are upset—and Jimmy saying "no" is upsetting—the old pattern of 'not staying' jumps out and takes over. We need to practice a new pattern if it is going to work when we are upset. Talking—that's the left side of the brain—about staying doesn't help us to stay. Visualizing—that's the right side of the brain where parenting patterns are—your staying with Jimmy can help. It can start a new pattern of being with Jimmy.

MARIE: *Doesn't make sense, but I'll give it a try.*

THERAPIST/SOCIAL WORKER/SUPPORT WORKER: *Thank you—I really appreciate your trying something new. Bring up, in your mind's eye, an image of you talking with Jimmy. Where are you? . . . Now, watch yourself suggesting to Jimmy that you and he watch a video together. Can you see that? . . . Then Jimmy says "no." . . . What happens inside you when he says "no?" . . . Can you feel that tightness now? . . . Just stay with that tightness and take a breath. What is happening now? . . . Watch yourself staying in the room, sitting down on the couch and turning on the video there in the living room. What do you see? . . . Now watch what happens next and let me know. . . .*

Imaging, as in the example with Marie, can be used to practice a new way of responding. It also can be used to help a parent calm themselves in order to respond in a more positive way to their children.

Ann & Sofia, 9 years old

> **BACKGROUND INFORMATION:** Sofia spends alternate weeks with each parent. Sofia responds to her mother's requests with yelling and often kicks or hits her. In the developmental assessment, Ann had reported that she has few memories of her childhood, and those she does have are negative.

ANN: *Last night I asked Sofia to clear the table—we have talked about this before. Just a simple thing like that. She refused and I insisted. Then she started yelling and stomping on the floor. I just shut down—I couldn't do anything. Eventually, she quieted down and I looked at her again. She made a face at me and went to her room. I had to clear the table. I was shaking. I know I should make her do it but I can't. Life is torture and it is getting worse.*

THERAPIST: [Feels tension and knows this tension needs to be shifted if she is to be able to hear Ann and Ann is to be able to hear her.] *Let's take a breath together. . . .* [Feels calmer and better able to think.] *Remember the image* you made in your head the last time we met—the image of the two of you drawing at the table. Bring that image back into your mind. What are you seeing? . . . What do you notice in your body?

ANN: *I'm calming down. My heart is settling.*

THERAPIST: *Let's try something. In your mind's eye see the situation from last night. You have asked Sofia to clear the table and she has refused. When you ask again she starts to yell. Do you have that picture in your mind? . . .*

ANN: [Tenses and dissociative stare starts to come in.] *It's there!!*

THERAPIST: *Describe it to me. . . . Where are you? . . . What is Sofia doing? . . . What do you notice in your body? . . . Now—shift over and look at the image of the two of you drawing at the table; you are still there in the room with Sofia and she is yelling but you are remembering the two of you drawing at the table. . . . What is happening in your body?*

(See Diagram 4.2.a—the memory of Sofia yelling is very clear and comes very easily, the calming image of Mom and Sofia drawing together is not nearly as clear, but as Ann and the therapist talk about it, it is able to take shape.)

ANN: *I'm taking a breath.*

THERAPIST: *Now, having taken that breath, what do you want to say to Sofia?*

ANN: *After you clear the table, we could draw together.*

THERAPIST: [Wants to be sure that the imaging is actually happening.] *Now take another breath and watch yourself telling Sofia that after she clears the table the two of you can draw together.*

ANN: *After you clear the table, we could do some drawing.* [Pauses.] *I said it!! I didn't close down!! She actually cleared the table. It's magic!*

THERAPIST: *Not magic—it's a new pattern you're teaching your brain—calming and remembering what you both like to do. Now keep going with the image—watch Sofia coming back to the table and watch the two of you drawing.*

Imaging can be very powerful, but it certainly is not magic. Parents need to be encouraged to practice the imaging if the neuronal patterns related to doing things in a new way are to strengthen. (See Diagram 4.2.b—although the tense moment is still strong, it is easier to bring in the calm moment.)

And they certainly need strengthening if the parent is to be able to access them in a tense moment. (See Diagram 4.2.c—the calm moment comes to mind more quickly and is able to be accessed during a tense moment.)

Parents can be encouraged to practice at home, but for many parents that is very difficult at the beginning. Practice together with us is important, then the practice at home. The chapters ahead will offer many ideas related to imaging.

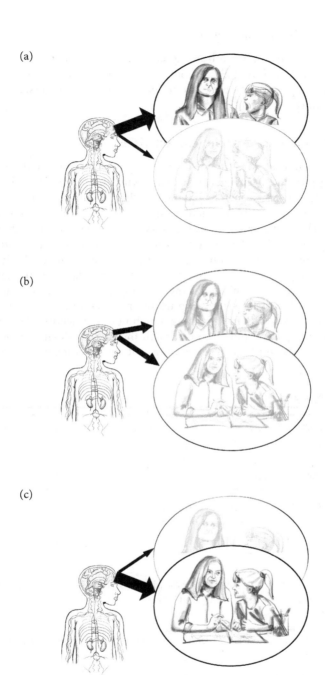

Diagram 4.2 Importance of practice—(a) Ann's brain from the example, (b) Ann's brain after several experiences of bringing in the shutdown image and then the drawing image, (c) Ann's brain after further practice with the negative and positive images.

Imaging for strengthening and learning new ways of interacting with a child can be used by child professionals without therapeutic training. Imaging that is going to probe the past or emotions should be used only by professionals with therapeutic training.

Nonverbal Interaction—Attachment Activities

Another part of building attachment is encouraging interactive activities. We can encourage parents to engage in eye gaze with their child. For the child who is resistant, eye games such as having the child name which eye the parent blinks or the parent naming which eye the child blinks can be used. Touch that does not feel too intimate such as thumb-wrestling, writing on each other's back, brushing each other's hair can be introduced. As both parent and child become more comfortable with physical touch, the parent can give body massages. Breathing together as well as other emotion-regulating activities (see Chapter 7, p. 192) can also help build more secure attachment. Movement or play that the child directs as well as singing and reading together in a noncorrective manner can strengthen a positive attachment connection. Within the therapy session the parent and child can, with the therapist's encouragement, create sand trays, drawings, or play act a difficult situation together (Booth & Jernberg, 2010[8]).

Alexandra & Mary

> **PRESENT SITUATION:** Alexandra has told Mary she will be leaving for a weekend away and that Mary will stay with her grandma. As Mary comes into the waiting room, she clings to her mom and hides her face. Mary doesn't want to go into the playroom.

PLAY THERAPIST: [Holds a puppet] *Oh! I can see a little girl here looking sad. Mom, why do you think this little girl is sad?*

ALEXANDRA: *I think she is sad because I will go on a weekend out and she is gonna miss me.*

MARY: [Enters the room but puts up her hand to stop her mother. She picks up a miniature dollhouse and a little doll.] *Don't come here! This is my home. Stay away!*

ALEXANDRA: [Stand by the door, picks up another doll.] *I want to stay with you! Let me in!*

MARY: *No! You go with your boyfriend!*

ALEXANDRA: *I will go out with him and then will return back home with you. I promise!*

MARY: *You lie! You left the baby with Granny! And you didn't come back!*

ALEXANDRA: *No honey, that happened a long time ago, when I was sick. I'm OK now; that's why I go to my work, and that's why I can bring you here, and that's why I have a boyfriend.*

MARY: [Leaves the doll and goes over to the support worker] *Sick moms don't have boyfriends?*

PLAY THERAPIST: *Sick moms need to take care of themselves so they can go back home and take care of their babies; they don't have the energy to have boyfriends.*

MARY: [Takes the doll and goes over to her mom.] *OK. Go with your boyfriend, but you must return on Sunday!*

ALEXANDRA: *I will. I promise. Now would you please let me in?*

MARY: *Ok. I forgive you. Come in.*

PLAY THERAPIST: *What if each of us makes a card? Mary can do one for Mom, so she can take it with her on the trip. Mom can make a card for Mary, so she can have it and remember Mom while she is out. And I . . .*

MARY: *Make a card for Mom reminding her she must come back!*

As we encourage these activities between the child and parent, the parent is not only having a new experience with his or her child but also learning activities and skills that can be used at home. As we notice not just the child's response but also the parent's effort and response, our own interpersonal relationship with the parent strengthens. Remember, many of these parents have not experienced strong secure attachments with their own parents. They need a positive attachment experience with us. This in itself will help them to be able to provide more secure attachment with their child.

Summary

As we have talked about attachment, we have focused again on our relationship with the parents and our attunement with the parents. We have looked at ways to bring mindfulness and mentalization into the work we do with parents and highlighted the importance of nonverbal work.

In particular, we emphasized imaging, which may be a new idea for some child professionals. But at the same time, we need to remember that we already, whether a teacher or a therapist, have many skills to help us as we interact with parents.

Chapter 4—Points to Remember

- Judgment from us increases a parent's fear and defensiveness.
- We need to synchronize our body and voice reactivity with the parent's spontaneous expressions of her or his internal experience—distress or delight.

- Left hemisphere stimulation does not change right hemisphere neuronal patterns.
- Only when we activate neuronal networks relevant to interpersonal functioning do we have the potential to change interpersonal patterns.
- New neuronal firing creates the possibility of new synaptic connections.
- Imaging for strengthening and learning new ways of interacting with a child can be used by child professionals without therapeutic training. Imaging that is going to probe the past or emotions should be used only by professionals with therapeutic training.

Notes

1 "Attunement" means to be 'in tune' both cognitively and somatically with another (see further definition, p. 85).
2 Words, in that they are directed by the left hemisphere, can more easily be directed by conscious thought, while facial expression, body posture, and voice tone have more connections to the right hemisphere and, thus, are under less conscious control.
3 The important exception to this occurs with "earned attachment" (Siegel, 2012) when an individual has sufficiently understood and processed early insecure attachment and/or has experienced subsequent secure attachment experiences such that the individual's internal working model of attachment has shifted.
4 "Coherent narrative" is a term that came into use with the development of the Adult Attachment Interview (George et al., 1985) to describe the manner in which adults who experience a secure attachment pattern talk about their life. Within a coherent narrative, individuals talk objectively about their past, both negative and positive influences, and reflect on how those influences have or have not affected them. The individual moves easily from memories to reflections and is able to give specific examples that support generalizations. There is a coherence between cognition and emotion, between explicit memory and what appears from implicit memory. It does not mean that the narrative is all positive but that enough sense has been made of the negative that it does not determine one's present interactive patterns. A coherent narrative of an early insecure attachment experience usually indicates that the individual has now an 'earned secure attachment pattern' (Siegel, 2012).
5 As the infant reacts in the moment to all of the changing sensations inside her body, the attuned parent changes his rhythms in space and time to match those of the infant. The infant expresses distress; the parent first matches that distress with facial expressions and tension, then slowly moderates his own expression ("exogenous sensory stimulation"). As he moderates, the infant moderates and the parent moderates further while at the same time seeking and, to a great extent at that point, sensing what it is the infant needs.
6 Adapted from Dr. Kristin Neff, "Self-Compassion/Loving-Kindness Meditation. Guided Meditations" http://self-compassion.org/category/exercises/. Retrieved on July 30th, 2015.
7 See Kestly (2014) for more ideas on encouraging parental play with children. She discusses "Serious Lego Play."
8 This reference is given as a good resource for ideas for parent-child activities; it is not given as an endorsement of theraplay in general for parents. There are many parents who, because of their hurt that has not been attended to, are not ready to participate in theraplay successfully.

CHAPTER 5

Using the Skills We Already Have

As child professionals, whether youth support workers, teachers, or therapists, we are aware of the importance of attuning with the child, helping the child regulate his arousal, validating his experiences and emotions, and providing new positive experiences for the child (present safety, internal resources, external supports, new learning). For those of us who work as counselors and therapists, we are trained in providing opportunities for processing the distress related to the past and helping children engage in new, healthier experiences. Each of these skills—skills we already have—can assist us as we interact with the child's parent.

Getting Starting

The parent, similar to the child, is feeling distress. This distress is related not only to what is happening now for his or her family which may be partially known, but also to what happened to the parent as a child, which is unlikely to be known. The parent needs to have the unknown early distress as well as the present known distress recognized in such a way that the parent feels accepted and supported. Naming the distress directly, as we understand it from the referral issue, may quite unintentionally push the parent into a defensive position. Much more may be happening—but how are we to know that at the beginning? Just as we do with children, we need at the start to respond to the tension in the room, to the tension in the parent, and to the tension in us.

Initially, let's look at a first session with one of the children and parents from Chapter 1 (Developmental Interview is already completed). This story with Marie and Jimmy could play out with a child therapist, a social worker who has specialized in working with children, or a child, youth, or family support worker.

> Marie (24 years old), mother of 9-year-old Jimmy, sits rigid on the couch as the 9-year-old stares at the therapist. [Therapist/support worker/social worker feels herself tightening inside—what's wrong, doesn't Marie see that Jimmy is frightened and unsure as to what he should do, doesn't she see that he needs reassurance, needs reassurance from her? No wonder he is creating stories about a fantasy world in which there are two parents and several siblings.]

106   Using the Skills We Already Have

We need information. How did the referral come about—was it the parents who wanted some help for their child, had the school suggested that they seek therapy, or was this a requirement set by the courts or child protection services? During the initial interview with the parents (see Chapter 2), we would have gathered information on the parents' concerns, the pregnancy and birth, the child's development and interactions with other people. We would have asked about family history related to mental health issues and the parents' early childhood experiences.

In a first session with the child, we observe the interaction between the parent and the child. We also pay attention to our reaction to the parent as well as our reaction to the child. Although this session is described as a time to get to know the child and for developing an initial hypothesis with regard to the child's experience, we are also developing initial hypotheses related to the parents and their experiences. With these hypotheses we can start to connect to the parents, to recognize what they need and what will be helpful for them. These initial hypotheses may or may not be revamped several times during our work with this child.

Marie & Jimmy, 9 Years Old

> **REFERRAL:** Mother called requesting an appointment following a suggestion from Jimmy's teacher. Jimmy had been talking in school about a fantasy family he lived with; he did not interact with peers; and he was resistant to instructions from the teacher.
>
> **BACKGROUND INFORMATION:** Marie had explained in the Developmental Interview that she had been raised by her grandfather, who was distant emotionally but had made sure she was fed, clothed, and went to school. She became pregnant when she was 15 and her boyfriend was 17. After Jimmy was born they tried living together, sometimes at grandfather's, sometimes at his parents', and sometimes on their own. There was considerable and very frightening domestic abuse, and Marie with Jimmy (1-year-old) moved back to grandfather's house. After inconsistent visits from Jimmy's father, Marie cut off that contact.
>
> **OBSERVED INTERACTIVE DYNAMICS:** Marie sits with a space between her and Jimmy. As Jimmy leans toward her, she very slightly leans away. Jimmy stares at the therapist and shows little response. He grabs at his mother when the therapist suggests that Mom go to the waiting area while he draws, has a chance to play, and answers some questions. Marie tightens. When it is agreed that Mom will stay in the room, Jimmy is able to move to the child's table. While he is able to complete the requested drawings (House, Tree, Person Projective Test[1]), he does not provide any stories for the pictures, does not engage in any play, and remains silent when questions are asked.

THERAPIST/SOCIAL WORKER/SUPPORT WORKER'S REACTION TO THE PARENT AND CHILD: Physical rigidity and also a sense of physically pulling back from both Marie and Jimmy occur. There is an impulse to tell Marie

Using the Skills We Already Have 107

to reach over and gently touch Jimmy, to reassure him that she will keep him safe. As the therapist focuses on Marie and Jimmy, she becomes aware of a sense of emptiness inside her.

> **INITIAL HYPOTHESIS:** Marie appears avoidant in her response to Jimmy, and Jimmy, at times, does not seem even to be in the room. Jimmy's presentation, which appears somewhat dissociative, leads the therapist to wonder whether the attachment pattern may not only be avoidant but also disorganized (Liotti, 2009; Wieland, 2015a). Marie had received limited emotional and physical comforting as she grew up and, thus, has little knowledge about emotional and physical comforting for children. Both Marie and Jimmy have experienced loss, chaos, and trauma. Jimmy's resistant behavior and telling of fantasies reflects his need to control his unsteady world—normal behavior for a child experiencing disorganized attachment.

THERAPIST/SOCIAL WORKER/SUPPORT WORKER'S WARNING TO SELF: Remember not to ask Mom to respond in ways that Mom does not know how to do. That would only set everyone—including herself—up for failure. If she asks Mom to reach over and reassure Jimmy, Mom may just stare at her, not understanding what she is asking, or Mom may reach over, but the tension in her body as she touches Jimmy would send him a message of avoidance, certainly not the moment of acceptance she visualized. And Marie, hearing her wish to have her be different, would also feel not accepted. Yes, asking too much is a set up for failure.

Attunement

While the background information and our hypotheses give us information on what is going on for Marie and Jimmy, it does not help us connect to either of them. The internal experience the social worker, therapist, or support worker is having of drawing back from Marie and Jimmy, of feeling empty inside, does, however, give considerable information about this boy and his mother. They have had little experience of closeness, they themselves are pulling back, they themselves are experiencing emptiness. While the reaction gives us information, we must not act on it—behavior based on that internal response (either a pulling back or an intrusive telling what to do) is exactly what they do *not* need! We need to take time with this negative experience. There needs to be some experiencing of their experience—that is the attunement—our experiencing their experience without acting it out. As discussed in Chapter 4, attunement is different from empathy in that attunement includes a physical resonance with the other person's somatic experience. Empathy is a cognitive understanding of the other person's experience.

As we pay attention to Marie and Jimmy and also to our own internal experience, we are using mindfulness (see Chapter 4). This mindfulness allows us to be aware of what is truly going on without reacting. If we move to judging the parent, to telling

108 Using the Skills We Already Have

the parent what to do—which is a natural reaction to Marie's behavior—we are unable to attune. But if we stay with the feeling in the session, even though it is a very heavy negative feeling, we are attuning.

While our automatic reaction is to want to make things right for the child—this, after all, is why we chose this profession—this is not helpful for the parent-child relationship. It is not the social worker, the therapist, or the support worker who can make things right—it is the parent whom the child needs. If we were to direct Marie to reach out and give Jimmy a hug, it might have provided a good moment between them. Jimmy might have become more present, but Marie would, very likely, have felt reprimanded, not good enough, and definitely not seen. For a parent with a strong, positive sense of self, this could have been a 'teachable moment,' but for Marie, who is already fearful of not being an adequate parent, attunement is far more important than teaching. Besides, without the attunement and the building of trust between the parent and ourselves, teaching is unlikely to be effective. Mindfulness directed not only to Marie and Jimmy but also to our own body response, thoughts, and sensations gives us some space with what is happening before reacting.

As highlighted in Chapter 3, mindfulness has been shown to activate the medial prefrontal cortex (mPFC) of the brain, and, as this area of the brain strengthens, the neuronal connections between the mPFC and the amygdala strengthen. As activity in the mPFC increases, activity in the amygdala decreases (Cozolino, 2010; see also Lazar et al., 2005), thus providing a calming for the individual. Thus, we gain a great deal from the practice of mindfulness. But what about Marie and Jimmy? Thanks to mirror neurons and to the reciprocal firing of body receptivity, Marie is going to benefit from our calming and, in time, Jimmy is going to benefit from Marie's calming.

Our reflecting on how our initial reaction to Marie's physical withdrawal from Jimmy was to tell her what to do gives us a moment. A very important moment! It allows us not to react immediately. Marie's mental state (avoidance of Jimmy) would likely have triggered our basic belief that parents should reach out to and reassure their children[2] and consequently would have led to the behavioral impulse to do something to make it right for Jimmy—tell Marie to reach out to Jimmy. This reflection gives us one more moment. Another important moment! Our mental state (disapproval of Marie and her behavior toward Jimmy) was going to affect Marie's behavior—this is our mentalizing, recognizing that our state of mind is going to affect Marie, her state of mind, and her behavior (see Chapter 4). Marie might or might not have been able to reach over and touch Jimmy, but she definitely would have felt our mental state—our reprimand—and would have pulled away from us and from the potential for help that she was seeking. She might or might not have come back for the next appointment. These moments of mentalization, moments of pause, help us to sit quietly.

THERAPIST, SOCIAL WORKER, SUPPORT WORKER: *It is hard to come to a new appointment.* [Relaxes rigidity but stays aware of the sensation of pulling away and quieting down her tone of voice.] *It is hard to come to a strange* *place with a strange person and not know what is going to happen. It may feel a lot safer just to pull away and observe. That makes sense. [Pauses. Picks up tone of voice a bit and sits up a bit straighter]. Let me tell you about this room, about myself, and about what we are going to do.*

That pause to notice our own reaction as well as Marie's reaction and then to shift away from the impulse to tell Marie what to do or to become overeager in our approach allows us time to attune. When we want Marie to reach out to Jimmy, we are wanting her to respond to his fright. We are wanting her to mentalize (engage in reflective thinking and responding). As discussed in Chapter 4, to be able to mentalize, one needs to have had the experience of being mentalized—not only being held in someone else's thoughts but having one's state of mind (not just one's behavior) understood by someone else (Fonagy et al., 2012). We want Marie to be able to do this with Jimmy. But she cannot do that until she, herself, has had the experience of being mentalized by someone else (something her grandfather did not know how to do). That someone else is going to need to be us, whether we are a therapist, a protection worker, a support worker, or a teacher. In any of these positions we can develop our own ability to mentalize, and we can provide the parents we work with the experience of having their state of mind—whether negative or positive—and their behavior—whether we approve of it or disapprove of it—understood. Parents are showing us behavior they were taught when very young, not behaviors that they chose. The early behaviors are impacted by family beliefs and values, which may be very different from our own beliefs and values.

The response noted above happened in session, but much of our mentalizing in relation to a parent—just as it would be for a child—likely happens outside the session. It may happen as we are writing notes—what was sitting in that session like for Marie? It may happen as we take a walk between sessions—Marie never had a chance growing up to learn about touching for reassurance, so she will not have that pattern of responding within her. Mentalizing may occur as we speak with a colleague for a brief consultation—how can I create an activity of interaction without asking Marie to do a physical interaction that is outside her present repertoire of responding? It may occur as we review our notes before the next session—how can I keep Marie's stated wish to interact with Jimmy more present in my mind than my observation of her physically pulling back from Jimmy?

Attunement, with both mindfulness and mentalization, helps us know when and how to intervene between the parent and child and when and how to help parents with guidelines.

Jessica, Paul & Julie, 7 Years Old

> **REFERRAL:** Jessica (Mom), Julie (daughter), and Paul (Dad) were referred by protective services for family support services because of the high level

> of verbal and emotional violence between the parents. Protective services were concerned about the effect this was having on Julie and also concerned that the violence could turn toward Julie.
>
> **BACKGROUND INFORMATION:** Jessica and Paul have a highly conflictual relationship, but neither of them wishes to leave the relationship. Jessica reported that her parents had fought vociferously and that her mother had been very critical and distant from her.
>
> **FAMILY SUPPORT WORKER WITH JESSICA AND JULIE:** The support worker had been meeting with mother and child at the beginning of each session and focusing on attachment activities. Both Jessica and Julie enjoyed this time, as did the support worker, and clearly the mother-daughter relationship was improving. At the beginning of this session, the support worker asks how the week has been.

JESSICA: *Really good week, everything was fine.*

JULIE: *No it wasn't! You two had a really big fight.*

JESSICA: [Voice raises and considerable tension is apparent in her body.] *Not so big, and it is not your concern—you shouldn't even be there!*

JULIE: [Voice also raises.] *I had to get between them and tell them to stop.*

FAMILY SUPPORT WORKER: [Feels a tightening inside—what is it like to be a mom who wants to downplay the violence so she won't lose her child, and then has her child highlight the violence—mindfulness and mentalization? Takes a breath.] *Mom, that's really hard.* [Tries hard to attune; deep breath to keep voice calm.] *You are right. Julie should not be there, and above all, she must not play the role of trying to stop the fights. That is not her job.*

JESSICA: [Voice even higher and eyes take on a hard stare.] *Then you tell her not to—I've already told her that.* [Clearly Mom did not feel any attunement—only criticism.]

FAMILY SUPPORT WORKER: *Yes, you have.* [Tries again to attune but misses the fact that her disapproval—lack of mentalization—has affected Jessica's attitude and behavior.] *The fighting just shouldn't happen when Julie is around. Parents are going to argue, but you need to wait for a time when Julie is not in the house.*

JESSICA: [Addresses Julie in angry, impatient tone.] *Now see the trouble you have gotten us into.*

FAMILY SUPPORT WORKER: [This is out of control, what happened? I joined with Mom, I recognized how hard the situation was. But I had to let her know that Julie being there was just not all right, that is something Mom needs to learn. And now it is even worse between Mom and Julie—why won't Mom listen?] *No one is in trouble.*

The support worker working with Jessica and Julie was careful to acknowledge how Mom would have felt *("That's really hard;" "Yes, you have")* but unfortunately missed Mom's raising voice, her body position, and her eye shift. Mom clearly had moved into overarousal—her defensive-aggressive sympathetic ANS (see Chapter 3) had taken over. While the therapist was absolutely right that Mom needed to be more aware of Julie and her needs as well as the effect of the parental arguments on Julie, Mom was not going to be able to hear any of that when she was in overarousal—just as she would not have been able to hear if she had been in underarousal—and outside her window of receptivity (see Chapter 3). Closer attunement would help keep Mom within her window of receptivity.

Mentalization by us would have alerted us to the danger of trying to teach the parent something when we are feeling disapproval and, therefore, Mom—because of normal nonverbal interconnectivity—is feeling our disapproval. Too often, we make the assumption that if we do not actively criticize, then the parent does not feel criticism. But the parent picks up our attitude toward her or him—this is why we have to work on our own attitude as much as we do the parent's attitude. Teaching should stay 'on hold,' not only until Mom calms but also until we calm our disapproval to the point that Mom can feel support rather than disapproval. Only then will Mom be able to hear us.

FAMILY SUPPORT WORKER: *That's really hard. Hard for you, hard for Julie.* [Takes a breath.] *What would you have liked to be able to do at that moment?* [Communicates belief in Mom.]

JESSICA: *Tell her dad to shut up. Take Julie and get out of there.*

FAMILY SUPPORT WORKER: *Yes, you would have done that, and how smart of you.*

If Jessica and Julie had been working with a counselor or therapist, he might have suggested that the two of them role-play the situation—the counselor/therapist could be the dad. If the meeting had been just with Jessica, imaging could be suggested.[3] Jessica would then have had some practice protecting Julie.

As we attune with the dynamics happening at the moment in the room, we need also to be aware of the other pressures a parent is experiencing. There may be economic stress—dealing with poverty and the ongoing anxiety related to poverty uses tremendous energy. There may be social stress—disapproval from family or friends, the challenges facing immigrants who come from different cultures. Investigation or the fear of investigation from child protection agencies creates insecurity, fear, and resistance. Isolation—lack of contact with extended family and friends—has been identified as increasing an individual's vulnerability (Perry & Szalavitz, 2006) and the likelihood of maltreatment within a family (Garbarino & Eckenrode, 1997). As discussed in Chapter 2, there may be marital stress (no support, active disapproval, domestic violence) or the stress of being on one's own. There undoubtedly is parenting stress (trying to settle an emotional, perhaps fearful child; trying to interact with an oppositional, perhaps physically aggressive child; trying to communicate with a withdrawn child). Parenting stress also comes from the parents' discomfort with their present manner of responding to their child—what Siegel and Hartzell (2003) refer to as the "low road" of parenting—as well as the disappointment that being with their child is not the positive experience they wanted. They may even not like their child. Parenting stress is compounded when the other parent, whether in the home or separated, takes a different approach to parenting. We may or may not be able to help parents with these stresses, but we do need to acknowledge and respect the struggle and, when possible, help the parent link to other resources.[4]

Recalling the effect of stress on both the brain (amygdala reaction, which triggers the HPA axis and a release of cortisol, which in turn has a negative effect on the responsivity of the hippocampus—memory processing and recall—and the frontal lobes—planning and reasoning) and the body (ANS sympathetic or dorsal vagal parasympathetic response) (see Diagram 3.2, p. 49), helps us remember to take time to provide the parent with some calming and reassurance before we ask them to shift their behavior. Parents need to experience calmness and reassurance before they are going to be able to calm and reassure their child.

Being aware of the many stresses parents experience and acknowledging them can help a parent feel less alone. Indeed, at those times, parents will need our support before they will be able to 'hear' any of our ideas. They need to experience our being aware of their struggles and how the struggles impact them. They need to experience our holding them with their very difficult reality in our minds.

Only while being mindful, mentalizing, and maintaining awareness of all the other stresses, are we able to attune with the parent. If we are working with the parent alone, we may want to name the emotional experience we are noticing. This needs to be done carefully (remember the parent did not come for therapy for themselves) and without judgment.

Marie & Jimmy (Continued from p. 105)

THERAPIST/SOCIAL WORKER/SUPPORT WORKER: When we met together with Jimmy, it seemed to me that maybe you were experiencing [slow, deliberate pacing of words] some closing down inside you or a slight pulling away from him. And yet I know [slight pickup in voice tone and speed] how important Jimmy is to you and how much you are wanting to connect with him. Did you notice any of that?

If we are aware of an emotional fragility, as certainly was the case with Marie, it is often better, when first working with someone, to link one's observation to something observed rather than to an internal experience.

THERAPIST / SOCIAL WORKER / SUPPORT WORKER: When we met together with Jimmy, Marie, I thought I noticed [slow, deliberate pacing of words] some tightening in your body. I don't know if you noticed that—sometimes it is really hard to notice what goes on in our bodies. I know how much [slight pickup in voice tone and speed] *you want to help[5] your son, so the tightening in your body, while it may have felt familiar, may have felt confusing.*

If we are working with the parent and child together, we need to be sure that what we say does not leave the parent feeling vulnerable with his or her child. Neither parent nor child must feel criticized but rather feel seen in some way and supported. Often naming first how the situation is difficult reassures the parent and child that having some difficult reaction would be expected and normal. If this happens early in therapy, as in the example with Marie and Jimmy, we can provide some information related to the situation.

THERAPIST / SOCIAL WORKER / SUPPORT WORKER: *It is hard to come to a new appointment* [slow, deliberate pacing of words] *with someone you do not know and also not knowing what is going to happen. It may feel safer to just pull away and observe. That makes sense.* [Pauses and slight pickup in voice tone and speed.] *Let me tell you about myself and about how we can spend the time. And then you can tell me what you are hoping can happen during our time.*

Attuning and taking time to slow down needs to occur before any difficult conversation begins.

Emotional Regulation

In our work with children, we help them learn to regulate their arousal, to move back from overarousal and to move up from underarousal—remember our discussion about the window of receptivity, p. 74. We provide ideas for slow breathing, offer opportunities to blow and catch soap bubbles, encourage them to blow pinwheels and to sing their favorite song for us. We may have them balance on yoga balls, stand on one foot, or show us how some animal walks. While parents are often reluctant to sing or stand on one foot, they certainly are willing to engage in slow breathing, blowing bubbles or pinwheels, and sitting on yoga balls. Their experience while doing it may be that they are helping their child, which indeed they are, but they also are having an experience of calming and engaging with their child. As we encourage them to feel the calming or alerting within their own bodies as a way to help their children moderate their arousal levels, we are helping them become more aware of and, therefore, have more control of their own arousal shifts.

Just as important as these calming or alerting activities for the child and the parent is our own process of emotional regulation—calming ourselves when we feel agitated (perhaps the child is having an emotional explosion or the parent is verbally attacking us) or alerting ourselves when we notice a closing down inside (perhaps the child is crawling under the table or the parent is nonresponsive). This process of calming or alerting is similar to what a responsive parent does with an infant or child—soothing the distressed infant/child and arousing the lethargic infant/child. Soothing and arousing must first occur in our own ANS, just as in the parent-child interaction it needs first to occur in the parent's ANS. Because of normal interpersonal reactivity (see Trevarthen, 2009), as our levels of arousal or reactivity are moderated, the arousal or reactivity level of the individual with whom we are working (parent or child or both) will moderate (see also Schore, 2012).

But moderating ourselves is not always easy. What happens when we are working with an angry parent, one who is in our office only because a protection worker has threatened to remove her or his child. The parent may verbally attack us and may reject all of the ideas we offer. The verbal attack will obviously activate our ANS and, depending on our own past experiences, we will feel like running away, or, alternatively, we will feel like giving an angry response. The rejection of ideas will discourage us, and we may find ourselves feeling numb and unable to think creatively. Or we may feel disrespect and find ourselves becoming more rigid in our thinking. Our system needs to be moderated before we can help the parent or child.

We need first to recognize that the parent's anger or rejection of ideas is *not personal* to us. The parent's way of reacting comes from her earlier negative experiences. The parent is frightened, and her anger at us is her effort to protect herself and her family, it is not about us. What reaction do we notice in ourselves (mindfulness)? Our immediate reaction likely comes from our own old experiences related to people being angry with us, people being dismissive of us and our ideas. This needs to be separated off—sometime outside of sessions we will need to do some processing of our own past experiences, but not now.

This situation, while directed toward us, is not about us. Our personal reaction—perhaps to challenge and respond with anger or to shut down and run away—does not need to be here. We do not want it to shape our response to this parent. The only way to be sure that it does not dictate our behavior is to be aware of it and set it aside. This personal reaction, referred to as countertransference, will be discussed in more detail in Chapter 8. At present, we need to take the deep breaths we have been teaching to the child and parent and move on.

Only after we separate the parent's reaction from us personally will we be able to start noticing the parent. The parent, just like ourselves, is reacting from old experiences with 'authority figures.' Just because we do not see ourself as an authority figure does not mean that the parent does not. Also, the parent is probably reacting from fear. What is this fear related to? Fear that the child is going to be taken away, fear that the family will be broken up, fear that he or she will not be the parent he or she was determined to be, fear that he or she will not be able to manage.

After taking another slow breath and separating ourselves from our old experiences, we can take a moment to wonder what the parent needs in order to recognize that this situation is not the same as her or his past experiences or even the present experiences with the many 'authority figures' in her or his life. Parents need to have a different experience with us—not one of disapproval and censure. We may not approve of the position they are taking with regard to the child, but that is not the same as disapproving of them. What are they needing? Can we name it? That would be attuning. What are they afraid of? Can we name it? That would be validating. What is a small step that can be taken, a step that includes the parent

Using the Skills We Already Have 115

in some manner? That step would be believing in the parent, the child, and also in ourselves. And now, we need to take another slow breath.

Kathy & Tommy, 7 Years Old

> **REFERRAL:** Mother placed a call to a therapy agency because of a requirement placed on the family by family protection services.
>
> **BACKGROUND INFORMATION:** Tommy was sexually abused by his older brother. The brother is out of the home but comes home for visits, and Tommy is increasingly afraid and extremely anxious. Kathy wants Tommy to 'settle down' so the family can be back together again.
>
> **OBSERVED INTERACTIVE DYNAMICS:** Initially Kathy had presented as very concerned about Tommy and had been very reassuring to him when they entered the room. When the therapist explained that, before reunification could be considered, it would be necessary to create a safer feeling for Tommy in the home and to understand how and why the abuse had occurred, Kathy became angry. She started yelling and demanding that the therapist produce a treatment plan that included the brother coming home. Kathy appeared oblivious of Tommy's presence and ignored him when he tugged on her jacket. Kathy had shifted from gentle caregiving to a neglectful and even abusive response to both Tommy and the therapist.

THERAPIST'S REACTION TO THE PARENT AND CHILD: [Experiences a strong desire to grab Tommy by the hand and get out of there. Feels furious but also intimidated, has no desire to engage with this woman. Takes a slow, deep breath.]

> **INITIAL HYPOTHESIS:** The disorganized dynamics and lack of safety in the home certainly played some part in the incidents of sexual abuse. Both would need to be addressed for Tommy to be safe. Kathy was clearly frightened (most anger comes from fright)—was this fright related to having the family broken up or to realizing she had not kept the home safe? Had something from her past been triggered?

The therapist was trying to grasp and hold in her mind what Kathy had experienced when the therapist had raised the issues of sexual abuse, lack of safety, and delay in family reunification and how all of that had led to Kathy's outburst. To do this the therapist had first to calm her own arousal—her reactive anger and her triggered intimidation. So much had to be done all at one time—mindfulness as to what was happening for herself, mentalization to help her understand what was happening both for herself and for Kathy. But none of this could be done until the therapist first calmed herself (see discussion on the importance of functioning from the ventral vagal ANS in order to engage in reflective thinking, pages 74–75). As our therapist calmed and then tried to attune with Kathy's experience, Kathy calmed. Her system had responded to the calming of the therapist's system (see Trevarthen, 2009). Her heightened emotions responded to being recognized even without anything being verbalized.

For attunement to happen, the therapist needs to recognize that Kathy's fears will not necessarily be the same as what the therapist assumes. One's greatest fears are linked with the values one has been taught and the situations one has experienced—Kathy's values and experiences are not the same as those of our therapist.

THERAPIST ATTUNEMENT AND EMOTIONAL REGULATION: [Attuning with Tommy is going to be easy—fright is the feeling coming in. Attuning with Kathy is going to be difficult. The therapist does not want to be with this woman. Takes a breath; she does not want to react from her state of anger and intimidation. Kathy's fright and anger has certainly affected the therapist's state of mind; she does not want this anger and intimidation to shape her behavior toward Kathy. Inside the therapist focuses on, *'Kathy's reaction is not related to me—Kathy is scared. What is she most scared about? I would be most scared about sexual abuse having happened in my family, but that is not what Kathy is talking about. She is talking about the family needing to be together—she is most scared about division in the family. I must focus on her fear, not what would be my fear.'*] How difficult to have the family split, to have Tommy's brother not with the family. How difficult to learn about the abuse having happened. [Uses an intense tone of voice matching Kathy's intensity but without anger. Takes a breath] You are hearing how much his brother wants to be back home and how he is promising that the abuse will not happen again. You are also realizing that Tommy is scared or else you would not be here with him. It makes sense that you really want Tommy not to be scared so his brother could come home. [Takes several breaths.] Having the family separated must be really hard for you, and now having me say that I cannot give you a plan for brother to be coming home would be even harder. What is your worst fear?

Regulating one's emotional response when with a parent who is in overarousal is certainly difficult. Equally difficult can be the regulation needed with a parent who is very discouraged, depressed, or dissociative. With this parent, we are likely to become equally discouraged and feel caught in an impossibly difficult situation. When with a discouraged or depressed parent, there is usually a heavy feeling in the room, and we often find we start to be distracted with other thoughts. When with a dissociated parent, we often find we become disorganized in our thoughts and our responses.

Ann & Sofia, 9 Years Old

> **REFERRAL:** Ann called the therapist for an appointment for her daughter because of her fear that she can no longer manage her daughter, Sofia.
>
> **BACKGROUND INFORMATION:** As a baby Sofia lived with mother but went to father's on visits ordered by the court. Mother would come to father's to nurse Sofia (it was very tense) and then leave. At present, Sofia spends alternate weeks with each parent. Sofia responds to mother's requests with yelling and often kicks or hits her. Mother has few memories of her own childhood, and those are negative. Sofia responds reluctantly but without the physical aggression at father's.
>
> **OBSERVED INTERACTIVE DYNAMICS:** Sofia is clearly angry with being at the appointment and glares at both mother and the therapist. Ann speaks in a monotone describing what had happened on the way to the appointment. The bus that came was not a double-decker, and Sofia refused to get on. She started hitting her Mother when her Mother took her by the arm. Ann closes her eyes for a moment, and then when she opens them she seems to be reorienting herself to where she is. The therapist notices this indication of possible dissociation and wonders inside her head if Ann had dissociated at the bus stop when Sofia started yelling and hitting. In response to the therapist's question as to what happened then, Ann replies that they waited for the next bus, which fortunately was double-decker. Sofia grins.

THERAPIST'S REACTION TO THE PARENT AND CHILD: [The therapist feels irritated by the child and even more by the mother. If Mother lets Sofia 'win' because of her behavior, of course she is going to behave that way. What does Mother expect? This feels hopeless.]

> **INITIAL HYPOTHESIS:** The attachment appears disorganized, with Sofia being the one in control. Mother is clearly triggered by her daughter's behavior and may be experiencing dissociation. Her closing down or dissociation would then trigger in Sofia a sense of being left.

Taking several breaths, the therapist becomes mindful of her own reaction—discouragement. Her body position (a bit of a slump) and voice tone (heavy and slower) are matching Ann. Then she realizes that her discouragement could increase Ann's discouragement. Yet if she becomes too positive or too energetic, she is not attuning with either Sofia or her mother. The therapist shifts to a slightly stronger position but without going so far (excitement) that she would lose Ann (lack of attunement). By regulating her ANS—avoiding both the underarousal of discouragement and the overarousal of excitement—the therapist maintains her ANS arousal within the window of receptivity. This is a modeling that encourages both Ann and Sofia

118   *Using the Skills We Already Have*

to experience the space of mid-arousal—a space that enables one to be open to other people and other ideas.

> **THERAPIST ATTUNEMENT AND EMOTIONAL REGULATION:** [Feels irritated with the mental health system; what can she do with the 10 sessions that were funded—this is way beyond what she can do. It feels totally impossible! Surely there must be some connection, some way forward, but where is it? *"I need to stay with this feeling, but it must not consume me."* Takes several breaths.] *You both had a really hard time this morning*—[The therapist's shoulders slump a bit, her voice tone is heavy, and she is speaking with some effort.] *Sofia with having to come here and then with the disappointment about the bus; Mom with Sofia yelling and hitting.* [Takes a breath.] *But I'm glad you are here*—[Sits up straighter, stronger voice but without excitement.] *both of you, because that's a start.*

Validation

Attuning with the parent and providing emotional regulation both for ourselves and for the parent is only the start. In a session separate from the child, it will be important to validate not only the parent's present experience but also the dream she had for herself and her family. This conversation can include the goals for therapy—what are the immediate goals (what needs to happen first) and longer-term goals?

Validation takes us a step further than attunement. With attunement, we are reflecting the parent's emotional state in that moment. With validation, we are recognizing what the parent is wanting/needing. This 'wanting' includes not only the parent's immediate goal—for Marie it is a child who is emotionally attached to her; for Kathy it is having her family back together; for Ann it is a child who does what she asks—but also the parent's dream of the family. For some parents this will include the dream the parent had before the child was even conceived, for others it will be a dream that started when the baby lay in their arms, for others there may have never been a dream.

Asking about early dreams for the family not only gives the child therapist information about the parent, it also highlights for the parent that he can still have dreams and that dreams can happen. For the parent who never dreamed about having a child, perhaps the parent who did not want to have a child, the answer to this question can help the therapist attune with the parent's present despair and confusion. For a parent who does very little thinking about his child, it introduces a new idea and perhaps one that might intrigue him. A dream infers that things can be different from now; it invites the parent to think beyond the difficult now.

Marie & Jimmy

> **THERAPIST/SOCIAL WORKER/SUPPORT WORKER:** *Did you ever dream, before having children, what being a parent, having a child would be like?*

MARIE: *I was 15—having a baby was not my plan! My friends stopped spending time with me. I was so alone.*

THERAPIST/SOCIAL WORKER/SUPPORT WORKER: *How difficult. How did you manage that time?*

MARIE: *I continued to live with Grandpa, did my courses through the internet, and spent time with the baby's father.*

THERAPIST/SOCIAL WORKER/SUPPORT WORKER: *What a determined person you are. What was it like when Jimmy was born?*

MARIE: *It's a haze. I remember very little—trying to take care of Jimmy, moving between lots of places, and lots of yelling and being hit.*

THERAPIST/SOCIAL WORKER/SUPPORT WORKER: *And you got yourself and Jimmy out of there. What is your dream for the two of you now?*

MARIE: *I want Jimmy to get help. I want him to listen to me and not be so negative to me.*

THERAPIST/SOCIAL WORKER/SUPPORT WORKER: *Sounds like you want more closeness between you and Jimmy—what an important goal.*

As we hear the parent's dream, we can validate the parent and what he or she wants. Of course some dreams will be unrealistic or outside the capacity of our work with the parent—have a child with no problems, be the perfect mother, have more money, find a supportive partner—and these can be talked about and reshaped into something that is feasible. Talking about the early or present dream can reconnect the parent to a part of her that has, at some point, been hopeful. This reconnection to hopefulness is important in that parents who come to therapy have, for the most part, experienced a great deal of discouragement and possibly a great deal of disapproval, not only from their own parents but also from professionals.

How are we going to be sure that this reconnection to the hopeful, positive parent part of them actually happens? We can 'talk' about this reconnection and the parent can talk about it also and even agree that this is what they want to have happen. However, talking and agreeing take place in the left hemisphere of the brain, not the right 'experiencing' hemisphere. Wanting to become a hopeful, positive parent is simply not enough to make it happen. The neuronal patterns in the parent's brain that holds the parent's own early experience of how parenting is done (i.e., her parent's way of parenting her) are far stronger than a neuronal pattern related to what she wants.

How can we help parents start to create or strengthen a neuronal pattern related to a more positive interaction with their child? As discussed in Chapter 3, this work needs to be a more active process than listening or even of listening and talking. It needs to engage the part of the brain related to attachment, the part that holds early interpersonal experiences—the deep cortical areas of the right hemisphere (Schore, 2012). Recalling that this is the part of the brain that works much more in images than in words, it is important for us, as support workers or therapists, to invite parents to work more in images—images that they, not we, create.

Marie & Jimmy

> **THERAPIST/SOCIAL WORKER/SUPPORT WORKER:** *Sounds like you want more closeness between you and Jimmy—what an important goal. If you were to picture the two of you doing something together, what might it be? Describe it to me.*

Ann & Sofia

> **THERAPIST:** *Did you ever dream, before having children, what being a parent, having a child would be like?*
>
> **ANN:** *I dreamt a lot—we would do things together, have fun together—but now she just yells and hits, and I get so angry that I have to move myself away from her. Nothing's fun.*
>
> **THERAPIST/SOCIAL WORKER/SUPPORT WORKER:** *If you were to create an image of the two of you having fun right now at the age she is now, what would it be?*
>
> **ANN:** *When she was little we used to draw together, sitting at the table. I wish we did that now.*
>
> **THERAPIST/SOCIAL WORKER/SUPPORT WORKER:** *Make a picture in your mind of what that looks like—you and Sofia—11-year-old Sofia—sitting at the table drawing. Describe it to me. . . . What do you notice about Sofia? . . . What do you notice about you? . . . Do you notice how present you are to her? . . . What is that like for you? . . . What is that like for her? . . . How is the image changing? . . . What do you notice now? . . . What a positive time for both of you!*

Clarifying the parent's dream helps to restore hopefulness. Interacting with parents and helping them expand and experience enjoyment with the image creates a new neuronal firing pattern within the parents' brain—a pattern that, albeit very slight, is more than they had before, is something they can bring into their minds outside of the session, and eventually something that can happen in their interaction with the child.

If the image goes to a negative interaction with the child, the therapist can help the parent stay with the image and work to resolve it in some way. While

Kathy & Tommy

THERAPIST: *Did you ever dream, before having children, what being a parent, having a child would be like?*

KATHY: *Family is really important. My kids wouldn't be like other kids, they would get along together, and we would go on family trips together.*

THERAPIST: *What an important dream. I see why you are so anxious to have the family back together.* [Validates.]

KATHY: [Tension coming back into voice.] *That's why I am here, and I need a plan NOW for Tommy's brother to move back home.*

THERAPIST: *And in that dream of Tommy and his brother together, what is the behavior each of them is showing to the other? Look at that image of Hunter and Tommy—what do you notice about Hunter, what do you notice about Tommy?*

KATHY: *They are squabbling—it is so awful. I hate it.*

THERAPIST: *So awful!* [Validates.] *But what brothers do. Is the squabbling all right, or is someone getting hurt? What do you see happening now?*

KATHY: *No one is getting hurt, but I hate the fighting—it's not right. I can see myself telling them to get out and go to their room—they share a room. Oh, no, do you think that is when the abuse happened?*

THERAPIST: *What do you think?*

KATHY: *I don't know. That would be awful. I would tell them they had to play together, and then they would fight, and I would get so mad, so I would send them away, and they were quiet.*

THERAPIST: *So in that image now, what could you do or say to them?*

KATHY: *I am so angry, I've got to stop the fighting or I will hit one of them. I could tell them to play separately. One could go to the room but the other stays where I am.*

THERAPIST: *So do that in your image, and what happens then? . . .*

The therapist would help the parent follow through with the image until the situation settles, until the parent's anxiety decreases, and the situation feels safe. And as the image develops, the therapist may be able to clarify that the dream has changed, as dreams do when situations change. And as the parent

122   *Using the Skills We Already Have*

images the change—with the therapist's support and assistance—the parent's brain has practice interacting with the child in a different way.

> If Kathy had not been able to recognize the possible danger in how her image developed, the therapist could wonder, *"Given what you know now about the sexual abuse, how would Tommy feel about going to the room with Hunter?"* Given that information, Kathy, with the therapist's assistance, could develop the image until Tommy was in a space that would feel safe for him and Kathy was experiencing less anxiety. Although the therapist is asking questions, it is Kathy who continues to struggle with the image—she, not the therapist, is creating a new pattern of responding with the boys. The imaging exercise does not mean that the problems are resolved, but it does mean that there has been neuronal firing within the parent's brain related to this new way of doing things.
>
> There is also a possibility the parent may have become overwhelmed with dream imaging—an old memory may have been triggered, or the realization that she had played some role in the abuse may have swamped her with guilt. The therapist would notice either a speeding up of speech and body agitation—activation of the parent's sympathetic ANS putting her above her emotional window of receptivity—or a shutting down and possibly some dissociation—activation of the parent's dorsal vagal parasympathetic ANS moving her below her window of receptivity (see Chapter 3).
>
> In these situations, we want to bring the parent back to the present moment, to her role of parenting, and to an internal steadiness—within the window of receptivity. More focus could then go, during that session, toward present problem-solving. The therapist would make a mental note to talk to the parent about some therapy for her or himself.
>
> There will also be some parents who refuse to dream.

Joan, Nathan, & Johnny, 10 Years Old

> **REFERRAL:** Joan (Mom) had called asking for appointments for her son, who was causing huge problems in the family because he would not listen. When he did not do what he was asked, Nathan (Dad) would yell, and then the whole household would become upset. Therapist invited Mom and Dad in for an appointment to gather developmental information. Mom said she would come but Dad was busy. Therapist suggested they wait until Dad could come as well since he was an important part of the family. Finally an appointment was set. Toward the end of the appointment, the therapist asks Dad what his dream of being with his son was like.

NATHAN: *That's a waste of time—dreaming.* [Voice takes on an impatient tone.] *We are here to get Johnny straightened out, to get him to listen to us!* [Voice takes on intimidating tone.]

THERAPIST: [Takes a breath.] *Yes.* [Uses similar voice tone to the parent but without the level of impatience or intimidation.] *You really want Johnny to listen, and moving a child from 'not listening' to 'listening' is not easy.* [Attunes.] *If it were, you wouldn't be here.* [Validates.] *Patterns get set in the brain—both in a child's brain and in a parent's brain. The patterns in a parent's brain—in your brain, in my brain as I parented—are from when we were children and our parents parented us. Some of those patterns from the way our parents parented we may want to keep, and some of those patterns—certainly for myself—we want to change. We may want our children to listen to us just like we listened to our parents, but we don't want them to do it out of fear like we did. And yet, we have within our brains, without our wanting it there, the pattern of forcing our children to listen. And Johnny doesn't respond well to being forced, does he?*

NATHAN: *But it doesn't work when I don't yell. I always ask first, but that doesn't work, so then I have to yell. If his mother would just not interfere, we would be all right.*

THERAPIST: *Sounds like you want it to be different, but with all the difficulty you have had, the pattern of asking by yelling has become even stronger. Our challenge is how to do it differently even when the asking by yelling patterns are already in your brain. Just wanting to change doesn't make it happen. We have to start new brain patterns. One of the ways to do that is to visualize ourselves doing it differently—watching ourselves, inside our heads, doing it differently. When you make an image you have started a different pattern of neuronal firing in your brain. Obviously, visualizing this once isn't going to change everything, but it is a start.*

NATHAN: *Well, I'm better thinking in words, not images, and, anyway, this seems to me just a waste of time.*

THERAPIST: *Then tell me in your words how you would like it to be. I appreciate your wanting a different pattern with Johnny.*

As the therapist backs away from his or her request but without getting sidetracked by Dad's challenging comment, Dad is more likely to move back from his position. And no, we do not achieve the ideal—parents watching themselves (neuronal patterns firing in the right cortices) do something different—but we do achieve a step forward—parent talking about doing something different (neuronal patterns firing in left cortices). Appreciation of parents is a major form of validation.

Asking about a parent's dream both from the past and from the present helps to reorient the parent from a place of discouragement and distress to one of hope and positive belief. So many of the people surrounding the parent—protection service workers, teachers, neighbors, even relatives—focus on the problems and thus reinforce negative neuronal patterns. Parents need someone who not only attunes with their distress but also believes that the parent and child can move toward a better experience, someone who believes in the parent's dream. This is a 'joining' that provides support for the parent and an 'engaging' that will provide support for the therapist.

After talking about dreams, the therapist and parent can talk about the goal of therapy and what needs to change for this goal to be reached. In many cases the parent may not know, or the parent may say, "For the child to get over it."

Kathy & Tommy

THERAPIST: *It makes sense that you want him to get over it. I wonder what Tommy needs to get over it.*

KATHY: *That's your job.*

THERAPIST: *[Takes a breath.] Absolutely, and Tommy and I will be working on this. What does he need at home? As we worked on that image, what did you notice helped Tommy? . . . Would that work at home?*

Again, we are having to regulate ourselves in order not to be irritated by the parent's irritation. Only then are we able to attune with the parent and join the parent in his or her dream/goal for the child.

But what about the situations in which what the parent is asking for is not in the best interest of the child?

Adele & Lorraine, 16 Years Old

> **REFERRAL:** Lorraine was referred for therapy following a disclosure of sexual abuse from her father.
>
> **BACKGROUND:** Lorraine and her brother had been moved to foster care because their mother, Adele, did not believe her husband would 'do such a thing.' In time, Adele did tell the children's father to leave, and the children were returned home. While Adele stated to the authorities that she believed Lorraine, Lorraine reported that at home Adele continued to call Lorraine a liar and to state that she herself met all her husband's sexual needs.
>
> **INITIAL HYPOTHESIS:** Lorraine's disclosure had destabilized her mother's fragile world and was triggering considerable fright, which activated both movement toward Adele's father (source of mother's security) and away from Adele's father (source of family danger). This disorganized attachment pattern predictably also existed between Adele and Lorraine, and undoubtedly existed between Adele and her parents—Lorraine's grandparents.
>
> **THERAPY DILEMMA:** In a case conference with the protective service worker, Mom asked for family therapy sessions in which the sexual abuse would

> not be discussed but she and Lorraine could learn better ways to communicate. Not only was Lorraine's therapist concerned that doing this would justify Mom's position that the abuse was irrelevant but also Lorraine would experience a clear dismissal of the anger and hurt she felt from her mother's denial of the abuse from Dad.

THERAPIST: [Experiences a strong anger reaction—how can a mother be so blind to what her child needs?—takes several deep breaths to emotionally regulate herself and steadies her voice] *I hear how much you want positive communication in your family.* [Attunes.] *That is something that is really important to you.* [Validates.] *How hurtful for Lorraine and how hurtful for you that the abuse happened. Lorraine's hurt leads to her yelling and running out of the house. Your hurt leads to your yelling and your disbelief of the abuse.* [Mentalizes.] *Your two hurts are very different, but both are very real. We cannot do work on positive communication—family therapy—until there is recognition of the hurts.*

Here the therapist is working to hear the parent and what the parent wants but does not move beyond what is therapeutically acceptable. To do this, the therapist first recognizes what the parent is asking for/what the parent's hurt is and what the child is asking for/what the child's hurt is; then moves backwards to a commonality between them—the hurt. This is, at times, like walking a tightrope. Let's go back to Marie and Jimmy for a moment.

Marie & Jimmy

MARIE: *I need a break. It is all just too overwhelming.*

THERAPIST/SOCIAL WORKER/SUPPORT WORKER: [Feeling a tightening and some fear inside—Jimmy needs closeness, not being sent away—but wants to be able to hear Marie's despair.] *Yes, you need a break. How can it happen in a way that Jimmy can still feel safe?*

We need to attune and validate what the parent needs/wants while still clearly stating the child's best interest. With both Adele and Marie, our therapist is acknowledging where she is and at the same time bringing in consideration of the child's needs. There is a better chance that the parent will be able to consider what the child needs if he or she first has the experience of having his or her needs heard.

Providing and Strengthening New Experiences for the Parent

Present Safety

Helping a parent experience a sense of safety is fairly straightforward with parents who want help for themselves, but what about the many parents who bring their child to therapy to have the child fixed and have no wish for help for themselves? This can be translated as, knowingly or unknowingly, being frightened to change. These parents may come for individual sessions as a part of the child's therapy but clearly state that they are here only to help their child, only to talk about their interaction with their child, and do not want any individual therapy for themselves. Engaging this parent in internal safety and strengthening work may be easier if parents experience this work as something they are doing to help their child, not for themselves.

Instilling the sense of a safe place is important for both child and parent. Coming to therapy is connected with something being wrong with the child. As a result, the child—at least in the beginning stage of therapy—is going to experience some distress arousal—activation of the sympathetic nervous system. The parent, experiencing distress related to having 'a child with a problem' and perhaps distress related to having someone in a position of authority[6] 'judging' them, will also experience an activation of the sympathetic nervous system.

We can explain to parents that, although the parent is already providing his or her child with real world safety, it is often difficult for children—particularly children who have been frightened in some way as well as children who are anxious, children who have an impulsive nature, and children who feel disconnected—to hold inside themselves a sense of safety. We can invite the parent to work along with us to help build his or her child's internal sense of safety.

THERAPIST/SOCIAL WORKER/SUPPORT WORKER: *I am wondering, Jimmy, Mom, what might be your 'safe' place today—a place that feels 'safe' for each of you—maybe a place you visit all the time, maybe a place in nature, maybe a place you have never been, but a place that gives you a safe feeling inside you. Mom, what would be your 'safe' place today?*

As we ask the parents for a place where they feel safe, we have to be careful we do not ask for something they do not have. We can suggest places they often go, places in nature—mentioning some that fit the parents' locale and culture as well as places far away, thus enabling the parents to distance themselves from their real world if need be—or even places they have created in their minds. If the parent appears very fragile—that she or he may not be able to come up with even an imaginary safe place—we can ask for a place that is 'calm and peaceful' (Wieland, 1998). We would then ask the child for his or her safe (or calm and peaceful) place.

Having children and parents draw the safe or calm and peaceful place helps both the child and the parent increase their level of attending—remember, attention is crucial for rewiring and for strengthening neuronal connections (Doidge, 2007; see also Chapter 3)—and helps both the child and the parent engage their right hemisphere—remember, early attachment patterns are held deep in the right hemisphere (Schore, 2012; see also Chapter 3). Some parents may object to drawing. At those times we can simply ask them to picture the place in their mind's eye and to describe the colors and variations of light—not the objects—they see. We can be persistent in our determination to engage the right hemisphere, although flexible in how it is done.

If the parent suggests an idea or a change for the child's drawing, we will want to thank him or her for offering to help the child but explain that for a 'safe drawing' to be successful, it needs to come from the child's own thoughts. We can explain that we are working to create new neuronal networks in the child's brain just as we are in the parent's brain. As the child creates a drawing, he is showing us the neuronal networks already in his brain (his internal world) and only as—perhaps with our or his parent's supportive curiosity, not correction or criticism—new networks are stimulated will the child's internal world change. If a child follows our or the parent's suggestion, new neuronal networks may be created in our brains *but not* in the child's brain. We can also explain that the parent just sitting quietly with the child while the child is drawing and observing carefully what the child does provides a feeling of safety for the child. And for the scared or anxious child, those are new neuronal networks. The parent's observation without correction gives the child a positive sense of self. And for the discouraged or depressed child, those are new neuronal networks. The parent's ideas and corrections can be really helpful in some situations but are not a part of the work being done now.[7]

Then we can ask both the child and her or his parent to breathe slowly as they look at their drawing or internal image. We would ask them what they notice. They may notice details in the image, or they may notice the image changing in some way. Therapists who are trained in EMDR could add some bilateral stimulation at this time (Wieland, 2015b). Even if the images do not feel safe to us (a room with white walls; riding in the car), it is best to trust the individuals and just ask for more detail. Staying with their image reinforces that they are in charge and that they are capable. When the child's or the parent's images appear frail or frightening, we can ask what might make the images safer or calmer. This needs always to be followed by the direction that the child or parent bring whatever he or she has suggested into the image—naming something (left hemisphere function) does not mean that the individual is automatically visualizing (right hemisphere function) the object. Then check as to whether it actually happened. As either the child or the parent changes his or her image, is there any change to the feeling of the image, to the lightness or heaviness of the image? It is important to work with the parent or child until there is some positive shift in the image. If it is the child who is having difficulty with the image, we could ask the parent what she would suggest to help. We would not ask a child for an idea for the parent.[8] The parent could be asked what she thinks some adult who is a positive figure for her might suggest. The teaching of the child, with the parent's help, to create a positive image as a way to calm and strengthen the self is invaluable for the parent.

Engaging the parent's help can be particularly valuable with parents and children with separation anxiety.

Donna & Mila, 6 Years Old

REFERRAL: Mila has been brought by her mother, Donna, for therapy because Mila is not able to separate from Donna without extreme fear and resistance.

THERAPIST OBSERVATION: The therapist notices that when she suggests a new activity for Mila such as sitting on the large yoga ball, Donna reaches out to offer Mila support even though Mila has not reached for help. At the end of the session, Donna explains to the therapist that Mila had been very anxious and apologizes for Mila being so withdrawn during the session. This was not the therapist's experience of Mila; she had experienced a child who was quite engaged and engaging. Donna may have been describing herself—perhaps it was she who was having difficulty separating from Mila.

HYPOTHESIS: While Mila did become anxious each time there was a reference to Mom not being with her, more striking was Mom's need to comfort and help Mila. Perhaps Mom needed Mila to need her.

ESTABLISHING AND STRENGTHENING AN INTERNAL SAFE PLACE: In Donna's first image of safety, she has herself, her husband, and her three children snuggling in bed; in Mila's first image she has herself snuggling together with her mother and father in their bed. The therapist contacts Donna outside the session and lets her know that the therapist is going to ask her, during the next visualization of the safe place, to have each member of the family leave her image one by one, checking each time as to whether the individual who has left is safe and whether Mom, without that person, is safe, until Mom is alone in the image and still safe, and then one by one bring each individual back in.

During the next session, when Donna has completed that, the therapist asks Mila what she noticed about her mom when her mom was all alone. *Was she safe? What kept her safe?*

The therapist then asks Mila for her safe place, which predictably was herself snuggling with her mom and dad in their bed. The therapist asks Mila to have her dad go downstairs to make breakfast—having Mila cut Dad out of her safe place drawing and place Dad in the dollhouse kitchen—and checks for safety (both Dad's and Mila's), then asks Mila to have her mom go outside to do some gardening—having Mila cut Mom out and place her outside the dollhouse—checks for safety (both Mom's and Mila's), and then asks Mila to bring them all back together. The therapist then asks what Mom noticed about Mila when she, Mom, wasn't there. *What was it that kept Mila safe? And what did Mom notice about herself when Mila wasn't there—was she safe, what kept her safe?* In this way, Mom's need for Mila was addressed at the same time as Mila's need for Mom.

Feeling some safety inside creates an internal calming—a shift to the ventral vagal parasympathetic ANS (Porges, 2009). Irrelevant indicators of danger are less likely to be perceived, and, as a result, the individual is better able to engage in reflective thinking (Hughes & Baylin, 2012).

Asking the child and parent for their safe place is not a one-time exercise. Initially, the image that comes up may not seem to the therapist to be either safe or comforting—the child or parent who sees his or her house from the outside and without any people in it; sees a hotel room where he or she took a holiday in the past; sees him- or herself in a car. When this happens, several of the ideas discussed earlier may be used. During subsequent sessions, we can ask what the safe place for that day will be, thus creating freedom for both the child and the parent to look inside afresh. The therapist can gain a sense of both the child's and the parent's ongoing sense of safety from the safe place images evoked. As the internal safety increases and the images show greater security, the therapist may use this time to mention some of the past safe places they have imaged. Mentioning their past images lets the child and parent know that the therapist is holding them in his or her thoughts—an important part of being valued. At the same time, we invite the child or parent to go to whatever place feels safe and right for them today.

When working with the parent or parents who experienced unsafe (emotionally or physically) times as a child, it will be important to help them connect with the ways in which their real world now is safer than it was then. If their world is not safer, other referrals and help need to be found for them. This work needs to be done separately from the child.

Strengthening an Internal Resource

Building internal resources is an important part of this stage of therapy. Once again, using the parent as a model for the child provides parents with an opportunity to notice something positive about themselves. And once again, we need to let the parent know in a phone call before the session that we are going to pose this type of question.

What is something that Mila likes about herself?
What is something Mom (Donna) likes about herself?

When the child is unable to answer, the therapist would ask the parent what she notices. In situations where the parent has expressed highly negative emotions toward the child, we would have informed the parent by a phone call before the session that we are going to be asking this question and, if need be, help the parent come up with some ideas. Some parents will not be able to do this even with a therapist's assistance. In those situations, we can make an observation from what we have noticed about the child.

When the parent is unable to think of something positive about him or herself, we would comment on something we have noticed. As with the work with the safe place, a child is not asked to 'care for' the parent. That is the job of the parent, the parent's adult supports, or ourselves, the professionals working with the child and parent. Therapeutic work with a parent and child needs always to provide a healthy model for interaction in the home.

Marie & Jimmy

> **THERAPIST:** *Jimmy, what is something you like about you? Maybe it is something you do with others or something you do alone or a feeling you get inside?*
>
> **JIMMY:** [Stares. Mom also seems detached.]
>
> **THERAPIST/SOCIAL WORKER/SUPPORT WORKER:** [Remembers the initial referral when Marie reported that Jimmy had talked about a fantasy family he belonged to—wanting a connection to other people is an important feeling and strength inside Jimmy.] *Having created a fantasy family tells me that you, Jimmy, like to feel connected with other people. That is something important, a positive strength in you. What could be a symbol for this positive strength inside you of wanting connection?* [Alert signal goes off inside us—what if Jimmy chooses the fantasy family as his symbol?] *Jimmy, would you go over to the sand tray and pick out an object that could represent—stand for—your wanting to feel connected to other people.* [Waits a moment while Jimmy goes over to the sand tray or does not go—continues.] *Mom, you decided to bring Jimmy here, to work together to help him feel better—that is a positive strength inside you—making a decision to help things get better. Mom, would you please pick out an object from among the sand tray objects that symbolizes your making decisions to help things. . . . Mom, what can your object do with Jimmy's object?*

Here the therapist/social worker/support worker is highlighting something in Jimmy and something in Mom that is a strength. Asking Mom as well as Jimmy to pick out a sand tray object brings in an element of playfulness—an important aspect of parent/child interaction (Hughes & Baylin, 2012; Kestly, 2014). The therapist is tempted to take these ideas further by adding a 'wish to connect' or 'work together' but is aware that little steps are more likely to be successful than big steps. Also, at this point, some physical interaction which may activate a positive internal experience for either Jimmy or Mom, or possibly both, is far more important than words.

For parents who feel very insecure, it can be helpful to suggest an internal image of a positive moment between the parent and child. This would provide an image parents could go back to when feeling discouraged either about how the child is doing or how they, as the parent, are doing.

Using the Skills We Already Have 131

Trina, Diego, & Jacob, 13 Years Old

> **REFERRAL:** Protection services had been called by the school because of comments Jacob had made at school.
>
> **BACKGROUND:** Trina and her younger sister, Jacob's mother, had been raised in a neglectful and chaotic home. When Jacob's mother became involved in a lifestyle of parties and drugs, Trina and her husband (Diego) took guardianship of Jacob and his sister. Although Trina had been able to establish a healthy adult relationship, she, like her sister, was very insecure, and the children's negative behavior would trigger in her a feeling of either anger or desperation. She was wondering if she should turn the children over to protection services. This conversation takes place after several sessions between Trina and the protection worker.

TRINA: *I can't manage, I don't know what to do. I promised my sister I would take care of the children, but everything is so hard.*

PROTECTION WORKER: *Yes, it is hard.* [Attunes.] *Jacob and his sister are both very demanding children. Their constant demands and the squabbling between them would be exhausting.* [Validates.] *Are there any good moments? . . . I do remember your mentioning that you liked driving them to school because they always turned around and waved to you before they went into the school. And what about the time you and Jacob went to Dairy Queen for some ice cream?*

TRINA: *Well, yes there are some times. It's just so hard to remember anything good when Jacob starts taunting his sister, and then she cries and he laughs, and it is just so awful. Then I get upset and say things I wish I didn't—things my mother said to me.*

PROTECTION WORKER: [Chooses to stay with the 'good times' topic, knowing that Trina needs some strengthening before she is going to be able to do the work to change her parenting style.] *Those good times are hard to remember, but they have happened and they can keep on happening. Which of those events is most special for you? . . . Let's make an image—a picture inside your head—of Jacob and Sally waving to you after you drop them off at school. Where are you? . . . Where are they? . . . What do you notice about them when they wave? . . . What are you doing? . . . What do you notice in your body at this moment? . . . Enjoy that moment, hold that image in your mind's eye.*

Talking with parents about positive things that have happened is not enough. Talking about a good time helps to reinforce that particular memory network in the brain, but we want to do more than that. We want to connect the positive time with the neuronal network that is holding the feeling of desperation. If we were working with a child, we might ask the child to draw a picture of the positive memory. With the parents, we can ask them to make an image inside their mind's eye. While the conversation has initiated some synaptic 'firing' related to the children waving at Trina in the left hemisphere, the image is going to initiate synaptic 'firing' in the right hemisphere. This focusing is helpful and does strengthen the memory network, and there is much more we can do.

PROTECTION WORKER: *Now let's try something—can you bring up a picture of Jacob and Sally fighting?*

TRINA: *That's easy.*

PROTECTION WORKER: *And watch yourself sending each of them to their room. What's the feeling you notice in you?*

TRINA: *Well, first it was anger, and now I just feel desperate—this will never get better.*

PROTECTION WORKER: *Watch yourself standing there in the kitchen feeling desperate. Now bring in the image of Jacob and Sally waving to you after they get out of the car at school. Focus really hard on the image we were working on just a moment ago. Notice their smiles. Now what are you doing? . . . Yes, you are waving—what do you notice in your body now? . . . Now for a moment go back to that feeling of desperation. . . . A really awful feeling; now go back to the image of Jacob and Sally waving at you. What do you notice?*

TRINA: *I don't feel quite so awful. They always smile when they wave—they look like healthy normal children. Why can't they be like that all the time?*

PROTECTION WORKER: *Sounds like the desperate feeling is increasing again.* [Trina nods.] *Bring the image of the children waving back in. What do you notice?*

TRINA: *It's better.*

Here we are working to form a connection between the desperation and a positive moment. Remember Hebb's proposal—"cells that fire together, wire together" (Hebb, 1949). In fact, Freud first introduced this concept in the late 1800s, stating that when two neurons fire simultaneously, they become associated (Doidge, 2007).[9] What we want is for Trina's mind, when swamped with desperation, to trigger the neuronal network holding the memory of the children waving.

Building the positive image and connecting it to a negative feeling or event is only a start. *After* practicing it numerous times in session, the parent can be encouraged to practice the image at home.[10] Then, in time, he or she can focus on

Using the Skills We Already Have 133

bringing up the positive image when negative things are going on (see Diagram 4.2). Some parents will be able to do this, and some won't be able to do it without our direction. Letting parents know that practicing an image at home may be much more difficult helps them not to become too discouraged when they have difficulty. Encouraging the parent to take a photo of the positive image—for Trina, a photo of the two children waving—or draw the positive image on a sticky note, and then post the photo or sticky note somewhere it can be easily seen when the desperation feeling comes up, can be helpful.

Building External Supports

As we help children and their parents build internal awareness of safety and strength, we will become aware of a parent's need for more supports in the external world. Although we, ourselves, are unable to resolve most external stresses, we can work with the parents as an advocate or a support.

Rebecca & Andy (12) & Veronica (15)

> **REFERRAL:** Andy and Veronica had been referred for therapy due to sexual abuse over several years by their father.
>
> **BACKGROUND INFORMATION:** Dad has had no contact with the children based on a 'no contact' order. This order has now run out, and Veronica's and Andy's therapists are quite concerned that Dad may try to contact the children. Mom was working extra hours to support her family as well as attending sessions with each of the children's therapists. Many suggestions given by the therapists had not been followed. At first, the therapists felt this was a result of Rebecca being overwhelmed. However, when Rebecca repeatedly failed to go to court to have the 'no contact order' renewed, the therapists became increasingly frustrated and concerned that Rebecca wanted the father back in her life.

At a Session with Andy's Therapist

> **THERAPIST:** *I'm noticing that again this week you did not get a new 'no contact order' against the children's father. I'm wondering if you are missing him and are thinking, perhaps, of spending some time with him.*
>
> **REBECCA:** *[Becomes quite agitated and increasingly nonresponsive to Andy's therapist.]*

At a Session with Veronica's Therapist

> **THERAPIST:** *[Speaks slowly in a way that suggests effort.] I've been thinking about how difficult it has been for you to go to the court building and file*

134 *Using the Skills We Already Have*

for a 'no contact order.' That can be a really hard thing to do. For some moms, there is a wish that this would all just go away and they could see their partner again. For others, the court building and all the forms to be completed are confusing and intimidating.

REBECCA: *Everyone starts talking so fast and they use words I don't understand.*

VERONICA'S THERAPIST: *How difficult! People certainly are not born with a guideline for how to go to court.* [Rebecca stares at her with a surprised gaze.] *Of course you didn't understand the process. The people at the courts should have helped. I am sorry I was not helpful. What if we roleplay your going to the court to ask for what you need?* [Rebecca nods but seems quite worried.]

VERONICA'S THERAPIST: [Starts a roleplay by describing the layout of the court building as Rebecca would experience it as she was walking in. She asks Rebecca to visualize it—the guard she would have to speak to for directions, where she would then go, whom she would speak to, what words she might use, what questions she would ask. They focus on Rebecca's body posture and tone of voice, taking many breaks to breathe slowly and calmly. The therapist checks on how Rebecca is feeling inside—this reinforces the concept that anxiety and feeling unsure is normal, not something wrong with Rebecca.]

The next week, when Rebecca brought her children for therapy, she reported that she had filed for the new 'no contact order.'

Role-playing, similar to imaging, can provide an experience that stimulates new neuronal connections. This provides the parent with both a knowledge and experiential basis on which new ways of behaving can be built. Some parents may need more assistance than Rebecca did. We may need to accompany them as they navigate systems that are quite foreign to them. At such times, we will want to play a supportive, not an active, role. Building external supports may mean our making contact with other professionals who are working with the family or our attending meetings together with the parent with protective services or with the school.

Summary

Our training as child professionals with its attention to attunement, validation, and emotional regulation has prepared us well for working with parents. Each of these skills not only strengthens our relationship with the parent but also strengthens the parent.

Parents who have not experienced attunement cannot attune with their child. Parents who have not experienced validation cannot validate their child. Parents who did not have a parent who helped them regulate themselves emotionally may not be able to provide emotional regulation for their child. Some parents are able to find positive experiences in school, through sports, within a church, or in the general neighborhood. But there are many others who come to parenting equipped only with the negative patterns taught to them as their parents parented them.

It is these parents who are the most challenging to work with but also the ones who need our help the most. Whatever the parent experiences from us will begin the process of them being more equipped to better provide for their child.

But even as we are doing all of this work with the parents, many of the children we work with will continue to misbehave and be resistant to their parents or may even become more resistant. The parents we work with are going to be discouraged and, very likely, will revert to or continue in old negative parenting patterns. Even when parents want to parent differently and decide to parent differently, old patterns persist (see Diagram 4.1). This is to be expected—old patterns come from well-used neuronal networks inside the parent's brain.

Chapter 5—Points to Remember

- Parents need to experience calmness and reassurance before they are going to be able to calm and reassure their child.
- We, ourselves, need to develop our ability to mentalize.
- If we are feeling disapproval, we convey disapproval (nonverbal interconnectivity).
- We need to find a place of mutual agreement with the parent before we will be able to truly attune with the parent.
- There needs to be some experiencing of their experience for there to be attunement—our experiencing their experience without acting it out.
- Never discuss with parents in front of children something a child could use against the parent at a future time when the child is angry.
- Appreciating the parent is a major form of validation.
- Even if children/adults are safe, they may not feel safe. Creating a sense of safety with us is one of the most important things we can do no matter what our role is with the parent.
- Do not try for too much; *small* successful steps are best.

Notes

1 House, Tree, Person Projective Test (Buck & Hammer, 1969) is used as projective drawings that help a counselor or psychologist recognize the personal and environmental issues relevant for the child.
2 See Chapter 8 for further discussion of how our beliefs can impact both negatively and positively our reactions to the children and parents with whom we work.
3 While other child professionals can certainly use imaging with parents, when a parent is as reactive as Jessica, it would be wise for imaging to be used only by a professional with therapeutic training.
4 One possible resource would be individual therapy for the parent when those resources are available and affordable. And while individual therapy for the mother and/or father is definitely an advantage, the challenge, as the child's therapist, to work productively with the parent continues to be considerable. Parents so often experience our 'helpful' comments as judgments and reprimands.

5 It would be tempting to use the words "feel close" to Jimmy here because that is what we would normally say, but for Marie, feeling close does not feel safe—it is not part of her safe experiences—and thus the word "help" is less likely to overactivate her system.
6 As mentioned earlier in this chapter, we may not see ourselves as 'figures of authority,' but many, many parents do see us as authority figures. And while we may state that we do not 'judge,' given our own experiences of being judged as we grew up, we may convey judgment as we interact with the parent. And, given the parent's experiences growing up, he or she may feel judgment even when it is not happening.
7 If a parent persists in correcting, we might wonder if they received a lot of correction when they were children and what it was like for them when that happened. Correcting was something their parents taught them to do—not a behavior they freely chose (see Chapter 1).
8 Asking the child to help the parent places the child in a caregiving role to the parent—a place we want to move the child out of.
9 Freud's use of free association as an avenue to uncovering unconscious thoughts is based on this concept of 'association by simultaneity'—when an individual with a thought or sensation activates a particular neuronal pattern in the brain, other neuronal patterns previously associated in some way with that thought or sensation are triggered.
10 Asking a parent right away to practice something at home is unlikely to be successful and, thus, should be avoided.

CHAPTER 6

Helping Parents Move Out of Negative Interactive Patterns

Parents come with their children (and sometimes without their children) to our offices, playrooms, and schools, and they invite us into their homes, because they want something to change. They want their child to be happier, not to be anxious or frightened, to be less demanding, not to have temper outbursts or emotional meltdowns, to achieve more. Their focus is on their child changing, not themselves.

As we meet with parents to learn about their child, we also ask questions about the parents and their growing up (Chapter 2). These questions introduce the idea that they, the parents, and their reactions play a role in how the child is doing. The questions also introduce the concept that the way in which we parent is a pattern taught to us when we were very young. And because we had no control over what we were taught, we may have patterns of parenting that we not only do not want but also that we are not aware we have. And then, perhaps the most important concept, we introduced the idea that parenting patterns can change. But even with all of these ideas, parents are still intent on changing their child, not themselves.

We have talked about ideas for initiating more secure attachment interactive patterns between the parent and child and between the parent and ourselves (Chapter 4). In the last chapter we talked about attuning, validating, emotional regulation, and strengthening. All of this is important work, but it is not always enough. Many parents are caught in very strong negative interactive patterns with their child. Some parents recognize these patterns and want to change them, while others do not recognize the negative patterns, or they recognize the patterns but not that they have a role in the patterns.

Recognizing a pattern is only the first step to changing the pattern. Interactive patterns have underlying habits, beliefs, and emotions. As we have already discussed, much of our parenting comes from patterns taught to us when we were very young—habits we may not even know we have. Some parents are able to observe themselves and become aware of negative parenting habits and are able to shift them. Others observe and become aware but do not shift the negative habits. They may not feel that it is possible to change, or they may not know what change to make. Other parents neither observe nor are aware. For them, the negative habits continue.

Although habits are mostly behavioral, the belief systems or values underlying these habits are more intrinsic. They likely come from the spoken and unspoken messages parents heard both in their family of origin and in society as they grew up. Which are the beliefs they want to pass on to their children, and which are the beliefs that do not fit with the way they want their child's life to be? Another interference in the way parents may want to parent are the emotions they experience when they interact with their children. Sometimes these emotions relate to the child, but often these emotions relate to other people or situations in the parents' worlds. Often these emotions relate to themselves as they were as children.

In this chapter, we will look at how we can help parents recognize habits and, more importantly, shift the habits they do not want. We will then look at the belief or value systems parents may be holding with regard to parenting, to gender, to what constitutes success, or to their child in particular. These beliefs often relate (are similar or are opposite) to the parents' own experiences when they were children. Ways to question these beliefs without the parent feeling judged will be discussed. Hearing the emotions that may be underlying negative interactive parenting patterns is imperative. We will consider how we can, without becoming the parents' therapist, assist them with separating those emotions from their interactions with their child. We will then look at some of the factors that frequently block positive interacting between parents and children and discuss ideas for assisting these parents.

Habits Underlying Negative Parenting Patterns

During the assessment session, we listened to the parents' description of their own growing up. What were the habits of their parents that they might be carrying forward to the next generation? Habits include not only the patterns we cultivate to assist ourselves with daily living—flossing our teeth—but also behaviors and thought patterns developed (often unconsciously) to lessen anxieties or stress—biting nails—and behaviors and thought patterns we learned from our parents' behaviors and attitudes toward us—I am stupid. It is this last group that we are concerned with here.

Because the patterns we are talking about are unconscious (implicit), the first step is to make them conscious or explicit. This can be done with a very direct question:

"Do you ever find yourself saying things, doing things, or even thinking things about your child that your parent said, did, or thought about you as you grew up?"

We might ask a question in regard to a particular behavior that we observe:

"How did your parent handle that type of situation?" "How did your parent respond to you when you were frightened?"

Or it can be a more general question:

"Are there things from your growing up that you want the same, that you want different?"

Helping parents understand why they are responding in ways similar to their parents even though they did not like what their parents did is important (see Chapter 2). Then we can let parents know that the best thing about habits or patterns that have been taught to us is that we can teach ourselves new habits and patterns. All new learning needs new neuronal networks in the brain. And these new neuronal networks need practice. To change old patterns, new neuronal patterns need to occur and then need to be practiced in the same areas of the brain in which old parenting patterns are held (see Diagram 4.2).

At this point, we need to remind ourselves that *talking* about parenting with parents does not necessarily activate the part of the brain holding parenting patterns. As discussed in Chapter 3, attachment and other primary interactive patterns are held primarily in the deep right cortices of the brain (see Chapter 3 and Diagram 3.1). If parents are to change these patterns, they need experiences that activate neuronal firing in those areas of the brain.

The parent needs some nonverbal experience (right hemisphere functioning) of a new response pattern. With some parents we can explain that early patterns of behavior are held primarily on the right side of the brain—that part of the brain which is activated with observing, feeling, and experiencing—while our conversation about wanting to change occurs primarily on the left side of the brain. We may know that we want to do something differently, we may talk about doing something differently, but if negative experiential patterns are the only available response within the right hemisphere, as soon as our system is activated—as happens with difficult parent-child exchanges and with new parent-child interactions—we will respond according to the old pattern. To shift out of that old pattern we need to practice the new pattern in the same area of the brain that is holding the old pattern—the right hemisphere (see Diagram 4.2). For right hemisphere engagement we need to experience this new responding in some way. Imaging can help us do this (see Chapter 3, pages 68–72) and can help us experience the emotions and body sensations that are part of the new pattern of responding.

For some parents, talking about brain functioning (as we described in the previous paragraph) helps them accept the suggestion for imaging. For others, a less academic explanation is more helpful:

SUPPORT WORKER/PROTECTION WORKER/TEACHER/THERAPIST: *So often we talk about what we want to do, but when a tense moment comes, the new idea does not occur to us. We end up doing things just like we always have. That's because words and talking happen in one part of our brain* [points to own left hemisphere] *and early patterns of behaving happen in another part of our brain* [points to own right hemisphere]. *To change the early pattern we do not want, we need to practice the new pattern with the right part of our brain. We can do this by making an image of the new pattern—this happens in the brain right where the old pattern is* [points again to own right hemisphere].

Then, with the parent's agreement, we can move ahead to start the imaging:

Make an image in your mind's eye of that situation. . . . Where are you? . . . Who else is there? . . . What is happening? . . . What is happening inside you? . . . What does that tell you?

Take a breath—how is it that you wanted to respond? . . . Now watch yourself doing that. What do you notice? . . . What do you feel in your body? . . . What is the emotion coming up in you? . . . What is your child doing? . . . How is that different? . . . What is happening now?

Judy & Lucy, 17 Years Old

> **REFERRAL:** Adoption services recommends that Judy and Lucy receive some assistance from a support worker, a counselor, or a therapist because of the increasing tension in the home. Lucy refuses to talk to anyone, but Judy comes for appointments.
>
> **BACKGROUND INFORMATION:** Lucy grew up with a depressed mother who was unable to attend to her emotionally. A number of abusive men were in and out of the house. Lucy was taken into care at 6 years old and adopted at 7 years old by Judy, a single woman. Judy had grown up with severe, demanding parents who, according to Judy, would lecture on and on. They were very disrespectful toward Judy. There has been increasing tension over the years between Judy and Lucy, and Lucy has become increasingly abusive in her language and demanding in her behavior with Judy.
>
> **HYPOTHESIS:** Lucy comes to this relationship with a longing for something positive but had herself been taught negative patterns of how people should behave—withdrawal (her birth mother's pattern) or abuse (mother's boyfriends' pattern). Judy comes to this relationship with a demanding/lecturing parenting style, high tolerance for disrespect, and a longing for someone to love her.

JUDY: [Describes situations in which she and Lucy become engaged in verbal fights and Lucy is verbally abusive.]

SUPPORT WORKER/THERAPIST: *I'm noticing, as you describe that verbal fighting, how much you want Lucy to engage with you. I'm also noticing that, as you try to engage Lucy, you talk on and on—sounds like the parenting pattern you described your parents as having. That makes sense because your parents taught you that that was the way children should be handled. What was it like for you when your parents went on and on?*

JUDY: *It was awful. I would stop listening—oh, that's what Lucy does to me . . .*

SUPPORT WORKER/THERAPIST: *How would you like the conversation about chores to go?*

JUDY: *I'd like to just tell her the expectations and then have that be the end of the conversation. But what if she starts calling me names? That's what she usually does.*

SUPPORT WORKER/THERAPIST: *And how would you like to respond then?*

JUDY: *I'd like to tell her that that language is not acceptable.*

SUPPORT WORKER/THERAPIST: *Then what do you want to do?*

JUDY: *What do you mean?*

SUPPORT WORKER/THERAPIST: *Do you want to keep talking about it or have that be the end of the conversation?*

JUDY: *Oh, I see—I need to just say it and walk away.*

SUPPORT WORKER/THERAPIST: *You have done some really good thinking and deciding about this, but well-reasoned thinking may not come up in the moment with Lucy. That thinking and reasoning occur in a very different part of the brain—the left part—than where the old parenting pattern of lecturing is—the right part. To have this new way of doing things—saying things only once and walking away—become a new pattern in parenting Lucy—it needs to be practiced, and it needs to be practiced in the part of the brain—the right part—that has the old pattern. The right hemisphere is the part of the brain that works more with images and body sensations than with words. I suggest that we do some imaging to practice what you are saying you would like to do. Is that all right with you? [For some parents, as described earlier, this explanation would include fewer references to brain.]*

JUDY: *Sure—anything that will help.*

SUPPORT WORKER/THERAPIST: *Bring up in your mind's eye—you can have your eyes open or your eyes closed, whichever you prefer—an image of you and Lucy talking about chores. Do you have it? Describe it to me. . . . What are you noticing about her? . . . What are you noticing about you? . . . Listen to yourself, what are you saying?*

JUDY: *I'm telling her that she needs to do the vacuuming and I expect it done by Friday, which is when I give Lucy her spending money.*

SUPPORT WORKER/THERAPIST: *What's happening now?*

JUDY: *Lucy starts to argue—oh no, it's the name-calling again.*

SUPPORT WORKER/THERAPIST: *Yes, that is her pattern. What's happening in you? . . . What do you feel in your body? . . . What do you feel in your head? . . . Okay, take a breath—what is the new behavior you talked about—what do you see, feel yourself doing?*

JUDY: *I'm walking away. I didn't even get upset—what a relief; I'm back in my office working at the computer.*

142 Moving Out of Negative Parenting Patterns

Judy reports that, during the past two weeks, she was able to walk away from the various chore discussions with Lucy. It had been great, and Lucy actually came and sat with her while she was watching TV, and they talked about the show.

SUPPORT WORKER/THERAPIST: *Really nice, did you congratulate yourself?*

JUDY: *But then I gave her money even though she hadn't done her chores, so of course she never did them. I just am no good at this.*

SUPPORT WORKER/THERAPIST: *One thing at a time—sounds like you are lecturing yourself.*

JUDY: *I deserve it.*

SUPPORT WORKER/THERAPIST: *What about what you did well? Would you bring an image in your mind's eye of the part of you that did really well with Lucy and the part of you that is lecturing you?*

JUDY: *I'm shaking my finger at me!!!*

We can work with Judy using the image her brain has created—the two Judys. The content of this image shows how completely Judy took in the parenting her parents had done. We can help Judy congratulate herself for what she did well—talking without lecturing. This provides modeling for a new way of parenting—not just the talking without lecturing but also a pattern of complimenting someone for something done well. Judy reports that the self-complimenting brings up a strange feeling, not a bad feeling but a really strange one.

Two weeks later, Judy reports that she and Lucy are still getting along better but that the name-calling has increased again and she then starts to lecture. Also, Lucy is not doing her chores, but Judy is giving Lucy her spending money.

SUPPORT WORKER/THERAPIST: *I'm realizing that we did not do any practicing with avoiding lecturing last time—I am sorry. Old habits do not change by wishing them different, they do not change without practice.* [Asks Judy to make an image of herself and Lucy having a conversation about chores. In the image, Lucy starts calling Judy names, Judy makes short, clear statements and walks away.] *Do you want to do some work on that habit of giving Lucy money even when she has not done what was agreed to?*

JUDY: *My parents never gave me my allowance if I had not done everything. I didn't learn that from them.*

SUPPORT WORKER/THERAPIST: *My guess is that the habit of giving the money comes from you wanting so much to make Lucy's life better and from wanting so much for Lucy to love you. Does that make sense?* [Judy nods.] *Bring up an image of Lucy coming and asking you for money. Where*

Moving Out of Negative Parenting Patterns 143

are you? . . . Where is she? . . . Now what is happening? . . . Hmmm—is that the old habit of lecturing coming in again—remember what you did when your parents lectured? . . . How could you do it differently from your parents? . . . What happens if you ask a question rather than making a statement? Try it, what happens? . . . We will continue to practice this here, and when you feel ready, you could practice the image at home.

In this example, our support worker or therapist did introduce a suggestion related to parenting. But note that the support worker/therapist uses the suggestion—posing a question rather than making a statement—as she talks with Judy. The support worker/therapist then encourages Judy to image herself using the suggestion, thus giving Judy practice with using questions rather than statements. Both the modeling and the imaging stimulate neuronal networks in Judy's right hemispheres.

This example with Judy highlights that there are reasons for negative behaviors other than early learned behaviors. We shall be looking at that after the next example.

Larry & Billy, 5 Years Old

> **REFERRAL:** Larry referred himself and his son for therapy because of Billy's angry and aggressive behavior toward Dad following the parents' separation.
>
> **BACKGROUND INFORMATION:** Billy's mother had experienced postpartum depression after his birth. It was a time when Dad was very busy. Dad and Billy's mother have now separated after a difficult few years. Billy is living primarily with his father but having every other weekend with Mom. Dad's mother was a teacher and the dominant parent in the home. Dad expresses considerable admiration for her and for how she had parented. He also expresses insecurity as to whether he could do well enough as a father.
>
> **OBSERVATION OF PLAY:** Dad attends closely to Billy's play and then gives Billy a new idea for something Billy could do. Billy brings Dad a sand cupcake to eat. Dad expresses a lot of pleasure and then asks about putting some frosting on top. Billy starts a drawing with a pencil. Dad tells Billy how nice the drawing is and then hands him a marker, telling Billy that the color will make the picture even brighter.

THERAPIST: *Dad, I notice how well you attend to Billy and how much you support him in what he does. I'm also noticing how you are adding an idea to every idea he has. I wonder what that is like for him?* [Encourages mentalizing.]

LARRY: *What do you mean?*

THERAPIST: *If someone added something to every idea you came up with, what would you start to think?*

LARRY: *Oh, that my ideas were not good enough. But aren't we supposed to teach our children to do better and better?*

THERAPIST: *You're right—we might call it 'teacher-parenting.' I remember you telling me that your mother was a teacher. I imagine that may have been the way she parented. But Billy experienced an early time when neither his mother nor you were able to be very attentive with him. And now, over the last few years, both of you have been, quite understandably, distracted. He is likely feeling insecure and unsure of himself. That may be where his angry behavior is coming from. You are, as I mentioned, so good at watching him and appreciating what he does.* [Validates.] *What would happen if you just stopped after the appreciative comment?*

LARRY: *I guess he might be left with a good rather than an inadequate feeling. I could do that.*

THERAPIST: *Yes, you could!!*

Because Billy is in the session, Dad can right then practice not adding suggestions. If it had been a separate session with Dad, our therapist could suggest that Dad make an image of himself watching, commenting, and not making any further suggestion.

Beliefs Underlying Negative Parenting Patterns

We all hold beliefs related to parenting and related to how we want our children to be. Some of these beliefs come from our experience of being parented, and some come from the messages handed down within our families. These messages—some spoken and some unspoken but very apparent—may relate to how girls/women or boys/men are supposed to be, what role children play in a family, how children are to be disciplined, whether negative emotions are permitted, what makes someone a strong person, and many more. We absorb these beliefs—both positive and negative. Over time we may recognize these beliefs and go along with them without ever questioning them, or we may reject them and construct a new set of beliefs. And then there are the beliefs that we are not even conscious of having. All of these beliefs affect our parenting. Some of the beliefs of the parents we work with agree with our own, and some do not.

If we want parents to show respect to their children, then we need to show respect to them. The conversation we had with parents during the assessment interview (Chapter 2) can help us know what their beliefs and values may be. It is easy to talk about those beliefs we agree with but much harder to discuss with respect beliefs with which we do not agree.

Noel & Andrew, 7 Years Old

> **REFERRAL:** Following a parent-teacher interview between Noel and Andrew's teacher during which Noel mentioned that Andrew was hitting his sister a lot, the teacher spoke with the school counselor. The counselor called Noel and invited him to come in.
>
> **BACKGROUND INFORMATION:** Andrew's mother is separated from Andrew's father, Noel, because of domestic violence. The children live alternate weeks with each parent. Noel is willing to be involved in the therapy. He has stated that he is concerned about the level of his son's aggression toward his sister but also is very concerned that Andrew be able to stand up for himself with other kids and with adults. Noel grew up in a variety of foster homes, all of which he described as abusive.

SCHOOL COUNSELOR: *How would you describe Andrew's behavior toward his sister?*

NOEL: *Well, given his size and strength, it is a problem. I'm glad he does not let her get away with being a whiny girl, but I don't want her to actually get hurt.*

SCHOOL COUNSELOR: *Why do you think he is so rough on her?*

NOEL: *She sure whines a lot; it gets on my nerves as well. I tell her not to whine, but I don't hit her, so I don't know why he is so rough. Andrew's mom complains that I taught him to hit his sister—absolutely not!! I know there was the fighting between his mother and me before the separation, but what was I to do, his mother was cheating on me. I had to let her know that was not all right.*

SCHOOL COUNSELOR: *Sounds as if hitting is the way men/boys let others know that their behavior is not all right. You mentioned that you had lived in several different foster homes growing up—what were they like?*

NOEL: *You don't want to know! I got hit a lot—mostly by my foster moms and the other foster kids. I was a small kid and didn't know how to stand up for myself. I've taught Andrew to stand up for himself!*

SCHOOL COUNSELOR: *That's tricky: you want Andrew to stand up for himself—an important way to be—but you want him to stop beating up his sister—another important way to be. What are some of the ways you've taught Andrew to stand up for himself?*

NOEL: *He is really good at using his fists—we play fight a lot. No kid is going to take advantage of him, and no adult either.*

SCHOOL COUNSELOR: *How are you wanting him to decide when to use his fists and when not to use his fists?*

NOEL: *Well, I guess if someone threatens him.*

SCHOOL COUNSELOR: *That makes sense. If someone threatens him, he needs to keep himself safe.* [Validates.] *Absolutely! But is his sister threatening him?*

NOEL: *Well, his sister should stop whining—I've told her that. And his mother, what can I say—she is a nag.*

SCHOOL COUNSELOR: *Whining and nagging—they certainly are irritating. But the hitting, do you want Andrew to be like those foster siblings you grew up with? Didn't sound like they were much fun to be with.*

NOEL: *Certainly weren't!! They were bullies—Andrew's not like that* [voice rising]!

SCHOOL COUNSELOR: *I really hear you that you do not want Andrew to be a bully but you want him to stand up for himself.* [Attunes; speaks with a questioning tone in his voice.] *A 7-year-old boy beating up a 4-year-old girl—sounds 'bullyish' to me even when you do not want it to be. I'm wondering—could Andrew stand up for himself without using his fists?*

What is our school counselor doing here? Although he probably has his own theory—and it is probably pretty accurate—as to why Andrew is beating up his sister and hitting his mother, he is staying engaged with Noel and wondering about Noel's ideas. If he had presented his theory, challenged Noel on what Noel felt he had taught Andrew or criticized Andrew, Noel would have undoubtedly become defensive and maybe even aggressive. A shift to a defensive or aggressive position means increased arousal, and Noel's ability to think (functioning from his prefrontal lobes) will decrease, and his emotional reactivity (functioning from the limbic system) will increase (see Chapter 3). Once this shift occurs, the possibility of Noel thinking more objectively—or even thinking at all—about Andrew's behavior decreases.

What does the school counselor do? He starts with several questions encouraging Noel to consider his son's behavior a bit further—a definite effort to engage Noel's thinking (prefrontal) system. He does not, at this point, ask questions that challenge either Andrew's or Noel's behavior. The school counselor does verbalize the belief he recognizes related to males and their behavior, but he does not pursue it. At that point, he links back to Noel's growing up and invites more information on what that experience was like for Noel. He has made an accurate judgment that Noel's growing up affected his present belief structure. Again, he clarifies Noel's beliefs without judgment but highlights how they contradict each other. Rather than pushing this idea, which could lead Noel into defensiveness, he again asks questions. From those questions, Noel states a position with which the school counselor can agree. This allows the school counselor to form a link with Noel. With that linkage as a base, the school counselor is now in a better position to start challenging Noel's son's behavior. Each response from the school counselor after that starts with

Moving Out of Negative Parenting Patterns 147

the counselor supporting something Noel has said. He follows the supportive statement with a question that challenges the behavior Andrew has shown.

Parents are not always as accommodating as Noel—providing information with which we can agree. The important skill to observe here is that of keeping the parent within his or her window of receptivity and therefore able to engage in thinking not just reacting. What if Noel had reacted negatively to our counselor?

SCHOOL COUNSELOR: *Whining and nagging—they certainly are irritating. But the hitting, do you want Andrew to be like those foster siblings you grew up with? Doesn't sound like they were much fun to be with.*

NOEL: *Don't you make a comparison between those guys and my son—my son is smart!!! He is just teaching his sister and mother a thing or two, and they need to learn it.*

SCHOOL COUNSELOR: *[Startles . . . the conversation had been going so well. Takes a breath.] I apologize, I certainly did not mean that Andrew is like them. What I am noticing is that he is hitting a lot, which concerns both me and you.*

NOEL: *And if his sister and mother would change, then the hitting would stop.*

SCHOOL COUNSELOR: *You mentioned how the whining irritates you, but you aren't hitting your daughter. How are you avoiding that? [Takes a position of curiosity.]*

NOEL: *I don't want protective services at my door!!*

SCHOOL COUNSELOR: *Absolutely not. And you have found another way of responding rather than hitting—that's the helpful part.*

NOEL: *I talk, well, yell maybe, at her.*

SCHOOL COUNSELOR: *What happens then?*

NOEL: *She cries.*

SCHOOL COUNSELOR: *Why do you think she cries?*

NOEL: *I scare her—I really don't want to scare her, just don't want her to whine—I hate it.*

SCHOOL COUNSELOR: *[Continues to be curious.] Why do you think she is whining?*

NOEL: *I don't know. It's usually the end of the day—maybe she is tired.*

SCHOOL COUNSELOR: *Makes sense to me. That gives you something else to do about the whining—putting her to bed. Can we give Andrew something else to do when her whining bothers him?*

NOEL: *I suppose if he told me then I could put her to bed.*

SCHOOL COUNSELOR: *That would be quite a change from what is happening now. And big changes can be hard if we don't have some practice first. Talking about something is not really practice, because it happens in a different part of the brain from where our behavior patterns are. Creating images of you doing something new is practice. Images happen in the same part of the brain as behavior patterns. Could we do some of that now?*

NOEL: *Sounds airy-fairy to me. Like all that inner child stuff people go on and on about.*

SCHOOL COUNSELOR: *You're right, it does sound airy-fairy. But it actually is brain-based. The behavior patterns we use with our children tend to be held in the right side of our brain while all the talking you and I have been doing is pretty well based in the left side of the brain. Imaging is part of what the right side of the brain does; that is why I'm asking you to do imaging. I think it could be very helpful for you, so I am hoping you will just give it a try.*

NOEL: *Guess it won't do any harm. But I warn you, I don't believe in it.*

SCHOOL COUNSELOR: *Bring up a picture in your head of you telling Andrew how his sister's whining bothers you but that you are going to try a new solution. Then watch yourself in that image asking Andrew to tell you when her whining bothers him. Let him know that you will help her stop the whining by putting her to bed so she gets enough sleep and is not so tired. In fact, why don't you let Andrew, in your image, know that once his sister goes to bed, you and Andrew can have some time together—just the two of you. Now, in that image inside your head, go to sometime when you hear Andrew's sister whining, remind Andrew that he can tell you about sister's whining—watch what happens, tell me about it. . . . And now that you have sister in bed, what are you and Andrew doing?*

Apologies are important and also very helpful. If the counselor had tried to explain what he meant, the focus on the disagreement would only have highlighted the tension between him and Noel. Instead, our counselor directs the conversation back to his and Noel's mutual concern (Andrew's hitting)—a way to decrease the distance between them caused by the counselor's earlier comment. The counselor tries to engage Noel by asking how he handles the whining. While Noel's responses are not very helpful, they do allow the counselor to continue with his questioning, which encourages Noel to reflect on his daughter and why she behaves in a certain way (mentalizing). The therapist then finds a way to support Noel's thought and uses this to introduce the idea that Andrew could be encouraged to do something other than hitting.

Our counselor then asks Noel to image himself talking to Andrew. Noel is quite put off by the suggestion. Our counselor responds, not by correcting him,

Moving Out of Negative Parenting Patterns 149

but by agreeing with him and then providing a simple explanation as to why imaging could be helpful. The more detailed imaging with questions related to body sensation and emotions that we have talked about before may be more than Noel is willing to participate in. Better to keep things simple and end with a positive scene.

Jill & Roberta, 17 Years Old

> **REFERRAL:** Jill self-refers because of her high anxiety with Roberta going away to university.
>
> **BACKGROUND INFORMATION:** Jill has explained that it is not just her fear for Roberta's safety in that open environment but also her fear that, although Roberta had done well in high school, it had been because she worked so hard. University studies were likely to be more difficult than Roberta could manage. Jill was the youngest child in a professional family. While her parents had encouraged her siblings to continue their education and seek professional skills, they had tried to discourage her from further education because of the academic challenges. Despite their lack of support, Jill had continued her studies. She told the therapist that her parents' negative belief in her had always been hard to cope with.

JILL: *I am so worried about Roberta, and I know she can pick up my worry. I don't want her starting out on this new adventure full of anxiety.*

THERAPIST: *How wise of you. What worries you most?*

JILL: *So far Roberta has done really well. But I just know she is going to come up against demands that are way beyond her capability. Then she is not going to be able to manage.*

THERAPIST: *That idea of someone's ability not being enough to handle new challenges sounds familiar.* [Takes a position of curiosity.] *Where have you heard that before?*

JILL: *What do you mean?*

THERAPIST: *Sounds to me like the way you described your father.*

JILL: *Oh no!! You're right—I'm just like my father—what an awful thought!!*

THERAPIST: *What do you wish your father had believed about you?*

JILL: *That I was smart and capable and would be able to manage in some way whatever I took on. So maybe I got in over my head, but I would have been able to figure out what to do.*

THERAPIST: *What would it be like to feel that way about Roberta?*

JILL: *That sounds great, but what do I do about the fear inside me?*

THERAPIST: *What would happen if you talked to the part of you with that fear and let yourself know that that is actually only a 'thought habit' your father taught you? What if you bring up an image of Roberta in your mind's eye and place around her all the wonderful things you know about her? . . . What do you notice?*

JILL: *She looks like Athena. Is she ever strong! Yes, she will manage. I don't know how—but I don't need to know how, that is up to her.*

This is a very different situation from the one with Noel and Andrew. In our work we are going to come across a myriad of negative beliefs or values that can cripple parents in their wish to be supportive with their children. Our job is not to point out the inaccuracies or the possible negative impact, but to wonder where those beliefs or values came from and whether the parent wants them. Only when the parents recognize that their negative beliefs came from outside themselves, that they do not need to continue them, that they can do something new—something based on a new belief—can they change.

Values Underlying Negative Parenting Patterns

The values of the parents with whom we work may be similar to our own or may be diametrically opposed. Having chosen a profession that focuses on helping children, we are likely to have a set of values that gives high importance to children and how they are treated—children are to be respected and listened to; children are to be cared for and not hurt; children need a consistent and caring family; children need physical reassurance and safety. Having chosen a profession that requires a sense of responsibility, we likely place high value on personal responsibility—each person is responsible for his or her own reactions and behavior; others are not to be blamed for our mistakes; people should carry through on commitments they make. These values, both those taught to us when we were little and the ones we have learned as adults, may differ significantly from the values held by the parents with whom we work. This can be particularly problematic when working with families from different ethnic backgrounds than our own.

Hua & Duyi (8) & Daiyu (6)

REFERRAL: Hua and her children were referred to social services after the school had noticed bruises from the father having hit the children. The father had moved out of the house, as stipulated by social services. Hua was very distressed and continued to state that her husband had a right to hit the children when they did not behave. It was the children with their disobedience who were the problem, not her husband.

THERAPEUTIC PLAN: The social worker described during consultation how she would be explaining to Hua that children must not be hit—Hua needed

> to realize that children being hit was child abuse. The consultant suggested that it might be more helpful to view this as a cultural conflict rather than a conflict over treatment of children. Was there some position on which the social worker and Hua could agree?

SOCIAL WORKER: *But she needs to accept that hitting children is wrong if we are to be able to trust her.*

CONSULTANT: *I am concerned that places the two of you in opposition rather than as a team to help the children and to help the family. I wonder what it is like for her to live in a country that has a very different view regarding the discipline of children than the country in which she was raised.*

SOCIAL WORKER: *But she needs to accept that this is not the way it is done here.*

CONSULTANT: *Yes, but that is different from wanting her to change her values related to child rearing. The issue becomes how to raise the children in a different culture rather than whether her values are right or wrong.*

SOCIAL WORKER: *It has to be really difficult adapting to different ways and different values.*

As our social worker changes his emphasis from correcting Hua to exploring her experience, Hua is going to have a different and, most probably, a more positive experience of the appointments with the social worker.

Values are going to differ. If we focus on changing a parent's values, we are not only disrespectful but also likely to be unsuccessful in our work with the parent. If we move back from the difference in values—where there is disagreement—to an underlying issue—where there can be agreement—we will be able to work more positively and successfully with the parent. The better we can become at recognizing where our beliefs or values may be causing a conflict between ourselves and the parent, the better able we will be to avoid conflict and find a common concern to focus on.

Emotions Underlying Negative Interactive Parent-Child Patterns

At the beginning or end of our appointment with a child, there may be some time to meet with the parent alone, or we may schedule separate sessions with the parent. At these times, we can ask the parent about the difficult times between the parent and child. Here we want to focus not only on the child's behavior but also on the *parent's experience of that behavior*. What happened inside the parent when the child refused to do what the parent asked, when the child started yelling or hitting? What was the sensation in his or her body, what was the emotion that came up?

Negative moments between a parent and child flare up very quickly, and they are awful for both the parent and the child. A parent does the best he or she can at that moment—this is a very important position for us as the professional working with the child to hold. Parents do not want to be bad parents. As we look into a parent-child interaction from the outside, we may see all sorts of 'errors.' We can point out these 'errors,' we can give suggestions as to how the parent might handle those 'errors.' For some families—healthy families—this may be helpful, but for many families—the families we meet in our work—not only will it be unhelpful, it may increase the parent's anger toward the child, toward us, or even toward him- or herself.

Rather than pointing out 'errors,' let's help parents experience the negative moment a bit differently. We can, as we are talking with them, ask them to redo the negative moment but have them slow down the moment in order to have time to observe what is happening. What did they experience at different points in the moment—the body sensations, the emotions, and whatever thoughts came in or, indeed, what thoughts might have been blocked from coming in?

Bob & Andrew, 15 Years Old

REFERRAL: Bob referred his son for therapy because of the high anxiety Andrew was experiencing related to school attendance.

BACKGROUND INFORMATION: Andrew spent every other week with his mom and the alternate week with his dad. Andrew had started refusing to attend school at the end of the previous year and was spending more and more time playing video games. Although it was presently summer, Dad hoped that therapy would help Andrew be ready for the fall term. Mom did not wish to be involved in the therapy and said it was Dad's issue, not hers. Dad, who also struggled with anxiety, had become fearful that Andrew would never finish school and would be caught in a 'dead-end' job or, worse, never find a job or have a family. When Dad had tried to avoid situations as a child, his parents had insisted that he do the activity, and although it had led to some frightening times, he had done as he was told and had, in the end, been successful in school.

INITIAL THERAPY: The therapist met with Bob for the developmental assessment. Andrew had been invited to that session but chose not to attend. The therapist then met with Andrew a few times, helped Andrew identify his fears, did some problem-solving around the fears, and taught him a number of skills for calming. They also discussed the pressures of living in two very different homes. What Andrew really hated at this point was the fights with his father—if Dad would just leave him alone, he would be okay. Meeting with Bob, the therapist learned more about the fights. When Andrew was at Dad's, he was spending most of his time in his room playing video games. When he would emerge, Dad would ask him to do the agreed upon chores, and Andrew would say he would do them later, grab some food, and start to leave. At that point, Bob reported, he would raise his voice—not yell. And

> then, suddenly, he and Andrew would be yelling at each other—it was awful. Bob reported that he would say things he didn't mean, and what Andrew said was awful. Each time, Bob reported, he would tell himself he wasn't going to yell, but what could he do—Andrew needed to get out of his room and do stuff.

At this point the therapist could gather more information as to whether Andrew did the chores later, about how they decided on chores, and as to whether there were guidelines around computer use. In fact, there is no limit to the amount of information that could be gathered and much of that information could be really helpful. As professionals trained to work with children, we have excellent suggestions related to how families can talk about and specify chores, we have excellent suggestions related to guidelines for the use of electronics. But is this what the parent needs most? Indeed, most parents have already heard the suggestions many times.

What are the emotions Dad is experiencing? Could his emotions be getting in the way of a healthier interaction between him and Andrew? But Bob's conversation so far has not included mention of emotions; it has been very factual. For the therapist to immediately start talking about emotions is unlikely to engage him.

THERAPIST: *Sounds really awful for you* [Attunes]—*and awful for Andrew—sounds like neither of you like it. Let's see if we can figure out what happens. Blowups happen really fast. Let's go through it in slow motion and see if we can figure it out. Where are you when Andrew comes into the room? . . . Can you see yourself there?* [Encourages imaging in order to engage right hemisphere functioning.] *In your mind's eye, see him coming into the room; what do you notice happening in you?*

BOB: *I get all tense inside—I mean, wouldn't you? I can see it coming.* [Bob responds from right hemisphere orbital-medial prefrontal cortex recognition communicating through limbic system to body (see Chapter 3); but then shifts quickly to left hemisphere dorsal-lateral prefrontal cortex functioning with rationalization.]

THERAPIST: *Yes, makes sense* [Validates Bob's left hemisphere experience]. *Where do you feel that tension* [Returns to more right hemisphere-body engagement]?

BOB: *In my arms and in my jaw.*

THERAPIST: *What do you think that tension—the tightness in your arms and in your jaw* [Repeats in effort to keep Bob engaged in right hemisphere functioning]—*is about?*

BOB: *I don't want to fight, I really don't. But something has to change. He has to do something. He can't just sit there at the computer all summer.*

THERAPIST: *I hear a lot of emotion in your voice* [Again, tries to keep right hemisphere active]—*what do you notice?*

BOB: *What if he does nothing, what if he doesn't go back to school? What if he ends up like the kids you read about in the paper! I have to get him out and doing things.*

THERAPIST: *Sounds like a lot of fear—fear that he will end up a 'no-good kid.' No wonder you start yelling.* [Names an emotion but then shifts back to validation in order to keep Bob engaged and avoid a defensive reaction.] *Fear makes us either run away or start to fight or just freeze up—not what we want to do, but that is the way the body works.* [States factual information to maintain engagement through the more problem-solving area of the brain—dorsal-lateral prefrontal cortex—with which Bob is more comfortable (see Chapter 3, p. 78).] *Tell me more about your fear* [Wants to keep the medial prefrontal cortex active but, recognizing Bob's greater comfort with left hemisphere functioning, asks Bob to 'tell' about the fear not 'feel' the fear—more a right hemisphere function].

Once a parent (or therapist-parent combination) identifies the emotion behind a response, we can help her or him look at it and understand it better. As in this example, the exploration can be more of a cognitive task for parents who are less comfortable with emotions, but for parents more comfortable with emotions it can be a more sensation-based task (*"Where do you notice the fear in your body?"*). Often the emotion coming up is related to something earlier in their life or to some present event quite separate from the child. If this is the case, we can help them recall some positive experience with their child separate from the past or present event as a way to help disconnect the child from the negative emotion and reconnect the child with a positive emotion. If the emotion is actually connected to the child (the minority of situations), we can help them understand the emotion, provide them with ways of calming, and then help them find new ways of experiencing their child.

BOB: *Yeah, afraid he'll turn out no good—won't go to school, won't graduate, will end up just floating, maybe even on drugs—there's so much out there.*

THERAPIST: *This fear of Andrew not doing well, is it a new fear, or does it feel like you have had it for a long time?*

BOB: *I guess I didn't think about it before, I left it to his mother. But since we separated he has withdrawn more and more, and she won't do anything about it* [Voice rising]. *And I end up harping on him.*

THERAPIST: *Sounds like you are worried not just about how Andrew is going to manage but also about parenting on your own* [Attunes]. *And also maybe some anger at Andrew's mother* [Shifts to position of curiosity to open a new area]?

Moving Out of Negative Parenting Patterns 155

BOB: *Sure, but how do I get Andrew to do something* [Acknowledges emotion but quickly moves away from emotion and back to the behavioral issue]*?*

THERAPIST: [Stays with the fear of not parenting well—since this fear was not originally mentioned it is probably the more basic of the two and needs attention before the fear of Andrew not doing things can be addressed—but also recognizes Bob's need for something more concrete than a discussion of emotions. Shifts to resourcing.] *Have you had any good moments of parenting since the separation?* [Bob nods] *Tell me about them. . . . Can you make an image of those times in your mind? Describe one to me* [See Chapter 5]*. . . .* [Remembers the importance of bringing the positive image together with the negative experience if the parent is to be able to make a positive behavior shift outside of therapy.] *Now, go back to Andrew coming into the kitchen and your fear that he'll turn out 'no good' and your fear of not parenting well. Do you have that feeling—the tightness in your arms and your jaw? Now bring in the image of that good time you had with Andrew last summer when you went camping. What happened then? . . . What do you notice yourself saying to Andrew now?*

BOB: *I asked him if he remembered the camping trip. And we started talking about it—he didn't go back down to his room. Maybe we need to do that again—we could fit it in before school starts again.*

THERAPIST: *What about the tightness in your arms and jaw?*

BOB: *I'm not noticing it. Huh? It's gone!*

THERAPIST: *Sounds as if remembering the good times with Andrew helps to relieve the tension you feel related to his present behavior with video games. But we both know that that tension in your arms and jaw is going to come again. Negative situations with Andrew are going to happen; after all, he is 15. The positive memory from camping and the possibility of other positive times can help alleviate but won't erase the tension. But it does let you and Andrew have some good connection.*

What has the therapist done? He has helped Bob notice the physical sensation—the physical sensation is more concrete than emotion and therefore easier for Bob to connect with. The therapist then connects the physical sensation (and also the voice tone) with expression of an emotion. He does not ask Bob to acknowledge the emotion (that might push him beyond what he can do) but invites Bob to examine (a cognitive task he is good at) the emotion—is it new or old?

As Bob examines this question, the therapist is able to recognize another fear—a more basic one—his fear that he will not be a good enough parent. This is the fear that needs attention before addressing the fear of Andrew not engaging in school, chores, or other activities. Bob's quick movement back to his upset with Andrew indicates that he is not ready at the moment to pursue the fear of not being a good enough parent. Making a mental note that this is something to go back to (does it come from his experience with his father; does it come from messages he received from others—perhaps his ex-wife?), the therapist moves toward helping Bob with problem situations. He provides some positive resourcing for interacting with Andrew—interesting that the resource also addresses Bob's fear of not parenting well.

The final step in this interaction is the very important one discussed earlier of linking the positive resource (a neuronal network related to positive interaction) to the negative experience (a neuronal network related to negative interaction) if we want the parent to be able to bring up the resource when the negative experience happens. Encouraging the parent to get out some photos from last summer's camping trip as a reminder and encouraging the parent to practice remembering positive times he has had with his child can be helpful. The major step, however, is being able to bring in (link together) the positive thought (positive neuronal network) when the negative situation (activated negative reactivity) is happening.

What would have happened if the therapist had suggested that Bob and Andrew needed to do more things together? Bob might have taken the suggestion, and the two might have gone off camping together. More likely, Bob would have felt the therapist had dismissed his concern. Bob's underlying fear of not being a good enough parent would not have been acknowledged and, therefore, might not have shifted even though the activity in which they were participating—camping—was the same.

Negative parenting patterns do not shift with one exploration. Negative interactions are going to continue to occur between Bob and Andrew. But Bob does now have another way to view the interactions and a clearer sense of his own vulnerabilities. He may want to pursue this conversation further with Andrew's therapist or with his own therapist. Bob also has some resourcing—recall of positive times—on which he and Andrew can build some new positive experiences.

Ann & Sofia

ANN: *Last night I asked Sofia to go down and get the mail out of the box. She refused, and I reminded her that that was one of her chores. With that she started screaming at me and pushing her fists into my face as if she were going to hit me. I don't get it: it was really awful when I was growing up, but I did what I was told; why can't Sofia be like that? I'm working so hard to get through my own stuff, but it is all still awful.*

THERAPIST: *Yes, you are working hard* [validates] *and I can see why it feels discouraging* [attunes]—*you are keeping Sofia safe from yelling and drinking—the things that made your growing up so unsafe—but even so her behavior is out of control* [again validates]. *What happened in you when she was yelling at you and pushing her fists in your face?*

ANN: *I froze inside. I closed down.*

THERAPIST: [Recognizes that Mom may be dissociating—makes sense that Sofia yells—if she does, she doesn't have to go get the mail. And every time Mom dissociates, Sofia probably gets frightened. That's going to lead to more yelling by Sofia to try to get Mom back. Wait—I am going away from Ann—just what she is doing to Sofia. I need to hear Ann, be with Ann!] *That's hard!* [Pauses.] *That's an old response, isn't it? That closing down inside makes sense given your experiences growing up. Any idea what the emotion was that you were needing to keep out?*

ANN: *Hatred—I don't want to hate her!!!*

THERAPIST: *No, you don't, and I really admire that. Whom do you think the hatred is attached to?*

ANN: *Her father, my mother, all the people who hurt me.*

THERAPIST: *How is Sofia different from them?*

In this situation, the mother is willing to pursue the emotion. Indeed, an important part of therapy for dissociation is helping the individual, bit by bit, recognize the unwanted (dissociated) emotions and unwanted (dissociated) memories (Howell, 2011; van der Hart et al., 2006). Because we, as child professionals, are not necessarily trained in providing therapy for adults who dissociate and we do not have agreement with the parent to address their dissociation, our interaction should focus not on the parent's past experience but on her present dissociation when with her child. We would, however, encourage the parent to pursue her own therapy.

As Ann lists the ways Sofia is different from other people, the therapist asks her to make an image of the child that highlights these differences—right hemisphere activation—and asks what words go with the image—left hemisphere activation—words that highlight how the child is different from those other people. Remember that one of the differences the child has is that Ann, who wants so much to connect with Sofia, is her mother.

THERAPIST: *You have told me of several ways in which Sofia is different from your mother and different from your ex-partner, her father. Can you bring up an image in your mind that represents these differences?*

ANN: *Sofia is standing in the middle, and my mother is on one side and her dad is on the other side.*

THERAPIST: *What do you notice?*

ANN: *Well, Sofia is really small. She's just a kid. But there is all sorts of yelling that is going on over her head—yeah, it is yelling by my mother and her father—they are just the same—my mom, her father. How did that happen? I said I would never be with someone like my mother, and there I was with Jim—Sofia's father. How did that happen?*

THERAPIST: *It would have felt so familiar to you—all the yelling—my guess is you just closed it out. Jim's paying attention to you—different from your mother—would have felt good. Let's go back to the image of Sofia and your mom and Sofia's dad. How is Sofia different?*

ANN: *Well, she is little and they are big. And she is looking for me—they aren't even noticing me. Why can't Sofia see me? She is getting scared because she can't see me! Her eyes are darting around. Why can't she see me? She needs me. Oh, my goodness, she needs me.*

THERAPIST: *Have you dissociated—gone away—because of the yelling? Then Sofia gets scared because she is alone, and maybe she yells to get you back?*

What is important here is that the therapist uses imaging to keep Ann connected to the emotional part—right hemisphere processing—of her experience with Sofia and does not get diverted (for too long) to talking about why she was attracted to Jim.

It is important that the parent actually brings up an image in her mind's eye and does not just talk about the image. For parents who rely more on logic and factual reasoning in their interactions with the world as opposed to sensing and observing, not only the concept of imaging but also the importance of imaging may seem very strange. Explaining how the brain works and the importance of engaging all of the brain as they work to improve their interactions with their child may be helpful. Also helpful are questions that increase the parent's ability to access a more nuanced image:

"What is the body sensation that comes with that image?"

"What is the emotion you notice with that image?"

Once the parent has connected to a healthier image—Sofia being smaller and looking for Ann—the therapist would encourage Ann to go back to the difficult situation—the negative neuronal pattern of Sofia yelling and Ann dissociating—that the therapist wants the new image—Sofia looking for Ann, Sofia needing Ann—to connect to. The therapist would have Ann image Sofia yelling at her, would encourage Ann to notice the negative emotion—hatred—and then invite Ann to bring in the image of the small Sofia looking for Ann. What is the emotion Ann is noticing now?—being needed, wanted, feeling important to someone—and then staying there, not dissociating.

It will be important to go through this exercise several times, reminding the parent that each time she goes through it, she is stimulating that new neuronal pattern in her brain. And new neuronal patterns do not mean that the old ones disappear. It does mean that the old ones are not being reinforced. And each time the new one is practiced, it is getting a little bit stronger.

Ann might have identified fear rather than hatred coming in. Our approach would be the same—

THERAPIST: *Whom do you think the fear is attached to?*

ANN: *Her father, my mother, all the people who hurt me!*

THERAPIST: *How is your world now different from the way it was when you were a child living with your parents; how is your world now different from the way it was when you were with Sofia's father? How are you different now from how you were then? What is the picture or object or even a color that represents you and your world now?*

ANN: *That's easy to think about here, but what about at home when Sofia explodes?*

THERAPIST: *You are right—much easier to do here. But the more we practice it here and then when you are at home and things are calm and you practice bringing in that positive image of Sofia, the more likely it is to come in when things are difficult. Remember each time we go through it here or you go through it at home, you are teaching your brain a new way of responding. The closing down is a habit your brain learned to do when things got scary; now you are teaching it a new habit. Could we practice it again now?*

Those of us trained in EMDR could add slow bilateral stimulation while the parent is practicing the positive image (Shapiro, 2001). For those trained in hypnosis, this exercise could be taken a step further by anchoring (connecting) the positive image, sensations, and emotion to a particular spot on the body (Mason, 2014). In the future, when the parent touches that spot on her body, the thought of the image, or maybe even the image itself, will come to mind.

Now let's go back to Judy and Lucy and Judy's wish to be loved:

Judy & Lucy

> **SEVERAL WEEKS LATER:** Judy is doing a better job with guidelines around spending money, but she is still buying things for Lucy whenever asked.

JUDY: *It is prom time and I bought her a dress; it was really expensive. And now she wants shoes to go with it and yet she does nothing around the house.*

THERAPIST: *What's the hardest thing about saying "no" to Lucy?*

JUDY: *Well, it is her prom and she wants to enjoy it. She says she can't wear the dress if she doesn't have shoes to go with it.*

THERAPIST: *Sounds as if you don't want her to be disappointed. And, yes, this is important for her. And important to you for her to be happy* [attunes].

What does buying everything for her do to your relationship with her? [Brings in curiosity.]

JUDY: *She might be grateful. She means so much to me, but I don't think I mean anything to her—she is so disrespectful. She blames me that she isn't happier. If I hadn't adopted her, her life would have been good.*

THERAPIST: *Sounds as if you are feeling guilty* [Attunes]. *Is it guilt that talks you into buying everything for her* [Again is curious]?

JUDY: *I wanted to be a good mother and I'm not. It is so hard.*

THERAPIST: *Your lecturing is less. I call that a 'good change in mothering.' Can you tell yourself that inside your head?* [Tries to resource.]

JUDY: *I can say it, but I don't believe it. I just see Lucy screaming at me.*

THERAPIST: *And what are you doing when she starts screaming? Watch yourself.*

JUDY: *I'm walking away.*

THERAPIST: *Wow!* [Validates.] *Good change in mothering!!!! What is Lucy doing* [Again is curious]?

JUDY: *She stopped screaming.*

THERAPIST: *What do you want to do now?*

JUDY: *I could come back and we could talk.*

THERAPIST: *You are trying very hard at this difficult task of mothering* [Validates]. *That effort you are making needs to be put together with the feeling of guilt that so often seems to take over.* [Has momentary debate—use some imaging replacing guilt with the effort she is making or pursue curiosity?] *Why is Lucy still living with you and hasn't run away?* [Pauses as Judy looks bewildered.] *You are providing something really important for Lucy; let's focus on that. What is the image that comes into your mind's eye now?—focus on that.*

Here the therapist is trying to figure out why Judy is so caught in the pattern of buying things for Lucy. It certainly is not creating a healthy experience for either her or Lucy. First, it appears to be Judy's wish to be loved, and then it appears to be guilt—neither one a healthy motivator. Judy needs a positive place to stand in her relationship with Lucy. Rather than focusing on the negative motivation, our therapist is trying to give Judy an internal resource that will strengthen her ability to respond more reasonably to Lucy. To be sure, there is a need for some psychoeducation related to the effects of intermittent reinforcement and the effect of boundaries never adhered to, but that education will be of little help without some assistance with the negative parenting patterns taught by her parents and negative self-concept resulting from the way Judy's parents treated her.

Moving Out of Negative Parenting Patterns   161

Blockages to Positive Parenting Patterns

Triggers

In Chapter 3 we talked about 'triggers' and about the two brain pathways for transmitting information from the outside world to the amygdala: fast route: thalamus (gateway for sensory stimuli—she is raising her hand) → amygdala (alarm center for the brain—I'll get hit); slow route: thalamus (gateway for sensory stimuli—she is raising her hand) → hippocampus (memory function—people raise their hand to wave 'hi') and frontal cortex (analysis function—this person could be safe) → amygdala (alarm center for the brain—feels safe and able to take in this new information). (See Chapter 3, Charts 3.2 and 3.3.) If the sensory information is dangerous, the fast route is very important. The amygdala prompts the individual to a fast reaction intended to keep the individual safe. If, however, the information looks dangerous but actually, when checked with memory (hippocampus) and thinking (frontal cortex), is safe, that fast reaction may cause trouble.

Sally & Peter, 6 Years Old

> **REFERRAL:** Sally referred her nephew and adopted son, Peter, for therapy because of angry and aggressive behaviors, particularly toward her.
>
> **BACKGROUND INFORMATION:** For Peter's first two years he had lived in a chaotic setting with considerable domestic abuse. When Sally and her husband learned about this, they offered to adopt Peter. Sally and her sister, Peter's mom, had similarly grown up as part of a large sibling group in a chaotic and abusive setting, but as adults had followed two different paths: Peter's mom—alcohol and drugs, Sally—no alcohol and drugs.
>
> **INITIAL THERAPY:** Therapy initially centered around sessions for Peter. At one point therapist asked Peter what made him feel safe. He responded that his room at home made him feel safe, cuddling made him feel safe, and Mom (Sally) slapping him made him feel safe. Therapist was at first confused as to why being slapped would increase someone's sense of safety then realized that it might have, for Peter, connected him back to the very early days with his birth mother when violence and safety occurred together, but it also might have 'settled' Peter's brain when in turmoil in the same way that self-injury can settle the ANS (Yates, 2004). But Peter growing up with the perception that slapping was positive would lead him very quickly into abusive behavior with partners. What was happening for Sally, someone who had worked so hard and was so committed to avoiding violent environments? Was something triggering her? But, of course, Peter's hitting would have been a trigger back to Sally's very abusive childhood, when she had to fight with her siblings for food and for attention.

THERAPIST: *Peter's yelling and hitting, particularly when it is directed toward you, must be so difficult. What happens in you when Peter starts hitting you?*

SALLY: *It is like I see red!! I feel trapped, and it is rage that comes up. It is very scary! I don't mean to hit him. It does stop him, but I know that's not the way to do it. I know he needs reassurance that he is safe, but I just can't stop myself—I slap him.*

THERAPIST: *Sounds like a trigger response. Peter's hitting reminds your system of when you were little, and the only way to survive in your house was to hit back. With his hitting, your system goes into danger mode and responds just as it did when you were little.*

SALLY: *That makes sense, but how do I stop it? I know I shouldn't do it.*

Helping a parent to recognize the trigger is a first, but not sufficient in and of itself, step in moving away from triggered behavior. Knowing that slapping is not good parenting is in Sally's left hemisphere, but slapping as a way to respond to hitting is an early neuronal pattern deep in her right hemisphere. Being an earlier and more often repeated neuronal pattern of responding, it will supersede the later and less basic learning of what is good parenting.

A second important step to pay attention to before triggered behavior can be shifted is safety. An individual needs to *feel* safe and needs to communicate that safe information to all the parts of herself. In brain terminology, that would be increasing the internal sense of safety—held in the right hemisphere—such that the amygdala does not move into hyper alert when something similar to an old experience occurs.

THERAPIST: *How is your world different now from how it was when you grew up? . . . What makes your 'now world' safe? . . . How are you different now from how you were back then? . . . What do you know now that you didn't know then? . . .*

ANOTHER THERAPIST POSSIBILITY: *What is something physical about you now that you did not have back then? . . . Touch the ring on your finger and feel the safety it represents* (Dolan, 1991).

ANOTHER THERAPIST POSSIBILITY: *Now, bring an image that represents the now safety into your mind's eye. . . . Now bring yourself—the now you—into that image. And when you are there, describe it to me. . . . Now bring Peter into the image with you; describe what is happening.*

SALLY: *We are cuddling—that's not a problem, we both love those times.*

THERAPIST: *Move away from the cuddling for just a minute. I am asking you to bring in the image of Peter exploding and starting to hit you; let yourself feel the 'red' come in with that trapped feeling and all the rage. Now touch your ring—that object that reminds you of now. What is happening inside?*

SALLY: *I am settling down. It's Peter. I tell him that he is not to hit me. If he hits me, I shall leave the room. I am leaving now.*

Here the therapist is helping the parent to link to a sense of safety just as we do when we work with children who are experiencing trigger responses (Wieland, 1997, 2015a). Feeling safe is absolutely essential for the thalamus-amygdala fast route not to create an eruption.

It can also be helpful to explain to parents how situations in the child's world now, even though the child is safe, may trigger the child back to a time when the child was not safe—perhaps to a time when domestic violence was happening, to a time when the mother was experiencing depression, to a time when some trauma or other frightening event occurred—and the child explodes (or shuts down). It may seem to the parent as if there is no reason for the child's explosion (shutdown)—the parent is unaware of what the child is remembering at an unconscious level—and the parent responds with exasperation and discipline. Understanding trigger responses enables the parent to help the child better and, when possible, to eliminate triggers until further therapy is done (Wieland, 1997).

Let's also remember that we as child professionals may also have trigger responses. Something within a situation, perhaps some behavior on the part of the parent or the child, is similar in some way to an unprocessed negative experience we had as a child. Recognizing a trigger response within us is very important. Once recognized it is easier to put the response aside for thinking about later and to reorient ourselves to the child, the parent, the session. We shall talk more about this in Chapter 8.

Mismatched Temperaments

There is an extra challenge when working with a parent and child whose temperaments or sensitivities are very different. It is harder for these parents to recognize what their child needs and then exceptionally hard for them to provide what the child needs.

Janet & James, 7 Years Old

> **REFERRAL:** Janet had referred her son to the school counselor at the request of the school.
>
> **BACKGROUND INFORMATION:** The teachers reported that he was constantly touching the other children, and mother stated that at home he annoyed his younger sister by always standing or sitting really close to her. Dad worked and lived in another city but would call about once a week. Janet would not provide any information about her growing up.
>
> **INITIAL COUNSELING SESSIONS:** When the therapist met with James, he stood close to her and from time to time leaned against her. When the school counselor met with Janet and James together, there was little physical contact between them.
>
> **HYPOTHESIS:** Janet had learned an avoidant style of attachment and, therefore, had an avoidant way of interacting with others. James clearly

experienced a need for physical touch as reassurance, and Janet was not able to meet this need.

DILEMMA: How to help Janet develop some ability to be closer physically with her child while not asking for physical touch, a request that would probably cause resistance.

SCHOOL COUNSELOR: *I am noticing from your description, the teachers' report, and from James' behavior that he has a high need for physical contact. Some children have a higher need for reassurance from physical contact than other children. It seems, however, that close physical contact is uncomfortable for you.* [Janet pulls back.] [Recognizes Janet's defensiveness and probably a shift out of the 'window of receptivity,' so decides not to pursue an uncomfortable topic. Does some concrete problem-solving, the type of thinking with which Janet is more comfortable.] *I was thinking that perhaps as we spend time together, James could sit in the rocking chair, you could wrap the blanket around him, and then you could sit next to the chair and rock the chair. He experiences a sense of closeness and connection and you are able to decide for yourself how close feels right for you.* [Janet relaxes and agrees.]

Recognizing the two different needs—one for closeness and the other for distance—we are challenged to find an activity that will meet both needs. An ability to be creative is certainly one of the necessary qualifications for a child professional.

Kent & Jacob, 8 Years Old

REFERRAL: Kent and his wife referred their adopted son, Jacob, because of continuing out-of-control and aggressive behaviors.

BACKGROUND INFORMATION: Jacob, the son of two parents with high-level ADHD, had experienced early chaos and neglect. He experienced numerous moves until he was adopted at age 4 by Kent and his wife, both in their fifties. Over the years, Jacob had learned some emotional regulation, but even his normal level of activity was considerably higher than that of his parents. Kent, who has a very quiet demeanor, would become agitated/frightened by Jacob's boisterous way of doing things. Dad and Jacob could have positive calm moments together, but then Jacob would jump up and knock against Dad. Dad would reprimand Jacob, and Jacob, sensing Dad's disapproval and Dad's fright, would escalate. Dad would then move away from Jacob, and Jacob's negative behavior would escalate even more.

> **HYPOTHESIS AND DILEMMA:** Kent and Jacob were two individuals who cared very much for each other, but each of them had a very different physiological system—each creating anxiety in the other.
>
> **OBSERVATION:** In a session with Kent and Jacob, the therapist has them throwing a cushion back and forth as the three of them talk. Kent recoils when the cushion comes too close to his head. Each time that happens, Jacob laughs. Jacob then starts throwing the cushion to the therapist.
>
> **THERAPY INTERACTION:** The therapist, recognizing that it is important that she not be more successful than Dad when interacting with Jacob, invites Jacob to throw the cushion just as hard as he could but into the empty chair next to the therapist. He would grab it from there and throw it back to Jacob. If Jacob made a mistake and threw the cushion directly at the therapist, the game would stop. After a bit, the therapist invited Dad to take his place. Jacob threw the cushion into the chair next to Dad; Dad grabbed it and threw it back.
>
> In this manner, our therapist created an activity that had a high pace—meeting Jacob's need for movement and speed—but distance from Dad's face—allowing Dad to relax and feel safe. The need of each to be in contact with the other was met but in very different ways. Our therapist recognized a similar need—to be in contact—and two separate needs—high activity for Jacob and a safe distance for Dad—then devised an activity that met these three requirements. This activity was particularly successful because Kent and Jacob could repeat it at home.

As illustrated with these two examples, activities for a parent-child dyad where each has very different needs because of different temperaments and/or physiological arousal levels need to be individually designed. With careful observation of the differing needs, placement of those needs side by side, we can then create an activity that meets both needs.

Rejection of Ideas Presented

As trained child professionals we have had the opportunity to do considerable reading, discussion, and thinking in the area of child development and family functioning. Not only is it highly likely that we have read more books and heard more lectures on parenting than most parents, we have the advantage of doing this reading and listening in a non-emotional state—that is, a mental state that is receptive to new ideas. Parents trying to resolve negative child behaviors or family situations often are in a highly activated state when reading a book or listening to a YouTube talk on parenting. This activated state makes it harder for them to take in new information.

Not only are parents worried about their children, but they also may be caught in the fear of not being a 'good enough parent.' Because of the activated state, the parent's limbic system is more reactive and the prefrontal system needed for clear thinking is more sluggish (see Chapter 3). This same activated state—limbic system more active, prefrontal less active—is often there when parents come into our offices.

George & Jack (13), Justin (12), Joey (7)

> **REFERRAL:** George and his three boys were referred by protective services because of concern that Dad needed assistance in learning parenting skills.
>
> **BACKGROUND INFORMATION:** The three boys had been removed from their parents' care because of neglect and the use of drugs in the home. Since then, Dad had separated from Mom and had successfully completed a treatment program for his addiction. The boys had been returned to his care, but he was having difficulty getting them to school and following through with other outside programming. In a case conference together with Dad and protective services, a plan for summer programs in the city had been agreed to.

GEORGE: [Voice rising.] *They are making us stay here in the city this summer. The boys need fresh air and to be out in the country with their grandparents—not here!!! My parents are a really important part of the boys' lives, and I'm going to take them there—you people can't stop me!*

FAMILY SUPPORT WORKER: *You may remember we all agreed to this plan when we met together. No one is forcing you to change your plan. We all agreed that working together with a summer camp schedule here in the city would help you organize better. And protective services is funding the camp programs—lots of work has gone into that, and you had agreed. There is the soccer camp and then the outdoor camp—think about all of the new things they will learn and new friends they will make. You were wanting them to get away from video games, and these camps do that.*

GEORGE: [Interrupting.] *I never agreed. They forced me into this. They are my boys, and I'm going to decide what they do.*

Our support worker is absolutely right about what he says—Dad had been part of the planning discussion, he had said he wanted the outdoor programs but could not afford them. A lot of work had been done to make these plans happen and Dad had agreed. While Dad may be hearing what the support worker is saying, he is not processing it. He is not functioning from his prefrontal lobes—his limbic system is in high activity. And remember, the higher the activity in the amygdala, the lower the possibility for activity in the prefrontal lobes (Kern et al., 2008, see also Chapter 3).

Trying to explain something when the parent is upset, no matter how good the explanation or how gently we present it, is unlikely to be successful.

Dad's voice tone, his agitated manner, and his darting eye movement can tell the support worker, even before the tirade, that Dad is functioning primarily from his limbic system. It is this system, not the decision-making system of the prefrontal cortex, that needs to be addressed.

GEORGE: [Voice rising.] *They are making us stay here in the city this summer. The boys need fresh air and to be out in the country with their grandparents—not here!!! My parents are a really important part of the boys' lives and I'm going to take them there—you people can't stop me!*

FAMILY SUPPORT WORKER: [Takes a slow breath.] *Not only does it feel like we're not listening to you, it feels like we are controlling what you have to do* [Attunes]. *That's hard* [Validates].

GEORGE: *Sure is! The boys need to be out in the country with their grandparents.*

FAMILY SUPPORT WORKER: *Contact with family is important to you.*

GEORGE: *Sure is!* [Voice calming.] *And I need the time out of the city.*

FAMILY SUPPORT WORKER: *Yes, you do.* [Recognizes from Dad's voice and words that his system has slowed down a bit; shifts to a stance of curiosity in an effort to engage Dad's prefrontal system, which is now more available.] *I wonder how the boys could do the planned summer activities and all of you could also get some time out of the city with your parents?*

Including an activity like slow breathing or breathing to different parts of the body (particularly if it is a regular part of each session) or, for families from a First Nations community, a smudge, can provide calming. Then, attunement and validation of each person's experience of what has happened provides another pause before ever considering the problem that needs solving.

If the parent or another professional in an agitated state starts the session with problem-solving, it would be our job to ask for a pause and do some settling and attuning before proceeding. Not only will this help the session go better, it is modeling for the parent the importance of slowing down agitated interactions such as they have with their children before trying to discuss problems.

Grandmother Alice & Jonathan, 5 Years Old

REFERRAL: Grandmother referred Jonathan because of his 'evil ways.'

BACKGROUND INFORMATION: He had been removed from his parents' care as a result of neglect and the parents having been involved in robbery. Alice, Dad's mother, and her husband, agreed to take Jonathan into their home. The referral came following an incident during which Jonathan had taken some candy from the corner store.

GRANDMA: *So he stole the candy. When I found it, I couldn't believe it—robbing at 5 years old! I told him he's just a 'no good kid' like his dad. We went right back, and I insisted he tell the store keeper and apologize. I paid for the candy, and Jonathan will now have to do chores to pay me back.*

COUNSELOR: [With each word, "stole," "robbing," "no good," his stomach gets tighter and tighter—this is a 5-year-old—and a 5-year-old with a lot of deprivation and very poor modeling—not a juvenile delinquent. Focuses on Alice's vocabulary—this needs to shift or the child will be labeled before he is even in school.] *Those are really harsh words—"stealing," "robbing," "no good"—what if we noticed how hard it is to want candy and not have it? He is feeling so alone right now, and 'taking things' is a behavior we often see in children who feel alone—it is like trying to fill the hole they feel inside. And Jonathan did a good job with apologizing.*

GRANDMA: [Voice rising.] *Good job!! I had to force him to apologize. He is not going to behave that way and live in my house—who is going to want a little thief?*

COUNSELOR: [Stomach tension gets worse—he is offering grandmother an alternative way to talk with Jonathan and it is an approach that could teach Jonathan about having to delay a treat—wasn't that what Grandmother wanted to teach him?]

As counselors, we can see the child's dilemma, we can empathize with a 5-year-old who is feeling alone and needs something positive. But we are not talking with the 5-year-old, *we are talking with Grandmother*. She is the person we need to be empathizing and attuning with. She is the person who needs to have something positive. Jonathan may be feeling frightened, but so is Grandmother. She is having to acknowledge that her son is not able to be the person she wants him to be, and now her grandson seems out of control—and he is only 5.

GRANDMA: *So he stole the candy. When I found it, I couldn't believe it—robbing at 5 years old! I told him, he's just a 'no good kid' like his dad. We went right back and I insisted he tell the store keeper and apologize. I paid for the candy and Jonathan will now have to do chores to pay me back.*

COUNSELOR: *You certainly handled that well—taking Jonathan back to the shop, having him pay the store keeper, and now he needs to repay you. You are highlighting that each of us needs to be responsible for our behavior.* [Validates.] *What an important value!* [With this compliment, he aligns himself with grandmother and shifts to curiosity.] *I wonder where the behavior of taking the candy came from?*

GRANDMA: *His no-good dad!!*

COUNSELOR: *That's hard. Not how you wanted things to turn out for Jonathan's dad.* [Attunes.] *And you are right, Jonathan had modeling* *that taking things is an okay activity.* [Validates, compliments, joins with grandmother.] *That is something you and I can help Jonathan with.* [Notices some relaxation in grandmother's shoulders indicating that she is back within the window of receptivity.] *Also, I'm thinking of how deserted and alone Jonathan may be feeling right now, and taking things is something kids who feel alone often do—it's like trying to fill the hole they feel inside them.*

Not only is our counselor validating Grandmother, he is talking about him and Grandmother being a 'team.' That is important recognition and also very true. The most effective therapy for a child is when the parent and the counselor function together as a team. As a teacher, a counselor, or a social worker highlight a concern both they and the parent have, they are building the idea of a 'team.'

"We certainly share similar concerns about Jonathan's behavior."

"I think it will be really good for Jonathan to know that you and I are working together to help him. He may complain, because that is his habit, but having important adults work together just for him will be something new, and it makes him important—something he needs."

"Please send me an email or text when you notice something related to Jonathan and school that you think I should be aware of. That will help us be able to function more as a team in our work with Jonathan."

Parents may present with parenting habits that are detrimental to the child and legally actionable. While reporting a parent to protective services is necessary by law in specific situations, helping a parent learn another way of responding is far preferable.

Beverly & Ricky, 7 Years Old

> **REFERRAL:** Ricky had been referred at the request of the school. He was aggressive toward other children, particularly when he felt they were being unkind to him.
>
> **BACKGROUND INFORMATION:** Ricky had lived with relatives since he was a toddler but had several visits each week with his mother, Beverly, and his half-brothers. During a visit, Ricky had become very aggressive, and when Beverly tried to discipline him, Ricky bit Mom. Mom then bit Ricky to "show him how it felt." On return to his uncle's house, Ricky kept talking about his mother having bitten him. His uncle contacted Mom, who stated that she had to teach Ricky not to bite, and if Ricky bit her, she would bite him. There had been quite a dispute, with Mom very adamant in her position. Uncle contacted the therapist.

THERAPIST: *Sounds like it was a really difficult visit* [Attunes]. *Tell me about it.*

BEVERLY: [Angry voice] *I know they told you!! Ricky bit me, so I bit him back. I had to stop him—I wanted him to know how it felt. I know what you are going to say—that's what his uncle and his grandparents told me, but if Ricky bites me, I'll bite him.*

THERAPIST: *You are absolutely right that Ricky's biting needs to stop* [Validates]. *My concern is that hurting a child teaches . . .*

BEVERLY: *I have to stop it. All my parenting groups have said that when a child bites, biting the child lets the child know that it hurts. I need him to stop biting.*

THERAPIST: *Yes, you do need to have him stop biting* [Validates]. [Feels lost as to how to approach this, remembers that questions are the best way to go.] *How else might you stop the biting?*

BEVERLY: *Nothing else stops it, and nobody is going to tell me how to manage my child!*

THERAPIST: [Takes a breath and pauses—realizes he needs to activate Beverly's dorsal-lateral prefrontal cortex, which engages in problem-solving, and thereby decrease some of her emotional reactivity.] *How have you stopped other negative behaviors?*

BEVERLY: *Time out—but we were at the park. What else could I do? My mom did it to me.*

THERAPIST: *No wonder this is confusing* [Attunes]. *And your mom shouldn't have done it to you* [Supports Beverly]. *Good question—what else could you have done* [Compliments and agrees with]? *There needs to be some gesture that lets Ricky know that biting is not all right.*

BEVERLY: *With his little brother [2½ years old], I put my hand over his mouth.*

THERAPIST: *What about trying that with Ricky? Can you see yourself doing that* [Wants to activate the area of the brain that holds old parenting patterns]? *Let's go back to that time last week in the park. Ricky and his brother were playing, and Ricky was getting too rough* [Remembers that, for the new neuronal wiring to be activated when needed, it needs to connect with the neuronal wiring that has the negative behavior], *so you very wisely told him to stop* [Compliments]. *Then, when you started to separate them physically, Ricky bit you. Can you see this in your mind's eye? . . . Now watch yourself put your hand over his mouth, and what are you saying? . . . Then what happens?*

The therapist's first response is to be supportive in some way to Beverly ("You are absolutely right"). Beverly is already agitated—outside her window of receptivity. The therapist's first concern is not the biting but to help Beverly calm enough that she can think more clearly about the issue.

Our therapist is then choosing not to use the term "biting" in his response because he does not want to oppose Mom. Opposition facilitates overarousal. Our therapist recognizes something he can agree with—stopping the biting. This is not the time to do teaching (*"Biting a child does not teach a child not to bite"; "Parenting courses do not support biting a child"*). Rather, it is a time to try to engage the parent's thinking system with something she has already done successfully.

Beverly brings in her own experience of her mother biting her. At another time this would be helpful for the therapist to talk about—parenting received teaches parenting—but here the more important response is Beverly's question—*What else could I do?* This opens a door for more productive thinking. Once again the therapist is able to support Beverly—an experience Beverly seldom has with regard to her parenting of Ricky. Knowing that talking about how Beverly could respond is not enough to change a behavior, our therapist introduces the idea of imaging. Notice that it is introduced in a very informal way. An explanation with regard to brain functioning would distract both Beverly and the therapist from the important issue that a parent biting a child does not teach a child not to bite.

'Preaching' Parenting

As adults, we are very used to providing information to children. After all, they do not have the experience and knowledge that we do—if they engaged in more helpful and sharing behavior rather than hitting, they would have more positive experiences; the house is safe, so they do not need to be scared at night; if they steal, they will end up with less rather than more. All of this is true, but in all of these conversations, it is the parent, not the child, who is doing the thinking. Hopefully the child has heard the parent, but that only means the part of the child's brain that interprets audio sound waves has been functioning. There is no guarantee that the child's thinking system has been involved. How can the parent activate the child's thinking? Perhaps a better question for us to be asking is: "*How can we activate the parent's thinking?*"

George & Justin, 12 Years Old

GEORGE: *Every time I go out, Justin asks if I am coming back. So I explain again—of course I am coming back. And I do it so carefully, just as I've been told to—I tell him I'm going to the grocery store, I tell him why I'm going to the grocery store, I tell him what I am going to be doing there, and then I tell him that I am coming back. And remind him that his brother is here at home with him. Why can't he remember that? It gets so tiresome and everything takes so long, I get impatient, and I know he can hear that in my voice, and then he gets tense and his behavior gets worse. Then I just get furious, start yelling but end up taking him with me. It's just a vicious cycle.*

FAMILY SUPPORT WORKER: [Speaks slowly—attunes.] *That's tiring. What's happening here is that you are doing all of the thinking for him. You are explaining the situation—giving him all that information so he never needs to do it on his own. He is hearing what you are saying but he is not actually thinking about it, figuring it out. Why don't you try . . .*

[Wait—our support worker is doing exactly what he is telling the parent not to do. The support worker is doing the thinking for the parent.]

FAMILY SUPPORT WORKER: *You are working so hard to give Justin all the information he needs* [Validates]. *But we don't even know if he hears it. What would happen if you asked him questions rather than giving him information?*

GEORGE: *He asked me a question, so I am answering it.*

FAMILY SUPPORT WORKER: *And that certainly makes sense* [Validates]. *But who is using the thinking part of the brain—you or Justin?*

GEORGE: *Well, I am.*

FAMILY SUPPORT WORKER: *What would happen if you responded to Justin with questions? What would happen if he had to come up with the answers?*

GEORGE: *I guess then he would have to do the thinking.*

FAMILY SUPPORT WORKER: [Continues to be curious.] *If he had to do the thinking, I wonder, would he be more likely to remember the information?*

GEORGE: *Well, yes he would.*

FAMILY SUPPORT WORKER: *Let's practice. I'll be Justin and you have just told me you are going out to the store. "Dad, are you coming back?"*

GEORGE: *Of course I'm coming back.*

FAMILY SUPPORT WORKER: *Wonder how could you turn that into a question? Just as you gave him all those pieces of information—where, why, what then—to reassure him, how could you get him to think of all those pieces of information and to tell you?*

GEORGE: *Justin, do you remember where I told you I was going?*

FAMILY SUPPORT WORKER: *Yeah, you're going to the grocery store.* [The roleplay is continued, with George changing his statements to questions.]

Just like the parents, we need to learn to do our interactions with parents with questions rather than statements if we want them actually to think through solutions—and if we want them to learn a new way of interacting. Note, the support worker used roleplay in place of imaging. Because of the interactive action in roleplay, the right cortices—not just the verbalization areas of the brain—are being activated.

Overactive Therapist

As child professionals we want so much to improve the home situation. If the parents would just recognize this, if they would just do what we suggest—their child would have a chance to settle and everyone would be happier and the temper tantrums, both the child's and the parent's, would decrease. All the books we have read and workshops we have attended have given us multitudinous ideas—ideas we want to share. The danger is that we may flood the parent.

Ronald, Dorothy, & Mica, 12 Years Old

> **REFERRAL:** Ronald and Dorothy had self-referred themselves to a local family service organization. They were referred for some parental support and parenting ideas.
>
> **BACKGROUND INFORMATION:** They have three birth children (ages 13–18) and adopted Mica five years ago. She had come from a very abusive birth home and then had experienced a series of very strict and rather demeaning foster homes. She has received several years of therapy and, while her tantrums have settled, she continues to experience high fright related to public places, family gatherings, and her mother, Dorothy, leaving.

FAMILY SUPPORT WORKER: *You have done so much for Mica* [Validates]. *Let's see if we can problem-solve some of the situations that are still feeling out of control.*

SESSION: As Dad and Mom describe Mica's reactions in various situations, the support worker realizes that Mica may be highly sensitive to noise and suggests they purchase some ear phones for her. The support worker talks about the positive effect that has been found for children listening on ear phones to Mozart (Tomatis, 1991). When Mom talks about what happens when they go to family gatherings, the support worker recognizes that Mica feels unsafe at these gatherings. The support worker suggests that, before they get out of the car, Mom could remind Mica that this is a safe group of people. When, during the gathering, Mom notices Mica becoming agitated, Mom could take Mica aside and again review the safety. For the distress related to Mica's upset each time Mom leaves, the support worker suggests Mom and Mica draw a comic strip of Mom going away and then coming back that Mica could look at both before Mom left and when she was gone. Dad then starts talking about how Mica purposefully holds onto her anger and releases it on him when he comes home. Support worker notes how Mica is not doing this 'purposefully,' she is caught in some old pattern. The hour seems to just fly by.

RONALD: *Thank you so much, this has been so helpful—so much to do.*

FOLLOW-UP: *Ronald and Dorothy canceled their next session and did not reschedule.*

What went wrong? Our support worker's ideas were excellent, but it was just too much. This is a busy family—four children and one with very high needs. Maybe one or, at the most, two of those ideas would have been enough for one session. When there is too much to do, parents become overwhelmed. Then, when parents quite reasonably can't accomplish everything, they feel a sense of failure or guilt—both exhausting feelings that drain their ability to be available to Mica.

And, there is another problem with all this problem-solving. We have been talking about the importance of being aware of which part of the parent's brain is being activated. We need to be aware of our own brain functioning. When we are focused on problem-solving, our dorsal-lateral prefrontal cortex is very active. Parents need our medial prefrontal cortex—we need to practice mindfulness and mentalization. Parents need our attunement and our validation; they need us to be present with them. When we focus too much on problem-solving, we may miss being with the parent.

Parent Exhaustion

Raising children is exhausting. Raising a child who is distressed in some way—experiences anxiety or difficulty learning, has attention deficit hyperactivity disorder or autism, has been traumatized within or outside the family, has experienced a family breakup or parental distress, is engaging in destructive or withdrawal behaviors—is doubly exhausting. This exhaustion is often intensified by a feeling of failure for parents—what did they do wrong that the child is like this?

And the problems do not end there. A child with difficulties raises tension between parents. Often there is disagreement as to what is wrong, why it happened, and how it should be handled. Should there be more flexibility in discipline or less flexibility? In some families, both parents become overinvolved with the child and lose the connection between themselves; in other families, one parent becomes overinvolved and the other parent feels excluded. Marital stress is a frequent byproduct of child problems (Marshak & Prezant, 2007) and, in turn, creates even more exhaustion for the parents.

Not only may there be disapproval and antagonism coming from the one of the parents toward the other, a parent may experience considerable impatience and disapproval from teachers, day care providers, camp counselors, relatives, and from society in general. The judgmental looks and comments from total strangers can be hurtful and very upsetting.

Poverty, insecure or unsatisfying employment, single parenting, lack of friends or family support, personal mental health issues or addictions, anger with others or with life in general—so many things can add to a parent's exhaustion. While we may be able to connect parents to some other supports, we cannot solve these problems. What we can do is recognize how difficult and exhausting it has been to parent their child. We may not agree with how they are speaking to their child or how they treat their child, but we need to appreciate that they are still there and they are trying. If they were not trying, they would not be in our offices or us in their homes.

Exhausted parents need someone who believes not only that they want their child to have a happier, healthier experience but that, with very few exceptions, they want to be part of that positive experience. They need someone who believes their family will get better. And we can be that person.

"Sounds like a really hard week. How are you doing? Have you had any time to take a breath and notice that you actually got through the week?"

"I felt my body tensing just now as you described that situation. You must have felt tremendous tension when it was actually happening. [Breath] You and Joey both got through it, maybe not the way you wished—and we will continue trying to figure that out—but you got through it."

"When he gets like that it must be hard to remember how much he loves you and actually is feeling desperate to connect to you."

"That is so hard when other people are staring and don't understand. What were you able to do to reassure yourself?"

"Thank you for coming today. I admire all the effort you are making to help your child. It makes a difference."

Another form of exhaustion is discouragement—the feeling that things will never get better. Some parents bring their children to see us after the child has already seen several other support people and there has been no substantial improvement. They have had to tell the story of child dysfunction/family dysfunction so many times, they have had to spend hours in waiting rooms and in consultation rooms, they attended parent-teacher interviews until they were so discouraged they just did not go anymore. They may be in our office not because they think things can get better but because protective services or the court or social pressure has pushed them there.

Josie & Serina, 10 Years Old

> **REFERRAL:** Josie has called for an appointment at the insistence of protective services.
>
> **BACKGROUND INFORMATION:** She tried living with Serina's father for a year after Serina was born, but there was constant yelling and considerable pushing. After Serina's father started to use drugs in the home, Josie moved out with Serina. Since that time Josie has had numerous boyfriends, but none of them actually lived in the home. As she said, she was keeping Serina safe. Josie stated that she was able to manage Serina's rather bizarre behaviors when Serina was little, but once Serina entered school, teachers complained and insisted that Josie take Serina for help. They had gone to four different counselors or other support people over the last four years and now they were here.

JOSIE: *Just to let you know—I don't really expect anything from this. We've been to all sorts of professionals and nothing has changed. Serina is a bit bizarre, and that's how she is, nothing's going to change that. It's her father's fault, but of course he is off having a great time with his new family and I am stuck with his daughter.*

SCHOOL COUNSELOR: [Resists urge to explain how she thinks she can help.] *Sounds like you are really exhausted* [Attunes].

JOSIE: *Putting it mildly!! Now let's get on with this so I can go home. It's really expensive having to miss work hours.*

SCHOOL COUNSELOR: [Resists urge to problem-solve Mom having to miss work hours.] *I'm impressed that you are here* [Compliments]. *You have not found the previous counselors helpful for you or Serina, and yet you are here. I realize that protective services has put pressure on you to come, but I appreciate that you decided to come.*

JOSIE: *Yeah, well, I'm here. What now?*

SCHOOL COUNSELOR: *Tell me a bit about Serina and tell me what it is like to be Serina's mom.*

Our counselor is resisting the urge to justify counseling and the urge to problem-solve. Josie says she doesn't want protective services peering over her shoulder, but she is clearly invested in Serina being bizarre. If one difficulty is resolved, another will occur. Our counselor is also resisting focusing on Josie even though it is clear that Josie is feeling needy. Josie would likely reject any direct focusing on herself—she is there only because of Serina. Our counselor focuses on appreciating Josie. For Josie to be able to shift to a position of supporting Serina, she is going to need to experience some supporting herself.

SCHOOL COUNSELOR: [Remembers importance of ending on a positive note.] *Josie, I appreciate your coming today. Serina is certainly a handful* [Validates] *and you have done so much to keep her life stable* [Compliments]. *It is you, not us, the professionals, who make the difference for Serina. And as we finish today, knowing how exhausting it can be to be Serina's mother, I would like to take just a few minutes to breathe quietly together. . . . I look forward to seeing you with Serina next week.*

As our counselor ends the session, she continues to focus on appreciating Josie. It is tempting for her to talk about how she is hoping this counseling experience is going to be different, but she is aware that that may push Josie into defending her belief that professionals cannot help. Rather, the counselor offers an experience of calming—a very limited experience, but each experience stimulates new neuronal synapses and connections. If she had asked Josie to picture a positive time with Serina—an excellent intervention with a parent who is not as negative toward her child—Josie would likely have resisted. We must respect a parent's discouragement and her lack of belief in therapy.

Summary

To help parents with negative parenting patterns, we need first to recognize the habits, beliefs, and emotions that may be underlying these patterns. We do not want to challenge the habits, beliefs, or emotions but rather help the parents identify them, where they came from, and how the parent wants to be with their child in the future. We always want to find some area of agreement with the parent—parenting their child is really difficult, a behavior like biting needs to be stopped, living in a community with different cultural beliefs is challenging. This gives us a healthy place from which to start our work together.

In our discussion we highlighted the importance of using questions, of complimenting the parent, of giving apologies, and of not trying to do too much all at once. We talked again about the importance of helping a parent calm before discussing something difficult and of shifting between analytical (more left brain dorsal-lateral prefrontal activity) and emotional (more right brain orbital-medial prefrontal activity) processing to help the parent stay focused with us.

And then we looked at some of the blockages to more positive parenting—trigger reactions, temperaments that differ from their child's, parents' need to defend themselves and their vulnerabilities, and their exhaustion. Through dialogs between our child professional and the parents, we explored ways to move through these blockages.

Even more challenging is working with adoptive parents. This shall be explored in the next chapter.

Chapter 6—Points to Remember

- Wondering about a behavior is more likely to lead to change than criticizing a behavior.
- Many negative parenting patterns are unconscious (implicit); we need to make them conscious or explicit.
- To change old patterns, we need to create new neuronal networks in the brain areas holding the old patterns.
- Apologies are important for maintaining connection between ourselves and the parent.
- When exploring new areas such as emotions or body sensations, alternate with conversation more within the parent's comfort area (perhaps analytical left brain activity) in order to avoid a defensive reaction from the parent.
- The ability to be creative is a necessary qualification for a child professional.

CHAPTER 7

When the Home is an Adoptive Home
Sandra Baita

During the previous chapters, we have been focusing on the importance of helping parents understand the role their experience of being parented has on their current parenting. When working with adoptive parents, there is even more these parents need to become aware of.

The adopted children and their adoptive parents that we talk about in this chapter have experienced varied and serious trauma. Fortunately, this is not what many adopted children experience. What we will focus on in Chapter 7 is the importance of the child professional gaining a clear understanding of the different dynamics that do exist in the adoption relationship. With this understanding we are able to provide more support to both the child and the parent, whether we are a child support worker, a teacher, a therapist, or an adoption social worker. This understanding will help us appreciate and attune with the parents' concerns, their complaints, their fears, and their needs.

In this chapter we will cover some specific aspects of the experience of adoption, both from the perspective of the child's story and from the perspective of the adoptive parents' expectations, that can help child professionals attune to parents. We will highlight what kind of information, different from what has been covered so far in this book, will be relevant for our work, and how to help parents understand the uniqueness of their child's emotions, behaviors, and relationship to their past. Aspects regarding disorganized attachment and how the child's behavior can disorganize parents, or even trigger disorganized attachment patterns in parents themselves, will be covered.

At the end of the chapter, we will take a brief look at working with foster parents. While many of the difficulties that can arise when working with parents who have adopted children are similar to those that occur with parents who are fostering children, there are several unique situations, and we will discuss some of those.

The Meeting between the Child's Previous Experience and Parents' Expectations

Adoption is an encounter between two different interpretations of 'love.' Adoptive parents are convinced that adopting a child is an act of love. *"Love will be enough; love will cure anything; having a lot of love to give will suffice"* are common thoughts and beliefs about adoption shared by most adoptive parents. At a first glance, it seems easier to adopt a baby or a newborn. The younger the child, the easier it will be for the baby/child to adapt and bond to the new family and the family to bond to the child.

But what happens when the adopted child is already 1, 2, or even older? What happens when the child comes with a radically different experience of what a family is from the adoptive family, this adoptive family that is to imprint a new, healthier and safer experience on his brain and body? Most of the time these children come with a negative experience of parenting: Most of them have learned that living within a family means abuse, neglect, violence, abandonment, or loss. Because of these early learnings, they will start relating to their new parents based on the internal working models (see Chapter 3) of insecure attachment they have already developed. Their brains do not recognize the new parents as 'new=different,' but rather as 'new=the same.' For these children, 'love' means something quite different from what it means to the parent. Based on their previous experience, to be loved by someone could even be potentially dangerous. This is a very different understanding of 'love' than that held by the parent.

On the other side, adoptive parents bring into their parenting not only their own stories and previous experiences, but also their own specific expectations about adoption. Maybe they expected to adopt a newborn or a toddler, instead of an older child; maybe they expected to adopt a single child instead of a child with his siblings; maybe they expected to adopt a 'healthy' child instead of a child with severe behavioral problems. In most situations these expectations are changed by the reality of adoption—maybe they have waited so long for a child, and *this* child is their only chance to become parents; maybe they feel selfish if they reject a child who has been waiting for a family, and so they go ahead and adopt a child or children different from their original expectations.

Most of the time parents can 'imagine' that the children and teens they adopt—especially older ones—have had complicated, troubled, and sad events in their lives. However, the real story of these children may be beyond what they have imagined. The more they come to know about the child or youth, the more they feel overwhelmed. This may lead them to reconsider adoption or even—in some cases—to deny the truth of the child's experience.

During the first meetings between the child and parent, often the child's most disruptive behaviors—defiant, overtly aggressive, or sexualized—are hidden from the parents. Parents often describe their first impression of their child as someone who has captivated them—"She was so polite and educated"; "He was so affectionate"; "He was so shy"; "She won us over when she first greeted us." In some situations, the parents may even have heard these positive comments from the professionals who were previously working with the child. Sometimes, feeling pressure to find a home for a child, professionals overemphasize positive qualities when introducing a child to potential parents.

When the child starts living with the new parents, the child quickly shifts to a different and more complicated child. Once in the home, the polite and educated girl becomes an aggressive and defiant girl; the affectionate child rejects any tenderness coming from the adoptive parents, and the shy boy detaches and distances himself from others. Parents understandably feel puzzled—what happened to their child? What has changed?

The parents were expecting some trouble, but not *this* kind of trouble and not *this* much. The parents ask, "*Why is he acting like this now that he has a family?*" They feel overwhelmed, tired, confused, and in despair. They may even regret having adopted this child. This is a feeling they struggle with while, at the same time, they are determined to love the child. Other parents don't give the adoption a second chance—they send the child back to the system. The parents may look for the worker involved in the adoption process, wanting to know why the child is now behaving in such a different way than they expected. They may feel embarrassed if the child behaves at school in negative ways such as stealing things from others. They are afraid teachers and other parents will judge them as bad parents. If they do take the child to therapy, they expect things to change quickly and feel frustrated and betrayed if change does not happen as soon as expected.

What other expectations do these parents have regarding the adoption of this child? For many parents, parenting this child means to give him everything he did not have and he deserves to have—shelter, food, clothes, toys, structure, routine, discipline, education, pleasure through different activities, an extended family. This will mean more love for the child, friends, and a place to belong. They likely think the child just needs some time to adapt to this new structure and do not want to overwhelm the child by adding therapy sessions. They see helping the child to adapt to his new life as their job, not that of outsiders. The parents want their child to be part of their normal life as soon as possible. And this is a good wish, a legitimate one. However, in trying to give these children a 'normal' life, parents might not know that for the child, this 'normal' life can only be assimilated slowly, piece by piece, as severely malnourished babies receive their milk—not with a bottle but rather with a teaspoon.

All child professionals can play a role in helping the adoptive parents accept their child. But first we need to understand how difficult that can be—accepting a child. This is not the child they had dreamed about, not the child they had counted on. We need to keep that in mind and to know that the parents cannot learn from us until we help them grieve the loss of the child they don't have and accept the child they do have.

John, Susan, & Patrick F., 5 years old

> **REFERRAL ISSUE AND BACKGROUND INFORMATION:** Patrick had been adopted by John and Susan at the age of 4. At the time of his adoption, he had been considered as delayed but had not been assessed for fetal alcohol syndrome (FAS). Following the adoption, he was assessed and was then diagnosed as having FAS and placed in a special education class for children with severe delays. The school suggested that a school behavioral specialist work with the parents at their home to teach them some strategies for child behavioral management. Although the parents clearly understood the

> strategies when the specialist was explaining and demonstrating them, the parents reported that they had chosen not to use any of the strategies.
>
> When the specialist reported this to the teacher, the teacher wondered if the parents had accepted the diagnosis of FAS. After all, that was not what they planned on when they adopted a child. If they did not accept the diagnosis, it made sense that they didn't accept the strategies. The teacher invited John and Susan to come in for a meeting.

JOHN: *My wife and I want Patrick to have a normal life. He went through a very difficult time before living with us, and we don't want him to be treated as a different child only because of his past or that he was adopted. The specialist talked to us as if Patrick were retarded.*

TEACHER: *What a wonderful wish for Patrick.* [Attunes.] *He is fortunate to have you as his parents.* [Appreciates the parents.] *I understand that recently Patrick received a complete assessment.* [Although she knows the result of the assessment, she realizes that John and Susan being able to articulate the diagnosis will be difficult but necessary.] *What did they tell you after the assessment?*

JOHN: *Well, they gave us this label, "fetal alcohol syndrome," but he is just a little boy who has had some bad experiences, and we are going to make that better. We know the specialist is trying to help, but we are not going to treat him any differently than we would have before that label was put on him.*

TEACHER: *That is a very hard label to hear—that something happened to your son before you came into his life, and that you cannot change it.* [Validates.] *What do you—as parents—think Patrick needs?*

SUSAN: *We think he just needs some more time to adjust, that's all. Then he will settle down, and he will be able to learn and to behave.*

TEACHER: *Patrick has been living with you for over a year, am I right? Tell me some about his adjusting process to his new life with you both. How was he when he first went to live with you?*

JOHN: *Well, not too much different from now.*

SUSAN: *No, Honey, you don't remember. He had trouble falling asleep, he used to stumble a lot. This is no longer happening. . . . He is doing so much better now. . . .*

TEACHER: *That is definite progress, nice work on your part.* [Supports.] *Tell me, who referred your son to this special education class?*

JOHN: *Well, it was the social worker at the adoption agency. She said Patrick's mom was an alcoholic, and sometimes children coming from alcoholic mothers might need a special education program.*

When the Home is an Adoptive Home 183

TEACHER: *That must have been difficult to hear.*

JOHN: [Interrupts and smiles nervously.] *We swallowed it pretty quickly, we had to move on.*

TEACHER: [Turns to Susan.] *Mrs. F., I notice a lot of sadness in you as we talk about this.*

If a child professional who had received therapeutic training was working with Susan and John, they would pursue this feeling of sadness further. Given that a teacher does not have that training, she just notices and acknowledges that the feeling is there.

SUSAN: [After a brief silence . . .] *I'm not sure I have swallowed it. But there is nothing I can do now. He is our son. We accept him just as he is, but not the FAS. The FAS isn't important.*

TEACHER: *What is so important for Patrick is being accepted by you, his parents. And accepting a diagnosis like FAS is very hard. What you would never have wanted to have happen to your child's brain has already happened. And some of the negative brain functioning—like the fright when something happens now that reminds him of the past—can shift and change as he has good experiences with you. But some of the brain functioning—like the poor attention and focus—can be improved but not totally changed even with all your love and care. Because of the alcohol that went into his system in utero some of the brain wiring he needed never happened—that is really difficult! Sometimes I feel like society puts a lot of pressure on us as parents. We are expected to act so perfectly that it seems we are not allowed to feel tired or hopeless or angry. I hear you both talking about facing this diagnosis of your child, and I was thinking how many different feelings must have come up for you when given the FAS diagnosis. I'm wondering, did you receive any support at that time?*

JOHN: *The doctor talked to us about a support group for parents of children with FAS, but we didn't think we needed to talk to other parents. We needed to just get on with giving our child a good life.*

SUSAN: *I think we could have tried. I don't know, maybe going once or twice and see. But John thought that was like giving up before even trying.*

JOHN: [Talks to the teacher.] *Don't you think it is really discouraging to sit along with other couples sharing your child's difficulties? I don't need to know about others' struggles; this makes things look even worse. Patrick has spent four years of his life in an ordeal. Now he is our son. He will spend the rest of his life being our son. We will give him a normal life; we're gonna make it.*

TEACHER: [Takes a deep breath to steady herself—he is just not hearing her.] *I get your point, Mr. F., and you have a huge task at hand—giving a healthy life to a child who not only had four scary years but also nine months inside an* unhealthy womb. It's a big challenge! And I'm thinking it would be helpful to have someone 'translating' for the two of you which are the behaviors that come from his trauma and which are the behaviors coming from the FAS, and how the two of you with all the love and care for him can help him with each of those.

JOHN: *Well . . . I certainly want to help him. I just don't want to label him.*

TEACHER: *I think Patrick's experience—both before birth and after birth—is so far from what any of us wished, that sometimes it feels better just not to think about it.* [Validates.] *I'm wondering if you had the chance to talk about any of this with the specialist the school sent to your home?*

JOHN: *Well, not really. She came to our home, and she seemed to have a plan already established. She started saying "Kids with FAS . . . ." I don't like that approach. It is so distant; it is so what we do* not *want.*

TEACHER: *Makes sense. I could arrange for a meeting with her and you both here at the school; I would be more than glad to be part of that meeting and talk about what FAS means and what it does not mean. And most importantly, just as you two have been saying, it is not all of Patrick, he is a lot more than the FAS diagnosis. But we can help him with the difficulties he is having and the difficulties you and he are having together because of the FAS. I think we can all make a good team for Patrick.*

JOHN: *I think we could try. You seem to understand.*

So often we, as child professionals, feel so much pressure to get the work done, to sort things out as soon as possible, that we inadvertently forget that having a child with a negative diagnosis is very difficult for parents, and particularly for adoptive parents. Our teacher seems to understand this in that she does not start the meeting trying to convince parents about the need for them to work with the specialist on managing their child's behavior. She understands Patrick's parents are in denial; they want their child to have a normal life—be a normal child—and they think giving him time to adjust will be enough.

Our teacher talks instead about the challenges and difficulties of raising a child with problems coming from a story these parents did not create. She does not insist that they accept the diagnosis of FAS but does continue to talk about it. By engaging—not forcing—the parents in this conversation, she is helping them on the road to accepting FAS. Only after having both parents share with her a bit of their experience of learning about the FAS diagnosis does she come up with the idea of starting again with the school behavioral specialist. But now she adds a new perspective. She suggests she could be present at the meeting. For both John and Susan, the teacher's presence could be reassuring and supportive. The teacher has reframed the work as 'teamwork.' In doing so, she gives the parents the feeling of external support without being judgmental. John's final statement seems to support her reasoning—he *feels* she understands them—attunement in motion.

When the Home is an Adoptive Home 185

For parents to realize and accept that their child's wounds go beyond disruptive behaviors and dysregulated emotions, they will need a great deal of support. There may be a great deal of talking that they need to do as a way to process this information. And much of the talking needs to be between the parents, but that will not happen until an outside person, one of us, starts the conversation and lets them realize that talking, acknowledging, and just being with the reality of the child's world is a way to process their grief.

At some point it might be easier for parents to understand that alcohol during pregnancy has affected the child's brain circuitry. But how can we help parents understand that their child still feels in danger when there is obviously not danger in his or her surroundings? How can we help them understand that when their child has difficulty attaching to them, it is not because *of them*, but rather because the child has learned that closeness and care come with abuse and harm?

The neuronal patterns holding danger and distrust created early on in the brains of these children do not shift to safety and trust because the child has shifted places. This is a common misunderstanding of adoptive parents. Change in brain patterns requires many new experiences (Perry, 2006), and even more repetition when the new experiences are very different from the old experiences. Just as parents need lots of practice to change their own behaviors, so do children. They need many experiences to change their internal working model of themselves and of the world and then lots of practice to change their behavior patterns. While parents may use words related to safety, this is left hemisphere communication. The lack of safety—experiences these children suffered when with their first attachment figures—is held in the right hemisphere in implicit memory (Chapter 3, p. 62). Words alone will not be enough to help the child feel safe now. Until new safe experiences within a nontraumatizing family occur over and over again, the child will behave, interact, and relate based on his old experiences. Conflict between the child and parent easily arise and escalate. This is all too likely to confirm the child's expectation—"I won't be loved, I don't deserve love, I will only be abused"—and, in turn, reinforce his old behavior patterns. These behaviors increase the parents' frustration—towards the child and sometimes towards themselves as well.

This is usually the moment when either the parents seek help or are referred by the school or day care for some help from a child professional. Some come wanting the child support worker, social worker, doctor, or therapist to 'fix' their child. Others come hoping the professional can 'erase' the child's past. It may be their last effort before sending the child back. Others come recognizing that not only does the child need help, but also the entire family.

To help parents understand why their children behave and relate the way they do, it is necessary for the parents to understand the type of experiences the child has had. Many parents cannot even imagine the kinds of lives their children have had. Some parents may know the headline of the child's story but lack detailed information about their experiences. Sometimes they feel afraid of knowing too much and actively avoid receiving such information.

However, parents need some of this detailed information to help them recognize that their child's negative behaviors make sense; their child is not just a 'thief' or a 'liar.' Parents also probably need information about posttraumatic and dissociative symptoms[1] that most probably manifest through the child's expression of emotions and behaviors. Psychoeducation, however, does not fix parent-child interactions or create new ways to help the child engage in healthier relationships. Psychoeducation must be given with attunement and careful attention to the parent's situation as well as attention to emotional regulation if the parent is not to be left feeling either helpless or like a failure.

Jane & Max, 9 years old

> **REFERRAL ISSUE AND BACKGROUND INFORMATION:** Jane and her husband tried seven unsuccessful fertility treatments before deciding to adopt a child. Jane was reluctant to adopt a toddler or a child; she wanted to adopt a newborn that she could raise from the very beginning. It was her husband who convinced her to adopt Max two years ago. During Max's first year of life, his birth parents fought a great deal. When Max was 1 year old, his birth mother left the home, and shortly after that a neighbor reported the father to protective services as abusive and exploitative with his son. Over the next three years there was considerable involvement from social services, and when Max was 4 years old, he was taken into care. Three years later, Max was adopted by Jane and her husband. Following several recent instances of sexualized acting out, the school had requested that Max receive therapy.

JANE: *When I heard you say at our first session that many of Max's issues were probably related to the things he went through before living with us, I freaked out. I remember a few things from what the social worker at the adoption agency told us about his past. I remember that there was a moment in which I found myself trying not to listen to her. I recall having had nightmares that night, and when I woke up I felt we were just making a mistake. I never shared those feelings and thoughts with my husband; he was so happy with the adoption plan. When Max started misbehaving and we came here, I knew you would want to discuss his past. It was me, it is me, who doesn't want to discuss his past.*

THERAPIST: *I can imagine how hard it must have been for you to listen to what the social worker was telling you and your husband about Max's life.* [Takes a deep breath to allow time for the attunement with mother's feeling to settle in.] *I am wondering if you knew why knowing about his past was so important.*

JANE: *Well, I'm not saying his past is not important, I'm just saying I don't want to know about it. This is one of the reasons I wanted to adopt a newborn;*

they don't have too much past to know about. [Moves uncomfortably on the couch, avoids looking at the therapist.]

THERAPIST: [Notices Jane's shift out of her 'window of receptivity.'] *I'm sorry, I wasn't clear with my statement. I certainly realize you consider your son's past important. What I was thinking was that the adoption worker and I have not explained clearly why it is important for you and your husband, as parents, to know some of the specifics about Max's past. I would like to explore this idea with you, if that's okay, even before jumping into what Max experienced. How might it be helpful for you, for your parenting task, to know about Max's past?*

JANE: [Surprised.] *Well, I didn't think about this from that viewpoint. I guess Max's past has forged somehow his personality. Maybe, we could understand why he feels or acts in a particular way. It makes sense, I guess.*

THERAPIST: *Did Max ever talk to you or your husband about his past?*

JANE: *Oh God, yes! Every time we are at the table! It looks like he wants to upset us. And he tells in such a natural way the most horrible things! It's not that he says so many things, maybe something related to a place where he hid with his mom or that they didn't have enough food.*

THERAPIST: *And what do you or your husband do when he starts telling these things?*

JANE: *We let him talk a bit and then we change the subject. I feel so upset that sometimes I lose my appetite, but I don't let Max see me feeling this way.*

Although the therapist does not know much about Max's experiences from his past, there is a strong likelihood that Max's misbehavior is linked to those experiences with his biological parents. The link between this behavior and the past may be of great help in working toward changing it. And, of course, it would also be helpful for Jane and her husband, as Max's parents, to know and understand that link so they can actively support Max's work and effort in therapy. However, our therapist has a lot of work to do with Jane before talking about Max's past. Jane's fear of knowing about Max's past activates her limbic and autonomic nervous arousal system. As she shifts out of her 'window of receptivity,' she is not able to be emotionally available—prefrontal cortex activity—to Max when he is talking about his experiences. How are we able to be of help to Jane?

Gathering Information: What Do We Need to Know and How Can We Use This Information?

At the beginning of this chapter we stated that adoption is the encounter of two different ideas about love. The child's experience previous to the adoption will influence the adoption experience itself as much as the parents' previous experience of being parented will shape their parenting role. Thus, when working with adoptive parents, professionals need to have two important pieces of information: they need to know about the child's past, and they need to know the reason parents are adopting. Depending on the role and skill level of the professional, the information gathered will be extensive or less so.

Regarding the child's past, it will be important to know what kind of traumatic events the child experienced before being adopted, at what age and for how long they lasted, and who was the offender. This will give the child worker an idea of the possible extent of the trauma and the kind of behaviors that can be expected (i.e., sexualized acting out usually occurs when the child has experienced sexual abuse). It will also be of help to know how long the child stayed in foster care, if there were multiple placements, and the reason for them (Yehuda, 2016). This information gives the professional an idea of what type of obstacles the child is facing in terms of attaching to his new parents.

Now, let's see what we need to know about parents. We understand that the parents' parenting pattern will be affected not only by their own experiences of being parented but also by why and how they decided to adopt. Was the adoption decided on due to infertility issues, and, if so, how did they deal with the stress of that situation? Did both parents agree with the adoption, or was one of them reluctant at first? What were their differences? How did the reluctant parent change his/her viewpoint about adoption? Were they supported by their relatives/friends, or were there negative ideas about adoption? How did they deal with these negative opinions? If they were supported, what kind of support did they receive, and is this support still available?

We also need to know, as part of the information gathered about the reason for adoption, what were the parents' expectations of the adoption? How long had the parents been waiting to adopt a child? Do they have other children? Are these biological or adoptive children? What is the age difference between their biological children and the adoptive one/s? How did they talk with their other children about the arrival of the new—adoptive—sibling? Did they ever find themselves making comparisons between their biological and adoptive children? As discussed earlier, had they wanted a child who was different in some way from the child they received? How much information were they given on the child's past? And how much do they know about the behavioral or emotional distress the child was experiencing in relation to the adoption? Did the child or did the parents receive support, counseling, or therapy prior to the adoption? If so, did they find the support they received successful, insufficient, not helpful?

Gathering all this information will help us understand the level of anxiety and distress the parents experienced before and around the adoption process and how much of this anxiety and distress is still there. While understanding a parent's expectations is important in all work with parents, it is especially important in working with adoptive parents. When things do not work out as expected, adoptive parents may blame the birth parents, genetics, or even the child. Sometimes they blame themselves as well. Their motivation for remaining engaged in a support or therapeutic process with their child may be lower.

Jane & Max (Continued)

THERAPIST: *Jane, I would like to know what do you do when Max yells at you, "I hate you!" It would be upsetting.*

JANE: *Well, I try different things. Sometimes I count to 10, I breathe, I try not to react. Other times I go to another room of the house and just stay away from him. Then there are the times I cry. It's so unfair. I don't know why he yells those things at me! Does he hate me? Really? I don't think so, but I don't know what to do. Then Max comes to me and says "I'm sorry, Mommy!" He is so cute that I forget all the yelling, all the nasty words.*

At that point our therapist might have asked, "Why do you think he tells you this?" but avoided it in that it might have made Jane feel she had indeed done something to make Max hate her, that she was a failure, a bad mom. Instead she decides to validate Jane's feeling of being lost as to how she should respond to Max:

THERAPIST: *Yes, you are right. It's so different if you know, then you can be prepared and your mind doesn't boggle and get stuck with the thought, "This is because of me, I'm not doing things well."*

In our work with the parents, it can be helpful to ask them what would have helped them most at the time they adopted this child (for Jane and her husband this would have been two years ago). This question can help relieve the parent of guilt feelings and of feeling they are not adequate to the task of adopting. It may also help both them and us formulate a clearer idea of what they need from us now to help them.

THERAPIST: *If you could go back to the moment of the adoption, to the moment you and your husband brought Max home for the first time to live with you as a family, do you have an idea of what might have helped you then?*

JANE: *They told us he might have some 'adjusting problems' during the first few months. I didn't ask what kind of problems, and they didn't elaborate further. . . . Now I am thinking that when Max tells me he hates me, maybe it is because of what he has lived through before our family and not because of me, not because he feels my fears and reluctance around the adoption.*

Even though the referral issue was related to the parents' concerns about Max acting out sexually, it has become clear that there are attachment issues to be worked on before Max and Jane are going to feel secure enough to address the behavioral issue. The old cycle of Max yelling, "I hate you," Jane removing herself from him either emotionally or physically, Max saying he is sorry, and Jane then cuddling him needs to shift. Undoubtedly this cycle plays out in a number of different ways, and Max's fear of being left is reinforced. Our therapist decides to focus back on why it might be so important for Jane to know about her son's past—something she has been trying to avoid.

THERAPIST: *You have mentioned that now, knowing that Max's past experiences affect his present behavior, you are wondering if his yelling at you that he hates you, might, indeed, be because of his past. What things in his past do you think might make him yell at you like this?*

In this way, our therapist is helping Jane reflect on other reasons for Max's feelings and behaviors. In doing this, the therapist is helping Jane to mentalize (see Chapters 3 and 4). Our therapist is encouraging Jane to hold Max's mind within hers as a way to understand *his* motivations and how these motivations may be linked to his past experiences of being in a relationship with a parent. This recognition can help Jane move from the idea that *she* was the one who caused his reaction—triggering guilt and shame about herself, which caused her to involuntarily distance herself from Max's suffering—to the idea of something about the present parent-child relationship reminding him of his past and causing his reaction.

JANE: *Well, his birth mother abandoned him. This would have been so terrible for my little boy.* [Visibly touched, takes a deep breath.] *I can't understand how she did this.*

THERAPIST: [Takes Jane back to holding in mind Max's experience—mentalizing]. *I wonder how a child would relate to a new parent when his own birth parents abandoned him. Sounds like a very difficult task!*

JANE: *Yes! You are right! Do you think he feels like I will abandon him? I don't want him to feel like this.*

THERAPIST: *How do you think you could help Max feel you will stay with him?*

JANE: *I can tell him. . . . In fact, I've told him this several times. But it doesn't seem to work!*

THERAPIST: *Words go to a part of our brain that is somehow disconnected from the feelings and sensations of the past. The feelings and sensations from the past are held in another part of the brain, the one that reacts without knowing that things in the present are different.*

JANE: [Interrupts with some excitement in her voice. Her facial expression has changed.] *Do you mean that he doesn't really hate me because I was doubtful about adopting him?*

THERAPIST: *It sounds to me like Max has enough reasons in his past to have strong feelings towards a 'mom' figure in his present. He may feel afraid to become attached to you because he is afraid of abandonment. Because of*

> his early experiences, he is afraid of attaching, and he is also afraid of losing you; that's why he runs towards you to ask for your forgiveness. (See later discussion on phobia of attachment loss, p. 209.)

At this point our therapist acknowledges Jane's need for reassurance. Jane is very anxious and needs confirmation that she is not the real cause of Max's hatred and hostility. The therapist provides a short piece of information—left hemisphere processing. In that way, the therapist approaches the issue Jane has been strongly avoiding—her son's past and how this past has the key to understanding the way he behaves as he does today. Even though the sexual acting out—the referral issue—has not yet been addressed, the link the therapist is making between Max's past experience of a 'mom' with his now relating to a 'mom' is crucial for allowing attachment and bonding to happen. Max's experience of being parented has been one of abandonment, and Jane's expectations about being an adoptive parent were related to raising a child 'with no past.' The information gathered by the therapist at the beginning related to Max's past and Jane and her husband's expectations about adoption and the experiences surrounding the process of adoption is extremely helpful for understanding what is needed to build a more secure attachment. Without this, any further work towards changing Max's sexual acting out would be unsuccessful. A more secure attachment will provide both Jane and Max with the strength to work through and resolve issues around sexualized behavior.

Helping Adoptive Parents

Attach to Their Children

In Chapter 4 we talked about the importance of the attachment relationship when working with children and parents. When working with traumatized children, the work with the attachment system gains even more relevance, as the work with Jane and Max has shown us. These children were traumatized *within* the attachment system. They have learned to stay tuned to signals of what Blaustein and Kinniburgh (2010) refer to as 'relational danger'—the danger of being harmed again within a caretaking relationship. Helping the adoptive parent manage her own affect responses and attune to her child's story, needs, and behavioral manifestations and their meaning is essential for building a new attachment relationship for these children. But why is this so important?

We know from the trauma field that an adoptive child coming from a traumatic/traumatizing environment will display a consistent pattern of dysregulation across several domains: emotions, somatic responses, behaviors, ability to attend, ability to relate to others (Baita, 2012; Spinazzola et al., 2013). They may have learned that 'not feeling anything' is self-protective in that it avoids a flood of emotions they are unable to manage, and they may also have learned that 'feeling everything' keeps them alert of possible dangers around them. They may go back and forth between feeling nothing and feeling too much. The balance between these two patterns of hypoarousal and hyperarousal is emotional regulation, which seldom develops in children growing up in traumatizing environments. The importance of emotional regulation is that it enables the child to adjust to disruptive external and internal experiences. In normal nontraumatic development, an infant's emotional regulation is first achieved through outside regulation (the presence of an adult protective figure who regulates him- or herself). This calming is then achieved through the presence of a transitional object (i.e., a stuffed toy or blanket) and then to the child's own system of self-regulation. The big challenge for adoptive parents will be to become the secure and safe attachment figures these children never had. Love and/or therapy alone cannot teach a child self-regulation. No child can improve his self-regulation skills without the attuned presence of a self-regulated and caring caregiver. If a child did not have that in infancy when he needed and deserved it, he will need it once he has finally been adopted. And adoption by itself does not provide self-regulation skills; the parents self-regulating and then attuning to the child does teach self-regulation skills.

Parents who can self-regulate their own internal states will be more able to attune to their child's needs and soothe her when overaroused or engage her when underaroused. The new experience for the child of being soothed by an adult who will not harm her will, in turn, enhance bonding. The repetition over time of this new experience of soothing creates a new attachment experience for the child.

Blaustein and Kinniburgh (2010), in their work with traumatized children,[2] highlight the importance of caregivers managing their own affect, attuning to their children's needs, and being able to respond consistently to their children as the three core aspects of building attachment. They suggest specific exercises that help parents achieve these goals. These exercises highlight experiencing through interactive activities, which fits with our proposal throughout this book of involving the whole parent's brain—right hemisphere as well as left hemisphere.

If we are to ask a caregiver (birth parent or adoptive parent) to provide soothing for the child, we need to be sure the parents know how to calm themselves. How do they manage their affect in general situations, how do they manage their own affect when facing the most challenging and complicated situations with their children (especially their disruptive behaviors)? Whenever we find the parent is having a difficult time managing her own affective states, it will be important to help her self-regulate (see Chapter 5, p. 113).

As discussed earlier, adoptive parents' own self-regulation will be key in their role as the new regulators of their child's affective states. These skills will be especially important when facing the child's anger—anger the parents may misinterpret as directed toward them (remember Jane)—or the child's longing for his past (as we will see later in this chapter)—a feeling adoptive parents often misinterpret as a child's lack of connection, not loving them, or 'ingratitude' towards his new 'better' life. Parents' self-regulation is necessary if they are to be able to provide calming and soothing to their dysregulated child. It is a key component for the parents to be able to attach in a secure pattern to their child and to help the child attach in a secure way to his parents.

Attachment also requires the parent to attune with the child (Chapter 5, pages 107–111). However, as Blaustein and Kinniburgh (2010) assert, the child's trauma-derived behaviors—inability to communicate needs, inability to identify and manage emotions, and use of maladjusted behaviors to express needs and emotions—challenge even the most skilled parent's attunement. Developing reflective thinking and compassion toward self and toward the child can help adoptive parents attune to their child.

Reflecting upon the child's behaviors, the patterns underlying the behaviors, and how these patterns come from their past experiences—not actions *willingly and consciously acted against* the new parents—will help parents not react against the child. A reaction against himself is what the child expects from his previous experiences. It fits with his bruised internal working model of self—*"I'm bad, I don't deserve being loved, I will get hurt"*—and the world—*"They will hurt me as my birth parents did"; "I can trust no one."* Parents engaging in reflective thinking are encouraged as we, in our work—as a teacher, a social worker, or a therapist—engage in reflective thinking with parents. This skill can also be developed and encouraged through brief mindfulness exercises with the parent (see example later). But first we need to help parents understand their children's emotions and behaviors.

Understand Their Child's Emotions and Behaviors

Some adopted children come from abusive and neglectful environments. There are several things they may feel angry about—the abuse they suffered, the unmet needs, the separation from their birth family, school, and neighborhood. Even though the family may have been abusive and neglectful, we need to remember that this was the child's place in the world, and this was his first attachment. Children may feel angry at the judicial system for what it did (separating them from their birth parents) or for what it did not do (speed up the adoption). They may feel angry towards foster parents and foster placements, they may feel angry towards previous—failed—adoptive families, and they may feel angry at their current adoptive parents because they did not adopt them sooner.

How will these children display their anger?—through outbursts, stealing, rejecting, defying, controlling, manipulating, acting out (Moreno, 2011). And whom are they going to address their anger to?—mostly their adoptive family. Why? Because they do not want to risk attaching to other people who might abuse them, neglect them, hurt them. They will act out with their adoptive parents the attachment patterns learned from their previous experiences, not because they want to but because these are the patterns held within their brains, these are the patterns that helped them survive the ordeals of previous attachment traumas. These attachment patterns helped them regulate their approach to and avoidance of the early dangerous attachment figures.

This explanation sounds very logical for us as child professionals, especially for those of us who have received trauma training, but it is far more difficult for adoptive parents to understand. They immediately ask, "But why is he acting like this with me? I'm not going to hurt him! Doesn't he see that life has changed, that he is safe now, that things are really different from then?" The answer is, unfortunately, simple: "He understands only what he has experienced." Understanding for the child is not about 'knowing,' but rather about 'experiencing' something. In order for this to happen, parents need to understand that lecturing the child is less important than *being with* the child, *accepting* the child, *validating* the child, and *attuning to* the child. And we need to remember that for the parents to be able to do this *our* lecturing the parent is less important than being with the parent, accepting the parent, validating the parent, and attuning to the parent. We need to do for the parent what we want them to do for the child.

Affective states in children can only be soothed through a loving, calming, and reassuring presence—this is the primary feature of a secure attachment. Fear is better relieved through a tender hug (right hemisphere to right hemisphere communication) rather than an explanation. A parent's fear is better relieved through thoughtful listening and attuning than an explanation. And our job will be to help the parents experience that which we want them to offer to their child. Along with this, we will want to help them understand the child's emotions and behaviors—where they are coming from and how to attune to them.

Rose, Chris & Patricia, 11 years old

REFERRAL ISSUE: Rose and Chris sought therapy for their oldest adoptive child due to her lying and stealing behavior. Before getting married, both of them had attended a group that worked with people in disadvantaged conditions. When they learned they were unable to have children of their own, they decided to adopt a child and stated that they were not scared about the story behind the child they would adopt. They had, before the adoption, asked for the records of the case and read them and, therefore, knew many of the situations the three siblings had experienced. Rose and Chris were able to report a timeline of the different traumatic events their children had suffered.

BACKGROUND: Patricia was the oldest of three siblings who were adopted two years earlier by Rose and Chris. Patricia had lived with her drug addict mom and two siblings, moving in and out of shelters until age 5. Patricia and her siblings were taken into care and placed with a foster family, where she was sexually abused. They were then placed with another foster family until she and her siblings were adopted.

THERAPIST: *Rose, you were talking about Patricia's anger. You said she was angry all the time. That would be so difficult for you and Chris.* [Attunes and validates.] *Could you give me some examples? What is she angry with?*

ROSE: *Everything and everybody. She is angry with her siblings, she is angry with my family, she is angry with me, with the judge, and with her biological mother.*

CHRIS: *She doesn't want us to refer to her birth mother as her biological mother. She claims we should call her by her name.*

When the Home is an Adoptive Home 195

ROSE: *We disagree with that. Her biological mother was a poor young woman with a very sad history. She was abandoned by her own mother, she was forced into prostitution; I can understand that she was unable to handle having children of her own.*

THERAPIST: *Yes, this is probably the case.* [Takes a breath.] *I'm curious, what do you do when Patricia says she wants you to refer to her birth mom by her name?*

ROSE: *We tell her she should be more empathic, she should understand her mom didn't want to hurt her or her siblings, it was just she couldn't handle them. Her mom wasn't as lucky as Patricia and her siblings, because no one adopted her.*

THERAPIST: *And what's Patricia's reaction to your words?*

CHRIS: *She gets worse. She insults Rose.*

THERAPIST: *And what about you, Chris? Does Patricia turn against you?*

ROSE: [Interrupts with evident discomfort.] *I'm her target. She adores her father, or at least she says she does.*

CHRIS: *I don't know if she adores me, but she really seems to dislike Rose.*

THERAPIST: [Notices Rose's discomfort and movement out of the 'window of receptivity' and slows down the conversation with some attunement.] *It must be really upsetting for you, Rose, to feel that you are the target of your daughter's anger. Do you have any idea of why this might happen?*

ROSE: [Continues in an agitated tone.] *It's easy. Kids always turn against the parent they spend more time with. My husband works all day, and when he gets back home, I only tell him the most relevant things of the day. I am with the three kids the whole day. And Patricia is very jealous of her siblings. She wants me to focus my attention only on her.*

Rose and Chris are very well-informed parents. As opposed to Jane, Max's mother, they were willing to know all the facts; they were able to explain to the therapist detailed information about the things Patricia and her siblings had been exposed to. Yet connecting these facts with Patricia's behavior and mood had not happened. Rose's interpretation of Patricia's anger toward her because she is the parent spending more time with the children makes our therapist wonder what Rose did with all the information she knew about Patricia's past. Is there anything in Rose's background blocking this understanding? Is she feeling defensive, observed, judged as a mother? These are questions arising in our therapist's mind while thinking how to address efficiently Rose's anxiety related to Patricia. Besides the stealing and lying behavior of her daughter, she is informing us that the relationship between the two of them is highly conflictual. Rose and her husband came looking for help with their daughter's disruptive behaviors. They want these behaviors to stop, 'because they are unacceptable.' And they are right. However, are Rose and Chris ready to understand the connection between these behaviors and Patricia's past? Can Rose understand why Patricia is so angry towards her birth mom and apparently toward her adoptive mom as well? Is there any road to follow to help these parents start to connect all this information?

THERAPIST: *Rose, would you please tell me a little bit more about Patricia taking things and telling stories?*

ROSE: *I don't know which of the two behaviors is the worst one. She lies about her life in a way that is puzzling for everyone. She once said at school that I had cancer! When we confronted her about this, she denied she had said such a thing. If we confront her about something missing, she denies having anything to do with that. And later we find whatever was missing in her bedroom. Even then she keeps saying she has nothing to do with it.* [Softens her tone of voice.] *I understand she might lie about her life because it's better to create a fantasy around it rather than remembering the awful things she lived. But the stealing, I really can't understand that.*

THERAPIST: *I can understand . . . this must be really upsetting.*

ROSE: [Interrupts.] *It's more than upsetting, it's outrageous! I don't want a thief in my home! I don't want her to be such a bad example for her siblings!*

THERAPIST: [Feels the tension tightening in her stomach, breathes in and out, and notices Chris with his head down. Is he feeling and thinking the same way Rose does? Wonders where Chris thoughts are going—to Patricia's behavior or to Rose's feelings? She needs to phrase a very open question so she does not direct his answer.] *Chris, I was wondering how you feel about all of this?*

CHRIS: *Of course, I disagree with Patricia's behavior, but I think Rose is being so harsh. I don't think Patricia is already a thief; we have argued about this. Rose thinks I'm too soft. The most perplexing fact is that she steals money to buy gifts for us!*

ROSE: *These are not gifts; she is trying to buy our love!* [Crying.] *I'm such a horrible person, I feel like I don't want her around me.*

Now we have more information. The behavior these parents are concerned about is developing within the attachment system—their daughter steals from *them* to buy gifts *for them*. But these parents are only able to see the behavior, quite isolated from any other facts. They are worried about the present (for Rose, Patricia *is* already a thief) and the future (for Chris, Patricia *might become* a thief) but are not connecting this to their daughter's past—where did Patricia learn to steal, and what experiences made her feel that she had to give gifts to have their love? The anger in Rose's statement lets us know that some attachment issues need to be addressed as soon as possible in order to help Rose be the supportive but firm, attuned parent Patricia needs.

Rose is very angry toward Patricia, and it seems like she will not be open to understanding the meaning of Patricia's behavior—either the stealing or the anger towards her birth mom and her present mom—until some connection can be made between past experience and present affective state and displayed behavior. Rose's rage towards Patricia (*she is a thief*) has led to a feeling of self-hatred (*I'm a horrible person*). Our therapist can try a brief exercise of self-compassion meditation and loving-kindness to help Rose gain some perspective and sooth her emotions.[3] Self-compassion means to be kind to ourselves when confronted with our own personal failures and inadequacies (Neff & Dahm, 2015). Practicing self-compassion and loving-kindness opens the door to be compassionate towards others' failures. As Rose is able to be kinder to herself, she will be able to be kinder and more understanding in her judgments towards Patricia. We need to be careful in explaining to parents that being kind does not mean accepting the behavior but rather accepting their child as she is, even with this 'failure.' For parents who have adopted older children, this is a very important step. They need to accept a child with a story previous to their existence within the new family.

Before parents can feel kindness and understanding for their child, they need first to experience both kindness and understanding for themselves.

THERAPIST: *How sad it is for you being caught in this situation. Sometimes we feel so frustrated that we jump from feeling angry towards our kids to feeling angry towards ourselves for feeling that way. I'm sure you want Patricia to be better. I'm sure we will find the meaning of Patricia's behavior, because there certainly is some meaning in what she is doing. But for now, what if we try to see if it is possible to stay for a moment with this unease you are feeling . . . just noticing without trying to change anything . . .*

ROSE: *Sounds weird . . . what do you mean "without trying to change anything"? I don't really like to feel this way . . .*

THERAPIST: *I hear what you are saying, Rose. But you know what? Sometimes the more we try to change what we feel, the bigger it becomes! The harder we try to avoid something, it does not disappear, and when it comes back we find ourselves feeling exactly the same way. I was thinking of trying a brief exercise called "loving-kindness" . . . It's about spending a moment being kind to ourselves and our feelings just as they are at this moment. What do you think?*

ROSE: *I guess I could try.*

THERAPIST: *OK . . . we will start by sitting in a very comfortable position, taking good care of our body, releasing the tension, breathing in and out. Try to stay with this unease you are feeling and see how it feels in your body. Now* say to yourself, "this hurts," . . . take a breath . . . stay with this feeling as it feels in your body. Now say to yourself, "I'm not alone. We all struggle with our lives." Now could you put your hands on your chest, feel the warmth of your hands around your heart. Now say to yourself, "May I be kind to myself."

Our therapist could also have said "Say to yourself 'May I be patient' or 'May I forgive myself' " depending on which words best fit the situation she is working on with the parent.

Neff and Dahm (2015) state that self-compassion has three elements: mindfulness (being aware of the negative experience and the feelings surrounding it without trying to change them or avoid them), common humanity[4] (acknowledging the universal quality of suffering), and self-kindness (giving ourselves a kind, warm, and understanding gaze instead of ignoring or harshly judging our inadequacies and failures). The practice of mindfulness helps our brain shift from a reactivity mode to a reflective mode (see Chapter 3). The practice of loving-kindness helps our brain shift from a resentful mode to an accepting one. Our therapist is using Rose's acceptance of her own suffering and that of others as a way to build closeness between Rose and Patricia. While doing this exercise, the therapist may want to include Patricia in the practice:

THERAPIST: [Adds a few words after having Rose say *"I'm not alone in my suffering . . . we all have struggles in our lives." "Patricia is also struggling with her life."*] *Now, can you put your hands on your chest, feel the warmth of your hands around your heart? Now say to yourself, "May I be kind to myself." . . . And now gently open your eyes, giving yourself a moment to come back to our conversation.*

Understanding the parent's experience with this exercise is an important part of it. It lets us know what adjustments should be made when repeating the exercise.

THERAPIST: *How do you feel now, Rose?*

ROSE: *The most striking part of this exercise was the part in which you said Patricia is also struggling with her life. Maybe she IS trying to communicate something and she doesn't know how to do it in a good way. She needs to learn, and I need to learn.*

However, these insights might not be a result of the exercise:

THERAPIST: *How do you feel now Rose?*

ROSE: *Better, I guess. . . . Before this exercise I thought I didn't even want to talk to her when we get back home. I feel I can talk to her now. Keeping some distance, of course.*

THERAPIST: *This seems to be a good start. Feeling a little less angry will give you some room to think more clearly about what you want to do and how you want to do it. When we are caught by our emotions, we can't decide what to do. Our emotions make the decision.*

ROSE: *A little bit less angry. . . . Yes, this is how I feel right now.*

THERAPIST: *Let's see if it is possible to stay with this feeling for just one more moment. You don't have to do anything, just observe. . . .*

ROSE: *It's easy here with you. At home, I don't think I could.*

THERAPIST: *Yes, you are right, it is easier here. But for now let's just stay with what is going on right here, right now.*

For now, the target of the therapist intervention has been the intense anger Rose has been feeling towards Patricia because of the stealing. This intense emotion certainly prevents Rose from approaching her daughter, who, in turn, will read her mother's response as confirmation of what she already expects, "Mom doesn't like me, she doesn't love me." With this exercise, Rose has been able to slow down the intensity of her feeling. Now, the therapist may see if it is possible to go a little further and use the same kind of exercise, but now including Patricia.

THERAPIST: *Rose, I would like to try another exercise with you, one that might help us understand a little bit of Patricia's anger. I would like you to bring to your mind a moment of distress, it can be a current situation or even a situation from your childhood or your adolescence, maybe one in which you felt upset or angry. Try to bring this moment to your mind right now and see what emotions come up while you remember the situation. Where in your body are you feeling these emotions? . . . Let yourself stay with these emotions and how they feel in your body for a moment.*

ROSE: *What comes to my mind is the first time I knew Patricia had stolen money from my purse. I can still feel the anger.* [Rubs her chest.]

THERAPIST: *Try to see if it is possible for you to stay with that feeling in your chest for a moment; try not to change it or erase it. Now bring your hands on your chest and see if you can feel the warmth of your hands around your heart and try to say these words to yourself, "May I be peaceful. May I be free of suffering."*

ROSE: *Do you mean that I have to forgive her for what she did?*

THERAPIST: *No, this is not about forgiveness. For now, we are just trying to bring some loving-kindness to you, seeing if it is possible for you to send warmth and kindness to your own suffering. We are not trying to change anything right now.*

ROSE: *It feels good, having some peace.*

THERAPIST: *Sure, we all need some peace in the middle of the storm; we are all human beings, we all have moments of pain and despair. This is something we all share. This is human experience. Now I would like you to bring to your mind a picture of Patricia in a moment of distress for her, maybe a moment during which she was already living with you and Chris, maybe a moment of her years before she knew you.*

ROSE: [Cries quietly.] *I have always tried to imagine what it was like for her to live on the streets. She was just a baby!*

THERAPIST: *Try to stay with the emotion that comes with this picture of your daughter wandering on the streets as a child. Remember it was before she met you and Chris. Try to stay with that picture in your mind's eye and bring your hands to your chest, try to feel the warmth of your hands in your heart and see if it is possible for you to send this little Patricia some loving-kindness, saying words like "May you be safe. May you be peaceful."*

ROSE: *I'm her mom now. She will always be safe with me.*

THERAPIST: *Yes, she is no longer on the streets, but she* still *needs to learn deep inside that you are her mom and she is safe now with you.*

ROSE: *I want her to feel safe.*

THERAPIST: *Try to stay with that wish you have for her for a little while, having in your mind a picture of Patricia now being your daughter. And send to her loving-kindness through these words, "May you be safe. May you be free of suffering." . . . Now let's try something else. Try to bring to your mind a moment when you and Patricia were angry toward each other. You don't have to remember the reason, just the feeling of anger toward her and knowing she is feeling the same toward you. Remember she is struggling with this feeling as much as you are with yours. Try to stay with that feeling for a moment and see if it is possible for you to send loving-kindness to both of you, saying words like, "May we both be peaceful. May we both be kind to ourselves. May we both accept ourselves as we are."*

ROSE: *Wow. That was so intense. I feel there is so much work to do with her. And with us!*

THERAPIST: *Yes! Being a parent is a full-time job! And you and Chris have been Patricia's first experience of having parents able to take care of her. She spent so many years without knowing what that was like.*

ROSE: *Yes! I've never thought about this in the way you describe it. But, how are all these things we are doing here going to prevent her from stealing?*

THERAPIST: *This is a very wise question. Why do you think Patricia takes money to buy gifts for you?*

ROSE: *As a way to show her gratitude towards us for having adopted her? Is she trying to win our heart? I don't know. I really don't know. Oh my*

God! Now I remember something I read in her files! When she was on the streets with her birth mom, this woman sent her to steal money for food so they could have something to eat! This is where she learned that misbehavior!

Now Rose seems more open to understanding that her daughter's behavior is a learned one within a past relationship with her birth mom. The misbehavior is no longer seen isolated from the context that created it:

ROSE: *I would like to tell her I now understand why she did this. Do you think that could be helpful?*

THERAPIST: *Well, it sounds interesting. What would you expect from doing that?*

ROSE: *I guess it would be a way to apologize to her, a way to tell her, "I know you now and I understand you better."*

THERAPIST: *Could you visualize yourself saying this to your daughter?*

ROSE: *[Closes her eyes, nods.] If I had been there with her mom, I also would have been angry at her mom.*

THERAPIST: *It seems that Patricia didn't have a very good mom-experience in her life.*

This is a long way from the mom who lectured Patricia on having empathy for her birth mother. Now Rose has made some connection between her daughter's emotion, her behavior, and her past (being angry at a mother who makes her steal food or money), the therapist wants to move further:

THERAPIST: *Rose, could you picture yourself in a situation in the near future when you have found out that Patricia has stolen something?*

ROSE: *I forgot this was not over. But I get your point. Well, I can see myself in a situation like the last one.*

THERAPIST: *Can you picture yourself doing something different than what you did the last time?*

ROSE: *I feel the tension in my stomach but I am not yelling at her. I am asking her, "Why did you do this? You don't have to buy us anything, you don't need to." Yes, I would tell her, "You don't need to." I wish I could hug her.*

THERAPIST: *Try to remember another time in which you hugged her or in which you felt physically closer. . . .*

Rose understanding the origin and meaning of Patricia's misbehavior and anger towards Rose does not necessarily change them, but it does create a template for a new way of responding to Patricia. Rose's former hostile reaction towards her daughter's misbehavior would have reinforced Patricia's belief that she was unlovable. Over time the reinforcement of the child's negative belief would reinforce the child's misbehavior. That, in turn, would reinforce Rose's attitude, and again Patricia's negative belief—a never-ending cycle . . . the kind of cycle that, too many times, ends up in sending the child back to the child protection system.

Helping the Child Mourn the Past and Attach to the Present

Some adoptive parents wonder how their adopted child could miss his or her birth parents after physical, sexual, emotional abuse or neglect has been experienced.

But it is not that simple. Traumatic attachments create a complicated paradox, and part of our job as a child professional working with adopted children is to understand this paradox so we can help parents understand it. Children form an attachment to their primary caregiver (Schore, 2009). Even if the primary caregiver abuses them or leaves them in danger, the child looks to—builds an attachment with—that individual. The child's attending to the birth parent may be an effort to avoid abuse or to seek a bit of goodness. This is all part of the child's survival. In order to preserve whatever goodness there might have been from the abusive parent, these children separate off these good bits or 'hoped for good bits' from the abuse and neglect they suffered. That is why, sometimes, these children puzzle everyone trying to help them by wanting to go back to their birth parents after the abuse has been disclosed. They may try to protect their birth parents from jail even if means that they need to recant abuse allegations (Baita & Moreno, 2015; Rozanski, 2003). This is all part of the heritage of disorganized attachment. Relationship trauma is not just an event that *happens to* children. It eventually is *who they think they are*. Traumatized children do not expect to be adopted by a good mom and dad one day. Their expectation of parents includes being hurt in some way. When they are adopted, their lives suddenly change, and they are expected to leave behind all memories—good and bad. That is an impossibility.

Paul, Janine, & Jackson, 8 Years Old

REFERRAL ISSUE: Jackson was referred to his school counselor by his teacher after he had been talking in class as if his birth father was his present father. The school counselor had attended extra training on working with adopted children. Otherwise, the school counselor would have referred Jackson and his parents to an outside counselor knowledgeable in the area of adoption.

BACKGROUND: Paul (50) and his wife Janine (45) adopted Jackson when he was almost 7 years old. They had been married for five years before the adoption and because of concerns related to Janine's health, decided to adopt a child. They were eager to accept an older child rather than a baby—

> "We are a little bit old for diapers," Janine said. Jackson had been referred at age 5 to protective services because of high drug use by both parents and extremely exploitive behavior by his father. Jackson had been in foster care with a single foster mother for the last two years.

SCHOOL COUNSELOR: *Tell me more about Jackson talking about his birth dad. Was the school situation the first time he did this?*

PAUL: *Well, outside of our home. Yes, it was the first time*

SCHOOL COUNSELOR: *I'm curious. What do you mean when you say "outside home"?*

JANINE: *Well, it was really odd, you know? A few weeks after Jackson came to our home, he started talking or asking about "daddy Mike." I first thought he was confused, that he meant "daddy Paul," as he had been calling my husband from the beginning. But one day at dinner Paul was talking to Jackson about his manners, and the boy said something like, "You're not daddy Mike."*

SCHOOL COUNSELOR: *And how did you react, Paul?*

PAUL: *I guess I was furious inside of me, but I tried to stay calm, and I told him something like "No, I'm not daddy Mike, I'm your father Paul." But I feel a tension in my stomach every time he says something about this daddy Mike, you know!*

SCHOOL COUNSELOR: *I can certainly imagine your tension. Did Jackson ever tell you what he was longing for with his birth daddy?*

PAUL: *Longing?! What do you mean "longing"? How could a normal child possibly miss a bastard like that or all the things his father put him through?*

SCHOOL COUNSELOR: [Notices that she has moved too quickly with her question. Takes a deep breath.] *Yes, you are right. It seems quite impossible, doesn't it? From our viewpoint, it really is. But from Jackson's viewpoint—what might be going on inside of him that makes him miss all that ordeal?*

PAUL: [Interrupts and is clearly very anxious.] *Look, I know you are the expert, but we don't need to know Jackson's viewpoint about this. Is there any chance that you could just help him forget his past? I think talking about it will only keep him stuck in his past. He has new opportunities now in his life. We both love him. He has whatever he wants. We can give him a good home, a good school, a safe place. I think he needs to focus on his present.*

Our school counselor may have several hypotheses about Paul's reaction. He is feeling rejected as a father by his son. He is the one who may be feeling not loved, inadequate, and unfairly compared to a man who was a drug addict and abusive father. It is easy to empathize with Paul. He wants his son to focus on the present because in the present he, Paul, can offer Jackson a world far safer than "daddy Mike" did. But all of this is left hemisphere reasoning. It is reasoning that makes no sense to Jackson. In Paul's despair, no matter how reasonable it looks, no matter how much we may empathize with him, Paul is forgetting and dismissing the most important thing—how does his son feel inside?

Very wisely, our school counselor does not want to confront Paul or try to explain to him what she meant. Her work with these parents is just beginning. The counselor wants to engage these parents and determine what issues she will need to work on with Jackson. Paul seems to want the counseling to focus on helping Jackson live in the present rather than thinking about the past; he even wants the counselor to help his boy forget his past. As child professionals who have educated ourselves about the issues facing adopted children, we know this is not possible. At this moment, Paul is caught in his emotions. Recognizing the importance of providing Paul with some time to calm, the counselor decides to turn to Jackson's mother.

SCHOOL COUNSELOR: *I see your point, Paul. What do you think, Janine?*

JANINE: *I want Paul to be okay. He is a good dad, he really is. When Jackson rejects him as his dad, Paul really suffers. Paul is right. There is nothing good in Jackson's past. Going there means only suffering for all of us. As a parent, you don't want your child to suffer!*

Janine wants to support her husband. She has been with him far longer than she has been with Jackson, a boy who is having trouble relating to his new parents—an experience so many adoptive children have. She does not want to suffer, does not want Paul to suffer, and does not want Jackson to suffer. And she is right, of course: Jackson's past is full of pain and harm. But erasing it is not possible. We need these parents to be able to connect and attune with their son, not only to their own needs. If they are to be able to attune with Jackson, then we need to be able to attune with them. There is a reason for Jackson doing this, and we know that the answer to the question regarding what drives his behavior lies mostly in his past experiences.

SCHOOL COUNSELOR: [First validates Janine and then is curious as to why Jackson's behavior is happening.] *Of course you don't, I agree. The challenge we have here is to understand what Jackson's behavior that is causing you all so much suffering means. Why do you think Jackson is acting this way; what ideas do you have?*

JANINE: *We both think it is Jackson's way to defy his father as an authority at home. His birth father used to constantly break the law, and this is something Jackson is proud about! From time to time he brags of all the "good things" daddy Mike used to do, like stealing things without being caught.*

SCHOOL COUNSELOR: *Does he ever talk to you about other things from his past, like not having his birth mom around, or ways his birth father mistreated him?*

PAUL: [Surprised.] *No, never. He has scars on his skull! We were told these were from a time his father beat him but never took him to the hospital despite the injuries. Poor child.* [Seems to be connecting to Jackson's experience for the first time.] *Do you think it's strange that he doesn't talk about these other things?*

JANINE: *I remember having read in Jackson's files that he told the protection worker his birth dad was good to him only when Jackson brought him things Jackson had stolen at school.*

SCHOOL COUNSELOR: *Hm. Interesting. It looks like bragging about stealing things reminds Jackson of times his birth dad didn't abuse him.*

This may be a good moment to give these parents some information about why our brains do seemingly weird things—taking as 'good' the less bad moment or situation. Having that knowledge will not create a connection between these parents and the child they adopted, but it might open the doors to some new thinking.

PAUL: *So. What you are implying is that Jackson doesn't hate me or reject me, but rather he is trying to preserve a good memory from his past?*

SCHOOL COUNSELOR: *How does this sound to you?*

PAUL: *But isn't this going to block his bonding with me?*

SCHOOL COUNSELOR: [Validates Paul's feelings.] *I know this might sound scary and even threatening, but it's impossible to erase our pasts. We are who we are and our pasts are part of that. It doesn't necessarily mean that we are determined by what happened in our past. We can always learn something from the worst situations . . .*

PAUL: [Voice rising.] *The fact is that we don't want Jackson to learn anything from his past and especially not that being a thief is something to be proud of.*

SCHOOL COUNSELOR: [Notices the change in Paul's voice and the increased tension in his body.] *Of course you don't want Jackson to learn that stealing things is a good behavior! This is something that makes you completely different from daddy Mike.* [Notices that Paul relaxes a bit and is able to lean back on the couch. Takes a breath, and only then continues with the earlier thought.] *It sounds like Jackson learned in the past that he could make daddy Mike not abuse him if he stole things for Mike. I heard Janine say that Jackson brags of Mike's stealing behavior. I'm curious, has he stolen anything since he has been living with you?*

JANINE: *No, never! Maybe we are afraid of him doing it because of his past?*

PAUL: *Yeah. Probably.* [Turns to the counselor.] *Wouldn't you? Isn't it logical that we are afraid of him becoming a thief? He has already learned how to do it.*

The 'ghost of the past,' for many adoptive parents, is their fear that their children will behave as their birth parents did—abusing, breaking the law, drinking, taking drugs. They may read any signal from their children's behavior as confirmation of their worst fear. Even if the child does not presently engage in the behavior itself, adoptive parents want to prevent it from happening. The problem is that expecting something to happen makes them misread the cues. In the same way that traumatized children read danger all around them, the parents of these children misread cues and think that their children's 'nature' is stronger than the nurturing they can provide. By focusing their attention on this possible 'danger' they unintentionally see misbehaviors in their children.

SCHOOL COUNSELOR: *And for some reason he didn't do it in the entire time he has been with you....*

PAUL: *Sure, because it would be an inadmissible behavior.*

SCHOOL COUNSELOR: *Yes, that could be one reason, but he never stole anything at home or at school. How could he learn that stealing was inadmissible if he never behaved this way with you?* [After a brief silence, both parents seem surprised.] *What other reasons do you think might have prevented Jackson from stealing since living with you?*

JANINE: *We love him. I tell him every morning when I wake him up "I love you, sunshine." We don't yell at him, we don't abuse him; his first grades at school were not really good, and we never beat him for this and we didn't scold him for this. He is our son.* [Tears up.] *We could never abuse our son. Never.* [Paul puts his arm around Janine's shoulder, nodding.]

When parents are haunted by these 'ghosts from the past' they may focus on only one idea or thought that explains why the behavior they are expecting did not happen, for example, "*It was only a matter of luck.*" What trauma-informed models of therapy like EMDR[5] teach us is that traumatic information remains stuck in our brains, blocking our natural possibilities of processing new information in adaptive ways (Shapiro, 2001). Helping parents think about other possibilities as to why the feared behavior did not happen opens their brains to new information, information that expands their understanding of the problem.

The next step will be to help these parents respond in a more positive way to Jackson when he brags about the negative behaviors he learned from his daddy Mike or when he confronts Paul with, "You're not daddy Mike." We want parents to respond in a way that can help Jackson differentiate past from present and that can help him mourn the loss of the part of his birth father he felt was awesome.

SCHOOL COUNSELOR: [In this session, the School Counselor encourages Paul to share any changes he has noticed in his parenting of Jackson.]

PAUL: *Last weekend I had to tell Jackson several times that his time with the computer was over. And again he told me, "You're not daddy Mike." My first reaction was to walk away, but then I remembered your question—the one I didn't like—and turned back and asked Jackson, "Tell me, son, what do you miss about your daddy Mike?" Jackson stared at me. And then he started crying. I was shocked. I didn't know what to do. I was afraid I was doing the wrong thing. Janine was at her yoga class; I was alone with our son. I really didn't know what to do. I didn't want to screw it up.*

SCHOOL COUNSELOR: [Feels the intensity of that moment and takes a deep breath.] *What an intense moment it must have been for you! You made a really good decision in not walking away. Tell me, what happened next?*

PAUL: *He first said he didn't know. Then he said he missed the time daddy Mike bought him presents when he was 5 and he got the scar on his head. I just swallowed. I have this rage towards this guy. It was so difficult not to yell or swear. So I counted to 10—Janine helped me with this idea. Then I asked Jackson why that time was so special for him.*

SCHOOL COUNSELOR: *And what did Jackson answer?*

PAUL: [Cries.] *He said it was the time daddy Mike spent the most days without hitting him. I hugged him and was only able to say "Don't worry, kiddo, no one will ever hit you again." Did I do it right?*

SCHOOL COUNSELOR: *You did a huge thing right! You let your son talk about what he missed of his past, of his birth father. By controlling your own reactions, you gave him room to talk and share with you. You let Jackson understand that you accept him just as he is, and with your words and your hug you reassured him that his present world is safe. I think you made great progress.*

As we have stated throughout this book, our brains learn new patterns through repetition. We hope this new way of responding with Jackson will be stronger than the old reactions, but remember, the old reactions have happened more often. How can we be sure the neuronal connections underlying this more positive way of reacting are more easily available when needed?

SCHOOL COUNSELOR: *I would like to try an exercise with you, Paul, if that is ok. It is an exercise that might help you to have this kind of response to your son more available.* [See Chapters 3 and 6 for other examples on the use of imaging.]

PAUL: *OK . . .*

SCHOOL COUNSELOR: *I would like you to go back to the moment in which you heard Jackson telling you what he longed for from his past—the moment that brought up the wish to hug Jackson. See if it is possible for you to bring back the sensation in your body when holding your son . . .*

PAUL: *I didn't want to let him go . . .*

SCHOOL COUNSELOR: *And where in your body do you notice this feeling of not wanting to let him go?*

PAUL: *It's like a strength in my arms.*

SCHOOL COUNSELOR: *Good, let's see if you can stay with that feeling in your arms for a moment.* [Sits quietly for a moment.] *If the strength in your arms could say something to Jackson, what would this sensation tell him?*

PAUL: *I'm here for you, always, anytime.*

SCHOOL COUNSELOR: [Remembers that the good moment, good sensation, good words need to be able to occur in Paul at the same time as Jackson is defying or rejecting Paul.] *These are really good words. It will certainly be good for Jackson to feel the strength of your holding arms when he feels so sad or scared. Let's try to go further. I want you to try to stay with this feeling, this body sensation and the words stemming from both, and visualize a moment in which Jackson says again, "You're not daddy Mike."*

PAUL: *It makes me feel really tense.*

SCHOOL COUNSELOR: *Feel this tension coming from Jackson saying, "You're not daddy Mike." Can you see the scene in your mind's eye?* [Pauses and watches Paul's face to be sure he is there.] *Now, see if you can move your attention to your arms and visualize yourself hugging Jackson. See if you can bring back the feeling of the strength in your arms and your words, "I'm here for you always, anytime."*

PAUL: *Yeah. I can get that feeling. But the tension is not relieved.*

SCHOOL COUNSELOR: *You're right, it isn't. It's so much easier for our brains to go to known places—like the anger tension—rather than new places, even if the new places look and feel so much better. Try to see if it is possible for you to stay with the hugging sensation no matter how much your tension is pulling you away from it. Now repeat for yourself your words, "I'm here for you always, anytime."*

PAUL: *I'm not sure how this is going to help me?*

SCHOOL COUNSELOR: *I remember, Paul, your telling me you were afraid Jackson wouldn't bond with you. This exercise helps build the bonding. Bonding needs practice. It's always easier to bond during the peaceful times. The challenge is to keep this bonding during war times—during the times you feel the anger tension in yourself!*

Many times adoptive parents, as well as biological parents, are skeptical when we suggest exercises that include noticing body sensations and creating visualizations (see Chapter 6) and we encourage them to practice at home. We need to stay attuned to parents and suggest only exercises we think they can do. We do not want to add more discouragement to what they are already feeling.

The work done with Paul opens the door to his understanding and accepting his son's longing for what was a good memory of his birth father. Accepting this memory, instead of fighting against it or trying to erase it, creates the pathway for Paul to stay with his son emotionally while he mourns his past experiences. This unconditional presence and acceptance is also part of the secure attachment he is trying to build for himself to his son and for Jackson to him.

Understanding the Role of Disorganized Attachment

Children coming from abusive, neglectful and violent environments are most likely to fall into the disorganized/disoriented category of attachment. Research conducted in the late '80s found that more than 80 percent of abused children develop disorganized/disoriented attachment patterns (Carlson et al., 1989). Children develop disorganized attachment when the attachment figure becomes simultaneously the source of danger and the source of calm, putting the child in a paradoxical situation referred to as 'fear without solution' (Main & Hesse, 1990). Since attachment is a "strong, inborn, evolved disposition" (Liotti, 2009, p. 53), seeking the attachment figure when tension rises, especially during the first years of life, is always going to happen. The problem for the child in a situation of chronic interpersonal violence is that he is seeking for safety the very person who hurts him. Thus, every time tension rises and the child perceives himself in a stressful or even dangerous situation, his brain pushes him to look for proximity with the individual who is the very source of the tension or danger. This child spends a great amount of time with a parent who shifts without transitions into different states of mind. One of the parent's states of mind can be that of an affectionate parent, even if this state is transient and immersed in a pool of harm, violence, and neglect. As we saw in the example with Jackson, the child tries to preserve a good memory of the birth parent even though the memory may be linked with abusive behavior toward the child. To keep the good memory Jackson had disconnected—dissociated—the memory of the abusive behaviors.

This disorganized/disoriented attachment pattern shows itself through different behaviors and actions. One of them is the "phobia of attachment"—the need to avoid both attachment needs and attachment figures—in that both the needs and the people can become a source of danger. Another behavior is its counterpart, the "phobia of attachment loss"—the need to seek the attachment figure (van der Hart et al., 2006). The child brings this internal model of attachment with its contradictory behaviors into his new family, where a new attachment experience needs to be built. However, the child comes only with the old disorganized experience of attachment, and this is what the child believes will happen now. He desperately wants something different but is unable to believe in something he does not know. He cannot believe something good will happen; faith in a new good world does not work when complex trauma has been the previous experience. Disorganized/disoriented children are caught in an approach/avoidant dance of attachment that they continue dancing in their new family. Adoptive parents do not expect this.

Child's Disorganized Attachment May Activate Parents' Old Disorganized Attachment Patterns

But there is still more to add to this conundrum: What if the adoptive parents themselves had developed disorganized/disoriented attachment patterns when they were children? Some children growing up with abuse are able, with good experiences, to develop positive adult attachment relationships and manage well. But then the disorganized behaviors from the child may trigger those old negative attachment patterns (see Chapter 3, pages 50–52).

Lynn & Mia, 4 Years, 8 Months Old

> **REFERRAL ISSUE:** Mia was referred with her adoptive mom, Lynn, by her pediatrician due to the child's constant crying and difficulty separating from her mom. This started suddenly a few months earlier when Mia's adoptive father moved out of the home.
>
> **BACKGROUND:** Lynn is a successful professional who was married to Thom for 10 years. Unable to have children of their own, they decided to adopt a child from a developing country in South America, where they were living because of Thom's job. Mia was adopted at the age of 2. She was severely undernourished and needed extensive medical treatment during the first four months after adoption. With Mia's high medical needs and constant fright, she required considerable care. She showed no bonding to either Lynn or Thom. The couple experienced considerable conflict due to Thom's lack of involvement with Mia's care.
>
> Two weeks after Mia's third birthday, Thom filed for divorce. Lynn decided to return to her home country where she could be closer to family and friends, find a good job, and raise Mia by herself. During the first interview, Lynn looked self-sufficient, highly efficient, but rather distant emotionally and physically from her daughter. She explained the circumstances of her divorce in a matter-of-fact tone of voice.

THERAPIST: *You were talking about the moment you realized Thom was with someone else.* [Tries to attune with Lynn.] *This must have been hard for you, given the circumstances.*

LYNN: *I'm sorry, what circumstances?*

THERAPIST: [Feels confused.] *Well, you were alone in a foreign country without any support and with a little child facing medical decisions. When you adopted your daughter, there were two parents to face these decisions together.*

LYNN: [Stares at therapist as if she is listening to somebody else's story.] *I'm sorry, I got lost.*

THERAPIST: *I can see. Where did your mind wander?*

LYNN: *My mind never wanders, actually. I guess I was probably checking my schedule for the rest of the day.*

As the therapist starts to discuss loss and notices Lynn's emotional detachment, she makes a mental note to herself to return to this at a later time, always keeping a slow pace.

THERAPIST: *Tell me more about Mia's crying outbursts.*

LYNN: *I can't tell you much. It is so unbearable that I end up locking myself in my bedroom.*

THERAPIST: [Struggles to control her bewilderment. Takes a breath.] *Hmm, and for how long do you stay there?*

LYNN: *I don't know, I just fall asleep.*

THERAPIST: *And what happens with Mia?*

LYNN: *I guess she falls asleep as well, because sometimes when I leave my bedroom I find her lying in front of my door. Poor baby, I understand, it must be exhausting to cry like that.*

THERAPIST: *And how do you feel when you find her asleep lying there in front of your door?*

LYNN: *How do I feel? It's hard to say. Sad, I guess. But then she wakes up and looks pretty normal.*

THERAPIST: *Normal how?*

LYNN: *She just ignores me. I try to play with her, engage with her in what she is doing, and she ignores me. Sometimes she is bossy; I tell her I don't like her to be this way with me, but she keeps doing it, so I leave the room. I leave her alone because she needs to understand I'm her mom, not anyone else.*

By this point Lynn looks as unfeeling as she had appeared when discussing her emotional state during her divorce. Our therapist feels blocked and at the same time trapped in harsh feelings towards Lynn. She feels she needs to find a connection with Lynn, otherwise her work with both mom and daughter will certainly fail. But it is hard to try to connect to someone who seems to be so disconnected from others as well as from herself. Neither asking about the divorce or Mia's state—the referral issue—brought forth much information or feelings. The therapist realized that Lynn likely offers little information, not because she does not want to give information but because it seems a good way to keep herself away from difficult feelings. The therapist hesitates with the next question—it may be too pushy for someone so disconnected—but it could open the possibility of understanding what is happening for Lynn.

THERAPIST: [Takes a breath and settles the anxious feeling inside herself.] *Have there been other moments in your life where you found yourself locking yourself inside your bedroom in order to calm things?*

LYNN: [Tears in her eyes.] *My parents used to fight a lot. My father is an abusive man.*

THERAPIST: *I see this is upsetting, that makes sense. Do you think we can go on talking about it, or do you prefer to stop?*

LYNN: *I'm not upset. This is the past. My father died 10 years ago.*

This response gives our therapist a great deal of information about Lynn. She seems unable to recognize her own feelings even while feeling them—"*I'm not upset,*" while having tears in her eyes—and she spoke about her dead father as if he was still living—"*My father **is** an abusive man.*"

All the information gathered by now suggests that this woman likely was a traumatized child who tried to cope with life by becoming a successful professional, yet emotionally detached from intimate relationships. Her divorce may have triggered old abandonment memories and, together with the stress of adopting a child with many health issues, this may have pushed her into a place where she needed to dissociate in order to protect herself. We know that she had been referred to a psychiatrist but chose not to receive therapy because she had 'learned to deal with life by myself' and did not feel comfortable talking with a stranger about her issues. And remember that we are, for Lynn, a stranger. Lynn does not need assessment; she needs someone to hear her distress without confronting or criticizing her. She needs someone who will attune, validate, and help her with emotional regulation (see Chapter 5). She needs someone who will not just talk to her but will help her experience her child in a different way (see Chapter 6).

Working with this amount of disconnection—possible dissociation—is always difficult. It is always tempting as child therapists to want to limit our work, in these situations, to therapy with only the child. But helping these parents learn to connect—both within themselves and with their child—is doubly important.

THERAPIST: *I was wondering whether you have pictures of Mia. I always like to ask parents to bring in pictures of their children.*

LYNN: *Oh I like photos! I've taken hundreds of them since Mia came home with us. I also have some pictures of her at the hospital. Do you want me to bring all of them or just the happy ones?*

THERAPIST: *I think it would be good if we have pictures representing every important moment—happy and sad—of Mia's life. Will you bring them for our next appointment?*

In giving this suggestion the therapist is trying to find an alternative way to connect with Lynn and to help her connect with her daughter. Instead of pushing for any particular picture, our therapist wants Lynn to pick those that represent for her the most important moments of Mia's life. At the next appointment, Lynn brings an album full of pictures. She says she was unable to choose, so she decided to bring all of them.

THERAPIST: *Would you like to pick up a picture that represents a happy moment for Mia and another one that represents a sad one?*

While picking the picture that represents the sad moment, Lynn hesitates between two different photos: in one of them Mia is intubated at the hospital; in the second one Mia is smiling while sitting in her mom's lap on an airplane. There seems to be some relevant information expressed through Lynn's hesitation.

THERAPIST: *Tell me about those moments, both of them, and tell me why you think they were sad moments for Mia.*

LYNN: *Well, that's interesting. I thought they were both sad moments for her, and now I realize one of these moments was sad just for me.* [Points at the picture on the airplane.] *Here we were coming back home . . . without Thom. I guess she didn't know yet her dad was leaving us.* [Starts crying.]

THERAPIST: [Takes a deep breath, resonates with Lynn's sadness.] *What a difficult moment for a single mom—to do this trip all alone.*

LYNN: *I didn't want Mia to see me crying.*

THERAPIST: *I understand. How did you manage? I mean, you were on an airplane; it would be difficult to leave Mia alone, to lock yourself in the toilet to cry alone.*

LYNN: *I started singing a song my grandma used to sing to me when I was a little child. My grandma had this sweet voice, and it was so soothing when she sang for me.*

THERAPIST: *And what did Mia do?*

LYNN: *She fell asleep in my arms.*

THERAPIST: *Could you sing this song for me? I would love to hear it.*

LYNN: *I guess . . .* [Starts singing.]

THERAPIST: *This is so lovely! Do you still sing this song to Mia?*

LYNN: [Surprised.] *I thought she was too old for such a song. Do you think it's OK if I keep singing it for her?*

THERAPIST: *I would give it a try, especially at the moments Mia cries because she is upset. Maybe you could try to have a special moment before you go to your work to spend with her and sing the song for her. It may help her when you leave and help her remember you are coming back.*

What would be best for Lynn would be to have her own therapy process. Even if she has refused in the past, it does not mean we should give up suggesting therapy. Whether she looks for therapy for herself or not, given Lynn's own story of unresolved traumas, the first thing the child therapist needs to focus on is some connection between herself and Lynn.

Lynn was able to share with our therapist a good memory of her own childhood (Grandma singing to her), one in which an attachment figure would soothe her. She was able to use this same resource to soothe her own daughter at a moment in which she—as the adult—felt lost. As Lynn had said, Mia would probably not know or understand that her daddy was abandoning her while she was on the plane. It was Lynn who was letting in some of the sadness. What about Mia's crying when Lynn leaves for work? Would Lynn be able to connect with Mia's distress?

THERAPIST: *Tell me about this other picture* [Points to the one at the hospital].

LYNN: *Oh, it was so terrible. I was exhausted, I didn't have a bed at the hospital so I had to sleep sitting on a chair, my back ached, I couldn't take a shower, I ate poorly.*

THERAPIST: [Feels tense—Lynn is only talking about herself, but it was Mia who was having surgical procedures.] *And what about Mia?*

LYNN: *She was sedated. Well, I mean she didn't suffer like me because she was sedated . . .*

Again, Lynn has disconnected. The exercise with the first picture may have been too much for her.

THERAPIST: *I was wondering whether she was suffering before being intubated at the hospital. At some point in her life she must have felt hungry . . . .*

LYNN: *Oh sure! But that was before I adopted her.*

THERAPIST: [More disconnection. What else could be done?] *Tell me about your first experience when you had Mia in your arms. Can you remember that moment?*

LYNN: *Yes! She was so little I thought I was going to break her in pieces. I was so afraid.*

THERAPIST: *I can imagine. And what did you do to calm yourself down?*

LYNN: [Thinks and then smiles.] *You are not going to believe me. I sang to myself my grandma's song.*

THERAPIST: [Smiles with relief as she finally feels a connection with Lynn.] *It sounds to me that your grandma's song seems to be a good resource for soothing both Mia and you!*

Lynn's pattern of disconnection is so generalized that she has learned not to feel anything. However, having learned to 'not feel' does not prevent people from feeling something from time to time. But they know how—when that happens—to turn off emotion, detach themselves from the distressing situation, and go on automatic pilot. In order for Lynn to be able to understand Mia's distress when Lynn leaves and to be able to sooth Mia, Lynn will need first to learn to connect with her own feelings and, most importantly, remember the resources she learned during her childhood for calming. This will be needed before discussing Mia's past. While in the ideal situation Lynn would have her own therapist, she may, as she has done before, refuse her own therapy. In that situation, the therapist is going to need to return to Chapters 5 and 6 and to read some of the excellent resources on working with dissociated adults (Boon et al., 2011; Howell, 2011; Howell & Itzkowitz, 2016; van der Hart et al., 2006).

Child's Controlling Behavior May Disorganize Parents

By the time children with a history of disorganized attachment reach school age, they follow two different behavior patterns—both controlling. Their controlling behaviors may be punitive or may be caretaking, but both have the goal of keeping attachment figures at a safe distance—not too close, so they will not be hurt, and not too far, so they can be protected (Main & Hess, 1990). Adoptive parents are puzzled, astonished, and often fooled by the extreme changes in their children's behavior toward them. Remember Rose, Patricia's mother? This is how she describes Patricia's relationship with her:

ROSE: *I don't know what to believe. Am I being fooled by this girl? We had this wonderful weekend. We baked together, we played cards together, I helped her with her school work. She was so sweet. But this morning I was doing the laundry and I found this piece of paper in her trousers on which* she had written the most horrible things about me—calling me a bitch, saying that I was pretending to be a good mom but she knew I was just like her birth mom. I am so confused. I thought she loved me!

THERAPIST: [Attunes and validates.] *Sounds so confusing! What do you think is happening for Patricia?*

ROSE: *She says I'm pretending to be a good mom. I think it's the other way around—she is the pretender, not me.*

THERAPIST: *It feels like she is deliberately acting like a good girl with you?*

ROSE: *What else could it be?*

Parents may feel like they are caught in the middle of a power struggle. This happens particularly in situations where there are other siblings the child has been taking care of before the adoption.

ROSE: *I found out that Patricia has been telling her siblings to disobey us—to not do what we tell them to. It's like she is sabotaging all our efforts to become a normal family. I accepted this the first few months after they came to our home, but now this is just unacceptable.*

THERAPIST: *That's hard. What do you do when you realize this has been happening?*

ROSE: *Well I must say it depends on my mood. Sometimes I try to explain to her that I understand she felt she had to take care of her siblings when they were in shelters or on the streets. But now we are the adults, and we can manage. Other times I feel very sad and beg her to stop doing this. It's so painful for everyone, and it's confusing for her siblings. And other times I just feel so enraged that I punish her. I leave her alone while I take the others to the park.*

Rose's reactions are so variable. We can imagine how variable her feelings and state of mind have been when she responds to Patricia's behavior. If we put ourselves in Patricia's shoes, we can imagine how confusing Rose's reactions may be for her. Rose is able to describe how puzzling and challenging her daughter's behaviors and attitudes are for her, but is she able to realize how confusing her shifting reactions must be for Patricia?

THERAPIST: *Rose, what are Patricia's reactions when she sees you in these different states: understanding, sad, angry?*

ROSE: *When I try to explain to her that we are in control now, it's like she wants to trust but still can't. Most of the time she denies having told her siblings what to do, and I don't want to argue. So I just assume she told them and I don't let her know I'm mad. I try to look calm but firm. When I feel sad* *she gets this look in her eyes, you know? Like "I won." I feel like she enjoys seeing me there, begging her. And when I leave her alone, well. . . . Some time ago I used to yell at her, a lot, and sometimes I also said very harsh things to her. But I realized I didn't want to be like the other adults who had maltreated her; that's why I changed my strategy. I just leave her alone, without a word. I assume she knows why I'm doing that. And then, when I return back home, she has usually gone to sleep. It doesn't matter if it's only 3 in the afternoon. She is in her bed, sleeping, and sometimes it's impossible to wake her up, not even for dinner. So I let her sleep until the next day.*

Rose is able to describe clearly Patricia's changing reactions—reactions triggered by Rose's responses to Patricia's behavior towards Rose. This means that Rose is noticing Patricia's reactions and feelings. But nothing is changing. Something is not working. Rose is expecting Patricia to understand (dorsal-lateral prefrontal cortex activity) from Rose's reactions that her behavior hurts and needs to stop. But Patricia is experiencing many emotions arising from the time she was living with a very unstable mother (orbital-medial prefrontal cortex activity). Rose seems unaware of what is happening inside Patricia when she sees Rose's reactions.

THERAPIST: *I would like to try a game with you, Rose. I will be Patricia. Now you tell me the several different things you told me you say to Patricia and do all the things you said you do, like ignoring her and walking away. I want you to pay close attention to my face. Remember, I'm Patricia now.*

The aim of this exercise is to help Rose actually 'see' how Patricia feels with her mom's shifting behaviors. At the end of the exercise, our therapist asks:

THERAPIST: *What did you notice?*

ROSE: *It's confusing. I'm not sure I got your point.*

THERAPIST: *Yes, it's confusing. Now we will do it the other way around. You will be Patricia, and I will be you, Rose. Now I will say and act as you did, and you show me* **just with your face** *how you feel. All right?*

At the end of this exercise our therapist repeats the same question to Rose. She wants to know what Rose noticed.

ROSE: *Oh! Now I get it. She feels confused, puzzled, until she just wants to get away like I did.*

Because Patricia's experiences were full of contradictory interactions with her prior attachment figures, she expects Rose will act the same. What Patricia cannot know is that her own functioning is so confusing that it provokes in her mom the contradictory interactions Patricia was actually expecting from her. What will happen if Rose learns how to react in a single coherent manner no matter how confusing the situation is?

THERAPIST: *Let's try this. Now you are going to be Patricia again, and you will act as she does and say the things she says. I will be Rose and will try to act in a single way.*

The therapist is now modeling for Patricia how a mom of a traumatized child gives order and consistency, acts in a coherent manner, always communicating the same message, and not letting her child walk away from the interaction. Another way to achieve the same goal would be to use visualization and imagination.

THERAPIST: *I know that when children keep doing the things we want them to change it can be pretty frustrating for parents. We start stumbling into different strategies that don't seem to work effectively, and that adds more frustration. Am I understanding how you are feeling? [Rose nods.] We desperately want our kids to understand our point of view, which in your case, Rose, is obviously very clear and legitimate. What I have learned is that it helps to try to understand **their** point of view.*

ROSE: *Well it seems pretty obvious to me. She wants to keep control over things. She can't relax, she doesn't want to let it go.*

THERAPIST: *Yes, all of this is possible, but what we don't know is how Patricia is feeling inside herself when she confronts your different reactions. What might prevent her from 'understanding' your point of view?*

ROSE: *I see . . .*

THERAPIST: *Let's try to go into Patricia's mind, what do you think? [Rose nods]. Could you close your eyes for a moment and imagine that you are not Rose, but Patricia? Your now mom, Rose, has explained to you that there is no need for you to keep taking care of your siblings, that you and your siblings are now safe with your parents, and they can take care of all three of you. How is Patricia feeling inside of her while listening to her mom?*

Our therapist is asking Rose to practice mentalization—to hold her child's experience inside her own mind (see Chapter 4; remember how mentalization correlates with a secure attachment) and to do it while using imaging (see Chapter 3; remember how imaging can stimulate the right hemisphere of the brain, where neuronal networks related to attachment and the working model of self are held).

ROSE: *I guess relieved, but not 100 percent relieved, it's more like can I trust you? Or why should I trust you?*

When the Home is an Adoptive Home 219

THERAPIST: [Recalls the importance of somatic sensations for right hemisphere processing.] *And while feeling this way, how is her body feeling inside?*

ROSE: *It's kind of tense, like wanting to approach but not too much; she actually turns her head to the side, like this* [shows with her eyes closed].

THERAPIST: *And what is her body saying with this turn of the head?*

ROSE: *I don't trust you?*

THERAPIST: *And now, Patricia is in front of her mom who is begging her to stop telling her siblings to disobey. Her mother's voice sounds kind of sad and tired. What is the feeling that comes up in Patricia now?*

ROSE: *It's weird. . . . It's like she is both happy and sad.*

THERAPIST: *And then one day, Patricia finds that her mom has left together with her siblings without ever saying anything.*

ROSE: [Clearly anxious.] *Oh God. I see. I see.*

THERAPIST: *What do you see Rose?*

ROSE: *It's like not being loved, it's kind of a void here.* [Puts her hand on her stomach.] *It's really awful.*

THERAPIST: *And now, I'm wondering how Patricia feels—how her body feels, what thoughts race through her mind when she first sees her mother acting understanding and calm, then sad and anxious, then absent and probably mad at her . . .*

ROSE: *Now that you put things this way, it's rather confusing.*

Severely traumatized and disorganized children need consistency more than any other children; consistency brings predictability. Consistency and predictability together can create a secure base for the child. It is easy for parents to get engaged in the dramatic shifts of their children's controlling behaviors. They may relax when a child displays caretaking-controlling behavior rather than the fighting back or flying away that happens when the child displays the punitive-controlling behavior. But, in both cases, there is a possibility that the parent may become neglectful—assuming the caretaking child will cope with everything by herself—or abusive—acting out her or his anger on the punitive-controlling child. To avoid this pattern repeating within the new family, parents will need to learn consistent responses to their child's behaviors.

Hughes (1997) compares attachment to a dance. The child's needs are the music, while the interaction with the parent sets the rhythm. But for the rhythm to be followed properly, the interaction needs someone leading it, as happens in a tango dance. The one who needs to lead the interaction is the parent, energizing and calming the child's arousal as needed. This is the pattern of secure attachment, an attachment the children in this chapter never had but need to experience. These children learned to dance to a very different rhythm, let us say hip hop. So what happens when their parents want them to dance a tango? A mismatch. The dance of attachment does not occur, and both the parent and the child involved in the dancing feel highly frustrated. At this point we, as child professionals, can hear the parents' frustration and help them find a new rhythm that will fit both them and their children. For this to happen, we will need, no matter whether we are an educator, a social worker, or a therapist, to pay close attention to the story, the needs and expectations of both parent and child. At the same time, we need to keep an eye on our own expectations about what needs to be accomplished—just small steps at a time.

Working with Foster Parents

Many children are placed not in adoptive homes, but with foster parents. For some this may be an interim period while their birth parents are receiving help, and there is a plan for the child to go home. For others, it is a period during which child services is seeking an adoptive family. And for others, it is long-term care with or without contact with a biological parent. Family foster care is intended to be a family setting that provides the child with a primary parental attachment figure (Doran & Berliner, 2001). This is the main feature foster and adoptive parents share. Much of our earlier discussion also applies to work with foster parents. In this section we will highlight some of the **different challenges** foster parents encounter and how we can help them in these situations.

Foster Care is a Temporary Situation

Although some children may remain in foster care placements for long periods of time, it is usually considered a transitory situation. While the message underlying adoption is *"From now on you will be my son,"* the message with a foster parent is *"I will take care of you like a son as much as you need."* Because of this transitory situation, some foster parents do not want to truly connect with the child.

The wish not to overconnect with a foster child is usually a result of the foster parents' own experiences, their particular attachment style, misinformation, or a combination of all three. Some foster parents think that if they do connect with the child it will be more difficult for them to let the child go—either back to his birth family or to an adoptive home. Others think it is not part of their job to emotionally connect to the child; they are there to provide better care than what the child received from his abusive, neglectful parents. These foster parents feel effective if they are good providers. They consider being affectionate and bonding with the child as the role for the adoptive or birth parent, someone more stable in the child's life.

Pete and Bea, Foster Parents, & Sam, 11 Years Old

> **REFERRAL ISSUE AND BACKGROUND INFORMATION:** Pete and Bea are fostering a child for the first time. Their only birth child has moved to another city to go to university, and they decided they wanted to become foster

> parents to help other children cope with the challenges resulting from their difficult lives. They attend regular meetings with other new foster parents to gain support and further training. Sam, the child they are caring for, has been in a number of foster placements. The previous placement failed due to Sam's rage outbursts, the last of them ending in Sam injuring his foster mom. The social worker conducting the meeting wants to know how Sam and his foster parents are adjusting to each other.

PETE: *First thing was to make clear our house rules. We made a chart with his daily routines, because we read these children need structure and organization. We told him he cannot hurt anybody at our home. He is warned now that he cannot do whatever he wants, there are some limits.*

SOCIAL WORKER: [Feels tension inside as she hears Pete's distant and emotionally detached tone as he talks about an 11-year-old boy who has been displaced from home to home. Realizes she needs to help Pete and Bea start connecting in some way with the child Sam is.] *I am wondering how Sam reacted to these rules.*

PETE: *He had this "I don't care" attitude. But he wasn't disrespectful at all.*

SOCIAL WORKER: *Has Sam shown any distress since he has come to live with you? Maybe nightmares, or crying, or isolating himself?*

BEA: *Yes, the first nights he stayed with us, he used to cry at bedtime. He went to bed . . . looked very obedient; he accepted our turning off the lights and half closing his door, but when all the lights of the house were turned off, we could hear his crying. Now this is happening only from time to time.*

SOCIAL WORKER: *And what would you do when you heard Sam crying?*

BEA: *I stood at his door and asked him whether he wanted me to stay with him a little bit, until he calmed down. But he usually hid under the blanket, so I thought he wanted some privacy.*

SOCIAL WORKER: [Feels the tension in her belly increase, takes a slow breath.] *Sometimes children coming from abusive environments have learned that closeness can be dangerous. But it doesn't necessarily mean that they don't need closeness.*

PETE: *Bea and I have agreed that we can be warm and kind with him, but it is better not to be too affectionate. He could take advantage of that and start misbehaving, as with the other foster family.*

BEA: *And besides, we don't know how long he will stay with us. What if we become affectionate towards him and he engages with us and us with him? What if he must leave our home? That would be unbearable. For all of us!*

When the Home is an Adoptive Home

Our social worker remembers at this point that Pete and Bea started the process for becoming foster parents shortly after their only child left their home (see earlier discussion about the importance of knowing why an adoptive parent has decided to adopt). She wonders whether they are mourning their empty nest. She understands this group meeting is not the right place to address this issue, so she makes a mental note to think about how to help these parents be emotionally available for Sam. We will return to this case later.

Foster Parents are Often Overwhelmed by Multiple Demands

Foster parents often foster numerous children not related to each other. In these cases, foster parents may feel overwhelmed by the numerous, difficult situations with which they must deal. Quite reasonably, they may choose to put their energy in what they consider the most important problem at that moment.

Rosina and Robert & Matt (8), Leo (6), and Alba (6)

> **REFERRAL ISSUE:** Rosina (foster mother) was called by the school counselor after Matt acted out with another boy in the school bathroom. The counselor had already had contact with Rosina and Robert, as they have three foster children in their home who often need extra support.
>
> **BACKGROUND INFORMATION:** Rosina and Robert are fostering three children, each from a different home and with different experiences. Alba had been in a serious car accident, had required multiple surgeries, and is presently in the hospital.

SCHOOL COUNSELOR: [Recalls the many demands on Rosina and starts by empathizing with Rosina—attention to her window of receptivity (see Chapter 3)—before addressing the present problem.] *How is Alba doing?*

ROSINA: *She is recovering fast but still is in such pain. I'm exhausted with staying at the hospital. Robert is being very helpful in taking care of the boys and the house by himself. But I'm confused, I thought you wanted to talk to me about Matt, am I right?*

SCHOOL COUNSELOR: *Yes, of course.* [Takes a deep breath, recognizes that Rosina is really overwhelmed and might not have much time or patience to stay at this meeting.] *. . . I was concerned about Matt's recent behavior. You know he exhibited some sexualized misbehaviors against another kid* [reads from Matt's file] *"he took a younger child into a toilet stall, fastened the door, made the child suck his penis, and threatened the child that he would beat him if he told anyone . . ."*

ROSINA: [Interrupts.] *I think this is his way to get attention. Matt is a very jealous boy; he fights with Leo even for a piece of cake, and his misbehavior* has escalated since Alba arrived in our home. Maybe because she is a girl? I don't know.

SCHOOL COUNSELOR: *Yes, probably. However, I think this 'call for attention' is significant and Matt could really benefit from some therapy. My concern is that this behavior could repeat or even escalate. Then there would be a bigger problem.*

ROSINA: *Yes, I get your point, but we are now very busy with Alba recovering at the hospital; I am not sure we have the time and energy to take Matt to a therapist. These things always take so much time before you start seeing any results. Is it possible for you to have talks with him about what he did? Tell me, what do you want me and Robert to tell him at home; I think we can help somehow this way.*

Our school counselor understands these foster parents are really overwhelmed by the unexpected car accident suffered by one of the children they care for, and at the same time she knows Matt's situation is more complicated than a child just calling for attention. She knows she needs to keep a balance between her understanding and attunement to the foster family situation and the urgent need for some therapeutic work for Matt. Trying to find this balance, she accepts Rosina's idea without giving up her own suggestion.

SCHOOL COUNSELOR: *I think we can work together to help Matt with his behavior in the best way he might need. During the next week I will have several talks with Matt about this situation, and I would like to have a new meeting with you and Robert, let's say . . . one week from now? I would like to discuss with you both my impression of what is happening for Matt, and you can fill me in on what is happening at home. The three of us can work on ways to find therapeutic help for Matt. Would that work?*

ROSINA: *I'll check with Robert. He is very busy, you know?*

SCHOOL COUNSELOR: *We can call him from here and check.*

ROSINA: *Okay.*

Visits with Birth Parents

Many children in foster care have regular, court-ordered or agency-arranged visits with their birth parents. Foster parents, rather than dealing with a child's mourning for the loss of their birth family, as adoptive parents are, are dealing with the living, actual presence of the birth parent and the aftermath of the child's regular—or not so regular—meetings with him or her. Children in foster care often experience 'loyalty conflicts' due to having two sets of parents—the birth ones and the foster ones (Baker et al., 2013). For foster parents to be better prepared to deal with these conflicts, Baker et al. (2013) suggest foster parents should receive specific training to (1) recognize and eliminate behaviors on their own part that might cause these conflicts (for example, not competing with the birth parent for the child's love), (2) identify and address behaviors by the birth parent that would lead to loyalty conflicts, and (3) learn ways to help children deal with possible negative feelings triggered by the birth parent, without the foster parents denigrating the biological parent or encouraging the child to do so.

Susan & Rachel, 7 Years Old

> **REFERRAL ISSUE:** Rachel has recently been referred for therapy. Following removal from her birth mother and placement in a foster home with two younger (nonsibling) foster children, Rachel had initially been doing quite well. After visits with her birth mother started, Rachel became increasingly irritated, was getting into fights at school, and was aggressive and rejecting toward Susan, her foster mother. Rachel had been referred for therapy. The therapist is meeting with Susan from time to time.
>
> **BACKGROUND INFORMATION:** Rachel was the only child of a single mom with severe drug abuse problems. As the mother went in and out of rehab, she would leave Rachel either with neighbors or completely alone. Rachel was removed from her mother's care with contact subject to the mother's commitment to pursue a rehab treatment. Initially, Rachel connected very closely with Susan, and it felt to Susan like a positive relationship. Nine months after Rachel's removal from home, Rachel started to see her birth mother again once a week for two hours. The meetings were very erratic in that Rachel's birth mother often forgot the appointments. As noted earlier, Rachel's behavior at school and in the foster home changed. During an appointment with Rachel's therapist, Susan shares her frustration regarding the mood changes in her foster child.

THERAPIST: *What is the thing that you most dislike about your current relationship with Rachel?*

SUSAN: *I would say that Rachel was the foster child with whom I had the fewest problems. I was used to children who were highly conflictive or disruptive, but Rachel was so polite. Well, I'm not sure if she was so polite. She was very shy; she would spend hours drawing. There was the problem with her incontinence, and then the nightmares. She didn't want to go to the bathroom alone. But I could handle that. Now the problem is her shifting behavior. When we come home from the visits with her mom, she is an uncontrollable child. She yells, "I hate Tara" [her mother] and then "I hate all moms in the world! They are good for nothing!"*

THERAPIST: *This must be very intense!* [Pauses to take in the intensity that such a moment would have on Susan—attunes.] *What do you do when she starts yelling all these things?*

SUSAN: *I first try to calm her down, but it's like she is possessed! She doesn't listen to me. And at some point I feel she is right. Her mom should try a little harder. But it really hurts my feelings when she says all moms are good for nothing. I am a mom.*

THERAPIST: [Notices Susan is more inclined to speak about herself and her own feelings. She has left the question only partially answered.] *So you try to calm her down and nothing seems to work. Do you have a specific strategy to calm her down, or do you try different things? I would like to know how does this work?*

SUSAN: *Sometimes I try to divert her from those feelings and thoughts. I invite her to do something with me, like baking, so she can see it is not true that all moms are good for nothing . . . but some other times I can't deal with the feeling that she is mixing up things, that she feels her mother and I are just like the same, and this is not fair. So, at that point I guess I lose my mind, too, and then I tell her, "No, young lady, this is not true. I understand Tara does things that make you hate her, but it's unfair that you make me look like her. She is the one who doesn't show up, and I'm the one who is always there for you."*

THERAPIST: [Takes a deep breath to allow herself to calm down, tries to find the right words to help Susan shift the focus from herself and focus on Rachel's feelings.] *How frustrating it must be for you . . . and how frustrating it must be for Rachel . . . not to know when her birth mom is going to show up or not. What would you feel if you were in Rachel's shoes?* [Encourages mentalization.]

SUSAN: *I would feel the same, exactly the same, but with my birth mom, not with my foster mom.*

THERAPIST: *Let's take a look at this from a child's viewpoint. I'm Rachel, I'm a toddler, my mom goes in and out, she leaves me alone. I'm hungry. Is anybody there? Mom returns. For a few days, things are going well, and then . . . again she leaves. I'm hungry, I'm cold, I'm alone. Then she comes back, everything is fine. She is nice. She sleeps a lot but at least she is there.*

SUSAN: *You want me to feel the way she felt, I get the point, I feel as angry as she does. But it's unfair.*

THERAPIST: [Validates Susan's feeling.] *Yes, it seems so unfair. Let's go a little further. Now Mom finds her neighbor, she is willing to take care of me sometimes, she is nice but she is always in front of the TV. Mom is back, Mom is out, Mom is back again. Oh God! What can I expect from mothers?*

SUSAN: *That mothers leave their children on their own? So she feels I could be like her mother just because I'm a mom? This is what you mean?*

Notice how the therapist has not given direct answers to the parent. Although she is very aware of the types of experiences shaping Rachel's behavior, she is asking Susan to wonder about Rachel's experience. Asking questions and encouraging mentalization (see Chapters 4 and 5) activates the prefrontal lobes—both left (as she uses words) and right (as she creates a scene with sensations and emotions)—and involves Susan in the process of making sense of Rachel's behavior.

Our therapist has Susan on the right path. Now Susan seems to understand that Rachel—through her rage—is defending herself from the possibility of being abandoned again, by her, Susan. But is this understanding enough to change the way in which Susan will respond to future rage outbursts? Probably not. The therapist needs Susan to be more inclined to empathize and attune with Rachel's feelings rather than getting caught in Susan's own feelings.

THERAPIST: *It is really frustrating. And I am thinking it may also be puzzling for you if Rachel acts polite and warm towards her mom when she finally shows up, am I right?*

SUSAN: *Exactly! What am I supposed to do then? I feel like, "And now what? Did she forget that her mom dumped her last week? Why doesn't she yell at Tara as she did at me when we got home?"*

THERAPIST: *This is what you would like her to do, and maybe this is what you would do if you were in her shoes. But sometimes kids don't act the way we think they should. What is her biggest fear?*

SUSAN: *That her mother will never come back. Oh, so she doesn't dare yell at her mother.*

THERAPIST: [Speaks slowly and quietly.] *But the rage is still there.*

SUSAN: *So she yells at me. Oh—does that mean she trusts me?*

THERAPIST: [Smiles softly and nods.] *Kids just do the best they can. Rachel cannot control her mom coming in and out, so she needs to adapt to Tara appearing and being nice, and then to Tara disappearing without saying a word. This is a scenario that happens over and over again.*

SUSAN: *Poor kid. It is so unfair to her. She should be able to grow up without having all these worries in her mind.*

THERAPIST: *Yes, you are absolutely right. But in the meantime this is what she has to deal with. And* [Wants Susan to feel less alone in the job of parenting Rachel] **we** *are there to stay with Rachel, move forward with Rachel. What is the action that best represents for you the act of being with her even if you cannot change her circumstances?*

SUSAN: *Comforting her, soothing her, maybe saying "I understand what you feel." But is this enough?*

THERAPIST: *Having someone there soothing her and telling her "I understand what you feel"—it sounds to me like more than what she has received in her entire life. Would you make a picture in your mind of Rachel sitting next to you or on your lap? Perhaps your arm is around her—tell me what you see—and you are being there with her.*

Providing Ideas for Foster Parents

Although foster parents usually receive some training or information about foster parenting, research has indicated that foster parents are generally inadequately trained to manage the types of behavioral problems experienced by children in foster care (Dorsey et al., 2008). Because there is a negative association between behavioral problems and placement stability (James et al., 2004), this is a crucial issue. The information foster parents receive is seldom enough, nor does it cover all the possible challenges they will face while parenting.

Although some research indicates that it is not necessarily more difficult to engage a foster parent than a biological or adoptive parent in the treatment of her child (Dorsey et al., 2014), it is often difficult, and particularly so when we want to work with the parent on her own. A problem does occur with some foster parents who feel they are already skilled in the work they do and are not interested in meeting with another professional to learn more. As we noted with Rosina and Matt, sometimes foster parents have already developed their own approach (theory) as to why a child is behaving the way he is and what needs to be done. They leave little room for help from a child professional.

Dorsey et al. (2014) provide several ideas that can help us as we work to engage foster parents. (1) When working with foster parents, it is important to be aware of the parents' previous experiences with mental health professionals, particularly if these have been negative. (2) Rather than telling foster parents what is needed, ask them what they need for help with the child's problematic behaviors in the home. (3) Do some background research in order to be able to provide the parents with more information about the child's background. (4) Talk about how engaging in the treatment of the child could help alleviate some of the stress in the parenting work they are doing.

Rosina, Robert, & Matt

> **SEVERAL WEEKS LATER:** Our school counselor was finally able to set an appointment with Rosina and her husband. The counselor had several meetings with Matt during the intervening weeks. Although she realizes that Rosina and Robert have many things to attend to and that Rosina seems to have her own theory as to why Matt is behaving as he is, the counselor continues to be concerned that Matt needs more specialized therapy than she can provide.

SCHOOL COUNSELOR: [Realizes that even though she recognizes Matt's need for therapy, she needs first to engage Rosina and Robert in thinking about this.] *I have been thinking about what you said, Rosina, of Matt's behaviors at home—his jealousy, his misbehavior escalating since Alba arrived in your home. I am thinking that some therapy would help him with those behaviors, not just with the sexual acting out that happened at school. What do you think?*

ROSINA: *It would probably help, but is it really that necessary? I mean . . . we've been dealing pretty well with him until now.*

ROBERT: *We don't want him to be treated like a special child that needs a different type of attention. Neither Leo nor Alba receive therapy, and I wonder whether putting Matt in therapy wouldn't make things worse—make him feel different or as if there is something about him that we can't control. Isn't that a message we should* **not** *be giving him? Think how his behavior would escalate when he feels we cannot handle him?*

ROSINA: *I think we can handle him. I think this situation with Alba was unexpected and our routines have changed, but once Alba has recovered, everything is going to settle down again.*

SCHOOL COUNSELOR: [Feels frustrated—these parents are more focused on defending themselves and doing exactly what they want to do and are not focused on what the child needs. Makes an effort to see the situation from their perspective—mentalization. They are hearing her suggestions as challenging their ability, not as something the child needs. Shifts to a position of complimenting and supporting.] *You are right; once Alba is back home things will slowly return more to normal. You have developed such good skills at providing stability for the children.*

ROBERT: *That's what we pride ourselves on!*

SCHOOL COUNSELOR: *And you should* [Validates]*! The stability you are providing has enabled them to do so well. You have mentioned that even with all this stability, Matt had difficulty—became more demanding—when a new child came in. And you, with your skills, recognized that this was normal reacting and were working with it. But then, with the additional stress of the car accident and Alba's hospitalization on the family, more and unusual behavior—the sexualized behavior—appeared.* [Keeps her focus on including Rosina and Robert as part of the professional team.] *As you know, sexualized behavior may appear when a child feels upset or stressed, but the underlying source of that type of behavior is always a concern. It is this underlying source—what were his previous experiences that you and I* [Includes parents and self] *do not know about—that concerns me. This is still going to be there when Alba comes home.*

ROBERT: *You are thinking that he may have been sexually abused?*

SCHOOL COUNSELOR: *Like you [Recognizes Rosina's sensitivity and is careful to be respectful], I don't know, but some therapy with someone with more expertise than I have—working through whatever is underneath this behavior and learning new strategies to deal with the things he dislikes—could help. It could make life easier for the whole family and take some weight off you while [Moves back to validating their focus] you are doing your hard work of adapting to Alba being back home.*

ROSINA: *It sounds good, but—we have had experience with therapists with another foster kid. They lectured us! It is as if we were dumb. And it wasn't very helpful! In the end the situation was uncontrollable and the child was placed with another foster family—he lost us and we lost him—it was awful for everyone, the other kids as well.*

SCHOOL COUNSELOR: [Now is able to grasp some of Rosina and Robert's resistance and again realizes the need to recognize Rosina and Robert's skills.] *That would have been so hard, and I am impressed with how you recognized the effect on the other children in your home. That speaks to your skill as foster parents. Of course you don't need someone lecturing you. You are the ones spending a lot of time with the child, you know pretty well what is going on with him* [Validates both parents and their role in the life of the child they are caring for]. *What we* [Includes parents and self] *need is someone willing to collaborate with you as a family and someone to give Matt some space to work on his experiences as Alba comes back home. Then you as a family with the three children would be able to become more settled. We could work together to find a good therapist willing to cooperate with you and your child.*

Instead of directly confronting Rosina and Robert with the fact that Matt needs help—which they think he doesn't—or that they as parents need help—which reminds them of their previous negative experience—our school counselor works at validating Rosina and Robert, supporting them and being impressed with their expertise as parents. She links herself with them as needing more professional help. By offering herself to help them find a collaborative therapist, she acknowledges the negative impact of their previous experience with mental health providers.

Finding Out about the Foster Parents

As with adoptive parents, foster parents' own stories and past experiences influence their decision to do fostering. These past experiences will influence many of the issues we have already been discussing in this section:

- The foster parents' experiences and attachment styles will influence unconscious decisions related to their connecting or not connecting to the child.

- Unresolved past traumas in the foster parents' lives will challenge their ability not to engage in behaviors that may, unfortunately, encourage child 'loyalty conflicts.'
- Their story will certainly influence their ability to attune to the child, to be emotionally available, or to react in a positive manner to the child's most disruptive behavior.

For us to help them with their parenting, we need to know, just as we did with adoptive parents, something about:

- What was the motivation for fostering?
- What are their expectations about fostering a child?
- What do they know about the child's background?
- What information do they need in order to foster this child? Do they need to know more information about this particular child, about the effect of complex trauma on a child's behavior, about the resources within the community?
- What do they think or feel the child they are fostering needs from them?
- How do they see themselves accompanying a child in his meetings with the birth parent the child has been separated from?
- How do they see themselves saying good-bye to the child—whether he goes back to the birth parent or is adopted?

Some foster parents have been birth parents themselves. This may make them feel their previous knowledge about parenting is enough to foster a child. Instead of confronting them with the reality that their own children's stories are very different from the stories of the children they are fostering and that foster parenting itself entails many different and sometimes more complicated challenges, it would be better to ask them:

- Do they feel their parenting their own children was different in any way from parenting a foster child? How?
- What part of the parenting style with their own children are they bringing to the experience of fostering? How useful do they find it?

All these questions will help the child professional understand the foster parents' world, their resources, and the issues that might block or interfere with the experience of fostering. Let's go back to the case of Pete and Bea as foster parents of Sam to illustrate how we can use this information.

Pete & Bea, Foster Parents of Sam (Continued)

> **A WEEK LATER:** Our social worker made an appointment with Pete and Bea to discuss, in a more private setting, some of the issues she noted during the group situation—their need to be distant from Sam.

SOCIAL WORKER: *In the last group meeting we were talking about Sam's distress and the way in which you might soothe him. I thought it would be helpful to have this extra meeting so we can discuss more strategies for calming Sam when he is upset. Helping foster children calm is a very important part of their adjustment to their new home.* [Wants to engage the parents in the conversation.] *I'm impressed, Pete, with your concern in providing Sam with some structure. I remember you mentioned having read something. I was curious about it.*

PETE: *Other parents of the group suggested some readings on the internet regarding the experience of children like Sam and the things they might need. I can provide you with the links if you need.*

SOCIAL WORKER: *Thank you! That would be great. I was wondering whether you have used, with Sam, any of the strategies that worked with your own son when he was Sam's age?*

PETE: *Well, when he was a child, Patrick was diagnosed with ADD, and we were told that structure was helpful, so I guess this is something we already had in our parental repertoire.*

SOCIAL WORKER: *And you certainly did well with Patrick. I mean he is now at university. Structure must have been very helpful. When did he leave your house?*

BEA: *Eighteen months ago. A year and a half! For me it's like a century! I miss him so much!!! We both miss him so much, but I think Pete is tough, I'm weaker* [wiping tears].

By briefly diverting the conversation to Pete and Bea's birth son, the social worker finds a way to assess whether the departure of their child is still being mourned and is influencing their approach to Sam.

SOCIAL WORKER: *I can see how much you miss him. I think it's pretty normal* [Empathizes with Bea's feelings towards her birth son]. *How hard it can be to let our children grow up. I think I understand a little better your comment about not wanting to engage with Sam to avoid making his departure unbearable* [Makes the link between that experience and their approach now. Bea nods, crying, while Pete remains silent; the social worker turns to him.] *Do you, Pete, feel like Bea?*

PETE: *When Bea came up with the idea of fostering, I said to myself "Why not?" We were very young when Patrick was born, we are still young enough to parent. We were very close with our son, very present parents. And then when your child leaves the home to have his own life . . . there is this void. We have so much to give. Why not give to a child who needs it? But now, I don't know. I'm not sure it was a good idea. Maybe we were not ready yet.*

Our social worker is now able to understand what is happening. Pete and Bea's own state of mourning is preventing them from engaging with Sam. They have been surprised by this new experience and have few resources to provide emotional availability for Sam when he needs it. While providing structure to this child is certainly helpful, their distance is interfering with the most important issue involved in fostering a child—providing Sam with an *attachment* figure.

Until Pete and Bea work through their own feelings regarding the departure of their son, any training or psychoeducation regarding strategies to help Sam soothe while in distress will be unlikely to be successful. Either referral for separate therapy for themselves (if they will accept it) or continued support from the social worker (if she has the training or can get special supervision for this work) would be recommended to help them gain a better understanding of the link between their experience of living without their birth son while fostering a traumatized child whose needs for affection are as important as his needs for structure.

Summary

Being a parent entails a huge responsibility. It is not possible to be a perfect parent. Even if we do know, as parents, how we should act in certain situations, how we should respond, what we should avoid doing, we will still fail. While some parents have trouble seeing how their actions influence or impact their children's behavior, others look too much at themselves and feel guilt and shame—*what did I do wrong?* With adoptive parents, each of these extremes becomes even worse. They adopt a child with genetic information different from their own, and some rely on this to explain everything that happens with their children. When working with these parents, the biggest challenge will be to engage them as the 'nurturing force' able to shape the 'genetic data.'

When parents connect to the suffering their children have been through, they may feel they have to do everything well and not allow themselves to make a single mistake. They may start to feel that the child's lack of progress is their own responsibility. With these parents, the challenge is to help them understand—and experience—that secure attachment, and that always having positive interactions is not going to happen. Their job as a parent is more about repairing the asynchrony in parent-child communication that their child learned in the birth home and maybe even in foster homes. For the children in this chapter, communication in the past had always failed; asynchrony was all they knew.

The greatest challenge for child professionals will be to tune in to both parts of this interaction—to the child and to the parent. The child professionals may need to act as a translator of two different languages speaking about the same subject—love—experienced in two—sometimes radically different—ways. In order for new positive bonding to happen, we will need to work towards a new meaning of love: a meaning that allows for the bruises from the past and the mourning for what was lost but includes hope for an unharmed future. When working with foster parents where the future is unknown, there are even more challenges. We have discussed some of those challenges, remembering that we need to work with parents, not as experts, but as part of a team for supporting their children.

Chapter 7—Points to Remember

- Parents' and children's expectations can be dramatically different, one from the other, and the meeting between both can produce mismatches in the communication and bonding.
- Adoptive parents might want to avoid the previous story of the child, dismiss it, or even deny it. In helping them face the story of the child they adopted, parents are assisted in meaning-making of the child's behaviors.
- Encouraging parents to talk about a negative diagnosis or a disappointment related to their child helps them process and, with time, accept the diagnosis and disappointment.
- Helping parents understand and realize that the child's difficulty to attach to them is related to the child's past, not to them, can correct some of the mismatches in the communication.
- The child professional needs to gather information about the child's traumatic past and the parents' story surrounding the adoption process.
- Helping parents see their child in a compassionate, loving-kindness way—especially in what relates to the child's past experiences—will help them attune to the child.
- Child professionals need to stay attuned to parents and give them exercises they accept to practice. Remember that adoptive parents might feel easily judged, even more so than biological parents.
- Some adoptive parents might have disorganized attachment patterns in their own story. Knowing this in advance will be helpful in that some of the child's behavior might trigger these disorganized attachment patterns in his parents, adding to the bonding difficulties the child might bring.
- Helping adoptive parents be consistent and predictable with their children will assist them in not engaging in the shifting, controlling behaviors their children might display, and this will, in turn, help to build the new attachment.
- Recognizing how fostering differs from adoption helps us give foster parents the best help needed.

Notes

1 Children who have lived within situations of chronic interpersonal violence can develop complex posttraumatic and dissociative symptoms such as hypervigilance, affect and behavioral dysregulation, amnesia, depersonalization, derealization, dramatic changes in their moods and behaviors, and regressive behaviors. For a more complete explanation of the kind of symptoms the child might develop, the reader is referred to Silberg (2013) and Waters (2016).
2 The ARC model of therapy refers to the three core domains of intervention its authors consider the most important areas for working with traumatized children and adolescents: attachment, self-regulation, and competency. They suggest these three domains

should be worked across different contexts: individual (working with the child/adolescent), family, and social (Blaustein & Kinniburgh, 2010).
3 This exercise has been adapted from Self-Compassion Break exercise, by Dr. Kristin Neff. http://self-compassion.org/category/exercises/. Retrieved on July 30th, 2015.
4 Common humanity refers to the acknowledgement that 'suffering' is not just a personal and unique experience (like when one says and feels "why is this happening TO ME?") but rather a universal one. All people suffer; all people struggle with their lives. Compassion meditation training starts with exercising a focus in self-compassion to move towards compassion for others.
5 EMDR stands for Eye Movement Desensitization and Reprocessing, a model of therapeutics developed by Francine Shapiro, PhD, that has been empirically validated for the treatment of PTSD. For more information, visit www.emdria.org.

CHAPTER **8**

Our Experience

As we meet with parents, we are going to find there are some parents with whom we enjoy working, and then there are others whom we would prefer to avoid. This wish to avoid may come from the negative dynamics we observe between the parent and child, or it may come from the negative dynamics we experience between ourselves and the parent. In either case, it is a relationship issue, the very thing we have been talking about throughout this book. In previous chapters we have been focusing on how we can help parents shift the negative dynamics occurring between themselves and their child. In this chapter we are going to focus on the negative dynamics occurring between ourselves and the parent—why these dynamics happen, why they are important to pay attention to, and how we can shift them.

Within the counseling and therapy world, the reactions and behaviors displayed by an individual which reflect something from their past are referred to as 'transference.'[1] Then the reaction experienced by the therapist to the individual's reactions and behaviors is referred to as 'countertransference.' Within the nontherapeutic world, these dynamics are more likely to be referred to as 'reaction—counterreaction' or as 'behavior—response.' Whichever terminology is used, this interactive dynamic plays a major role in how helpful we, as professionals, can be with the individuals with whom we are working. We shall, in the present discussion, be using the term 'countertransference' to refer to our experience with a parent.

Countertransference has also been described as the entirety of the professional's emotional reactions to an individual within an interactive situation (Bouchard et al., 1995) or as the reactions in the professional as a result of the interaction between the professional and the individual (Gelso & Hayes, 2007). Our discussion will be based on the definition referring to the entirety of the professional's experience. Including all reactions in our discussion provides us with the opportunity to clarify which of these reactions we need to separate from our work with the parents, which reactions we need to recognize and better understand so that they do not interfere with our being attuned—and therefore of help—with parents, and which reactions can provide information that assists us in creating a more helpful experience for the parent.

There can be positive countertransference—this occurs often with the parents with whom we enjoy working, and less often (but there are still good moments) with those we prefer to avoid. Positive countertransference does not necessarily mean experiencing positive feelings when with the parent. Attuning with a parent who is feeling depressed or angry means holding inside oneself some level—although less reactive than that which the parent is experiencing—of depression or anger. This is attuning with the parent—feeling what he or she is feeling. That is what makes it 'positive.'

If the child/youth professional either knowingly or unknowingly counters the parent's experience rather than attuning with it, that is an error—that would be a negative countertransference. When a parent is feeling depressed or angry and we, unable to accept that the parent is justified in feeling that way, in some way reject the parent's feeling, that is a negative countertransference reaction. We are not attuning with the parent's experience but opposing it.

When parents behave toward us in a negative manner, similar to how they may have been treated by their parents or other negative individuals in their lives (negative replay of an early relationship experience transference), we may fall into the responding position in this negative pattern (negative countertransference). If, however, rather than falling into the negative interactive pattern, we become curious about their behavior, where it comes from, and how it helps or doesn't help them, we are responding from a positive countertransference position. This is positive because it is a position that opens a door to change.

An inability to attune with a particular person and at a particular moment may be a result of (1) what is going on in our own lives at that moment, (2) our past experiences, and (3) the dynamics within the relationship between ourselves and that parent. In this chapter we are going to talk first about those three factors—what they are, how we can be aware of them, and which we want to keep and which we want to eliminate. We will talk about why countertransference is so important to pay attention to and what happens if we do not pay attention to it. Then we will talk about how we can shift negative countertransference.

Where Countertransference Comes From; Why We Need to Pay Attention to It

What is Going On in Our Own Lives at That Particular Moment

We, like the parents, are human. Whether we are in our professional role or in one of our many personal roles, we are affected by what happens in our day-to-day world. It may be something very personal—a disagreement with someone important to us; a positive comment from a colleague or partner—or something completely outside ourselves—the sun shining; the eighth day in a row of rain. In either case, our autonomic nervous system is affected, which, in turn, activates our body and our brain, just as it does for a parent. Whether we are aware of this interference and what we do with the interference may affect how we view the parent and the comments and responses we make. It may affect the particular words we choose, our tone of voice, our body posture, or our eye contact.

A negative event is likely to create a heaviness in our bodies and, if there is any sense of threat to our physical or emotional safety, the fight-flight response would be triggered. While we may not consciously think of the event as a threat, the negative happening may at an unconscious level remind us of something that was experienced as a threat when we were a child. The release of adrenalin and cortisol (fight-flight response), even in low amounts, starts a cascade of physical responses (tightening of muscles, increased level of tension), cognitive responses (decrease in activation within the prefrontal and memory areas of the brain), and emotional responses (increase in activation of the amygdala fear/anger reactivity). Our words, tone of voice, body posture, and eye contact are affected.

A positive event, in contrast, would likely create a lightness in our bodies, and we would sit up straighter but without the stiffness that occurs with the negative event. Our voice tone would be lighter and our choice of words perhaps more positive even though the thought we are trying to convey is the same. We would be more likely to establish relaxed but consistent eye contact. In other words, a general sense of well-being is present.

But we do not want to respond to the parent or the child from where we are; we want to respond from where they are. We want to attune not with ourselves at that moment but with them. If there is time, we may be able to think through the reaction—body response, emotional reaction, cognitive thought—and then, very consciously, set it aside. But often there is no time or, at least, no adequate time. This is where mindfulness (see discussion, Chapters 3 and 4) can help us: grounding ourselves to this particular moment, noticing how our body is feeling, linking that feeling to what has gone on for us (the disagreement, the compliment, the lightness of the sun, the dreariness of the rain), and then reorienting ourselves to this moment and the parent or child with whom we are about to meet.

CHILD/YOUTH PROFESSIONAL: [Takes a slow breath. I am here now in my office/in my car/in my classroom. My body is feeling tight; something is not feeling right. I'm not sure why I'm not feeling right, but something is off. This 'off' has to do with me, not this child, this parent. I can be aware of this feeling and put it to the side, knowing that I can come back to it this evening and can pay attention to it then. Right now I can take a breath, I can notice the parent's way of being, and I can be with the parent.]

If we have difficulty putting our personal experiencing to the side, we can practice what we have been preaching—use visualization. In our mind's eye we can make a picture of the experience and then take that image, in our mind's eye, to the closet where we hung our coat at the beginning of the day and place it there to be recovered with the coat at the end of the day. If it is more a feeling or sensation rather than an actual experience, we can take that feeling and give it a shape and a color and then place the symbol in the closet with our coat, again reminding ourselves that we will spend time with it later. It will be important that we actually do that—go back to the experience or feeling at the end of the day, think about it, figure out where it came from and how it can be handled. If we ignore the events or feelings that affect us, they will intrude more, not less. Taking time to resolve personal issues is essential if we are to become skillful at separating ourselves from the impact of our daily events.

We are also going to be affected by fatigue, physical exhaustion, and illness and by illness in the people close to us. Our resilience (ability to stay with the interaction of the moment) at those times will be more limited, and we need to be patient with ourselves. We need to be aware when this happens and brainstorm with ourselves or colleagues as to how we can best handle these situations. In situations with negative personal experiences but where we are well rested and healthy, we are likely to experience more resilience. There is always this interaction between our physical and emotional selves. But all of this has to do with us, and we need to keep it out of the interaction between ourselves and the parents.

Difficulty attuning with a parent or keeping our mind on what is being discussed lets us know we are experiencing some interference. The first thing to check out, as we have discussed, is our personal situation, and we should set aside any issues that may be interfering. For those of us new to the field, this can be quite difficult. Remember, the more we practice it, the easier it becomes. And there are other factors to be considered when noticing difficulties in our relationship with a parent.

Our Past Experiences

Our past experiences can affect our reactions to parents or to the issues that come up in the work. It may be that the parent's present or past story is similar in some way to our own story—he or she experienced changes in family composition, violence within the family, neglect of him- or herself, need to take over caretaking, an alcoholic parent, frequent moves, or disrespect. As the parent tells about his or her experiences, our past experiences can be triggered. At other times, as the parent talks, we may find that our values—both those we learned growing up and those we have chosen as adults—influence our reactions. And, at times, it may be our personal vulnerabilities or insecurities that insert themselves.

Our Triggers

At times some event or person from our past comes into our mind. This is easy to recognize as something from the past having been triggered. We can wonder why it was triggered and how it can help us, or hinder us, in understanding the parent's situation. But at other times, our past is triggered only as an emotional or somatic reaction. This is harder to recognize as a trigger.

If we notice an unusual sense of comfort or discomfort in our interaction with a parent, this likely reflects something going on for us. If we notice ourselves behaving in a way that is unusual for us[2]—having intrusive thoughts or a high level of agitation during the session; having difficulty remembering the session when writing our notes; having drawn an unclear or inaccurate genogram; having thoughts related to a session intrude into our thoughts outside work or even in the middle of the night—and it cannot be explained by what is going on presently in our world, then we need to consider if an early issue of our own has been triggered.

Having one's own triggers is not all bad. These triggers can help us, if we are careful, recognize what the parent experienced. What we have to be sure of is that our triggers do not distort our understanding of the parent's experience. This means recognizing triggers, whether they take the form of a cognitive recall, an emotional response, or a somatic reaction; realizing that our experience of a situation is unique to us and would not be the same as the parent's; and placing our experience to the side while we stay engaged with the parent and his or her experience.

If, at that point, a trigger continues to intrude or bother us in some way, it is an indication we need to do more personal self-exploration. This exploration may be done with a professional or with ourselves, depending on which is most needed and available at that time. Meditation, mindfulness, journaling, and self-talk can all be helpful if the distorted negative internalizations regarding ourselves or the world that occurred because of early negative experiences (Wieland, 1997) have already been sorted through.[3] If we are experiencing or re-experiencing old negative internalizations such as feeling as if there is something intrinsically wrong with us or we are to blame for abuse that happened (Wieland, 1997)—not just recalling the old experiences—this is likely an indicator that we need to find some outside professional help.

Negative triggers may occur not only because of a story similar to our own but also from the parent being similar in some way to someone who played a negative role in our lives. If the parent's negative way of behaving, either to ourselves or to her or his child—gestures, words used, tone of voice—is similar to what we experienced as a child, we are likely to be triggered. And if the parent is similar physically to a negative figure in our lives, we are likely to be triggered. The difficult part can be figuring out what or who has been triggered. Indeed, the parent may even remind ourselves of ourselves, particularly some aspect of our younger selves that we would prefer to forget. Then, as noted earlier, we have the task of separating our experience from the parent and setting it aside while working with the parent. Then coming back to this 'figuring out' later and doing whatever personal reprocessing remains to be done. Being triggered does not mean there is something wrong with us or that we are in the wrong profession; it simply means we are human.

Once a trigger is identified, recognized by us as belonging to ourselves and not the parent, the irritation experienced by ourselves usually calms. Indeed, even when we are unable to recognize what has triggered us, just recognizing that the reaction belongs to us and is not something about the parent seems to be helpful.

Dotti, Isaac, & Danny, 6 Years Old

> **REFERRAL:** Dotti and Isaac had referred their son, Danny, to the school counselor because of his inability to separate from his mother without extreme protests and panic.
>
> **ASSESSMENT SESSION:** Both Dotti and Isaac attend the initial assessment session. The school counselor is struck by Isaac's tendency to withdraw. He constantly defers to Dotti and praises all the effort she has made with Danny. The counselor finds himself highly irritated by Isaac. He recognizes that Dotti is somewhat controlling and Isaac feels unsure of himself. This does not fit with his perception of how a couple should be—but why this level of irritation?!?

COUNSELOR PROCESSING: [Hears his voice take on an edge when he speaks to Isaac. Takes several slow breaths and relaxes his shoulders. Even with this level of attention to his internal state, continues to have a sharper response to Isaac than to Dotti. Throughout the next week, the counselor thinks often about Isaac—wondering of whom or what Isaac is reminding him. He pictures Isaac in his mind—it may be a physical resemblance that is triggering him—and how Isaac seems to withdraw—it may be a behavior that is triggering him. As he thinks about it, he has a memory come back of how his mother would seem to disappear whenever his father yelled at him. When he started grade 1, he had been afraid to go to school (like Danny) and his father made fun of him and yelled at him. But Isaac was not his mother. Isaac had his own reasons for being unsure of himself. Danny's dad, Isaac, was really going to need the counselor's belief in him.]

NEXT SESSION: Prior to the session, the counselor reminds himself that he is seeing Dotti and Isaac, Danny's parents. This is not his father and mother—this is separate from him and separate from his experiences. Curiously, as Isaac comes in behind Dotti, the counselor feels no irritation. Isaac is indeed being deferential to Dotti, but it feels like something to be observed and considered, not a cause of irritation.

The counselor's (1) awareness of his irritation, (2) recognition that the irritation belonged to him, and (3) effort to understand where the irritation came from provided enough processing that the irritation did not continue to intrude. If, however, the counselor had spent the week complaining in the staff room about a father who was 'weak' and deferential, we can easily predict that the irritation would have continued and the possibility of the counselor being able to be of assistance to Danny and his family would be minimal. (See example of Fran and Alex, p. 42, in which the therapist was not able to figure out what was being triggered, but because of her acceptance that the irritation belonged to her and her effort to understand where it came from, the irritation shifted.)

Our past experiences of events and of people can trigger personal reactions that need to be separated from the work we are doing with children or parents. Another stumbling block, and one that we do not usually label as a block, may be the values we hold.

Our Values

In that we chose to work with children we are likely to hold numerous values related to children and how they should be treated—children are to be valued and not hurt; children need a consistent and caring family; children need to be listened to and respected; children are to be loved and cherished; no one should give up on a child. These values provide a strong and important support for our work. But they can also make it difficult for us to hear and attune with a parent when his or her values differ from ours.

Danielle (Foster Mother) & Tony, 6 Years Old

> **REFERRAL:** Tony, who had been raised in a home with severe abuse and neglect until he was 3 years old, was referred for therapy at age 5. He was, at that time, living with a single foster mother who had applied to adopt him.
>
> **PRESENT SITUATION:** Although initially Tony responded well in therapy, his behavior had deteriorated since he started school. Danielle explained to the therapist that she still loved Tony but was becoming frightened by his behavior and was feeling that she should not be adopting him.

THERAPIST: [First startles with Danielle's comment, then feels frightened as to what would happen for Tony, then angry at Danielle—how could she give up on Tony? Parents are not to give up on their children. His voice takes on a sharp edge.] *We just need to meet more often and be sure that we are giving Tony all the support he needs.*

DANIELLE: *I am giving him every minute of my time and every ounce of my energy, and I have nothing left for me. I need to have a life, too, and as long as Tony is with me, I can't have a life.*

THERAPIST: *What with the new experience of school, he needs more reassurance from you right now. He needs to know that you will not give up on him.*

DANIELLE: *There is no more I can give him. He is going to have to go to another family.*

Our therapist became caught up in his values—children need a consistent family, no one should give up on a child—and in that process missed what was happening for Danielle. Rather than giving Danielle some support and space to think through her decisions (see Chapter 5 sections on attunement, validation, and emotional regulation), the therapist actually pushed Danielle further towards giving up.

If we challenge a parent's values, we are not only being disrespectful but also likely to be unsuccessful in our work with the parent. While our values are important—they offer us support in the work we do—we need to be careful they do not interfere with our ability to attune with a parent whose values may be different from our own.

THERAPIST: [First startles with Danielle's comment, then feels frightened as to what would happen for Tony, then angry at Danielle—how could she give up on Tony? Parents are not to give up on their children. **Notices his agitation inside**, takes a deep breath. Feels like Danielle is discarding Tony, and that is not all right. But that is his belief, his value—where is she coming from at this moment? Has fright taken over? Has loneliness taken over? Paces his words slowly.] *That's a huge feeling, would be a huge decision. Tell me about it.*

With this reflection and then response, the therapist is recognizing and acknowledging his agitation. This allows him to set it aside and focus instead on Danielle and what is happening for her—mentalization.

DANIELLE: *I am giving him every minute of my time and every ounce of my energy and I have nothing left for me. I need to have a life, too, and as long as Tony is with me, I can't have a life.*

THERAPIST: *Yes, you need a life, time for yourself. Let's look at how we can make that possible. It might even be possible while Tony is with you.*

DANIELLE: *Thank you for understanding. My friends just think I am being selfish, but I feel like I am being suffocated. I can't sleep, can't focus at work, don't have any fun.*

With this exchange, the therapist is able to maintain his connection with Danielle. Nothing has been solved, but there is more possibility for a solution that would be positive for both Tony and Danielle. The therapist is not shifting his values but also is not letting his personal values get in the way of his being able to hear and attune with Danielle.

Our Vulnerabilities

Because all of us are human and make mistakes, we have vulnerabilities—those areas in which we feel less secure. These vulnerabilities or insecurities are likely a result of how we were treated by our parents, siblings, teachers, peers, or by society in general. And now those vulnerabilities are going to be triggered at times by what happens at work with our colleagues or with the individuals whom we are trying to help.

Because of vulnerabilities related to whether we are liked, we may refrain from challenging some parents. If our vulnerabilities are related to being successful, we may find ourselves blaming parents or pulling away from work with parents when the therapy is not going well and relating better, as well as making more effort, with parents who praise us for the help we have given them. If being smart was emphasized in our family growing up, and particularly where our own capability was questioned, we may find ourselves more concerned about explaining theory to parents than being attuned to their emotional state. In each of these instances, and in dozens more, we need to be aware when our vulnerabilities are being triggered and we are responding from our own situation and not from that of the parent with whom we are working.

Having recognized and set aside reactions (countertransference) occurring because of what is happening in our own world at that moment, having recognized personal triggers, values, and vulnerabilities that come up in our thinking and evaluated how they can inform us but not distort our understanding of the parent, we are still left with numerous stumbling blocks in our work with parents. We may find ourselves reacting in negative or unusual ways with a parent—where does this come from?

Replay of Parents' Past Relationship Dynamics

We come to our work with children and their parents from different areas of professional training. All of us will have learned some about child development and family functioning. We may, however, have learned very little about the interactive dynamics that occur between people. Yet these dynamics are relevant to the work we are doing each time we meet, or don't meet, with parents. Most relevant are going to be the dynamics we have already been talking about—attachment dynamics.

Because the earliest interrelationship experience each of us has is the attachment experience, it is this pattern that continues to affect our personal interactions. In Chapter 1, we talked about the how the parents' early experiences with their parents taught them a pattern of interaction based on interactive attachment. We, like the parents and children we are working with, had our own early experiences with our parents that taught us a pattern of interaction based on interactive attachment. In Chapter 3, we talked about how these patterns are held in neuronal networks within the brain and replay themselves over and over unless meaningful different experiences intervene. In the present discussion we are going to focus on how a parent's experience of attachment dynamics, as well as our own, can affect the interaction between the parent and ourselves.

Davies and Frawley (1994), in their analysis of transference–countertransference, introduced the concept of interpersonal dynamics having two different positions—that of the individual acting on the other person and the 'other person' acting on the individual. Children experiencing—as all children do—a repetitive interactive child-parent pattern learn both of these positions. These positions are described by Davies and Frawley as reoccurring within therapeutic interactions between client and therapist. This is a somewhat different meaning of the term 'transference' than is generally used. Here the individual is taking on (replaying) a role learned from the early relationship as opposed to experiencing the other person as someone from their childhood. When the parent is in the child position and reacting to the other person as if they were the parent, this is the common usage of the term 'transference.' But when they are in the parent position, the term transference can be confusing. For this reason we shall use the term 'replay from early relationship.' The term 'countertransference' still applies in that we are reacting to the parent's replay.

Although Davies and Frawley (1994) were focusing on the dynamics that occur within an abuse scenario and were focusing on therapeutic interactions, their framework can help us understand the dynamics that are likely to replay within the interactions between ourselves and parents. Of particular relevance to our discussion will be the dynamics within attachment patterns—secure, ambivalent, avoidant, disorganized. We will also talk briefly about a few of the myriad different dynamic patterns that may occur between parent and child and, thus, between professional and parent.

Each pattern has two different positions: the 'child's position' and the 'parent's position.' Both of these positions are taught to the 'parent as child.' The 'child's position' is taught as the child experiences it; the 'parent's position' is taught as the child observes it (remember mirror neurons, Chapter 3). As we have discussed throughout this book, the parent's early attachment pattern taught by her or his parent is often repeated with the parent's own child. It is also likely to be repeated within the parent's adult relationships (Bartholomew, 1993; Levine & Heller, 2010; Mikulincer & Shaver, 2007) and, thus, with ourselves as we interact with them.

For parents raised within a secure attachment pattern, the parent now grown may enact the 'parent position' by checking that the other person in the interaction ('child position') is safe and attended to or, at times, may enact the 'child position' by looking to the other person ('parent position') for assurance that safety and assistance is going to be there. When parents feel safe in their work with us and can approach us for assistance, we will indeed have a secure helping relationship with them. This represents positive 'replay from early relationship': countertransference dynamics. The challenging situations for us will occur when the parent comes with an insecure attachment replay.

Ambivalent Attachment Pattern

As the parent plays out the 'parent position' or the 'child position,' we will find ourselves, all too often, falling into the opposite position. That is, as the parent plays out the parent's role within, for example, an ambivalent attachment pattern—sometimes becoming engaged in the work with us and sometimes pulling back from being engaged in the work—we will, unless we are careful, fall into the demanding child role of wanting more and more from the parent. We have seen what the parent can do, and that is what we want to encourage.

Gloria & Jacob, 12 Years Old

> **REFERRAL:** Jacob was referred to a youth support worker because of out of control behaviors at home and resistant behaviors at school.
>
> **SUPPORT PLAN:** The youth support worker spent time with Jacob and also met together with Gloria and Jacob in an effort to encourage more positive interaction between them.
>
> **INTERACTION:** Gloria spent most of the mother-youth time complaining about how obstructionist Jacob was and resisting the support worker's ideas. The youth worker met with his supervisor, and they spent considerable time talking about how the worker could best approach Gloria and planning activities for Gloria and Jacob to do together. The next few sessions went more smoothly, with Gloria and Jacob even having some laughs together. These sessions, however, always ended with Gloria complaining loudly about how Jacob behaved when the youth worker was not there. The worker was encouraged by the positive moments and continued to put considerable time into thinking about and planning for the joint sessions. He did additional reading on attachment and encouraged Gloria to spend more positive time with Jacob. Although Gloria continued to engage well in the joint sessions, she changed nothing else. With time, the support worker became discouraged and alternated between wanting more from Gloria and feeling totally discouraged and putting in less and less effort. They seemed to be just 'spinning their wheels'.

Although Gloria showed inconsistent responding to the support worker (the 'parent position' within an ambivalent attachment pattern—see Chart 8.1, upper left box), with good effort when the support worker was there and little effort at other times, the support worker—focusing on how well Gloria did during the sessions—pushed Gloria to change the way she was doing things at other times—the 'child position' of wanting, demanding more and more (Chart 8.1, lower left box). That, unfortunately, was beyond what Gloria was able to accomplish at that time. For Gloria, the experience of not being able to do what was asked of her would be a familiar situation, leading to discouragement and, as a result, increasingly inconsistent behavior by her (see left side curved-arrow in Chart 8.1 indicating the exacerbating effect the support worker's 'child position' behavior had on Gloria's 'parent position' behavior). As could be predicted from the ambivalent pattern, Gloria's inconsistent responding, despite all of the support worker's effort and well-meaning enthusiasm, leads to him feeling discouraged and, as a result, less consistent in his own effort.

The parent who was taught an ambivalent attachment style might, in other situations, play out not the 'parent's position' but the 'child's position'—wanting, demanding more and more from us. In that situation, we are all too likely to 'fall into' (countertransference) the parent's role of being inconsistent—sometimes attentive to the parent and thinking through what is happening and sometimes exhausted from all the demands and, therefore, putting less and less effort into working with the parent.

Raymond & Lisa, 14 Years Old

> **REFERRAL:** Lisa was placed in a behavioral support classroom because of her aggressive behaviors in the school. She was showing similar aggressive behaviors at home.
>
> **SUPPORT PLAN:** The special education teacher met with Raymond before Lisa started in his class. The teacher mentioned that he liked to keep in close communication with the parents of his students and, although he could not take calls during class time, he would always return a call before the end of the day.
>
> **INTERACTION:** Raymond called the teacher several times the first week Lisa was in the class, and the teacher returned the calls over his noon hour. Raymond would tell the teacher in detail about some disruption Lisa had made in the family and ask for the teacher's advice. These calls took more and more time from the teacher's only break from the classroom, and he decided not to respond at noon. He was then having to call Raymond in the evening and sometimes forgot.

In this scenario, Raymond played out the 'child position' of wanting more and more from the teacher (see Chart 8.1, upper right box). The teacher, finding himself unable to respond adequately, became increasingly inconsistent ('parent position,' lower right box) in his response to Raymond. Raymond's early experience that people could not be counted on to be consistently attentive to him was reinforced (right side curved-arrow). It is easy to hypothesize that Raymond felt let down by the teacher and, as a result, took on a negative attitude toward Lisa's teacher.

Ambivalent Attachment Pattern

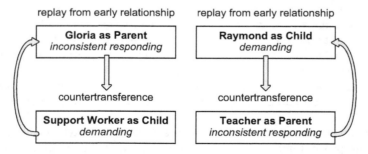

Chart 8.1 Ambivalent attachment pattern—parent's replay from early relationship experiences with our subsequent countertransference reaction.

As becomes clear in these two examples, both the support worker and the teacher became exhausted and discouraged in their interactions with the parent, as undoubtedly the parents did with them.

Responding to Gloria and Raymond's ambivalent behavior styles (replay from early relationship experiences), the support worker and the teacher fell into (countertransference) the ambivalent pattern presented by the parent. Their interaction with each parent would, unfortunately, have confirmed what the parent had already been taught—that people are inconsistent not only in their willingness to help, but also, as the 'parent as child' would have experienced it, in their belief in the parent-figure as a supportive, protective individual. In response to the support worker wanting more from Gloria and the teacher being inconsistent with Raymond (see curved-arrows in Chart 8.1), the negative responding by Gloria and Raymond would have increased, not decreased.

In other situations, a support worker or teacher might have shifted the guidelines established for his or her work with the parent or, alternatively, might not have carried through with the established treatment plan. In those situations, in which we are wanting to foster a more secure attachment between parent and child, we would instead have reinforced the parent's insecure ambivalent pattern.

We shall return later in this chapter to Gloria and Raymond, but for the moment we are going to look at how other attachment pattern dynamics may play out between ourselves and parents.

Avoidant Attachment Pattern

For the parents who were taught the avoidant attachment pattern when they were young, the parent may take the 'parent position' of pulling away as we try to engage them (see Chart 8.2, top left box).

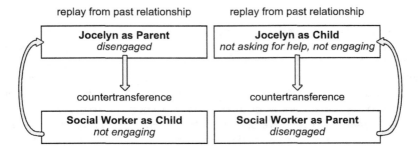

Chart 8.2 Avoidant attachment pattern—parent's replay of past relationship experiences with our subsequent countertransference.

Jocelyn & Delia, 13 Years Old

> **REFERRAL:** Jocelyn had been referred to a protection social worker over concerns related to how Jocelyn was disciplining Delia.
>
> **SUPPORT PLAN:** Jocelyn was to attend a parenting course and meet biweekly with the protection social worker to discuss issues that came up at home.
>
> **INTERACTION:** In the sessions with the social worker, Jocelyn showed little interest and offered only limited information. When asked questions regarding herself, she stated that that information was not relevant to the present issue. Jocelyn started canceling sessions and did not return phone calls. When Jocelyn did attend she was resistant to the efforts the social worker made to engage her in conversation. The social worker found himself feeling increasingly ineffective and dreading appointments with Jocelyn. Not knowing how to engage Jocelyn, he ended up spending most of the appointment time telling Jocelyn what she should be doing with Delia even though he knew that this was less effective than engaging with a parent to develop ideas (Chart 8.2, lower left box).

In other situations, a parent or even the same parent may enact the 'child position' within an avoidant attachment pattern—not asking for help and rejecting help even when having difficulty.

> **INTERACTION:** When Jocelyn did come to an appointment, she stated that she saw no reason for the individual sessions. She was meeting the requirements by attending the parenting course, and she was finding that she was able to manage Delia just fine. Although further sessions were not scheduled, the social worker encouraged Jocelyn to call him when a difficult situation did occur. And, as he said, difficult situations were normal for families with young teens. Six months later the school again referred the family to protection services—the difficulties with Delia had continued, and Jocelyn's method of responding had remained unchanged.

Quite logically, we may wonder why Jocelyn, who clearly needs help, pulls away from engaging with the social worker and, even when in situations of difficulty, does not ask for help (Chart 8.2, upper right box). Early experiences with an avoidant attachment pattern would have taught Jocelyn that needing help leads to rejection. Although this teaching was at an unconscious level, it affects Jocelyn's behavior when interacting with a helping professional—a role similar to that of a parent. We often refer to this type of behavior as 'defensive behavior.' The term 'defensive' has a pejorative sound to it, but it is totally logical—why would anyone invite rejecting behavior? The parent who grew up within an avoidant attachment pattern would link 'needing help' or 'asking for help' with 'being rejected.'

And what happened for our social worker when Jocelyn (in the 'parent position'—Chart 8.2, top left box) avoided him or (in the 'child position'—top right box) did not ask for help? As she distanced herself, the social worker found himself being less and less engaged in the work (see lower left box). The times they did meet, the social worker fell into a pattern of teaching—avoiding interaction. In that Jocelyn did not ask for help, the social worker contacted her less and less (Chart 8.2—lower right box). Jocelyn's pattern of avoidant relating (disengaged, not asking for help) continued and likely increased (Chart 8.2, side curved-arrows).

When working with a parent with an avoidant attachment pattern, we may find our mind wandering. We may find we do not follow through on issues. We tend to delay contacting these parents and are relieved when they do not show up for an appointment. Although normally we review our notes from the previous appointment before meeting with a parent, suddenly it will be time to meet, and we have not looked at the notes or even thought about the parent or child. We have avoided them.

We do not wear a badge that says "we have avoided thinking about you," but people are aware when the other individual is disinterested in them. Perhaps it is our body position—pulling back a bit—our tone of voice—boredom or fatigue creeps in—our eye contact is limited. If we do not pay attention, the parent we are working with is well aware of it. She or he has encountered it before and is sensitive to it.

Disorganized Attachment Pattern

The parent who experienced an early disorganized attachment pattern, without some assistance over the years, is likely to enact disorganized responding (both the 'parent position' and the 'child position') when working with a professional.

Alfred & Noah, 15 Years Old

REFERRAL: Noah was referred for therapy after being reported for having exhibited his genitals to a group of younger children. Alfred was a single parent raising Noah and his younger brother.

INTERACTION: During the Developmental Interview, when Alfred's therapist asked questions about what Noah was like as a child, Alfred started talking about Noah but switched to talking about himself and his various activities when he was 15 years old. The therapist, knowing that he needed to complete an assessment and treatment plan, explained why he was asking those particular questions and returned to the original question. Alfred became agitated and started asking how his son's behavior was going to affect what other people thought of him as a father. The therapist stated that they could talk about that another time, but today they needed to stay with the questions being asked. At the end of the session, despite being more controlling than his usual style, the therapist had completed only three of the ten areas required for the assessment report. He scheduled another appointment with Alfred.

At the beginning of the next appointment, Alfred asked what the treatment plan for himself and Noah would be. The therapist explained that first

> he needed to learn more about each of them and about the family. Alfred replied that he was so pleased to have this chance for therapy for himself but that they needed a plan immediately in that he would not be able to come in again for another month due to overtime at work. The therapist became agitated, stating that no treatment plan could be developed if Alfred did not cooperate. At the end, looking back on the session, the therapist wondered how it was that he had become so confrontational—this was not his usual way of being; why had it happened?

In both sessions, the therapist became disorganized (Chart 8.3). In the first appointment, in response to Alfred's disorganized and self-absorbed presentation ('parent position,' top left box), the therapist found himself becoming controlling ('child position,' lower left box) in an effort to complete an assessment. In the second appointment, rather than staying attuned to Alfred's experience (both controlling and disorganized—'child's position,' top right box), the therapist found himself feeling disorganized and off-balance ('parent position,' lower right box). As Alfred experienced the therapist's disorganized and controlling, as well as emotional responding, his own negative patterns would, unfortunately, have been reinforced (see side curved-arrows, Chart 8.3).

The therapist found himself responding in atypical ways. He was used to working with difficult cases and resistant parents—that was not the difficulty. The interactions with Alfred were disorganizing. The therapist felt like he had lost his bearings. His responses did not provide a clear structure for Albert. Rather than the therapist providing a new and healthier experience for Albert, Albert had disorganized the therapist. Albert's unhealthy way of interacting with others was reinforced (Chart 8.3, side curved-arrows).

Disorganized Attachment Pattern

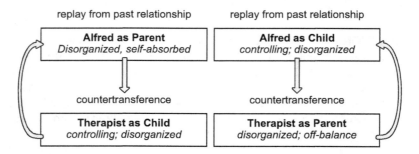

Chart 8.3 Disorganized attachment pattern—parent's replay of past relationship experiences with our subsequent countertransference.

While this discussion has focused on the three insecure categories delineated in attachment research, the reality of our parents' experiences is that they may have learned a combination of attachment patterns—secure attachment with avoidant characteristics; avoidant attachment with secure characteristics; and ambivalent attachment with disorganized characteristics being only a few of the many combinations that may occur. Parents may have learned different attachment patterns with each of their parents. These different patterns may then carry over to their interactions with professionals of the same gender as a particular parent. What is important here is for us to think about what attachment style the parent brings to the interaction with ourselves and how this may affect, unknowingly, the way we react to him or her.

There is another important piece to the attachment dynamics in the interaction between ourselves and a parent that we need to consider. We referred to this briefly in Chapter 2—what was the attachment pattern *we* were taught as young children? How does this play a role in our interaction with parents?

Our Attachment Pattern

Just like parents, each of us was taught an attachment pattern or, perhaps, some variation of several interwoven attachment patterns. Depending on this early experience, we will find ourselves falling more quickly and with less awareness into some interactive patterns than others. In the early work on attachment, Bowlby (1988) proposed that a counselor's level of emotional availability would play an important role in the success of any counseling relationship. This emotional availability, according to Bowlby, was related to the counselor's early attachment experiences. Knowing that many individuals in the helping professions choose, consciously or unconsciously, their profession as a way to resolve early experiences, we need to be alert to what we bring to any interaction.

We do, however, have an advantage. Our professional training, whether it is education, social work, child and youth care, or psychology, does encourage us to examine what happens in interrelationships—what causes the relationship to be the way it is, how it affects both ourselves and the other person, and how to recognize our contribution to the dynamic. Our training encourages us to work toward shifting patterns that are not helpful. Here our concern is with our contribution to the interactive pattern and our conscious effort to avoid falling into one of the insecure—ambivalent, avoidant, disorganized[4]—attachment patterns, whether as a result of our own attachment pattern, the parent's attachment pattern, or some combination of both of these.

If the pattern we experienced early in life was predominantly ambivalent, we are likely—if we are not observant—to bring an inconsistent style of responding to both personal and work interrelationships. Research has indicated that therapists with a preoccupied (ambivalent) attachment pattern are more likely to talk frequently during therapy sessions and are more likely to be overly deferential to as well as overly supportive of the client (Prout & Wadkins, 2014). While helpful in the initial stages of therapy, these characteristics are less helpful later in therapy. When meeting Gloria or Raymond, there is a high likelihood of our giving inconsistent attention to what is happening in the relationship and inconsistent effort to change that dynamic as well as other aspects of the work. With Jocelyn we would be less likely to fall too far into the avoidant pattern but may, on the other hand, become inconsistent in our efforts to stay engaged with her. Therapists with a dismissive (avoidant) attachment pattern have been found to be more likely to criticize or withdraw from the individuals with whom they are working (Mohr et al., 2005). If our own pattern were more of an avoidant one, it is highly likely that our level of engagement with a parent would be limited.

If, during our early years, we experienced a primary disorganized attachment relationship, we can hypothesize that we will have greater difficulty staying organized and focused in our work with parents without overcompensating by being controlling.[5] If we are working with someone like Alfred, who comes with a disorganized attachment pattern, this would be even more difficult.

The important point here is for us to be aware of any insecure attachment tendencies of our own and to notice when they intrude into our interactive pattern with a parent. As we hypothesize as to the parent's attachment pattern and are aware of our own attachment pattern, we can be far better at avoiding insecure patterns in our work with parents.

Other Early Parental Patterns

Attachment patterns are not the only patterns that may shape our relationship with a parent. Depending on what occurred within the parent's family of origin, numerous different interactive patterns may have been established. There may have been the critical parent and the no-good child; the demeaning parent and the inadequate child; the anxious parent and the anxiety-ridden child; the neglecting parent and the neglected child.[6] In other families there will be the supportive, encouraging parent and the courageous child; the self-confident, reassuring parent and the adventuresome child.

Tyler & Claire, 16 Years Old

> **REFERRAL:** Claire had been referred to the school guidance counselor because of defiant behaviors. She refused to attend, saying that it was her adoptive father, Tyler, not she, who needed to change. Tyler attended sessions with the school counselor during which they discussed the routine at home and a variety of rewards and consequences that might help Claire with compliance.
>
> **FAMILY SITUATION:** Claire had been raised by a neglectful and transient parent until age 5 and then placed in foster care. At 7, Claire was adopted by Tyler, a single father. It was a relationship full of friction from the beginning. Tyler, who had been raised by critical and demanding parents, was so thrilled to have a child, which he saw as a possibility for finally being loved by someone. Tyler gave Claire long lists of chores to do while at the same time giving Clair everything she wanted. Claire seldom did the chores and was disrespectful and cruel in her comments to Tyler, yet continued to demand special treats and clothing for herself.

Our Experience   253

TYLER: *I told her she had to complete her chores before she could have her allowance, but then the weekend came and she was going out and needed money but the chores weren't done. So I gave her the money on the agreement she would do the chores by the end of the weekend. But the chores weren't done. Guess I did it again; I shouldn't have given her the money at the beginning of the weekend. I just thought this time it would be different.*

SCHOOL GUIDANCE COUNSELOR: [Tyler did it again! So stupid! Of course she won't do the chores. He did it wrong again! Takes a deep breath as he is about to voice his thoughts—wait!!! This is just criticizing Tyler. Criticizing a parent doesn't change how parents do things—in fact, it often makes things worse—why was he about to do that? He isn't usually critical.]

As Tyler described a pattern of ineffective parenting (see Chart 8.4, upper box), the school counselor found himself reacting as the critical parent with whom Tyler grew up (lower box). Indeed, it is likely that many times over the years other people had fallen into the dynamics projected by Tyler's ineffective behaviors and had criticized Tyler. Tyler, being busy trying to shelter himself from criticism as he had to do so often as a child, never focused on how he could make a change.

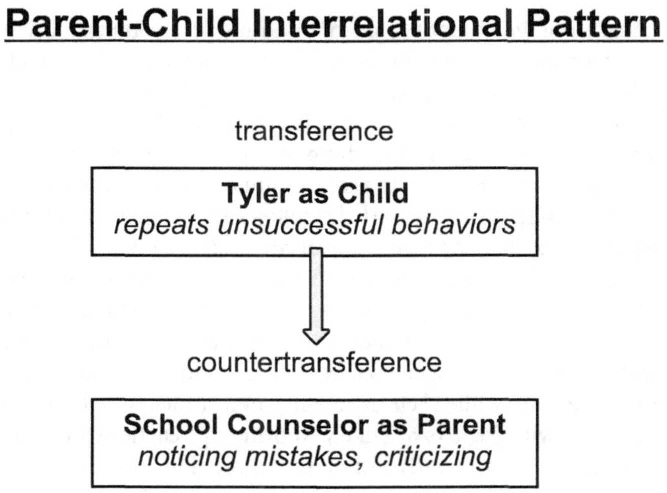

Parent-Child Interrelational Pattern

transference

Tyler as Child
repeats unsuccessful behaviors

⇩

countertransference

School Counselor as Parent
noticing mistakes, criticizing

Chart 8.4 Parent-child interrelational pattern—parent's replay of past relationship experiences with our subsequent countertransference.

Jade & Jordan, 11 Years Old

> **REFERRAL:** Jade referred herself for therapy. As a single mother of a difficult pre-adolescent son, she was becoming exhausted and was fearful that she would not be able to continue to parent Jordan.

> **THERAPIST'S EXPERIENCE:** [At the end of a particularly frustrating session with Jade, the therapist found himself thinking that Jade had blocked every idea he brought up, and then he thought, oh well, I'm not responsible for what she chooses to do or not do. Later, thinking back on the session, the therapist is struck by what an unusual thought that was—that he was not responsible. He could not remember ever having had that thought about a client before, not in the 20 years he had been working as a therapist. Of course, it is the individual who is ultimately responsible for what she does, but what a strange thought—separating himself that way from Jade and her experience. Why did that thought come up?]

An unusual reaction or thought—just as with the experiences of the support worker, social worker, teacher, and therapist in the cases discussed earlier—indicates that something unusual is going on. When we have an experience unlike ourselves and have checked out, whether it is connected with our ongoing life or our past experiences and values, we need next to look for what dynamic pattern is taking place and who in the parent's life we are playing out.[7] Only when we recognize this can we shift it.

Shifting Countertransference Reactions

As discussed earlier, if we do not pay attention to negative countertransference reactions, our reactions to the parent are all too likely to reinforce the parent's negative experiences. If we are responding from how we are feeling because of our own personal situation, we are not attuning with the parent. The parent will feel alone, an all too familiar feeling for most of the parents with whom we work. If, however, we are able to set aside what is happening for us, we will be able to attune. The attunement in itself may be a new experience for the parent. The work that follows attunement—whether increasing emotional regulation or imaging a new way of responding to her or his child—would definitely be a new and positive experience for the parent. That is the reason for our work—whether as a teacher, a support worker, or a therapist—with the parent.

Being triggered by a similar situation in our own life—either consciously or unconsciously—creates the danger that we will respond to parents as if their situation is the same as ours while their experience of a similar situation may be quite different from our own. Triggers are likely to bring up reactions in us that are not warranted (see example with Dotti) and make it difficult to accurately hear the parents and accurately understand their struggles. We are all too likely to see the parents' situations through our experience and, therefore, miss why they have become caught in what may be a negative cycle. Not understanding their experience—assuming it is the same as ours—we are unlikely to be able to help them.

If we become too entrenched in our values, we will have difficulty relating to a parent who holds different values. We are likely to become judgmental, which places us in opposition to the parent, rather than as someone working together with the parent to help the child. If our vulnerabilities—needing to be liked or needing to be successful—take over, we are less likely to question or challenge a parent.

When the parent with whom we are working is similar to someone with whom we had a negative experience, our way of responding may be shaped by that experience. We may become irritated with the parent, we may try to please the parent, we may feel intimidated by the parent—all reactions that are related to us, not the parent. What the parent experiences from us is 'not being heard' once again.

Only when we are able to set aside our emotional response—knowing that it belongs to us—but retain the situational information—knowing that it helps us understand the situation—can the similarity be helpful to us (Aponte & Carlsen, 2009). Timm and Blow (1999) talk about similarities between a therapist's story and an individual's story as providing both potential obstacles and potential strengths. They recommend that therapists explore the dynamics that happened within their own families and other important situations if they are not to be pulled into the negative dynamics of the people with whom they are working. While this exploration is particularly important for therapists, it can be of considerable help for any of us working in the helping professions. Understanding and processing distress from our past enables us to keep those experiences from taking over our perception of the other person's experience. Our experiences can then help us understand (have a higher level of empathy) but not distort how we relate with the parent with whom we are working.

Managing Countertransference

Gelso and Hayes (2007) suggest five different factors that play a role in the management of countertransference: self-insight, conceptualizing skills, empathy, self-integration, and anxiety management.

By *self-insight*, they are stressing the importance of professionals working within a helping role being aware of and having resolved to an adequate extent[8] the hurtful issues that have occurred in our lives. Also included in self-insight is a practice of reflection or meditation that allows us to be aware of what is bothering us. The greater our self-insight, the more likely we are to be able to catch ourselves before we become entrapped in a negative pattern with the parent (Gelso & Hayes, 2007). Also included in self-insight is self-care: we do not schedule several difficult families one after the other, we provide time in the evenings and weekends for activities that rejuvenate us, we spend time with family and friends. An additional part of self-care that we will be talking more about later in this chapter is finding some form of professional consultation to assist us in our work. Ideally, this will mean meeting with someone more experienced in work with parents—supervision— but when this is not possible, then meeting with peers to talk about difficult cases—peer-vision . . . and when that is not possible, talking with another part of ourselves, perhaps the professional observer part of ourselves for 'self-vision' (see pages 275–276). Taking good care of ourselves both personally and professionally enables us to be more present and, therefore, less reactive with others.

When talking about *conceptualizing skills*, Gelso and Hayes (2007) are referring to the theoretical frames we have for understanding child development, family dynamics, behavioral disturbances, and, of course, transference–countertransference interactions. Included in these skills are ideas for how we can be of assistance to the individuals with whom we are working (see discussion later). When we have ways of recognizing what is happening and then ideas for how to deal with what is happening, we are less likely to find ourselves responding to the parent in a way that is destructive to the help we are trying to offer.

Empathy represents our ability to understand another person's situation from his or her (not our) perspective. The stronger our empathy, the more these unusual reactions, feelings, or thoughts we have been talking about are going to stand out. They simply do not fit with what is going on in our interaction with the parent. If we are lacking in empathy—perhaps because of some personal issue or a high level of fatigue—we are less likely to notice our negative countertransference reactions.

The concept of *self-integration* refers to our knowing ourselves and being careful of the boundaries between ourselves and the parents with whom we are working. We become neither too connected nor too distant. We can identify with the parents, as is needed for strong empathetic understanding, but do not become enmeshed with them, which would cloud our being able to decipher the dynamics that are going on.

The last factor listed by Gelso and Hayes (2007), *anxiety management*, refers to our ability not to become so caught in anxiety that our thinking becomes cloudy. When we become anxious, we become protective of ourselves and less attentive to the parent with whom we are working.

But we need to do more than recognize and manage countertransference. Recognizing and managing countertransference means we will not fall into a negative pattern or interaction with the parent. Moving beyond that to working with and shifting a countertransference experience can provide the parent with a new and more positive interpersonal experience. This new experience means new neuronal network patterns are stimulated. A new way of interacting with her or his child becomes more possible.

If we do not shift negative countertransference experiences, we reinforce the negative patterns these parents learned when they were little and are now passing on to their children. If we do shift them, we are providing a new experience for the parent. Each new experience activates a new neuronal network within the brain. This is, to be sure, a very faint imprint, but it is an imprint and one that has a possibility of repeating. As we create a healthier interpersonal relationship between ourselves and the parent, we are creating the possibility of a healthier relationship between the parent and child—the most important goal in our work with parents.

We shall be considering two different types of responses for shifting our negative countertransference behaviors—relationship responses and intellectual responses.

Relationship Responses

As we notice within ourselves an unusual thought, reaction, or emotional response to the parent, we are alerted that something nonhelpful is happening. Gelso and Hayes (2007) encourage us at that point to engage in self-insight.

While their emphasis is on free-floating reflection, meditation, and self-care, not analytical thinking, they emphasize the importance of having 'conceptualizing skills'—informed understanding of what is going on in our interaction with the parent. We need a good understanding of what both the parent and we ourselves experience (see Chapters 1 and 2), of brain functioning (see Chapter 3), and of interactive dynamics (see Chapter 4 and the present chapter) to be able to decipher what is happening. It may be a reaction to a single interchange in a single session (see previous examples of Tyler and Jade) or a reaction to a negative pattern that has emerged over several sessions (see Gloria, Raymond, Jocelyn, and Alfred) that we are trying to decipher.

Looking back at Gloria, Raymond, Jocelyn, and Alfred, we notice that our professional missed the step of hypothesizing as to the parent's attachment pattern. Having missed that step, there was no warning as to which pattern of insecure attachment dynamics the parent and professional might fall into. Even with a warning, interpersonal dynamics are such that we often fall into them despite our best efforts. That is where recognition of negative countertransference and the resulting questions, *"Why did we fall into this pattern?"* and *"How can we get out of it?"* are helpful. We need to shift the relationship.

With Gloria, who is playing out the 'parent position' within an ambivalent attachment pattern, we need to shift out of the 'child position' of wanting her to do more and more.

Gloria & Jacob

> **YOUTH SUPPORT WORKER:** [Notices a discomfort in himself and the downward spiral in his relationship with Gloria; becomes curious as to why, given how much effort he made at the beginning, he is now making very little effort in his work with Gloria and Jacob. As he and his supervisor discuss the case, they notice his 'replay' of ambivalent responding. He was demanding ('child position') more of Gloria than she was able at that point to do, and she was becoming more and more inconsistent ('parent position'). He shifts his focus to the good work both Gloria and Jacob are doing in session and stops pushing for changes at other times. Both Gloria and Jacob become more engaged in their work with him.] *I am curious as to why the listening goes better when I am here than it does when I am not here?*
>
> **JACOB:** *Well, she listens to me when you are here but not when you are gone. Why should I listen to her if she doesn't listen to me?*
>
> **YOUTH SUPPORT WORKER:** *Hmmm—Mom, what do you think? What was it like for you when you were 12 and your parents didn't listen to you?*
>
> **GLORIA:** *They never listened to me!*
>
> **YOUTH SUPPORT WORKER:** *That's hard! Your parents never taught you that listening is part of parenting. But I've noticed that you listen when the three of us are talking.*

258 Our Experience

JACOB: *Sure, she wants to impress you, but she doesn't care about me.*

YOUTH SUPPORT WORKER: *Mom, what do you think about Jacob's comment?*

Our youth worker is taking himself out of the interaction between Mom and Jacob and is referring the situation back to them. This is far more respectful, a characteristic more consistent with secure attachment than ambivalent attachment. The worker is neither pleased nor displeased with the progress Mom and Jacob are making. Rather than pushing for more from Mom than she is able at that point to do, he is being an observer (see Chart 8.5, upper left box). He can be consistent within the role of observer, and Mom no longer experiences disapproval and inconsistent attending. Her response to the youth worker's respectful and consistent interactions is to become more consistent in her reactions with Jacob (lower left box).

The youth support worker has changed his relationship with Gloria—this is a 'relationship response' to negative countertransference. Being respectful of both Gloria and Jacob and being consistent in his interactions with them, the youth worker is providing a new relationship experience for both of them. This is a very small change in their lives, but it is a change, a new experience. For both of them it has the possibility of stimulating a new neuronal pattern related to interpersonal experiences. That neuronal pattern needs to be repeated many, many times before it is going to become dominant, but it is a start.

Our other parent caught in an ambivalent interactive dynamic was Raymond. Raymond's demands on his daughter's special education teacher were such that they fell into a relationship that reinforced the ambivalent interactive dynamics Raymond had experienced as a young child. Fortunately, the teacher had experienced many positive interactions as a child and was able to recognize that he needed to put some boundaries into his offer of being available by phone (see Chart 8.5, upper right box).

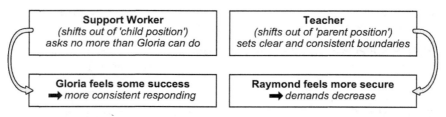

Chart 8.5 Relationship response for ambivalent attachment transference–countertransference.

Raymond & Lisa

SPECIAL EDUCATION TEACHER: [Anxious, he gets ready to phone Lisa's father, Raymond. It is two days since Raymond called him and he had, again, not returned the call on the same day as he had originally said he would. Feels irritated—how inconsiderate of someone to think a teacher could constantly return phone calls; after all his job is to teach Raymond's daughter, not hold Raymond's hand. Feels anxious because he does not want to make the situation in Lisa's home worse by irritating Raymond, and he does so hate confrontation. Decides to make notes on a pad as to what he is going to say before he calls.] *I realize that I am responding late to the call you made to me on Tuesday.* [Acknowledges what has gone wrong.] *I am sorry because I had told you I would return all calls on the same day. I am realizing with the high demands and exhaustion from my teaching, I am not able to do that.* [Takes responsibility.] *But I do want to keep the communication between us open.*

RAYMOND: [Voice rising.] *You think you are exhausted!*

TEACHER: [Takes a breath.] *You are right—we are both exhausted.* [Follows the notes on his pad. States clearly (specifically) how the situation can be shifted.] *In order that I can be of some help and you will be able to count on me, I am suggesting that I return two phone calls a week. If you want those calls twice on Monday or once on Monday and once on Tuesday, that is fine, but I would not return any other calls that week—not until the next Monday.*

With reasonable boundaries as to the number of calls that could be returned each week, the teacher was able not only to be consistent but also not feel resentful as he returned Raymond's calls. Raymond's calls decreased to the number set by the teacher (lower right box). A better relationship was established. With teacher and parent in good communication, they were able to present similar behavioral guidelines for Lisa. Her world stabilized and her behavioral upsets decreased. And Lisa was not the only one to profit.

Raymond had the experience of healthy, consistent, and reasonable guidelines consistently applied by the teacher. It was far better for Raymond to talk with the teacher less often but to know that when he did call (within the agreed-upon guidelines), he would always hear back from the teacher. With this as an example, Raymond found he was able to start giving Lisa clearer and more consistent guidelines related to behavioral expectations and to the rewards or consequences that went along with those guidelines. A more positive relationship between ourself and the parent provides a new neuronal pattern associated with relationships. This is only one small relationship among the many the parent may be experiencing, but improvement in one provides a possibility for improvement in others.

Remember Jocelyn, who was so avoidant of contact with the protection social worker? With the second referral, the social worker met with a consultant to review what had gone wrong before.

Jocelyn & Delia

PROTECTION SOCIAL WORKER: *Jocelyn kept refusing to give me information about herself and then would cancel sessions. I would try to engage her in talking about what Delia needed and what she herself needed, and she just kept blocking me, saying everything was fine. But we know it wasn't. And as things got worse, she didn't even ask for help.*

CONSULTANT: *What do you think her experiences were like growing up?*

PROTECTION SOCIAL WORKER: *She wouldn't tell me.*

CONSULTANT: *But the way she responded told you. What attachment pattern does her behavior remind you of?*

PROTECTION SOCIAL WORKER: *Definitely the avoidant attachment pattern! Oh, and then I avoided her with all my lecture-like behavior and not re-contacting her to find out how things were going. But how am I going to prevent avoiding her when she avoids me?*

CONSULTANT: *What do you think she needs? What do you think she is afraid of?*

PROTECTION SOCIAL WORKER: *Well, if I stay with the idea of avoidant attachment, she needs someone she can trust to be there no matter what happens, someone who is not going to bail on her even when she doesn't answer my questions.*

CONSULTANT: *Yes, and that is hard when she is blocking you! We can guarantee that she will block you again because that is what she knows how to do. That's the pattern she would have been taught and, thus, that's the pattern she has. Being open to you and trusting you is not something she knows how to do. How are you going to stay present to her when she doesn't trust you?*

PROTECTION SOCIAL WORKER: *What would happen if I talked about how hard it is to trust someone—I guess that would be the attuning, wouldn't it?* [Consultant nods.] *I could talk about how I made a mistake the last time we met of telling her what to do rather than working with her to figure out what could be helpful for her and Delia. I wonder if she has had any people in her past she could trust?*

CONSULTANT: *That's a question worth asking her, but don't expect her to answer it. If you don't expect her to answer and she does, that is great. But if you expect her to and she doesn't, she will pick up on your frustration and may feel you pull away—even if you are not aware of it—once again.*

If the protection social worker goes into the sessions with Jocelyn expecting avoidance, he is less likely to react negatively (avoiding) when Jocelyn does, indeed, avoid him. The social worker remaining open to her and even being curious about what is happening would be a new experience (see Chart 8.6, upper right box). If the social worker is able to hold this open stance, Jocelyn may learn to trust him a little bit—never expect an immediate or a large

Our Experience 261

shift—and there is the possibility, in time, of a new and more positive relationship forming. Until that happens, the social worker is going to need to stay available and interested in Jocelyn even when she is disinterested in him or in her own experience (upper left box).

Relationship Response for Avoidant Attachment

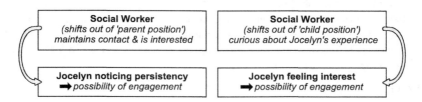

Chart 8.6 Relationship response for avoidant attachment: replay of past relationship experience–countertransference.

The therapist working with Alfred is even more challenged. Alfred's disorganized pattern of relating to others had disorganized the therapist. Carefully working out in his own mind what he would like to cover in a session would provide structure for the sessions. This structure alerts the therapist when the conversation starts to become disorganized and highlights for the therapist where the conversation needs to return. Attuning with Alfred's difficulty with staying with the topic allows the therapist to guide the conversation back to the structure without having to become overcontrolling (see Chart 8.7, upper left box).

For Alfred, having the therapist focus on Alfred rather than becoming entrapped in the therapist's own emotions and disorganization will be a new experience (upper right box). Experiencing someone attune with him allows Alfred to stay with his own emotions and not have to dissociate. But this does not mean that sessions will always stay organized. Disorganization is going to happen, and the therapist and Alfred can talk about where the disorganization came from. As the therapist works on being more patient with himself, Alfred may learn some patience with himself. Bit by bit, the sessions may stay more organized. And these sessions will offer Alfred a new experience.

Relationship Response for Disorganized Attachment

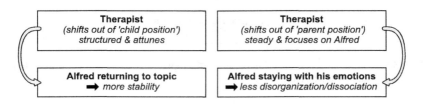

Chart 8.7 Relationship response for disorganized attachment: replay of past relationship experience–countertransference.

These are relationship responses—a change in the way the child and youth professional relates to the parent. And as the professional's behavior changes, the parent has a new and healthier experience. What about Tyler and Jade?

Tyler & Claire

SCHOOL COUNSELOR: [Feels something uncomfortable, why is he being so critical? Then recalls (thanks to a carefully done assessment, see Chapter 2) that Tyler had a very critical parent, wonders if he is falling into the role of the critical parent? How could he change that? What had Tyler done well this week? Certainly he could find something positive to comment on.] *You certainly figured that one out—well done.*

TYLER: [Startled.] *Do you think so? But I did it wrong.*

SCHOOL COUNSELOR: [Takes a breath of relief—how close he had come to re-enacting Tyler's old negative experience!] *But you noticed it, so next time you may be able to notice before you do it. I'll bet Claire asks for money next weekend.*

TYLER: *I bet she does.*

SCHOOL COUNSELOR: *Let's image that conversation* [see Chapter 6]. *Where might the two of you be? What might she say? And then what might you respond, and how will you handle that feeling of being sorry for her that always comes in?*

As the counselor steps back from the countertransference response of criticism, space is left for Tyler to try something new.

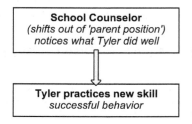

Chart 8.8 Relationship response for parent-child replay of past relationship experience–countertransference.

Jade & Jordan

THERAPIST: [Tries to figure out where this unusual thought—"not being responsible for the parent's decisions"—came from, remembers that Jade's mother never took responsibility for her children. When things got tense with Jade's father, she would just walk out for a day or months or a year—they never knew. What does Jade need to know from him?—that he can be counted on to keep working with her whether she keeps Jordan or not. No, he is not responsible for Jade's decisions, but he is responsible for being consistently available for Jade. He needs to track his thoughts and behavior carefully. He needs to be the responsible therapist he knows he is, not someone who shifts off his responsibilities, like Jade's mother.]

Our reactions to a parent can provide a new experience or can reinforce old unhealthy experiences. It is up to us, not the parent, to be aware of the dynamics that are occurring, whether it is a therapy session or a parent-teacher interview. Counselors and therapists are fortunate in that they have a number of different times to work with the parent, but also they are trying to shift deep patterns. Teachers have limited time with parents—sometimes only 15–20 minutes for parent-teacher interviews or short conversations after school. If, however, within that time the teacher stays aware of the dynamics that are happening and remembers to attune with the parent's experience of the conversation, then the parent will have a new experience. Each new relationship experience stimulates new neuronal firing.

Intellectual Responses

While a relationship response is always needed, there will be times when we can do more. As we become aware of having a negative—unhelpful—countertransference response to the parent's replay of learned behaviors, we might choose (1) to verbalize what has been going on between ourselves and the parent and accept responsibility for making a change, (2) to link the present experience to the parent's past experiences and notice how the present can be changed, or (3) to recognize the emotion beneath our response and again our responsibility for the handling of emotions. We refer to these responses as intellectual—as opposed to relationship—responses for shifting countertransference.

When we are experiencing negative countertransference, we may be tempted to say nothing, because "if we don't say anything, they won't notice." Those who grow up in dysfunctional situations are, however, very 'tuned in' to any negativity directed toward them. That was their means of survival when they were young. If we talk about the dynamics we see happening between ourselves and a parent, we are being honest and genuine, which is how we want parents to be with their children. We are modeling the importance of reflecting on the interactions between ourselves and others. We are modeling the importance of recognizing and naming when things go wrong; the importance of assuming responsibility when our reaction is not a healthy one; and the importance of correcting where we have made an error. We are talking about feelings and relationships. And perhaps most important of all, we are building connection with the parents and highlighting that change for the better can happen.

The second two types of intellectual responses—reference to the past and to emotions—should be used only by professionals who have engaged in training including therapeutic skills. As we will discuss later, it is important to stay within the boundaries of one's own training. Otherwise we can become entangled in what could be destructive dynamics for both the parent and ourselves.

1. Verbalizing What Is Happening

As we become aware of how we may have fallen into an ambivalent pattern with a parent, in addition to correcting our pattern of being inconsistent with the parent or of pushing a parent to do more and more (a relationship response), we can also reflect to the parent what we have noticed ourselves doing, how it has caused a problem, and how that problem has been discouraging for both of us. Ginot (2007), in his analysis of transference–countertransference interactions and neurobiology, proposes that a professional's "self-awareness of her own participation, followed by self-disclosure of her experience, promote[s] a conscious, verbally articulated encounter with the [parent's] unconscious relational styles, creating opportunities for emotional and neural integration" (p. 323) and repair.

Gloria & Jacob

YOUTH SUPPORT WORKER: [After a conversation with his supervisor in which they discussed how he had fallen into a pattern of 'overpushing' Gloria, the discouragement he was feeling and, now, his inconsistent attention to Gloria.] *Thinking back over our conversation about listening, I realize I, also, was not listening. Mom, I kept pushing you to do more with Jacob when the two of you were at home even though you had made really clear how tired you are. How can I ask you to listen to Jacob if I am not consistently listening to you? My error, and I apologize. I shall try really hard to listen carefully to both of you—that's my responsibility. We can focus on your joint activities during the time I am here.*

Not only is our support worker verbalizing where he made an error, he is also apologizing for it and, most importantly, taking responsibility for making a change. If we do not take responsibility for what went wrong, the parent may end up feeling guilty, which is likely to lead either to further despair in the parent or to anger—neither are productive places for encouraging change.

By verbalizing what had happened, the support worker is emphasizing the importance of listening, which is clearly part of what has been missing between Gloria and Jacob—what had been missed in the relationship between Gloria and her parents—and was now missing with the countertransference from our social worker's poor listening to Gloria.[9] How the support worker changes his behavior following this exchange is going to be most important. By 'listening' more carefully both to what Gloria's words and her behavior say about what she is or is not able to accomplish, the support worker will not be overdemanding and discourage both himself and her. With the experience of his consistent responding, Gloria has an opportunity to learn a more positive way of responding to her son.

The special education teacher, recognizing the impossibility of making a phone call to a parent every day, is tempted to call Raymond and tell him that his constant calling is an imposition on a teacher. Before doing that, the teacher decides to talk to a colleague just to get another perspective on what was happening (see further discussion on 'peer vision,' p. 275). His fellow teacher wonders if this is an old pattern with Raymond—asking too much of people and then being let down—and if there is another way the teacher could talk about it without anyone being to blame. After further discussion, the special education teacher calls Lisa's father.

Raymond & Lisa

SPECIAL EDUCATION TEACHER: [Names what has happened.] *Raymond, I realize I have not been consistent in returning your phone calls, even though I told you at the beginning I would return all calls. That's confusing and unfair to you.* [Apologizes.] *I am sorry about it. I also know that the demands of my job are such that I cannot speak with parents every night.* [Takes responsibility.] *I need to be the one to let you know what I can do.* [Names how he will change what he is doing.] *I would like to establish an agreement with you that I will return two calls each week. That way you can know what I will be able to do, and I will be able to be consistent in doing what I said I would do.*

The teacher was able to describe what had happened without placing any blame and, as the professional, took the responsibility of establishing clearer boundaries. He did not overstep his role as a teacher. Setting reasonable boundaries is an important step in any relationship and especially important with parents who did not learn appropriate boundaries as they grew up, a characteristic of insecure attachment patterns.

With parents caught in avoidant and disorganized attachment patterns, the content within a verbalization intellectual response is going to be different, but the steps (stating what happened, apologizing, making a change) are going to be similar.

Jocelyn & Delia

PROTECTION SOCIAL WORKER: [Names what has happened.] *Jocelyn, I am realizing that, after the first time we worked together, I did not follow up with phone calls to see how you and Delia were doing.* [Apologizes.] *I apologize* for that. *I was concerned that you would feel I was intrusive, but it may have felt like I wasn't interested, that I was avoiding working with you.* [Names how he will change what he is doing.] *I want to stay in touch and I want to help but not be intrusive.* [Takes responsibility.] *It is **my** job to find the right balance*

Again, our professional is taking responsibility for shifting what went wrong. Although we are aware that the dynamics are a result of both the parent and ourselves, we are the ones who need to make the change. That is the responsibility we take on as professionals.

Alfred & Noah

> **THERAPIST:** [Names what has happened.] *Alfred, our last few sessions have been quite disorganized.* [Apologizes.] *I apologize for the lack of organization.* [Takes responsibility.] *It is my responsibility to make clear to you what we are working on and* [Names how he will change what he is doing.] *then to stay focused on that topic.*

In some situations—for example, the school guidance counselor experiencing critical thoughts during his work with Tyler—it is not appropriate to verbalize what has happened. Tyler would have heard the criticism and might not have been able to set it aside as the counselor explained why those thoughts came up. If there is any possibility of the parent hearing only negativity and not hearing the professional take responsibility for the error, then the explanation should be avoided.

In the work with Jade, an intellectual response might or might not be helpful. It would depend on how capable the therapist thought Jade would be at recognizing how early family dynamics had affected her and also whether Jade would become distracted trying to defend her mother from criticism. If there is any doubt, it would be better to stay with the relationship response, as discussed earlier, for the countertransference experience.

2. Linking the Present with the Past

For those of us with training in therapeutic skills, what is happening in the present relationship can be explored further by our linking what we are noticing between the parent and ourselves to the parent's childhood experiences. Again, we need to take responsibility for this having happened and responsibility for changing our own behavior.

Gloria & Jacob

> **YOUTH SUPPORT WORKER:** [Meets just with Gloria.] *Thinking back over our conversation about listening, I am aware I have not been listening carefully to you, Gloria. I kept pushing you to do more with Jacob when you have*

made it really clear how tired you are. [Links to the past.] *'Not being listened to'* was an experience you had growing up, and one that never should have happened then or now. [Takes responsibility.] *My error, and I apologize.* [Names how he will change what he is doing.] *I shall try really hard to listen carefully to you.*

Talking about a parent's past experiences should *not* happen during a dyad session with the child. Such references with the child there could leave the parent vulnerable to negative comments from a resentful child.

Given that teachers will not have the same amount of information related to a parent's childhood as other professionals, Lisa's teacher will not be in a position where he can provide any linkage to the past for Raymond, nor would it be appropriate for a teacher to do that type of therapeutic work. It would be a possibility for the protection social worker—assuming he has had some therapeutic training—and Jocelyn and for the therapist and Alfred.

Jocelyn & Delia

PROTECTION SOCIAL WORKER: *Jocelyn, I am realizing that after the first time we worked together I did not follow-up with phone calls to see how you and Delia were doing. That may have felt like I was avoiding you—*[Links to the past.] *an all too familiar experience for you from when you were little—and unfair to you.* [Takes responsibility.] *It is my job to be sure that we stay in touch.* [Names how he will change what he is doing.] *When you are unable to attend or to answer a question during our time together, I shall continue to focus on how else I may be able to be of some support to you.*

Alfred & Noah

THERAPIST: *Alfred, I have been giving a lot of thought to our last few sessions and realize I have not been following through with my questions or even with my answers to your questions. This has made the sessions disorganized.* [Links to the past.] *This disorganization is too much like your experience growing up—your mother being very close and loving and then scary and distant. I certainly hope I have not been scary, but I certainly must have felt distant at times, and that is not what I want in our relationship. And most of all I do not want you to have a repeat of such disorganizing experiences* [Takes responsibility.] *AND it is my job, not yours, to make sure that does not happen.* [Names how he will change what he is doing.] *I shall work hard to keep us on topic and connected*

For parents for whom a linkage to the past is appropriate—see later—this conversation may highlight for them how past negative dynamics can replay in the present. This would help them become aware that the negative experiences they had with their parents may be repeating with their children. Because in each case the professional then took on the responsibility of changing the negative dynamics, the parent would also have the experience that it is the job of the more experienced individual—professional with the parent; parent with the child—to change the situation. Within insecure attachment dynamics, parents all too often blame children for the negative dynamics and state that the child is the one who has to change.

> There are clearly situations where this type of response is not helpful. The situation between Tyler and the school guidance counselor would be an example. Tyler, already overly critical of himself—a habit his parents taught him—would have been all too likely to focus on the criticism and not be able to understand the connection the counselor was trying to explain. When considering how to respond to countertransference, we need to project ahead—mentalize—as to how a parent will respond to our explanation.

3. Recognizing the Emotion Underlying Behaviors

Many of our countertransference experiences result from the emotions we pick up from the parent with whom we are working. So many of the parents we have been talking about in this book experience discouragement and disappointment. So many of them feel lonely, fearful, or angry. For those of us who are trained in providing therapy, if we do not acknowledge and talk about these negative feelings, they will undermine the work we do. We would be modeling exactly what it is we do *not* want parents to do—avoid their feelings. For those not trained in therapy, entering into conversations about emotions could lead to a negative experience for both the parent and the professional. This is the work of counselors and therapists and not the work of teachers and child care providers. For social workers and support workers, it will depend on the type of training they have received and the amount of supervision they are receiving. They may decide to acquire more training in attunement, validation, and providing emotional regulation (see Chapter 5). This work is always helpful for us and for the parents and children with whom we work. We always need to *consider carefully the level of our training and work only within our areas of expertise.*

When recognizing the emotions underlying the behaviors within an interaction, we can name the emotions, describe where they seem to be coming from, and talk about how this can be changed. While the examples here place these three steps close together, in a real session, they may be spread out over the hour.

Alfred & Noah at the Beginning of the Third Appointment

THERAPIST: [Names the emotions.] *I noticed so much confusion and frustration inside myself after each of the last two sessions. What was the feeling you came away with?*

ALFRED: *It was fine. Didn't accomplish much! A little weird to just sit and talk, but I guess that's what you people do.*

THERAPIST: *I was thinking back to our sessions and trying to figure out why I felt so confused.* [Explains where the emotion came from.] *I realized that I was letting our conversation jump from topic to topic. As different feelings came up, I let us jump from one feeling—a positive feeling about the chance to have therapy—to another feeling—anger that a treatment plan had not been done—without taking time to understand, much less even notice, each feeling.*

ALFRED: *Well, that's your fault, not mine.*

THERAPIST: *Thank you for stopping me—I certainly did not mean it was your fault. In fact, I don't think it was anyone's fault. We each . . .*

ALFRED: [Anger coming into his voice.] *Hey, don't include me in this.*

THERAPIST: [Notices a tightening in his body in response to the change in Alfred's voice tone, takes a slow, deep breath.] *My error, I can speak only for myself. And I have let us get sidetracked again. This jumping from topic to topic just increases the confusion in your life and in Noah's life, and there is already too much of that.* [Develops plan for changing the negative situation.] *Let's go back to your request for a treatment plan. What would you like to see in this plan? . . . Then let's look at what steps we need to tackle, one by one, to accomplish that. I'm going to stop us when we get off topic—I can keep a list of the other topics and feelings that come up that we can go back to later—but I shall, as best possible, keep us on topic.*

What a challenging job that is going to be for the therapist—staying on topic. When working with a parent with a disorganized or dissociative attachment pattern, the professional is going to need to think through each session ahead. These are not sessions that can be 'winged,' they need to be thought through and structured ahead. As we can observe from this dialog, the professional needs to overlook provocative comments and, in this case, countertransference emotions if he is to be able to stay on topic.

A discussion related to the anger the therapist noticed coming up in himself in response to Alfred's tone of voice may be important at another time, but not here. Here the therapist used a relationship response to the anger countertransference—calming himself; not being provoked. These are the moment-to-moment decisions—as opposed to becoming caught in one's own reactivity, probably the parent's early experience with others—needing to be made by a professional. For those who are trained in talking about emotions *and* in helping people contain emotions, these conversations can be helpful and can model for a parent a new way of handling emotions and, perhaps, of talking with their children.

The youth support worker, having received training with regard to talking with children and parents about emotions and after careful consideration with his supervisor, raises the topic of disappointment with Gloria.

Gloria & Jacob

YOUTH SUPPORT WORKER: [Names the emotions.] *Gloria, I am noticing a feeling of discouragement in myself as to how the work we are doing together with Jacob is going. You may be feeling it as well.*

GLORIA: *It's hopeless.*

YOUTH SUPPORT WORKER: [Explains where the emotion came from.] *Both of us were hoping the friction between you and Jacob would resolve more quickly. And, yes, it can be tempting just to give up. But, bit by bit, I think we are making progress and if we keep consistently at it, we will get there.* [Develops plan for changing the negative situation.] *So, even if you do not feel we are getting anywhere yet, I hope you will keep on working together with me. And if it feels I am pushing too fast or lagging too far behind in the work with Jacob, please tell me—this is something we can accomplish together. And when you get discouraged, tell me that as well—we'll try something else.*

The support worker is naming the negative feeling, identifying where it may be coming from, and asking Gloria to keep working despite that feeling. He emphasizes the importance of working together and talking about the discouragement as a way to keep going even when one does not want to.

In the situation with Alfred and Gloria, the negative feeling is one that both the professional and the parent share. This is also likely the situation with Jocelyn and the protection social worker—both of them feeling disengaged and perhaps even rejected. In this case, these would have been familiar feelings for the parent but, hopefully, not so much so for the therapist.

But the reality is that feelings of rejection and 'not being good enough' are common experiences. Many professionals will have had experience with these feelings growing up. And these feelings of rejection or not being good enough will create particular difficulty when working with parents who are avoidant and resistant to change. These are the situations where each of us needs the support of consultants or supervisors, as well as colleagues, in addition to positive self-talk (see discussion later) and, at times, our own personal therapy.

In contrast to the interactions with Gloria, Alfred, and Jocelyn, where the parent and the professional experienced similar feelings, Raymond and Tyler were more alone in their feelings. With the teacher not calling him, Raymond would probably have felt rejection as well as loneliness. The teacher, on the other hand, was feeling overwhelmed and probably guilty. While recognizing these feelings, the special education teacher without specialized training around the discussion of feelings is wise to stay with a discussion of what had happened and not venture into a discussion of these feelings.

Tyler was angry at himself and caught in a repetitive cycle, while the school guidance counselor was feeling critical. While the counselor did have the training to enter into a discussion of the emotions that had come up, he did not choose to do so since, as discussed earlier, Tyler was too likely to have focused on the counselor as having been actually critical of him and not on having had a countertransference experience.

The therapist's countertransference experience of dismissing responsibility for Jade's experience appeared not so much as an emotion but as a reflection of the mother-child dynamics. In talking about it, it was important for the therapist to state clearly that, even as this feeling came up, it actually was his responsibility, not Jade's, to do something about it. If this were not stated clearly, Jade's early negative experience might have been reinforced rather than the early negative experience being shifted.

How We Decide Which Countertransference Response to Use

In *all* situations, a shift to a healthier relationship dynamic—a relationship response—is important. But when should we follow this shift with talking about what has happened, linking what has happened to the parent's earlier experiences, or talking about the emotions experienced? As already discussed, this decision may be determined by the type of training the professional has completed. For those who have training in discussing, processing, and containing emotions, how might this question be answered?

With parents who tend to be very intellectual in their approach to life, and particularly those with an avoidant attachment pattern, it can be valuable to talk about emotions, thereby encouraging more engagement of the orbital-medial prefrontal lobes (Siegel, 2012) (see discussion in Chapter 3). For those who become very emotional and can benefit from engaging the dorsal-lateral prefrontal cortex in order to think through their experience, taking a more intellectual approach—discussing what has happened and how it connects with their past rather than the emotions coming up—can be more helpful.

If a parent appears particularly emotionally fragile—Jocelyn's avoidance of the social worker's questions likely indicates a emotionally fragility—this would not be the time to engage in a discussion of the past or a discussion of emotions. There needs to be considerably more trust before that happens. Pushing a parent far beyond his or her comfort zone will lead to more, not less, avoidance.

Connecting the present experience to the parent's experience growing up would not be appropriate early in the relationship between the professional and parent but could be extremely helpful after sufficient trust has been established. For parents who already have some understanding of their past negative experiences, this linkage between the present difficulty and the past can be helpful. It can, however, be detrimental with parents who have not accepted that their past may have had a negative influence. For those parents, this linkage by us could push them into a defensive position and should, therefore, be avoided. When parents are busy defending themselves or their family of origin, they are unable to hear new ideas.

Recognizing countertransference and deciding how to respond to countertransference can be very challenging. This is one of the many times during our work with parents that talking with a colleague or a consultant/supervisor can be very helpful.

Summary

In this last major chapter we have returned to the theme of the first chapter, 'The Parents and Us' and, in particular, the 'us' part of the equation. We have talked about countertransference and where it comes from—our ongoing world and our past experiences with their triggers, vulnerabilities, and learned values.

We took a look at how parents play out the patterns they learned—attachment patterns and multitudinous other behavior patterns. They may 'see' us—transference—as their parent and respond to us as the child to the parent, what we referred to as the 'child position.' Or they may replay the behavior they observed in their parents, what we referred to as the 'parent position.' And then, if we are not careful, we find ourselves in the opposite position—the parent to the 'child position' or the child to the 'parent position.'

Then came the question—how do we get ourselves out of there? We looked at examples of the relationship response and of various types of intellectual responses—naming what has happened, linking what has happened to the parent's earlier experiences, naming the emotions underlying the interactive dynamics. Most importantly, we looked at how the dynamics in the relationship between the parent and ourselves change when we change what we are doing.

Chapter 8—Points to Remember

- Negative countertransference is very important. It is not to be avoided but to be listened to and changed.
- We need to recognize and name when things go wrong, assume responsibility when our reaction is not a healthy one, and correct where we have made an error.
- If we do not take responsibility for what went wrong, the parent may end up feeling guilty, which is likely to lead either to further despair or to anger.
- Which intellectual countertransference response—if any—is appropriate depends on the level of trust already established and our level of training.
- Remember the part of the brain that holds the negative parenting patterns needs to be activated for change to occur in parenting patterns.
- All professionals need to consider carefully the level of their own training and work only within their areas of expertise.

Notes

1 A narrow definition of transference applies this term to an individual transferring their experience (positive or negative) of an earlier important person to the person with whom they are now interacting. A wider definition includes transferring earlier experiences (a replay of patterns learned early) to the present relationship. This is the definition we are using.

Our Experience 273

2 See discussion in Chapter 3 of the physiological response that occurs with triggers.
3 See Briere (1992) and Dolan (1991) for very helpful discussions regarding the negative and positive influences on an individual's ability as a therapist when having experienced early negative experiences similar to those of a client.
4 Different terminology is used for several of the attachment patterns when talking about adults and adult relationships—rather than avoidant, dismissive attachment pattern; rather than ambivalent, preoccupied attachment pattern.
5 The present discussion is based on conjectures from the research on attachment and clinical observation, not research that addresses these issues directly. Hypotheses are the starting point for research. It is our hope that the present discussion will contribute to the direction of future research.
6 Davies and Frawley (1992), in their discussion of transference and countertransference, list the interactive dynamics likely to arise when an individual has experienced sexual abuse. There is the neglecting parent and the neglected or unseen child, the sadistic abuser and the helpless victim, the idealized rescuer and the entitled child, and the seducer and the seduced child.
7 See Chapter 6, for an example of countertransference with dissociation—Ann & Sofia.
8 No one is expected to have totally resolved all issues; having issues and vulnerabilities is part of being human (Gelso & Hayes, 2007).
9 Our Chart 8.1 example of Gloria and the support worker showed Gloria in the 'parent's position.' The poor listening would have occurred when Gloria was playing out the 'child's position' of demanding relief and change that she could not yet do on her own, and the support worker's countertransference put him in the position of not listening.

CHAPTER 9

Concluding Thought—Super-Vision, Peer-Vision, Self-Vision

All of us, those new to our profession and those of us who have been working with children and parents for many decades, need assistance in understanding what is happening in our work. Working with other people, and particularly with people who are distressed and discouraged, is difficult. Working with people who are coming to see us not for themselves but because of their children or an outside mandate is even more difficult. It challenges everything we know about working with and helping others. It challenges our ability to be aware of our own reactions and responses. Getting tangled up in all of this is so easy.

Many agencies and institutions make provision for supervision or consultation from someone more experienced in the field. For those working in private practice or in agencies without provision for supervision, professionals often meet together—peer vision—to discuss cases. In either case, someone outside the interactive dynamics going on between ourselves and the parent is able to ask questions and make reflections about what is happening. This discussion—and particularly when it addresses countertransference—can help us see more clearly what is happening with us and the parent. Our supervisor, consultant, or peer is not tied into the dynamics and, therefore, is better able to see what is happening.

When supervision or peer vision is not available, and on those many days between supervision/peer vision hours, how are we to sort out what is happening? Here we can take advantage of the concept of ego-states (Federn, 1952; Watkins & Watkins, 1979). A part of us—our supervisor ego-state—can step back from our work with a parent and look at what was happening in a session. Rober (1999) refers to this as the inner conversation between the person-of-the-therapist and the professional role of the therapist. This is what we call self vision.

Our supervisor ego-state can ask the questions a supervisor might ask:

What was unusual in that exchange?
What are the dynamics from the parent's early experiences that were being played out? What are the dynamics from our present experiences or early experiences (triggers, values, vulnerabilities) that are being played out?
What are our personal challenges when working with this particular parent (Aponte & Carlsen, 2009)?

> What were the unusual sensations or thoughts that came up during the session?
> How can we be supportive of the parent but not take over?
> Am I doing enough emotional regulation and validation?
> How can we best activate new and healthier neuronal interconnections within the parent?
> Are my questions activating the part of the brain that holds negative patterns?

As we answer ourselves, new thoughts and new ideas are going to come up. These ideas can help us the next time we meet with the parent.

Why not make an image of that next conversation with the parent! And remember—bring in the parent's negative response to what we have done or said. Then image our responding in a new and different way.

Bibliography

Ainsworth, M., Blehar, M., Waters, E., & Wall, S. (1978). *Patterns of Attachment: A Psychological Study of the Strange Situation*. Hillsdale, NJ: Erlbaum.

Alexander, P. (1992). Application of attachment theory to the study of sexual abuse. *Journal of Consulting and Clinical Psychology*, 60(2), 185–195.

American Psychiatric Association. (2013). *Diagnostic and Statistical Manual of Mental Disorders* (5th ed.). Arlington, VA: Author.

Aponte, H. & Carlsen, C. (2009). An instrument for person-of-the-therapist supervision. *Journal of Marital & Family Therapy*, 35(4), 395–405.

Attunement. (n.d.). Dictionary.com. Retrieved January 5, 2016, from http://www.dictionary.com/browse/attunement.

Baddeley, A. (1992). Working memory. *Science*, 255(5044), 556–559.

Baita, S. (2012). Trastorno Traumático del desarrollo: una nueva propuesta diagnóstica. *Revista Iberoamericana de Psicotraumatología y Disociación*, 4(1). ISSN: 2007–8544. Retrieved from http://revibapst.com/data/documents/TRASTORNODESARROLLO.pdf.

Baita, S. (2015). *Rompecabezas. Una guía introductoria al trauma y la disociación en la infancia*. Ciudad de Buenos Aires, Argentina: Author.

Baita, S. & Moreno, P. (2015). *Abuso Sexual Infantil: Cuestiones relevantes para su tratamiento en la justicia*. Montevideo, Uruguay: UNICEF.

Baker, A., Mehta, N., & Chong, J. (2013). Foster children caught in loyalty conflicts: Implications for mental health treatment providers. *American Journal of Family Therapy*, 41(5), 363–375.

Bartholomew, K. (1993). From childhood to adult relationships: Attachment theory and research. In Duck, S. (ed.) *Learning about Relationships*. Thousand Oaks, CA: Sage Publications, pp. 30–62.

Beck, A., Emery, G., & Greenberg, R. (1985). *Anxiety Disorders and Phobias: A Cognitive Perspective*. New York: Basic Books.

Beebe, B., Jaffe, J., Markese, S., Buck, K., Chen, H., Cohen, P., Bahrick, L., Andrews, H., & Feldstein, S. (2010). The origins of 12-month attachment: A microanalysis of 4-month mother-infant interaction. *Attachment & Human Development, 12*(1/2), 3–141.

Behrmann, M. (2000). The mind's eye mapped onto the brain's matter. *Current Directions in Psychological Science, 9*(2), 50–54.

Blaustein, M.E. & Kinniburgh, K.M. (2010). *Treating Traumatic Stress in Children and Adolescents: How to Foster Resilience through Attachment, Self-Regulation and Competency.* New York: The Guilford Press.

Blizard, R. (2003). Disorganized attachment, development of dissociated self states, and a relational approach to treatment. *Journal of Trauma and Dissociation, 4*(3), 27–50.

Boon, S., Steele, K., & van der Hart, O. (2011). *Coping with Trauma-Related Dissociation: Skills Training for Patients and Therapists* (Norton Series on Interpersonal Neurobiology). New York: Norton.

Booth, P. & Jernberg, A. (2010). *Theraplay: Helping Parents and Children Build Better Relationships through Attachment-Based Play (3rd ed.).* San Francisco: Jossey-Bass.

Bouchard, M., Normandin, L., & Séguin, M. (1995). Countertransference as instrument and obstacle: a comprehensive and descriptive framework. *Psychoanalytic Quarterly, 64*(4), 717–745.

Bowen, M. (1972). On the differentiation of self. First published anonymously in Framo, J. (ed.) *Family Interaction: A Dialogue Between Family Researchers and Family Therapists.* New York: Springer, pp. 111–173. Reprinted in Bowen, M. (1978) *Family Therapy in Clinical Practice.* New York: Jason Aronson.

Bowen, M. (1978). *Family Therapy in Clinical Practice.* New York: Jason Aronson.

Bowlby, J. (1969). *Attachment and Loss: Vol. 1. Attachment.* New York: Basic Books.

Bowlby, J. (1971). *Child Care and the Growth of Love.* Harmondsworth, U.K.: Penguin.

Bowlby, J. (1973). *Attachment and Loss: Vol. 2. Separation*—Anxiety and Anger. New York: Basic Books.

Bowlby, J. (1980). *Attachment and Loss: Vol. 3. Loss, Sadness and Depression.* New York: Basic Books.

Bowlby, J. (1988). *A Secure Base: Parent-Child Attachment and Healthy Human Development.* New York: Basic Books.

Brandell, J. (1992). *Countertransference in Psychotherapy with Children and Adolescents.* Northvale, NJ: Jason Aronson.

Braun, B. (1988). The BASK model of dissociation. *Dissociation: Progress in the Dissociative Disorders, 1*(1), 4–23.

Bretherton, I. (1990). Communication patterns, internal working models, and the intergenerational transmission of attachment relationships. *Infant Mental Health Journal, 11*(3), 237–252.

Brewin, C.R. (2005). Remembering trauma. *American Journal of Psychology, 118*(1), 148–152.

Briere, J. (1992). *Child Abuse Trauma: Theory and Treatment of the Lasting Effects.* Newbury Park, CA: Sage.

Brown, K. & Ryan, R. (2003). The benefits of being present: Mindfulness and its role in psychological well-being. *Journal of Personality and Social Psychology, 84*(4), 822–848.

Buck, J. & Hammer, E. (1969). *Advances in the House-Tree-Person Technique: Variations and Applications.* Torrance, CA: Western Psychological Services.

Carlson, V., Cicchetti, D., Barnett, D., & Braunwald, K. (1989). Disorganized/disoriented attachment relationships in maltreated infants. *Developmental Psychology, 25*(4), 525–531.

Chapman, L. (2014). *Neurobiologically Informed Trauma Therapy with Children and Adolescents: Understanding Mechanisms of Change.* New York: Norton.

Chiron, C., Jambaque, I., Nabbout, R., Lounes, R., Syrota, A., & Dulac, O. (1997). The right brain hemisphere is dominant in human infants. *Brain, 120,* 1057–1065.

Cicchetti, D., Cummings, E.M., Greenberg, M.T., & Marvin, R.S. (1990). An organizational perspective on attachment beyond infancy: Implications for theory, measurement, and research. In Greenberg, M., Cicchetti, D., & Cummings, E.M. (eds.) *Attachment in the Preschool Years: Theory, Research, and Intervention.* Chicago: The University of Chicago Press, pp. 3–50.

Coatsworth, J.D., Duncan, L.G., Nix, R.L., Greenberg, M.T., Gayles, J.G., Bamberger, K.T., Berrena, E., & Demi, M. (2015). Integrating mindfulness with parent training: Effects of the Mindfulness-Enhanced Strengthening Families Program. *Developmental Psychology,* 51(1) 26–35.

Cozolino, L. (2010). *The Neuroscience of Psychotherapy: Healing the Social Brain* (2nd ed.). New York: Norton.

Damasio, A.R. (1994). *Descartes' Error: Emotion, Reason, and the Human Brain.* New York: Avon Books.

Davies, J. & Frawley, M. (1992). Dissociative processes and transference-countertransference paradigms in the psychoanalytically oriented treatment of adult survivors of childhood sexual abuse. *Psychoanalytic Dialogues,* 2(1), 5–36.

Davies, J. & Frawley, M. (1994). *Treating the Adult Survivor of Childhood Sexual Abuse: A Psychoanalytic Perspective.* New York: Basic Books.

Dell, P. (2009). The phenomena of pathological dissociation. In Dell, P. & O'Neil, J. (eds.) *Dissociation and the Dissociative Disorders: DSM-V and Beyond.* New York: Routledge, pp. 225–238.

Doidge, N. (2007). *The Brain That Changes Itself: Stories of Personal Triumph from the Frontiers of Brain Science.* New York: Penguin Books.

Doidge, N. (2015). *The Brain's Way of Healing: Remarkable Discoveries and Recoveries from the Frontiers of Neuroplasticity.* New York: Penguin Books.

Dolan, Y. (1991). *Resolving Sexual Abuse: Solution-focused Therapy and Ericksonian Hypnosis for Adult Survivors.* New York: Norton.

Doran, L. & Berliner, L. (2001). *Placement decisions for children in long-term foster care: Innovative practice and literature review* (Report No. 01-02-3902). Olympia, WA: Washington State Institute for Public Policy.

Dorsey, S., Conover, K., & Revillion Cox, J. (2014). Improving foster parent engagement: Using qualitative methods to guide tailoring of evidence-based engagement strategies. *Journal of Clinical Child & Adolescent Psychology,* 43(6), 877–889.

Dorsey, S., Farmer, E.M., Barth, R.P., Greene, K., Reid, J., & Landsverk, J. (2008). Current status and evidence base of training for foster and treatment foster parents. *Child Youth Services Review,* 30(12), 1403–1416.

Dorsey, S., Pullmann, M., Berliner, L., Koschmann, E., McKay, M., & Deblinger, E. (2014). Engaging foster parents in treatment: A randomized trial of supplementing trauma-focused Cognitive Behavioral Therapy with evidence-based engagement strategies. *Child Abuse and Neglect,* 38(9), 1508–1520.

Duncan, L., Coatsworth, J.D., & Greenberg, M. (2009). A model of mindful parenting: Implications for parent–child relationships and prevention research. *Clinical Child and Family Psychology Review,* 12(3), 255–270.

Federn, P. (1952). *Ego Psychology and the Psychoses.* New York: Basic Books.

Fonagy, P., Bateman, A., & Luyten, P. (2012). Introduction and overview. In Bateman, A. & Fonagy, P. (eds.) *Handbook of Mentalizing in Mental Health Practice.* Arlington, VA: American Psychiatric Publishing, Inc., pp. 3–42.

Fonagy, P., Gergely, G., Jurist, E., & Target, M. (2002). *Affect Regulation, Mentalization, and the Development of the Self.* New York: Other Press.

Fonagy, P., Steele, H., & Steele, M. (1991). Maternal representations of attachment during pregnancy predict the organization of infant-mother attachment at one year of age. *Child Development, 62*(5), 891–905.

Fosha, D., Siegel, D., & Solomon, M. (eds.) (2009). *The Healing Power of Emotion: Affective Neuroscience, Development & Clinical Practice*. New York: Norton.

Fraiberg, S., Adelson, E., & Shapiro, V. (1980). Ghosts in the nursery: A psychoanalytic approach to the problems of impaired infant-mother relationships. In Fraiberg, S. (ed.) *Clinical Studies in Infant Mental Health: The first year of life*. New York: Basic Books, pp. 164–196.

Frith, C. & Frith, U. (2006). The neural basis of mentalizing. *Neuron, 50*(4), 531–534.

Gallese, V., Eagle, M., & Migone, P. (2007). Intentional attunement: Mirror neurons and the neural underpinnings of interpersonal relations. *Journal of the American Psychoanalytic Association, 55*(1), 131–176.

Garbarino, J. & Eckenrode, J. (1997). *Understanding Abusive Families: An Ecological Approach to Theory and Practice*. San Francisco, CA: Jossey-Bass.

Gawain, S. (2002). *Creative Visualization: Use the Power of Your Imagination to Create What You Want in Your Life*. Novato, CA: New World Library.

Gelso, C. & Hayes, J. (2007). *Countertransference and the Therapist's Inner Experience: Perils and Possibilities*. Mahwah, NJ: Lawrence Erlbaum Associates.

Genogram. (n.d.) Merriam-Webster Online. Retrieved January 5, 2016, from http://www.merriam-webster.com/dictionary/genogram.

George, C., Kaplan, N., & Main, M. (1985). *Adult Attachment Interview*. Berkeley, CA: University of California.

George, C. & Solomon, J. (1999). Attachment and caregiving: The caregiving behavioral system. In Cassidy, J. & Shaver, P. (eds.) *Handbook of Attachment: Theory, Research and Clinical Applications*. New York: Guilford, pp. 649–670.

Gerittsen, J. (2010). The effect of Tomatis therapy on children with autism: Eleven case studies. *International Journal of Listening, 24*(1), 50–68.

Ginot, E. (2007). Intersubjectivity and neuroscience: Understanding enactments and their therapeutic significance within emerging paradigms. *Psychoanalytic Psychology, 24*(2), 317–332.

Goleman, D. (2006). *Emotional Intelligence* (10th ed.). New York: Bantam Books.

Gray, D. & Clarke, M. (2015). *Games and Activities for Attaching with Your Child*. Philadelphia, PA: Jessica Kingsley.

Grecucci, A., Pappaianni, E., Siugzdaite, R., Theuninck, A., & Job, R. (2015). Mindful emotion regulation: Exploring the neurocognitive mechanisms behind mindfulness. *BioMed Research International, 2015*, 1–9.

Grimminck, E. (2011). Emma (6 to 9 years old)—From kid actress to healthy child: Treatment of the early sexual abuse led to integration. In Wieland, S. (ed.) *Dissociation in Traumatized Children and Adolescents: Theory and Clinical Interventions* (1st ed.). New York: Routledge, pp. 75–96.

Grove, D. & Panzer, B.I. (1991). *Resolving Traumatic Memories: Metaphors and Symbols in Psychotherapy*. New York: Irvington.

Hariri, A., Mattay, V., Tessitore, A., Fera, F., & Weinberger, D. (2003). Neocortical modulation of the amygdala response to fearful stimuli. *Biological Psychiatry, 53*(6), 494–501.

Hebb, D.O. (1949). *The Organization of Behavior: A Neuropsychological Theory*. Hoboken, NJ: Wiley.

Hesse, E. (1999). The adult attachment interview: Historical and current perspectives. In Cassidy, J. & Shaver, P. (eds.) *Handbook of Attachment: Theory, Research, and Clinical Applications*. New York: Guilford, pp. 395–433.

Hesse, E., Main, M., Abrams, K.Y., & Rifkin, A. (2003). Unresolved states regarding loss or abuse can have "second generation" effects: Disorganization, role inversion, and frightening ideation in the offspring of traumatized, non-maltreating parents. In Solomon, M. & Siegel, D. (eds.) *Healing Trauma: Attachment, Mind, Body and Brain*. New York: Norton pp. 57–106.

Holmes, E.A., Arntz, A., & Smucker, M. (2007). Imagery rescripting in cognitive behaviour therapy: Images, treatment techniques and outcomes. *Journal of Behavior Therapy and Experimental Psychiatry*, 38(4), 297–305.

Holmes, E.A. & Mathews, A. (2010). Mental imagery in emotion and emotional disorders. *Clinical Psychology Review*, 30(3), 349–362.

Holmes, J. (2014). Where the child is the concern: Working psychotherapeutically with parents. In Holmes, P. & Farnfield, S. (eds.) *The Routledge Handbook of Attachment: Implications and Interventions*. New York: Routledge, pp. 53–64.

Holmes, P. & Collins, D. (2001). The PETTLEP approach to motor imagery: A functional equivalence model for sport psychologists. *Journal of Applied Sport Psychology*, 13(1), 60–81.

Howell, E. (2011). *Understanding and Treating Dissociative Identity Disorder: A relational approach*. New York: Routledge.

Howell, E. & Itzkowitz, S. (eds.) (2016). *The Dissociative Mind in Psychoanalysis: Understanding and Working with Trauma*. New York: Routledge.

Hughes, D.A. (1997). *Facilitating Developmental Attachment: The Road to Emotional Recovery and Behavioral Change in Foster and Adopted Children*. Lanham, MD: Rowman & Littlefield.

Hughes, D.A. (2009). *Attachment-Focused Parenting: Effective Strategies to Care for Children*. New York: Norton.

Hughes, D.A. (2011). *Attachment-Focused Family Therapy: Workbook*. New York: Norton.

Hughes, D.A. & Baylin, J. (2012). *Brain-based Parenting: The Neuroscience of Caregiving for Healthy Attachment*. New York: Norton.

Hyde, N.D. (1990). Voices from the silence: Use of imagery with incest survivors. In Laidlaw, T.A. & Marmo, C. (eds.) *Healing Voices: Feminist Approaches to Therapy with Women*. San Francisco: Jossey-Bass, pp. 163–193.

James, S., Landsverk, J., & Slymen, D. (2004). Placement movement in out-of-home care: Patterns and predictors. *Children and Youth Services Review*, 26(2), 185–206.

Jeannerod, M. & Decety, J. (1995). Mental motor imagery: A window into the representational stages of action. *Current Opinion in Neurobiology*, 5(6), 727–732.

Kabat-Zinn, J. (1994). *Wherever You Go, There You Are: Mindfulness Meditation in Everyday Life*. New York: Hyperion.

Kabat-Zinn, M. & Kabat-Zinn, J. (1997). *Everyday Blessings: The Inner Work of Mindful Parenting*. New York: Hachette Books.

Karterud, S. & Bateman, A. (2011). *Manual for Mentalization-based Treatment (MBT) and MBT Adherence & Competence Scale*. Oslo: Gyldenal Akademisk.

Karterud, S. & Bateman, A. (2012). Group therapy techniques. In Fonagy, P. & Bateman, A. (eds.) *Mentalizing in Mental Health Practice*. Arlington, VA: American Psychiatric Publishing, pp. 81–106.

Kaslow, F.W., & Schulman, N. (1987). The family life of psychotherapists: Clinical implications. *Journal of Psychotherapy and the Family*, 3(2), 79–96.

Keenan, J. & Gorman, J. (2007). The causal role of the right hemisphere in self-awareness: It is the brain that is selective. *Cortex*, 43(8), 1074–1083.

Keenan, J., Rubio, J., Racioppi, C., Johnson, A., & Barnacz, A. (2005). The right hemisphere and the dark side of consciousness. *Cortex*, 41(5), 695–705.

282   Bibliography

Kern, S., Oakes, T., Stone, C., McAuliff, E., Kirschbaum, C., & Davidson, R. (2008). Glucose metabolic changes in the prefrontal cortex are associated with HPA axis response to psychosocial stressor. *Psychoneuroendocrinology, 33*(4), 517–529.

Kestly, T. (2014). *The Interpersonal Neurobiology of Play: Brain-building Interventions for Emotional Well-being*. New York: Norton.

Kim, S.E., Kim, J., Kim, J.J., Jeong, B.S., Choi, E.A., Jeong, Y.G., Kim, J.H., Ku, J., & Ki, S.W. (2007). The neural mechanism of imagining facial affective expression. *Brain Research, 1145*, 128–137.

Kindt, M., Buck, N., Amtz, A., & Soeter, M. (2007). Perceptual and conceptual processing as predictors of treatment outcome in PTSD. *Journal of Behavior Therapy and Experimental Psychiatry, 38*(4), 491–506.

Lang, P. (1979). *A Bio-Informational Theory of Emotional Imagery*. Presidential address to the Society for Psychophysiological Research at its 18th meeting. Madison, WI: NIMH grant.

Lazar, S., Kerr, C., Wasserman, R., Gray, J., Greve, D., Treadway, M., McGarvey, M., Quinn, B., Dusek, J., Benson, H., Rauch, S., Moore, C., & Fischl, B. (2005). Meditation experience is associated with increased cortical thickness. *NeuroReport, 16*(17), 1893–1897.

LeDoux, J.E. (2000). Emotion circuits in the brain. *Annual Review of Neuroscience, 23*(1), 155–184.

LeDoux, J.E. (2002). *Synaptic Self: How Our Brains Become Who We Are*. New York: Penguin Books.

Levine, A. & Heller, R. (2010). *Attached: The New Science of Adult Attachment and How It Can Help You Find—And Keep—Love*. New York: Penguin.

Levy, T. & Orlans, M. (1998). *Attachment, Trauma and Healing: Understanding and Treating Attachment Disorder in Children and Families*. Washington, DC: Child Welfare League of America.

Liotti, G. (2009). Attachment and dissociation. In Dell, P.F. & O'Neil, J. (eds.) *Dissociation and the Dissociative Disorders: DSM-V and Beyond*. New York: Routledge, pp. 53–66.

Louridas, M., Bonrath, E., Dedy, N., Grantcharov, T., & Sinclair, D. (2015). Randomized clinical trial to evaluate mental practice in enhancing advanced laparoscopic surgical performance. *British Journal of Surgery, 102*(1), 37–44.

Lovett, J. (2005, September). Use of EMDR with traumatized children. Preconference workshop presented at the 19th meeting of the Eye Movement Desensitization and Reprocessing International Association, Seattle, WA.

Lyons-Ruth, K. & Jacobvitz, D. (1999). Attachment disorganization: Unresolved loss, relational violence, and lapses in behavioral and attentional strategies. In Cassidy, J. & Shaver, P. (eds.) *Handbook of Attachment: Theory, Research, and Clinical Applications*. New York: Guilford, pp. 520–554.

Lyons-Ruth, K. & Jacobvitz, D. (2008). Attachment disorganization: Genetic factors, parenting contexts, and developmental transformation from infancy to adulthood. In Cassidy, J., & Shaver, P. (eds.) *Handbook of Attachment: Theory, Research, and Clinical Applications* (2nd ed.) New York: Guilford Press, pp. 666–697.

Main, M. & Cassidy, J. (1988). Categories of response to reunion with the parent at age 6: Predictable from infant attachment classifications and stable over a 1-month period. *Developmental Psychology, 24*(3), 415–426.

Main, M. & Hesse, E. (1990). Parents' unresolved traumatic experiences are related to infant disorganized attachment status: Is frightened and/or frightening parental behavior the linking mechanism? In Greenberg, M.T., Cicchetti, D., & Cummings, E.M. (eds.) *Attachment in the Preschool Years: Theory, Research, and Intervention*. Chicago: University of Chicago Press, pp. 161–182.

Main, M., Kaplan, N., & Cassidy, J. (1985). Security in infancy, childhood, and adulthood: A move to the level of representation. In Bretherton, I. & Waters, E. (eds.) *Growing Points of Attachment Theory and Research (Monographs of the Society for Research in Child Development), 50*(1/2), 66–104. Chicago: University of Chicago Press.

Mancia, M. (ed.). (2006). *Psychoanalysis and Neuroscience*. New York: Springer.

Marshak, L. & Prezant, F.P. (2007). *Married with Special-Needs Children: A Couples' Guide to Keeping Connected*. Bethesda, MD: Woodbine House.

Mason, D. (2014). NLP Anchoring Techniques. Retrieved from http://www.key-hypnosis.com/Metaphor-Therapy/Metaphor-Techniques/NLP-Anchoring-Technique.php.

McGoldrick, M. (1982). Through the Looking Glass: Supervision of a trainee's "trigger" family. In Whiffen, R. & Byng-Hall, J. (eds.), *Family Therapy Supervision: Recent Developments in Practice*. New York: Grune & Stratton, pp. 17–37.

McGoldrick, M. & Gerson, R. (1985). *Genograms in Family Assessment*. New York: Norton.

McGoldrick, M., Gerson, R., & Petry, S. (2008). *Genograms: Assessment and Intervention* (3rd ed.). New York: Norton.

Messer, S.B. (2002). A psychodynamic perspective on resistance in psychotherapy: Vive la résistance. *Journal of Clinical Psychology, 58*(2), 157–163.

Mikulincer, M. & Shaver, P. (2007). *Attachment in Adulthood: Structure, Dynamic, and Change*. New York: Guilford.

Miller, M. (ed.). (2006). *Brain Development: Normal Processes and the Effects of Alcohol and Nicotine*. New York: Oxford University Press.

Mohr, J., Gelso, C., & Hill, C. (2005). Client and counselor trainee attachment as predictors of session evaluation and countertransference behavior in first counseling sessions. *Journal of Counseling Psychology, 52*(3), 298–309.

Moreno, P. (2011). La adopción de un niño severamente maltratado. *Revista Iberoamericana de Psicotraumatología y Disociación, 2*(1). ISSN: 2007–8544. Retrieved from http://revibapst.com/data/documents/ADOPCION%20MORENO%202011.pdf ba.

Neff, K. Self-Compassion Guided Meditations and Exercises. Retrieved July 30, 2015, from http://self-compassion.org/category/exercises/.

Neff, K.D. & Dahm, K.A. (2015). Self-compassion: What it is, what it does, and how it relates to mindfulness. In Ostafin, B., Robinson, M., & Meier, B., (eds.) *Handbook of Mindfulness and Self-regulation*. New York: Springer, pp. 121–140.

Ogden, P., Minton, K., & Pain, C. (2006). *Trauma and the Body: A sensorimotor approach to psychotherapy*. New York: Norton.

Parent [Def. 1]. (n.d.). Oxford Dictionaries Online. Retrieved January 5, 2016, from http://http://www.oxforddictionaries.com/definition/english/parent.

Parent [Def. 1a]. (n.d.). Merriam-Webster Online. Retrieved January 5, 2016, from http://www.merriam-webster.com/dictionary/parent.

Parent [Def. 2b]. (n.d.). Merriam-Webster Online. Retrieved January 5, 2016, from http://www.merriam-webster.com/dictionary/parent.

Perls, F. (1981). *The Gestalt Approach & Eye Witness to Therapy*. New York: Bantam Books.

Perry, B. (2006). Applying principles of neurodevelopment to clinical work with maltreated and traumatized children: The neurosequential model of therapeutics. In Boyd Webb, N. (ed.) *Working with Traumatized Youth in Child Welfare*. New York: Guilford, pp. 27–52.

Perry, B., Pollard, R., Blakley, T., Baker, W., & Vigilante, Domenico D. (1995). Childhood trauma, the neurobiology of adaptation, and "use-dependent" development of the brain: How "states" become "traits." *Infant Mental Health Journal, 16*(4), 271–291.

Perry, B. & Szalavitz, M. (2006). *The Boy Who Was Raised as a Dog and Other Stories from a Child Psychiatrist's Notebook: What Traumatized Children Can Teach Us about Loss, Love and Healing*. New York: Basic Books.

284 Bibliography

Pietromonaco, P. & Barrett, L. (2000). Attachment theory as an organizing framework: A view from different levels of analysis. *Review of General Psychology*, 4(2), 107–110.

Pochon, J., Levy, R., Fossati, P., Lehericy, S., Poline, J., Pillon, B., Le Bihan, D., & Dubois, B. (2002). The neural system that bridges reward and cognition in humans: An fMRI study. *Proceedings of the National Academy of Sciences of the United States of America*, 99(8), 5669–5674.

Porges, S. (2004). Neuroception: A subconscious system for detecting threats and safety. *Zero to Three*, 24(5), 19–24. www.frzee.com/neuroception.pdf.

Porges, S. (2009). Reciprocal influences between body and brain in the perception and expression of affect: A polyvagal perspective. In Fosha, D., Siegel, D., & Solomon, M. (eds.) *The Healing Power of Emotion: Affective Neuroscience, Development & Clinical Practice*. New York: Norton, pp. 27–54.

Porges, S. (2011). *The Polyvagal Theory: Neurophysiological Foundations of Emotions, Attachment, Communication, and Self-regulation*. New York: Norton.

Prout, T. & Wadkins, M. (2014). *Essential Interviewing and Counseling Skills: An Integrated Approach to Practice*. New York: Springer.

Ramachandran, V.S. (2011). *The Tell-Tale Brain: A Neuroscientist's Quest for What Makes Us Human*. New York: Norton.

Rempel-Clower, N.L. (2007). Role of orbitofrontal cortex connections in emotion. *Annals of the New York Academy of Sciences*, 1121, 72–86.

Rober, P. (1999). The therapist's inner conversation in family therapy practice: Some ideas about the self of the therapist, therapeutic impasse, and the process of reflection. *Family Process*, 38(2), 209–228.

Rozanski, C.A. (2003). *Abuso Sexual Infantil ¿Denunciar o Silenciar?* Buenos Aires: Ediciones B.

Schore, A.N. (1994). *Affect Regulation and the Origin of the Self: The Neurobiology of Emotional Development*. Mahwah, NJ: Erlbaum.

Schore, A.N. (2001). The effects of a secure attachment relationship on right brain development, affect regulation, and infant mental health. *Infant Mental Health Journal*, 22(1–2), 7–66.

Schore, A.N. (2003). *Affect Regulation and the Repair of the Self*. New York: Norton.

Schore, A.N. (2009). Attachment trauma and the developing right brain: Origins of pathological dissociation. In Dell, P.F. & O'Neil, J. (eds.) *Dissociation and the Dissociative Disorders: DSM-V and Beyond*. New York: Routledge, pp. 107–143.

Schore, A.N. (2012). *The Science of the Art of Psychotherapy*. New York: Norton.

Schore, J. & Schore, A.N. (2014). Regulation theory and affect regulation psychotherapy: A clinical primer. *Smith College Studies in Social Work*, 84(2–3), 178–195.

Schuengel, C., Bakermans-Kranenburg, M., van IJzendoorn, M., & Blom, M. (1999). Unresolved loss and infant disorganization: Links to frightening maternal behavior. In Solomon, J. & George, C. (eds.) *Attachment Disorganization*. New York: Guilford, pp. 71–94.

Shah, P., Fonagy, P., & Strathearn, L. (2010). Is attachment transmitted across generations? The plot thickens. *Clinical Child Psychology and Psychiatry*, 15(3), 329–345.

Shapiro, F. (1995). *Eye Movement Desensitization and Reprocessing: Basic Principles, Protocols, and Procedures*. New York: Guilford.

Shapiro, F. (2001). *Eye Movement Desensitization and Reprocessing: Basic Principles, Protocols, and Procedures* (2nd ed.). New York: Guilford.

Siegel, D. (2003). An interpersonal neurobiology of psychotherapy: The developing mind and the resolution of trauma. In Solomon, M. & Siegel, D. (eds.) *Healing Trauma: Attachment, Mind, Body and Brain*. New York: Norton, pp. 1–56.

Siegel, D. (2007). *The Mindful Brain: Reflection and Attunement in the Cultivation of Well-Being*. New York: Norton.
Siegel, D. (2010). *Mindsight: The New Science of Personal Transformation*. New York: Bantam.
Siegel, D. (2012). *The Developing Mind, Second Edition: How Relationships and the Brain Interact to Shape Who We Are*. New York: Guilford.
Siegel, D. & Hartzell, M. (2003). *Parenting from the Inside Out: How a Deeper Self-Understanding Can Help You Raise Children Who Thrive*. New York: Tarcher/Penguin.
Silberg, J. (2013). *The Child Survivor: Healing Developmental Trauma and Dissociation*. New York: Routledge.
Singh, N.N., Singh, A.N., Lancioni, G.E., Singh, J., Winton, A.S.W. & Adkins, A.D. (2010). Mindfulness training for parents and their children with ADHD increases the children's compliance. *Journal of Child and Family Studies, 19*(2), 157–166.
Snyder, R., Shapiro, S., & Treleaven, D. (2011). Attachment theory and mindfulness. *Journal of Child and Family Studies, 21*(5), 709–717.
Solomon, J. & George, C. (1999). The place of disorganization in attachment theory: Linking classic observations with contemporary findings. In Solomon, J. & George, C. (eds.) *Disorganized Attachment*. New York: Guilford. pp. 3–32.
Spinazzola, J., Habib, M., Knoverek, A., Arvidson, J., Nisenbaum, J., Wentworth, R., Hodgdon, H., Pond, A., & Kisiel, C. (2013). The heart of the matter: Complex trauma in child welfare. CW360° Trauma-Informed Child Welfare Practice, pp. 8–9, 37.
Steele, H. & Siever, L. (2010). An attachment perspective on Borderline Personality Disorder: Advances in gene-environment considerations. *Current Psychiatry Reports, 12*(1), 61–67.
Steele, H. & Steele, M. (eds.). (2008). *Clinical Applications of the Adult Attachment Interview*. New York: Guilford.
Swain, J.E. (2008). Baby stimuli and the parent brain: Functional neuroimaging of the neural substrates of parent-infant attachment. *Psychiatry* (Edgemont), 5(8), 28–36.
Swain, J.E., Kim, P., Spicer, J., Ho, S.S., Dayton, C.J., Elmadih, A., & Abel, K.M. (2014). Approaching the biology of human parental attachment: Brain imaging, oxytocin and coordinated assessments of mothers and fathers. *Brain Research, 1580*, 78–101.
Tachibana, A., Noah, J., Bronner, S., Ono, Y., Hirano, Y., Niwa, M., Watanabe, K., & Onozuka, M. (2012). Activation of dorsolateral prefrontal cortex in a dual neuropsychological screening test: An fMRI approach. *Behavioral and Brain Functions, 8*(1), 26–34.
Théoret, H., Kobayashi, M., Merabet, L., Wagner, T., Tormos, J., & Pascual-Leone, A. (2004). Modulation of right motor cortex excitability without awareness following presentation of masked self-images. *Cognitive Brain Research, 20*(1), 54–57.
Thomas, A., Chess, S., & Birch, H. (1968). *Temperament and Behavior Disorders in Children*. New York: New York University Press.
Timm, T. & Blow, A. (1999). Self-of-the-therapist work: A balance between removing restraints and identifying resources. *Contemporary Family Therapy: An International Journal, 21*(3), 331–351.
Tomatis, A. (1991). *The Conscious Ear: My Life of Transformation Through Listening*. Barrytown, NY: Station Hill.
Tomkins, S. (1963). *Affect Imagery Consciousness: Volume II, The Negative Effects*. New York: Springer.
Trevarthen, C. (2009). *Human Needs & Human Sense: The Natural Science of Meaning*. Presentation at the SAIA Seminar: Why Attachment Matters in Sharing Meaning in Glasgow.
Tronick, E. (1989). Emotions and emotional communication in infants. *American Psychologist, 44*(2), 112–119.

Tulving, E. & Craik, F. (eds.). (2000). *The Oxford Handbook of Memory*. New York: Oxford University Press.

Turkus, J. & Kahler, J.A. (2006). Therapeutic interventions in the treatment of dissociative disorders. *Psychiatric Clinics of North America, 29*(1), 245–262.

van der Hart, O. (2006). Structural Dissociation of the Personality: The Key to Understanding Chronic Traumatization and Its Treatment. Plenary presentation at the ESTD First Bi-Annual Conference in Amsterdam.

van der Hart, O., Nijenhuis, E., & Steele, K. (2006). *The Haunted Self: Structural Dissociation and the Treatment of Chronic Traumatization*. New York: Norton.

van der Kolk, B. & van der Hart, O. (1989). Pierre Janet and the breakdown of adaptation in psychological trauma. *American Journal of Psychiatry, 146*(12), 1530–1540.

van IJzendoorn, M. & Bakermans-Kranenburg, M. (1997). Intergenerational transmission of attachment: A move to the contextual level. In Atkinson, L. & Zucker, K. (eds.) *Attachment and Psychopathology*. New York: Guilford, pp. 135–170.

Waters, F. (2016). *Healing the Fractured Child: Diagnosis and Treatment of Youth with Dissociation*. New York: Springer.

Watkins, J. & Watkins, H. (1979). The theory and practice of ego-state therapy. In Grayson, H. (ed.) *Short-term Approaches to Psychotherapy*. New York: Human Sciences, pp. 176–220.

White, M. (2007). *Maps of Narrative Practice*. New York: Norton.

Wieland, S. (1997). *Hearing the Internal Trauma: Working with Children and Adolescents Who Have Been Sexually Abused*. Thousand Oakes: Sage.

Wieland, S. (1998). *Techniques and Issues in Abuse-focused Therapy with Children & Adolescents: Addressing the Internal Trauma*. Thousand Oaks: Sage.

Wieland, S. (2015a). Dissociation in children and adolescents: What it is, how it presents, and how we can understand it. In Wieland, S. (ed.) *Dissociation in Traumatized Children and Adolescents: Theory and Clinical Interventions* (2nd ed.). New York: Routledge, pp. 1–40.

Wieland, S. (2015b). Joey (11 to 12 years old)—Moving out of dissociative protection: Treatment of a boy with dissociative disorder not elsewhere classified following early family trauma. In Wieland, S. (ed.) *Dissociation in Traumatized Children and Adolescents: Theory and Clinical Interventions* (2nd ed.). New York: Routledge, pp. 191–260.

Wieland, S. & Silberg, J. (2013). Dissociation-focused therapy. In Ford, J. & Courtois, C. (eds.) *Treating Complex Traumatic Stress Disorders in Children and Adolescents: Scientific Foundations and Therapeutic Models*. New York: Guilford, pp. 162–183.

Yates, T.M. (2004). The developmental psychopathology of self-injurious behavior: Compensatory regulation in posttraumatic adaptation. *Clinical Psychology Review, 24*(1), 35–74.

Yehuda, N. (2016). *Communicating Trauma: Clinical Presentations and Interventions with Traumatized Children*. New York: Routledge.

Index

active memory 6
adoption: child's previous experience and parents' expectations 179–87, 233; gathering information 187–91, 233; helping adoptive parents attach to their children 191–3; helping adoptive parents understand their child's emotions and behaviors 193–202; negative diagnosis/ disappointment 181–4, 233; role of disorganized attachment 209–20; working with foster parents 220–32
amygdala 55–8, 65, 72, 73, 77, 108
anxiety management 255, 256
arousal level 63–4
attachment: ambivalent attachment 7, 51, 53, 244–7; avoidant attachment 51, 247–9; child professionals 251–2; as dance 219–20; disorganized attachment 7, 35, 51, 53, 209–20, 233, 249–51; insecure attachment 4, 6, 11; intergenerational transmission of 79–81; internal working model 52, 53, 63; nature/nurture effect 80; negative attachment patterns 210; negative parenting patterns 139; neuronal networks related to attachment patterns 47–52, 77; observing parent-child dynamics 35–8; patterns of 6–8, 12, 50; replay of parents' past relationship dynamics 243–52; secure attachment 4, 6, 7, 12–13, 49, 54, 77, 81–5, 137
attunement: child professionals relationship with parent 167; child professionals relationship with parent and 81, 107–13, 135; countertransference and 236; definition of 85; window of receptivity and 75
autobiographical memory 68
autonomic nervous system (ANS) 48, 55, 62, 63–5, 74–7, 129

beliefs 10, 23, 68, 81, 109, 123, 137–8, 144–50
birth parents 223–7
blockages: mismatched temperaments 163–5; overactive therapist 173–4; parent exhaustion 174–6; to positive parenting patterns 161–76; 'preaching' parenting 171–2; rejection of ideas presented 165–71; trigger reactions 161–3
'Book of Life' 67
brain: attachment and 47–52; autonomic nervous system 48, 55, 62, 63–5, 74–7, 129; brain development 10; internal working model of attachment 52, 53, 63; left hemisphere 71, 104; limbic system 55–9, 62; mirror neurons 53; neuronal

patterns 6, 49–56, 65–76, 139; orbital-medial prefrontal cortex (OMPFC) 56, 59–61, 65, 71–3, 74, 77; parenting patterns 6–7, 47–77; processing 55–65; right hemisphere 61–3, 66–71, 126–7, 139; therapeutic interactions and understanding 65–76
breathing exercises 86, 88, 102, 113, 167, 197
breathing rate 64, 70, 74

calming activities 71, 108, 113, 167
caregiving responses 49
central nervous system 10, 15
child professionals: attachment patterns 251–2; attunement with parent 81, 107–13, 116, 135; building external supports 133–4; building internal resources 129–33; caught in story 9–12; challenges for 232–3; connecting with children 11; countertransference and 235–6; countertransference response 271–2; cultural background of 9–10; day-to-day world experiences 236–328; emotional regulation 113–18; influence of other early parental patterns 252–4; learning about 17–44; our relationship with parent 81–5; overactive therapist 173–4; past experiences 238–43; 'preaching' parenting 171–2; providing sense of safety for parent 125–9; recognizing parent-us dynamics 39–43; relationship with child 4; role of 9; training 10–11; trigger reactions 238–41; validation 118–25; values 241–2; vulnerabilities 242–3; working with parents 12–14
children: adopted child's previous experience and parents' expectations 179–87; appointment for not listening 122–3; attachment patterns 4, 6–8; bedtime problems 69–70; calming activities 71, 113; child in the present 25–9; child's development 19–25; disorganized attachment 210–15; first session with 105–9; neuronal patterns 6–7, 13; parent-child dynamics 35–8; patterns of parent-child interaction 6–8; providing sense of safety for 127–9; trauma and 54, 67; visits with birth parents 223–7
Child's Helping System 8–9
'child's position' 243–6
cognitive therapy 68, 72
coherent narrative 81, 85
conceptualizing skills 255, 256

contingent communication 81–2
controlling behaviors 215–19
cortisol 55, 112
countertransference: characteristics of 235–6; deciding which response to use 271–2; intellectual responses 263–4; interpersonal dynamics of 235, 243–4; linking present with past 266–8; managing 255–71; negative countertransference 236; positive countertransference 236; recognizing emotion underlying behaviors 268–71; relationship responses 256–63; replay of parents' past relationship dynamics 243–52; shifting countertransference reactions 254–71; verbalizing what is happening 264–6; window of receptivity and 75
creativity 177
cultural background 9–10
curiosity 74

deep right cortices 65, 77
detachment 72
developmental interview: elements of 18–34, 106; present concern 19; questions about child in present 25–9; questions about child's development 19–25; questions about parent's early emotional experiences 30–4; questions about parent's own experiences 29–34; uncovering beliefs and values of parents 23, 144
dialog examples: adopted child's diagnosis of FAS 181–4; adopted child's instances of sexualized acting out 186–7; appointment at insistence of protective services 175–6; appointment for dealing with fantasy family 92–4, 98–9, 105–9, 118–20, 125–6, 130; call to therapy agency because of family protection services requirement 115–16; controlling behaviors of child 215–19; disorganized attachment 210–15; disruptive behavior at school 20–1, 27–9; foster care placement 220–1, 230–2; increasing tension in home 140–3, 159–60; not turning in any assignments 83–4; out-of-control and demanding behaviors 32–3; parent-teacher interview about abusive behavior of child toward sister 145–9; problems getting along with other children 25–7; referral because of aggressive behaviors in school/home 246, 259, 265; referral because of fear

that parent can no longer manage child 99–101, 117–18, 120–1, 156–9; referral because of out-of-control behaviors at home and resistant behaviors at school 245, 257–8, 264, 266–7, 270; referral because of separation issues 240; referral by protective services because of neglect and use of drugs in home 166–7; referral for aggression toward others by son 169–71; referral for continuing out of control and aggressive behaviors of adopted son 164–5; referral for dealing with negative behavior 89–91; referral for 'evil ways' of grandson 167–9; referral for father having hit children 150–1; referral for foster child acting out 222–3, 227–9; referral for high anxiety of son 152–6; referral for high tension in home 22–5; referral for play therapy and better parenting skills 94–6; referral for some parental support and parenting ideas 173–4; referral for talking in class as if his birth father was his present father 202–9; referral for therapy after exhibiting genitals to younger children 249–50, 266, 267–9; referral for therapy because of angry and aggressive behavior of child 143–4; referral for therapy because of negative thoughts 88–9; referral for therapy due to sexual abuse 133–4; referral for therapy of angry and aggressive behaviors toward foster parents 224–7; referral for therapy of angry and aggressive behaviors toward parents 161–3; referral of son to school counselor at request of school 163–4; referral to a protection social worker over discipline issues 248, 260–1, 265–6, 267; referral to neighborhood family service agency for support related to relationship with parent 86–7; referral to school guidance counselor because of defiant behaviors 252–3, 262; registration for after-school activity facility 36–7; request for play therapy 41–2; roleplay interactions with parents 171–2; self-referral for high anxiety 149–50, 173–4; self-referral for therapy 254, 263; single foster mother wanting adopt child with severe abuse and neglect issues 241–2; therapy for separation fear and resistance 128
disapproval 111, 114, 135
dissociation 54, 56, 65, 75, 116–17, 122, 157, 212, 215

dissociative identity disorder 54
dorsal-lateral prefrontal cortex (DLPFC) 60, 65, 73–4
dorsal vagal parasympathetic system 64, 112, 129
drawing 127
dyadic art 66–7

emotions: emotional communication 81, 84–5; emotional regulation 71–3, 81, 113–18; parents 3, 74; parent's early emotional experiences 30–2, 58; patterns of 8; underlying negative interactive parent-child patterns 151–60
empathy 41, 51, 85, 107, 201, 255–6
explicit information 66
explicit knowing 62
external supports 133–4
Eye Movement Desensitization and Reprocessing (EMDR) 67, 68, 127, 159

fathers: mindfulness training for 87; scheduling initial appointment with 18 *see also* foster parents; parents
fetal alcohol syndrome (FAS) 181–4
focus 73–4
foster parents: finding out about 229–32; foster care placements 220–2, 233; multiple demands 222–3; providing ideas for 227–9; visits with birth parents 223–7; working with 220–32

genograms 34–5, 40–1

habits 137–44, 169
hypoarousal state 75–6
hypothalamus-pituitary-adrenal axis (HPA) 55–6, 112

imagery re-scripting 68
imaging/visualization 67–71, 77, 127, 129–33, 139–40, 158
implicit information 66
implicit memory 61–2
infant development 49–50
insecure-avoidant patterns 7
insula 72
internal resources 129–33
interpersonal connectivity 81
interpersonal dynamics 235, 243–4

judgment 74, 85, 86, 103, 112

limbic system 55–9, 62

mentalization 71–3, 74, 77, 91–6, 108–9, 111–12, 135, 226
mid-brain areas 65, 77
mindfulness 71–3, 74, 86–91, 108, 112, 237
mirror neurons 29, 32, 53, 72, 84, 108, 244
mismatched temperaments 163–5
mothers: intergenerational transmission of attachment 80–1; mindfulness training for 87; scheduling initial appointment with parents 18; trigger reactions 58–9, 73, 75 *see also* foster parents; parents
motor activity 67–71

negative events 237
negative parenting: child professionals reactions with parent 66; helping parents move out of 137–77
negative parenting patterns: beliefs underlying 144–50; blockages to positive parenting patterns 161–76; emotions underlying negative interactive parent-child patterns 151–60; habits 137–44; helping parents move out of 137–77; making conscious/explicit 138–9, 177; unconscious/implicit 138, 177; values underlying 150–1
neuroception 64
neuronal patterns 6–7, 53–4, 65–76, 139, 177
nonjudgment 72
nonverbal interaction: attachment activities 102–3; imaging/visualization 97–102; play 96–7

orbital-medial prefrontal cortex (OMPFC) 56, 59–61, 65, 71–3, 74, 77, 108
overarousal 111

parasympathetic/slowing-down subsystem 64
'parent as infant' 49–51
parent-child dynamics: in home 37–8; in office 36–7
parent-figures 18
parenting patterns: drawing genograms 34–5, 40–1; learned parenting 2; negative parenting patterns 137–77; neuronal networks related to early attachment patterns 47–52; neuronal patterns related to 6–7, 53–4, 65–76; taught parenting 1–2
parents: adopted child's previous experience and parents' expectations 179–87; attachment patterns 4, 6–8; building external supports 133–4; building internal resources 129–33; caught in story 2–6; child in the present 25–9; child professionals relationship with parent 65–6, 81–5; child professionals working with 12–14; child's development 19–25; criticism of 12; definition of 1–2; disorganized attachment 210–15; early emotional experiences 30–2; emotions 3, 114–18; good parents 2; hypoarousal state 75–6; individual therapy for 13; learning about 17–44; 'low road' of parenting 112; mindfulness training for 87; negative parenting patterns 6–7; not being 'perfect parent' 3; own experience 29–34; parent-child dynamics 35–8; parent exhaustion 174–6; patterns of parent-child interaction 6–8; present concern 19; providing sense of safety for 125–9; recognizing parent-us dynamics 39–43; referral phone call 17–18; resistance 29–30; scheduling initial appointment with 18; uncovering beliefs and values of parents 137–8, 144
'parent's position' 243–4
parent-us dynamics: becoming aware of 39; becoming aware of experiences we had growing up 39–41; influence of our early experiences on experience with parents 41–3; recognizing 39–43; self-question for child professionals 43
peer vision 255, 275–6
perceptual processing 68
'perfect child' 3
'perfect parent' 3
peripheral nervous system 10
play 66–7, 96–7
'polyvagal theory' 64
positive events 237
positive interaction 23, 67–8, 77, 81, 119, 129–33, 156, 232, 258
posttraumatic stress disorder 68
problem solving 73–4
psychodynamic therapy 68

'ready-to-hear-their-story' stance 77
referral phone call 17–18
'reflective dialog' 82–3
rejection 165–71
repair 81, 83–4
resistance 29–30
right associative cortical areas 65, 77
right hemisphere 61–3, 66–7, 126–7, 139
roleplay 171–2

safety 125–9
sand-tray activity 66–7
self-image 26, 63
self-insight 255
self-integration 255, 256
self-regulation 51, 68, 77, 86, 192
self-vision 275–6
sensorimotor experiences 63
slow breathing 113, 167
'social engagement system' 64
Strengthening Families Program (SFP) 87
stress 111–12
supervision 255, 275–6
sympathetic/energizing subsystem 64, 112

therapeutic interactions: engaging deep right cortices—our relationship with parent 65–6; engaging dorsal lateral prefrontal cortex—focus; working memory; problem solving 73–4; engaging motor activity and right hemisphere processing—imaging 67–71; engaging orbital medial prefrontal cortex—emotional regulation; mindfulness; mentalization 71–3; engaging right hemisphere—dyadic art and sand-tray activity 66–7; regulating autonomic nervous system—window of receptivity 74–6
transference 235, 243–4, 256, 264, 272
trauma: adoptive children 188, 191–3; 'Book of Life' for children with history of 67; dissociative identity disorder and 54; use of imaging for survivors 68
trigger reactions 58–9, 73, 75, 82, 161–3, 210, 238–41

unconscious awareness of self-image 63
"unrepressed unconscious" 62–3

validation 75, 118–25, 167
values 137–8, 150–1

window of receptivity: autonomic nervous system and 74–6, 117–18, 122; emotional regulation and 113; overarousal and 111; shifting out of 164, 187, 195; skill to keeping parent within 147, 169, 222
working memory 73–4

Taylor & Francis eBooks

Helping you to choose the right eBooks for your Library

Add Routledge titles to your library's digital collection today. Taylor and Francis ebooks contains over 50,000 titles in the Humanities, Social Sciences, Behavioural Sciences, Built Environment and Law.

Choose from a range of subject packages or create your own!

Benefits for you
- Free MARC records
- COUNTER-compliant usage statistics
- Flexible purchase and pricing options
- All titles DRM-free.

Benefits for your user
- Off-site, anytime access via Athens or referring URL
- Print or copy pages or chapters
- Full content search
- Bookmark, highlight and annotate text
- Access to thousands of pages of quality research at the click of a button.

REQUEST YOUR **FREE** INSTITUTIONAL TRIAL TODAY

Free Trials Available
We offer free trials to qualifying academic, corporate and government customers.

eCollections – Choose from over 30 subject eCollections, including:

Archaeology	Language Learning
Architecture	Law
Asian Studies	Literature
Business & Management	Media & Communication
Classical Studies	Middle East Studies
Construction	Music
Creative & Media Arts	Philosophy
Criminology & Criminal Justice	Planning
Economics	Politics
Education	Psychology & Mental Health
Energy	Religion
Engineering	Security
English Language & Linguistics	Social Work
Environment & Sustainability	Sociology
Geography	Sport
Health Studies	Theatre & Performance
History	Tourism, Hospitality & Events

For more information, pricing enquiries or to order a free trial, please contact your local sales team:
www.tandfebooks.com/page/sales

The home of Routledge books

www.tandfebooks.com